MODERN ARCHITECTURE AND THE SACRED

MODERN ARCHITECTURE AND THE SACRED

RELIGIOUS LEGACIES AND SPIRITUAL RENEWAL

Edited by Ross Anderson and Maximilian Sternberg

BLOOMSBURY VISUAL ARTS
LONDON • NEW YORK • OXFORD • NEW DELHI • SYDNEY

BLOOMSBURY VISUAL ARTS
Bloomsbury Publishing Plc
50 Bedford Square, London, WC1B 3DP, UK
1385 Broadway, New York, NY 10018, USA
29 Earlsfort Terrace, Dublin 2, Ireland

BLOOMSBURY, BLOOMSBURY VISUAL ARTS and the Diana logo are trademarks of Bloomsbury Publishing Plc

First published in Great Britain 2020
Paperback edition first published in Great Britain, 2022
Selection and editorial matter copyright © Ross Anderson and Maximilian Sternberg, 2022
Individual chapters © their authors, 2022

Ross Anderson and Maximilian Sternberg have asserted their right under the Copyright, Designs and Patents Act, 1988, to be identified as editors of this work.

For legal purposes the Acknowledgements on p. xiii constitute an extension of this copyright page.

Cover design by Eleanor Rose
Cover image: Interior of the Mies van der Rohe's chapel on the IIT campus, Chicago, USA © Ross Anderson

All rights reserved. No part of this publication may be reproduced or transmitted in any form or by any means, electronic or mechanical, including photocopying, recording, or any information storage or retrieval system, without prior permission in writing from the publishers.

Bloomsbury Publishing Plc does not have any control over, or responsibility for, any third-party websites referred to or in this book. All internet addresses given in this book were correct at the time of going to press. The author and publisher regret any inconvenience caused if addresses have changed or sites have ceased to exist, but can accept no responsibility for any such changes.

A catalogue record for this book is available from the British Library.

Library of Congress Cataloging-in-Publication Data
Names: Anderson, Ross (Ross John), editor. | Sternberg, Maximilian, 1979- editor.
Title: Modern architecture and the sacred: religious legacies and spiritual renewal / edited by Ross Anderson and Maximilian Sternberg.
Description: London; New York: Bloomsbury Visual Arts, [2022] | Includes bibliographical references and index. | Summary: "This edited volume, Modern Architecture and the Sacred, presents a timely reappraisal of the manifold engagements that modern architecture has had with 'the sacred'. It comprises fourteen individual chapters arranged in three thematic sections – Beginnings and Transformations of the Modern Sacred; Buildings for Modern Worship; and Semi-Sacred Settings in the Cultural Topography of Modernity. The first interprets the intellectual and artistic roots of modern ideas of the sacred in the post-Enlightenment period and tracks the transformation of these in architecture over time. The second studies the ways in which organized religion responded to the challenges of the new modern self-understanding, and then the third investigates the ways that abstract modern notions of the sacred have been embodied in the ersatz sacred contexts of theatres, galleries, memorials and museums. While centring on Western architecture during the decisive period of the first half of the 20th century – a time that takes in the early musings on spirituality by some of the avant-garde in defiance of Sachlichkeit and the machine aesthetic – the volume also considers the many-varied appropriations of sacrality that architects have made up to the present day, and also in social and cultural contexts beyond the West"–Provided by publisher.
Identifiers: LCCN 2021051488 (print) | LCCN 2021051489 (ebook) | ISBN 9781350294356 (paperback) | ISBN 9781350098664 (paperback) | ISBN 9781350098718 (pdf) | ISBN 9781350098725 (epub) | ISBN 9781350098732
Subjects: LCSH: Architecture and religion. | Architecture, Modern–Themes, motives.
Classification: LCC NA4600 .M635 2022 (print) | LCC NA4600 (ebook) | DDC 203/.7–dc23/eng/20211028
LC record available at https://lccn.loc.gov/2021051488
LC ebook record available at https://lccn.loc.gov/2021051489

ISBN: HB: 978-1-3500-9866-4
PB: 978-1-3502-9435-6
ePDF: 978-1-3500-9871-8
eBook: 978-1-3500-9872-5

Typeset by Deanta Global Publishing Services, Chennai, India
Printed and bound in Great Britain

To find out more about our authors and books visit www.bloomsbury.com and sign up for our newsletters.

CONTENTS

List of illustrations	vii
Notes on contributors	xi
Acknowledgements	xiii

    Introduction
    Ross Anderson and Maximilian Sternberg   1

Part One: Beginnings and transformations of the modern sacred   11

1   Architecture and the question of 'the' sacred   13
    Peter Carl

2   Romantic *Kunstreligion* and the search for the sacred in modern architecture: From Schinkel's Altes Museum as 'aesthetic church' to Zumthor's Bruder Klaus Field Chapel as *Gesamtkunstwerk* and 'heavenly cave'   37
    Gabriele Bryant

3   The Ordinary as the extraordinary: Modern sacred architecture in Germany, the United States and Japan   56
    Kathleen James-Chakraborty

4   *Città dei Morti*: Alvar Aalto's funerary architecture   73
    Sofia Singler

Part Two: Buildings for modern worship   89

5   Light, form and *formación*: Daylighting, church building and the work of the Valparaíso School   91
    Mary Ann Steane

6   Reading, storing and parading the book: Between tradition and modernity in the synagogue   108
    Gerald Adler

Contents

7   Compacting civic and sacred: Goodhue's University of Chicago Chapel
    and the modern metropolis   125
    Stephen Gage

8   A diaspora of modern sacred form: Auguste Perret, Le Corbusier
    and Paul Valéry   143
    Karla Cavarra Britton

9   Structure for spirit in *The Architectural Review* and *The Architects'
    Journal*, 1945–70   159
    Sam Samarghandi

Part Three: Semi-sacred settings in the cultural topography of modernity   179

10 Revelatory earth: Adolphe Appia and the prospect of a modern sacred   181
    Ross Anderson

11 Anagogical themes in Schwitters' *Kathedrale des erotischen Elends*   196
    Matthew Mindrup

12 Modern medievalisms: Curating the sacred at the Schnütgen Museum
    in Cologne (1932–9)   208
    Maximilian Sternberg

13 Architecture, politics and the sacred in military monuments of Fascist Italy   222
    Hannah Malone

14 Atmosphere of the sacred: The awry in music, cinema, architecture   241
    Michael Tawa

Bibliography   255
Index   273

ILLUSTRATIONS

1.1	Alabaster altar of Tukulti-Ninurta I, Assur, thirteenth century BCE	14
1.2	Diagrammatic reconstruction of area surrounding Erechtheion, Acropolis, Athens, fifth century BCE	16
1.3	Apse mosaic of Santa Pudenziana, Rome, fifth century CE (and sixteenth-century repairs)	19
1.4	Ivory half-diptych, Constantinople, mid-sixth century CE, depicting archangel Michael in a festooned portal	21
1.5	Palatine Chapel of Roger II, Palermo, Sicily, twelfth century CE, combining Mediterranean Norman, Byzantine and Islamic ornamental practices	23
1.6	Caspar David Friedrich, *Sunset (Brothers)*, oil on canvas, circa 1835	26
1.7	Casa del Fascio, Como, 1936, view south across atrium from conference room with reflection	28
1.8	Casa del Fascio, Como, 1936, view of model of Sacrario	28
2.1	Karl Friedrich Schinkel, Altes Museum, Berlin (1823–30)	38
2.2	Schinkel, Altes Museum, view of the cupola room	41
2.3	Peter Zumthor, Bruder Klaus Field Chapel, Mechernich, Germany (2007), in its landscape of rolling hills, fields and forests	44
2.4	Zumthor, Bruder Klaus Field Chapel, on approach	45
2.5	Zumthor, Bruder Klaus Field Chapel, entrance passage	46
2.6	Zumthor, Bruder Klaus Field Chapel, the teardrop-shaped oculus	46
2.7	Zumthor, Bruder Klaus Field Chapel, an early sketch drawing	47
2.8	Zumthor, Bruder Klaus Field Chapel, under construction	48
3.1	Dominikus Böhm, Church of Christ the King, Bischofsheim, Germany, 1926	59
3.2	Erich Mendelsohn, Jewish Cemetery Chapel, Königsberg, 1927	61
3.3	Otto Bartning, Gustav Adolf Church, Berlin, 1934	62
3.4	Bartning, Gustav Adolf Church, interior	63
3.5	Eliel Saarinen, Christ Lutheran Church, Minneapolis, 1949	64
3.6	Saarinen, Christ Lutheran Church, interior	65
3.7	Togo Murano, Cathedral for World Peace, Hiroshima, 1954	67
4.1	Alvar Aalto, *Città dei morti, Lyngby-Taarbaek Funerary Chapels and Cemetery, Denmark, competition entry* (1951). Site plan	75
4.2	Alvar Aalto, *Trinitas, Malmi Funerary Chapels, Finland, competition entry* (1950). Exterior perspectives	76

Illustrations

4.3	Alvar Aalto, *Trinitas, Malmi Funerary Chapels, Finland*, competition entry (1950). Ground floor plan	79
4.4	Alvar Aalto, *Città dei morti, Lyngby-Taarbaek Funerary Chapels and Cemetery, Denmark*, competition entry (1951). Ground floor plan	80
4.5	Alvar Aalto, *Città dei morti, Lyngby-Taarbaek Funerary Chapels and Cemetery, Denmark*, competition entry (1951). Basswood model	82
5.1	Model of the Los Pajaritos chapel interior illustrating its 'equal' light	94
5.2	Model of the Los Pajaritos chapel exterior	94
5.3	Sketch of the liturgical celebration envisaged at the Los Pajaritos chapel	95
5.4	Section of the Los Pajaritos chapel project, looking south-east	95
5.5	Plan of the reconfigured church of Nuestra Señora del Tránsito, Corral	99
5.6	Diagonal view across the nave of the Corral church after reconstruction	100
5.7	Site plan of open-air oratory at the Open City, 2003	102
5.8	The Open City oratory looking west from the path that ascends towards it through a group of pine trees	102
6.1	Upper Berkeley Street synagogue, as depicted in the *Illustrated London News* in 1872	115
6.2	Upper Berkeley Street synagogue, present-day appearance	116
6.3	Heinz Reifenberg, Belsize Square synagogue, London (1958)	118
6.4	Belsize Square synagogue, View of choir gallery	118
6.5	Lyons Israel Ellis, South Hampstead synagogue. View of the *bimah* from the Ladies' Gallery	119
7.1	Chicago Tribune Tower	126
7.2	The University (Rockefeller) Chapel, completed in 1928	127
7.3	The University's Academic Avenue along the Midway	128
7.4	The University of Chicago Campus in the 1930s	129
7.5	'Proposed New Chapel for the University of Chicago, Plot Plan'	130
7.6	'Suggested Development of Chapel Site'	131
7.7	The chapel entrance on the Midway as completed	135
7.8	The University Chapel as seen in relation to the Midway Plaisance	137
8.1	Auguste Perret, Notre Dame du Raincy, Le Raincy, France, 1923. Interior	146
9.1	C. Holliday and L. G. Vincent, *Church at Stevenage*	162
9.2	Coventry cathedral interior perspective during design development, from Basil Spence, *Phoenix at Coventry*	164
9.3	Cecil D. Handisyde and D. Rogers Stark, Trinity Congregational Church, Lansbury (1951)	166
9.4	Peter and Alison Smithson, *Coventry Cathedral competition entry* (1952), model	168
9.5	Frederick Gibberd, Liverpool Cathedral	169
9.6	Selection of commended entries in the Liverpool Cathedral competition	169
9.7	Illustration from special edition *MANPLAN 5: Religion*	172
9.8	Francis Pollen, *Church at Worth Abbey* (1964–75)	172

Illustrations

10.1	Adolphe Appia, *Espace rythmique: The Diver* (1909)	182
10.2	Château de Glérolles, Lake Geneva	183
10.3	Photograph of *Appia's Espace rythmique: The Three Pillars*, taken by Frédéric Boissonnas in 1910	184
10.4	Heinrich Tessenow, Jaques-Dalcroze Institute for Rhythmic Education, Hellerau (1912)	184
10.5	The *Festsaal* in the Jaques-Dalcroze Institute, Hellerau (1912)	185
10.6	Rehearsals for Orpheus and Eurydice in the Festsaal (1912)	187
10.7	Frontispiece of *Der Rhythmus: Yearbook of the Jaques-Dalcroze Institute for Rhythmic Education* (1911)	187
10.8	Adolphe Appia, *Iphigenie in Tauris. Act II: Interior of the Temple of Artemis* (1926)	190
10.9	Mies van der Rohe, Chapel of St. Savior, IIT, Chicago (1952)	191
11.1	Kurt Schwitters, *Kathedrale des erotischen Elends* (1933)	197
11.2	Kurt Schwitters, *Das Merzbild* (1919)	198
11.3	Kurt Schwitters, *Haus Merz* (1920)	198
11.4	Kurt Schwitters, *Der erste Tag Merz-säule* (1923)	200
11.5	Kurt Schwitters, Gold Grotto (1925)	200
12.1	Schnütgen Museum, St Heribert Abbey, Room 10 'Gothic wood sculpture' (1932)	209
12.2	Applied Arts Museum, Cologne. Room 8 'Chapel' of the Schnütgen Wing (after 1925)	211
12.3	Poster for the opening of the Schnütgen Museum, St Heribert (1932)	216
12.4	Rudolf Schwarz, St Fronleichnam, Aachen (1930)	216
12.5	Rudolf Schwarz, Rothenfels Castle, refurbished communal room (1926)	217
13.1	Oslavia (1938)	228
13.2	Montello (1935)	229
13.3	Redipuglia (1938)	230
13.4	Redipuglia, detail	231
13.5	Monte Grappa (1935)	235
13.6	Monte Grappa	236
14.1	Gloaming space of shadow, dim reflection and obscurity. (War Memorial, Canberra)	242
14.2	Uncanny circumambience	242
14.3	Things go awry. (Lighthouse, Trial Bay)	243
14.4	Extensive porosity. (Mirror, Venice)	243
14.5	Indeterminate borderlines	244
14.6	Alien or deviant presence. (Bút Tháp Temple, Vietnam, thirteenth century)	244
14.7	Shudder. (Lighthouse keepers' cottages, Trial Bay)	246
14.8	Consilient discrepancy	246
14.9	Sigurd Lewerentz, St Peter, Klippan (1962–6), interior view from the western entry door towards the altar	250

ILLUSTRATIONS

14.10 Axial discrepancies in the plan of Sigurd Lewerentz's St Peter, Klippan   250
14.11 Lewerentz, St Peter, Klippan, interior view from the baptistery towards the southeast entry door   251
14.12 Lewerentz, St Peter, Klippan, brick-vaulted ceiling   251
14.13 Lewerentz, St Peter, Klippan, brick floor and baptistery   252
14.14 Lewerentz, St Peter, Klippan, baptistery   252

CONTRIBUTORS

Gerald Adler is Head of the School of Architecture and Planning at the University of Kent. He is currently writing a monograph on the German architect of 'silent modernism', Heinrich Tessenow, and has published on liturgical reform in the Church of England, seen through the work of the architects Maguire and Murray.

Ross Anderson is an associate professor of Architecture at the University of Sydney. Having completed his PhD at the University of Cambridge under Peter Carl, his research on modern German architecture and aesthetics has been published in various edited books and journals including *AA Files, The Bauhaus Annual* and *Art Bulletin*.

Karla Cavarra Britton is Professor of Art History at the Navajo Nation's Diné College. She specializes in modern and contemporary architecture and urbanism with an emphasis on sacred architecture and landscapes. Among her publications are the monograph *Auguste Perret* and the edited volume *Constructing the Ineffable: Contemporary Sacred Architecture*.

Gabriele Bryant is a German art historian with a PhD in History and Philosophy of Architecture from the University of Cambridge. She has worked as a lecturer and researcher at the University of the Arts in Berlin, the Central European University in Prague and Linacre College, University of Oxford.

Peter Carl is currently studying the place of architecture in cultural ecology. He has taught design and history/philosophy of architecture at Cambridge University for thirty years, at the CASS, London, for seven years and was a visiting professor, at the GSD, Harvard, for two semesters. He graduated from Princeton and studied at the American Academy in Rome for two years.

Stephen Gage is a lecturer in Architecture at the University of Reading. An architect and architectural historian, he was the inaugural Yale/Cambridge Bass Scholar and recipient of the RIBA President's Award for Research. His work investigates the evolution of cultural institutions, landscape and public space in the nineteenth/twentieth centuries.

Kathleen James-Chakraborty is Professor of Art History at University College Dublin. She has also been the Vincent Scully Visiting Professor of Architectural History at the Yale School of Architecture. Her most recent book is *Modernism as Memory: Building Identity in the Federal Republic of Germany* (2018).

Contributors

Hannah Malone is a researcher at the Max Planck Institute in Berlin. She is writing a book on Italy's Fascist cemeteries. Previously, she worked at the British School at Rome, Magdalene College Cambridge and the Freie Universität Berlin, and has published a monograph entitled *Architecture, Death and Nationhood* (2017).

Matthew Mindrup's ongoing research in the history and theory of architectural design locates and projects the implications that materials and found objects have in the design process. His new book *The Architectural Model: Histories of the Miniature and the Prototype, the Exemplar and the Muse* was published in 2019 with MIT Press.

Sam Samarghandi commenced his research on the subject of twentieth-century religious architecture in 2014 at the University of Sydney. He is seeking to understand the cause, meaning and historiographical implications of the persistent tension that exists between the discourse of religious building practice and the dominant constructs of the modernist movement in architecture.

Sofia Singler is an architect and Junior Research Fellow at Homerton College, University of Cambridge. She was previously a Gates Cambridge Scholar at the Department of Architecture, University of Cambridge, where she completed her PhD thesis on Alvar Aalto's Church of the Three Crosses in Vuoksenniska, Finland (1955–58).

Mary Ann Steane is Senior Lecturer in Environmental Design in Architecture at the Department of Architecture at the University of Cambridge. Her research considers the factors affecting human perception of the visual environment in order to examine architectural narratives concerning light. Her books include *The Architecture of Light* (2011).

Maximilian Sternberg is Senior Lecturer in History and Theory of Architecture at the Department of Architecture in Cambridge University. His books include *Phenomenologies of the City* (Ashgate 2015) and *Cistercian Architecture and the City* (Brill 2013). He is Fellow of Pembroke College, Cambridge.

Michael Tawa is an architect, and a professor of Architecture at the University of Sydney and the author of *Theorising the Project: A Thematic Approach to Architectural Design* (2011) and *Agencies of the Frame: Tectonic Strategies in Cinema and Architecture* (2010). His latest book *Atmosphere, Architecture, Cinema: A Thematic Approach to Design* is forthcoming.

ACKNOWLEDGEMENTS

The editors of this collected volume would firstly like to thank the individual chapter authors for their commitment to seeing the volume through to production, and for doing so in a spirit of collegial generosity. They all first gathered together at a symposium held in Spring 2017 at Pembroke College in the University of Cambridge to present their research into the vexed issue of the place and meaning of the sacred in modern architecture, and then developed those papers into the chapters that are to be found herein. Thanks are also due to Pembroke College for supporting the symposium with a generous grant and also for hosting it in the college's wonderful buildings and picturesque grounds. Stephen Gage was instrumental to the smooth running of the symposium and deserves warm thanks. So too does the School of Architecture, Design and Planning at the University of Sydney, which initially supported a number of the authors to travel to Cambridge, and afterwards assisted them with costs associated with the publication of their chapters. Finally, thanks are due to James Thompson and Alexander Highfield at Bloomsbury Academic for seeing this edited volume through to publication.

INTRODUCTION
Ross Anderson and Maximilian Sternberg

Collectively, the chapters that are gathered here as *Modern Architecture and the Sacred* present a reappraisal of the manifold engagements that modern architecture has had with 'the sacred'. While centring on Western architecture during the decisive period of the first half of the twentieth century – a time that takes in the early musings on spirituality by some of the avant-garde in defiance of *Sachlichkeit* and the machine aesthetic, through to the architecture of the sobering post-war years – it also considers the many-varied appropriations of sacrality that architects have made up to the present day, and also in social and cultural contexts beyond the West.

There are fourteen individual chapters, and they are structured into three thematically determined sections that capitalize on their commonalities.[1] These three parts are 'Beginnings and transformations of the modern sacred', Buildings for modern worship' and 'Semi-sacred settings within the cultural topography of modernity'. Collectively, the chapters in the first foundational section identify and interpret the intellectual and artistic roots of modern ideas of the sacred in the post-Enlightenment period, and they track transformations of these in architecture over time. The chapters of Part Two study the ways in which organized religion has responded to the challenges of the new modern self-understanding. While religious institutions in general often adopted a wary and defensive attitude, there are numerous examples of individual religious patrons embracing avant-garde experimentation and formal innovation that would influence modern architecture well beyond the realms of organized religion. Yet, ostensibly more secular patrons, politicians, academics or museum curators were attuned to the power of the sacred in conveying meanings in the architectural representation of their institutions. Part Three in particular investigates the ways that abstract modern notions of the sacred have been embodied in the ersatz sacred contexts of theatres, galleries, memorials and museums.

There are of course multiple ways of addressing the topic of modern sacred architecture, and this collection draws on some of the dominant approaches in current scholarship without committing to one of them in particular. One is the architectural monograph, whether focusing on notable individual architects and the religious ideas that they bring to bear in their architecture as a whole or in specific buildings.[2] By way of contrast, a second approach addresses sacred architecture by concentrating on focusing on one particular religious denomination or order, often in one region, thereby revealing what it is that architecture can teach us about church or monastic history and social religious history – especially as regards the architectural implications of liturgical reform and ecclesiastical responses to social or political change.[3] An approach related to this is pursued in some of the studies that come out of the discipline of religious studies, presenting theological insights concerning modernity and the modern, insofar as 'the sacred' and 'sacred space' are discussed principally in relation to how works of architecture come to either embody or respond to specific theological concepts and liturgical reforms.

By embracing multiple ways of tackling the subject matter, the chapters here provide a coverage of the topic that is deliberately more panoramic than it is comprehensive, selectively identifying and interpreting the variety of ways that questions of the sacred came to the fore in particular cultural, geographical and political contexts, as much as in the minds of individual modern architects. Moreover, there is no presumption of critical unanimity between the authors themselves. Rather, they evidence a range of methodological approaches as varied as their subject matter; some are driven by philosophy or theory, while others are impelled by archival findings and the conventions of art historical research.

Many of the chapters draw attention to the complexity of the cultural context within which architecture operates, and to the importance of the array of individuals who are inevitably involved – including patrons, clients and craftspeople – rather than fixating on works of architecture as the product of the imagination of individual 'genius' architects. Consideration is also given to those critics and scholars who write about buildings and condition their reception. This is a particularly important point, since even the ecclesiastical buildings and projects by the most notable of international architects, including, for example, Alvar Aalto, have tended to be either overlooked or ignored due to the awkward way that they sit within an otherwise apparently consistent œuvre.[4] They would have muddied the narrative of canonical Modernism that was largely codified in the middle of the twentieth century by figures including Sigfried Giedion with his *Space, Time and Architecture* (1942) and Nikolaus Pevsner with his *Pioneers of Modern Design* (1949).[5]

Then there are other architects for whom ecclesiastical commissions were the mainstay – including Rudolf Schwarz, Otto Bartning and Dominkus Böhm. It is largely for this reason that they tended to be overlooked altogether in more general histories of modern architecture, and it is only in more recent times that they have attracted scholarly attention as representatives of an 'other' Modernism.[6] Some of the chapters profit from these kinds of revisionist perspectives on Modernism and further extend their claims, offering new readings of the works both of some of the 'heroic' figures of modern architecture and of architects who have long been marginalized in the mainstream accounts.

As a corpus, the chapters contend that the substantial body of religious or semi-sacred buildings by modern architects should in fact be allocated a central rather than peripheral position in the history of modern architecture, and that close consideration of them might reveal some of those deep-seated yet under-discussed motivations behind the development of modern architecture in general. 'The sacred' is a persistent theme, even if it has long been deliberately or inadvertently marginalized, or considered anomalous; subject to misleading simplifications to the extent that it is discussed at all. Early writings on Modernism tended to downplay the significance of the sacred architecture of their time by dismissing these buildings as regressive or eccentric – difficult to situate – and therefore of only limited significance to the story of the otherwise onward march of modern architecture as a movement. And yet, architects of the stature of Peter Behrens, Le Corbusier, Mies van der Rohe and Alvar Aalto did themselves of course invest some of their energies into the design of churches and other buildings that harbour religious purposes and practices, such as cemeteries and mausolea. They also conversed in meaningful religious terms with the clients for these buildings, and held longer ongoing personal conversations with others – the Catholic theologian Romano Guardini in the case of Mies, whose books the architect had studied closely. Detlef Mertins recently wrote that 'of all the books in Mies's library, Guardini's *Letters* is the most heavily marked. Mies highlighted passage after passage with bold and rapid margin strokes and wrote key words diagonally and in large script across the first pages of many of the chapters'.[7] Then of course the architects put into practice the ideas they had been playing with. Le Corbusier, speaking in typically strident terms at the formal consecration of Notre Dame du Ronchamp, asserted that the sacrality he had summoned forth in the chapel transcended not only Catholicism but religion as a whole.[8] In addition to their engagement with explicitly religious themes, some of the architects had a more diffuse understanding of the sacred that took in primitivism, medievalism, orientalism and pseudo or semi-religious undertakings such as theosophy.

All considered, the focus here on questions of the sacred architecture is not simply to further elucidate one of the 'hidden' strands of modern architecture. Rather, it is conceived as a means to speak about the ways that the concerns of architecture can be seen to manifest a central tension within modern culture more broadly, namely that between the secular and sacred. This is the division that philosopher Charles Taylor goes so far as to assert in his book *A Secular Age* (2007) and which is the decisive one for the modern epoch.[9] Since it came to be consolidated as a discipline and profession during this epoch, architecture has certainly tended to view itself as both a medium and an agent of secularization.

Unable to self-evidently rely on conventional ways of conceiving and carrying out religious buildings, architects and their patrons turned variously to the hard sciences – following the logic of the Enlightenment and its dedication to reason – or to the fine arts that became the receptacle for all of that which hard reason either left out or viewed with suspicion, including religion. This tension between the apparently opposed concerns of the Enlightenment and of Romanticism persisted into the twentieth century, as, for example, Iain Boyd Whyte explored in his study of Bruno Taut that told of the architect's one-time commitment to Expressionism and then to *Sachlichkeit*.[10] Boyd Whyte made the point that modern architecture was in fact propelled by mystical and millenarian dreams as much as it was by pledges to function and rationality. Furthermore, even the concept of 'progress' that held a central place in early modern architectural discourse cannot be fully understood without acknowledging the extent to which it is a secularized adaptation of the theological ideas of redemption and divine providence.[11]

Part One of this book opens up some of these questions around the place of the sacred in the modern world that is ostensibly devoid of it. Peter Carl's wide-ranging chapter largely stakes out the terms of reference for those chapters that follow. He recognizes that once sacrality is freed from concrete religious practice, it becomes a general concept, a collection of vaguely defined attributes that can apparently be manipulated by scholars or artists as much as by political regimes enlisting art and architecture to its particular ends. The sacred might be conceived as a set of behaviours, aesthetic responses, or iconography and is regularly adduced in the ostensibly secular genre of modernist manifestoes, the Bauhaus 'cathedral of the future' merely being the most famous and frequently cited. With reference to terms such as Eric Voegelin's 'intramundane salvation', Carl identifies that post-Enlightenment culture has sought to preserve some of the original religious meanings in the midst of secularization – via notions like 'religious experience'. Perhaps rooted in a phenomenon first identified in Friedrich Schiller's remark in the ninth letter of *On the Aesthetic Education of Man* that 'the temples remain sacred to the eye, even though the gods have been declared ridiculous', Carl argues that architecture has been a major medium for expressing the ambivalent afterlife of the sacred in modernity.

The following chapter Gabriele Bryant's, couples Schiller's observation with Hugo Ball's quip that 'modern artists are gnostics who do things that the priests have long thought forgotten'. She goes on to explore the prominence in modern times of 'sacred' themes and architectural forms beyond the traditional realms of religion, most strikingly in art. Again, she identifies the historical foundations of modern '*Kunstreligion*' (art-religion) in German Romanticism, before it came to be embodied in architecture, most prominently in Karl Friedrich Schinkel's *Altes Museum* in Berlin – a museum built as a temple. She also addresses the enduring legacy of the contemporary relevance of the nineteenth-century notion of the *Gesamtkunstwerk* (total work of art) and its sacred connotations via a close reading of Peter Zumthor's *Bruder Klaus Field Chapel*, which 'makes a place for itself', standing *stele*-like in a landscape of rolling hills just outside Cologne in Germany.[12]

In Chapter 3, Kathleen James-Chakraborty asserts the importance of sacred architecture to the story of modern architecture more generally. She contends that modern architecture made earlier and deeper inroads in church and synagogue design than in almost any other area of building, especially in Germany. Designed by architects such as Dominikus Böhm and Eliel Saarinen – who in their day numbered among the most widely respected and influential members of their profession – these modern sacred buildings deployed abstraction and a deft use of light, coupled with modern technology (especially reinforced concrete) to create understated and inexpensive spaces that have been widely appreciated ever since by the congregations that worship in them. She stresses that by omitting structures such as Böhm's Christ the King in Bischofsheim (1926), Erich Mendelsohn's Jewish Cemetery in Königsberg (1929), Eliel Saarinen's Christ Church in Minneapolis (1949) and Togo Murano's Memorial Cathedral for World Peace in Hiroshima (1946) from the history of the mainstream of the history modern architecture, our understanding of the field as a whole is diminished.[13] That is, by ignoring the symbolic power of new forms, such histories exclude the many modern buildings that did not share an industrial aesthetic or a socialist purpose, overemphasizing the importance of a small number of architects based in a handful of countries.

Sofia Singler addresses one of those well-known architects, but does so through four of his projects that were never realized. Her chapter *Città dei Morti* focuses on Aalto's four funerary projects that she characterizes as 'epitaphs engraved in the wind'. It situates Aalto's funerary œuvre – which includes funeral chapels, crematoria and cemeteries – in relation to Nordic traditions, precedents and the works of his contemporaries, and contextualizes these projects within the framework of the historical, sociocultural, religious and political developments of their time. While Aalto developed an approach to cemetery design that drew upon motifs that are recurrent in his secular designs – notably his humanism and ideas concerning nature – his projects reveal subtle yet significant shifts in emphasis. Furthermore, Aalto linked his humanism ideas to those of pantheism, ritual and what Singler terms 'urban primitivism'. She thus shows that not only were sacred motifs able to be brought into a fruitful dialogue with modernist ideals but that the design of settings with religious purposes in fact also offered a privileged medium for the expression of meaning in Modernism.

Part Two opens with Mary Ann Steane's chapter, which addresses the ecclesiastical design-build projects by the Valparaíso School of Architecture in Chile. She explores the way that church building has shaped the school's pedagogical outlook into one in that apprehends architecture as an event that is enacted collaboratively rather than produced, and whose primary ambitions include the proper architectural expression of community and locality. The significance of light is explored not only for its phenomenal nature but also for the metaphorical connotations that attend it – moving beyond 'form' to *formación*. Typically translated as 'training', *formación* is more akin to the self-forming or self-education of *Bildung*.

In Chapter 6, Gerald Adler identifies that synagogue design since the Enlightenment can be read as a commentary on tradition and modernity, and the ways that it is embodied in building. By highlighting two particularly telling historical moments in Britain, he explores the paradoxical tendency towards mimicry of Christian building forms by reform-minded Jewish communities, as opposed to the continuation of traditional layouts that communicate a specific Jewish identity. The first of these is the late-nineteenth-century flourishing of synagogue building, echoing the eclecticism of contemporaneous church buildings. And the second is the mid-twentieth century, when Modernism produced two completely different synagogues at different ends of the tradition-modernity debate. During both of these historical moments it is the contested relationship between the *bimah* (the raised platform where the Torah scrolls are read) and the *Ark* (where they are stored) that is shown to in fact serve to define the configuration of each synagogue.

Stephen Gage identifies that Gothic Revival architecture enjoyed prominence in America into the 1930s, long after it had been eclipsed in England and Europe, but that since it was derided by Modernists, it remains a largely overlooked tradition. He presents a close reading of Bertram Grosvenor Goodhue's University of Chicago Chapel, with respect to the way that it can be seen to compact civic and sacred qualities and ambitions. The massive building was not only an exemplar of Goodhue's devoted search for a distinctive 'modern gothic' idiom but also a physical manifestation of leaders' desire for the university to become an epicentre of cultural life for all of Chicago. Conceived as a place for secular ceremonies and public gatherings, the project was seen first and foremost as a civic monument that would actively contribute to the life of the modern city; traditional religious symbolism was co-opted for civic purposes.

Karla Britton's chapter adopts and extends Vincent Scully's assertion that the attainment of the sacred was one of the well-hidden agendas of canonical modern architecture as a whole. She does so via analysis of key buildings and writings by Auguste Perret and Le Corbusier, two of the most prominent architectural thinkers of the twentieth century. Her discussion is bracketed by two key moments, the first is Perret's concept of the 'sovereign shelter' as expressed through the religious architectural language of his design for *Notre Dame du Raincy* (1923), and the other is Le Corbusier's phenomenological concept of 'ineffable space', which the architect first articulated in 1946. Both of these moments arose from the context of a modern French tradition of religious thought that pursued the expression of religious ideas beyond the predictable boundaries of architecture's material and technological concerns. Together, they serve to demonstrate how religious buildings often became the locus of significant innovation and experimentation within the wider modern project.

In Chapter 9, Sam Samarghandi presents a critical account of the presence of buildings for worship in the pages of two of the most important British architectural journals of the post-war period. He identifies that, particularly on account of the programme of post-war reconstruction of urban centres, the subject of church building featured regularly.[14] It was also a time of theological transformation, and both the buildings and the discourse surrounding them reveal that a transformation in the conception of new places of worship took place. Samarghandi's discourse analysis tracks the ways that church buildings were either absented within, or ran contrary to, the dominant modernist architectural historiography and its ideological impulses, and were consequently truncated from the larger narratives of Modernism and were treated separately.[15] He argues that despite their fettered associations to history and tradition, church buildings were a valid and indeed compelling subject in which to engage with Modernism, and that by the 1970s the simple dichotomies that had come to characterize early Modernism began to disintegrate among failed urban utopias and sober new political realities.

Part Three is made up of chapters that all have as their topic of concern those disciplines and their institutions that in the post-Enlightenment period have taken up the topic of sacrality that was previously the domain of religion. Often freighted with cultural and political ambitions, these semi-sacred settings include art galleries, museums and spaces for rituals and performances. Ross Anderson's chapter identifies the important and as yet undervalued role the Swiss scenographer Adolphe Appia played in the formulation of themes that would become pivotal in the modern architecture of Heinrich Tessenow, Mies van der Rohe, Le Corbusier and others, particularly as embodied in his austere yet mysteriously atmospheric *Espaces rythmique* drawings. Poised between melancholy and hope, these drawings, which were once described as being 'stripped of anecdote', guide our eyes over reiterated horizons that rise up from chthonic depths to meet a promising sky. Conceived as the fragmentary remains of a past culture, or the inauguration of one to come, the semi-ritualistic settings marry an atavistic appeal to primordial experiences with removed perspectival clarity and precision. This consideration of Appia's decisive contribution to the development of modern architectural 'space' provides insights into the underrated role of theatre in the emergence of the new semi-sacred sensibility that coupled an ethos of austerity with aspirations for cultural renewal.

In Chapter 11, Matthew Mindrup takes up the German artist Kurt Schwitters' remarkable *Merzbau* project as a vehicle to discuss the critical point of contact between sacred and modern architecture, within the realm of the domestic. Begun in 1923, and constructed over time using both found and pilfered materials, Schwitters invested his *Merzbau* project with meaning akin to the anagogical function of a Gothic cathedral, that is, to lead the mind from the world of appearances to the contemplation of God. Although unique in its expression, Schwitters' *Merzbau* is demonstrative of a broader trend in Modernism to adopt the Gothic cathedral as an exemplary architectural and cultural paradigm of aesthetic wholeness and integrity – as a *Gesamtkunstwerk*.

Maximilian Sternberg's chapter addresses the architectural and curatorial intent behind the Schnütgen Museum in Cologne during the 1930s. The Schnütgen holds one of the most important collections of medieval art in Europe. The now-lost setting of the museum in the 1930s at St Heribert was the first art museum curation to present a collection of exclusively medieval artefacts in an unabashedly modern manner that was radically pared back in both colour and décor, abandoning the whole ornamented wherewithal of the period room. While the distinctly modern curation of isolated exemplary artefacts in a succession of whitewashed rooms certainly aestheticized the sacred, it also sacralized the aesthetic.[16] It is this double movement that makes the Schnütgen Museum such an important window into some of the tensions around sacred and secular at the heart of Modernism.

In Chapter 13, Hannah Malone explores the way that Mussolini's Fascist regime in Italy attained its political ends through architecture that was both sacred and modern. She focuses on a group of ossuaries (bone depositories), which were built along the former battle front in north-eastern Italy to house the remains of Italian soldiers of the First World War. These ossuaries that were innovative in form and monumental in scale were intended to become secular sites of pilgrimage, merging religious symbolism with political ambition. Since Fascism operated as a 'political religion' within a deeply Catholic culture, the architects of the ossuaries borrowed tools of persuasion that belonged to the architecture and traditional imagery of the church, but since the regime also endorsed modern architecture as being in line with the future of the regime, both approaches were employed. This suggests how, far from disappearing from modern architecture, the sacred was reinvented in new and meaningful ways to serve ends both cultural and political.

In the final chapter of Part Three, and of the book, Michael Tawa recognizes the fact that normative oppositional thinking has left unexplored the constitutive identity between sacred and secular, with the consequence that the rational, secular project at the heart of modernity remains interminably haunted by the spectre of the sacred. Drawing on works of music, cinema and architecture, he analyses the agency of severance, dissonance and undecidability in the production of atmosphere; further, he shows how something like an atmosphere of the sacred can emerge through the essentially *tectonic* practice of suspended discordance – that is, through unaligned and dissonant yet strangely consilient compositional and material conditions.

Across the pages of *Modern Architecture and the Sacred*, the concerns, approaches and conclusions of individual authors are also not always concilient, deliberately privileging what Hans-Georg Gadamer termed 'the priority of the question'[17] over the answer. But what they do register collectively is that 'the sacred' is one of those persistent themes that underlie modern architecture, whether spoken about in terms that are religious or rather disclosed in words and buildings that are the result of ambivalent secularized legacies of sacred expectations and motifs.[18] In all, they suggest that the questions surrounding modern 'sacred architecture', or 'the sacred' in modern architecture, remain contested and therefore alive, open to future interpretative possibilities in contexts both secular and sacred.

Notes

1. The chapters derive mostly from the presentations delivered at a two-day symposium co-convened by the editors at Pembroke College in the University of Cambridge in April 2017, and one of them was subsequently written by a panel chair. The contributors to the symposium all engaged with questions of modern architecture and sacrality as individuals, yet their concerns were conversant and the topics and arguments presented here were sharpened through collegial discussion and reflection.

2. See, for example, the following works all dedicated to Le Corbusier: Debora Antonini, et al., *Le symbolique, le sacré, la spiritualité dans l'oeuvre de Le Corbusier* (Rencontres de la Fondation Le Corbusier, 2003); Jan K. Birksted, *Le Corbusier and the Occult* (Cambridge, MA: MIT Press, 2009); and Flora Samuel and Inge Linder Gaillard, *Sacred Concrete: The Churches of Le Corbusier* (Basel: Birkhäuser, 2012). And these books, all by Joseph Siry, each addresses one of Frank Lloyd Wright's religious buildings: Siry, *Unity Temple: Frank Lloyd Wright and Architecture for Liberal Religion* (Cambridge: Cambridge University Press, 1998); Siry, *Beth Sholom Synagogue: Frank Lloyd Wright and Modern Religious Architecture* (Chicago: Chicago University Press, 2012). See also Victoria M. Young's *Saint John's Abbey Church: Marcel Breuer and the Creation of a Modern Sacred Space* (Minneapolis: University of Minnesota Press, 2014).

3. See, for example, Kate Jordan and Ayla Lepine, eds, *Modern Architecture and Religious Communities, 1850–1970: Building the Kingdom* (London: Routledge, 2018); and Robert Proctor, *Building the Modern Church: Roman Catholic Church Architecture in Britain, 1955-1975* (Farnham: Ashgate, 2014). Some scholars have investigated the deployment of church building programmes in specific, and often charged, political contexts. See, for example, Holger Brülls, *Neue Dome. Wiederaufnahme romanischer Bauformen und antimoderne Kulturkritik im Kirchenbau der Weimarer Republik und der NS-Zeit* (Berlin: Verlag Bauwesen, 1994). This is a line of inquiry also pursued in a number of chapters in the current volume, most prominently in Hannah Malone's chapter on the monumental ossuaries built by the Italian Fascists along former battle lines to become secular sites of pilgrimage.

4. The same might be said of earlier 'transitional' architects including Hendrik Petrus Berlage, Otto Wagner and Jože Plečnik and others. The ecclesiastical works of Theodor Fischer meanwhile have received more attention, for example in Maite Kröger's *Theodor Fischers*

architektonisches Prinzip am Beispiel der Ulmer evangelischen Garnisonkirche (Munich: Grin Publishing, 2012). Sofia Singler and Maximilian Sternberg's forthcoming article 'The Civic and the Sacred: Alvar Aalto's Churches and Parish Centres in Wolfsburg, 1960–1968', *Architectural History* 62 (2019), will address the issue in regards to Aalto's architecture.

5. Sigfried Giedion, *Space, Time and Architecture* (Cambridge, MA: Harvard University Press, 1942); Nikolaus Pevsner, *Pioneers of Modern Design: From William Morris to Walter Gropius* (New York: Museum of Modern Art, 1949). And to a lesser extent, see Kenneth Frampton, *Modern Architecture: A Critical History* (London: Thames and Hudson, 1980); and William J. R. Curtis, *Modern Architecture Since 1900* (Oxford: Phaidon, 1982).

6. See Wolfgang Pehnt and Hilde Strohl, *Rudolf Schwarz, 1897-1961: Architekt einer anderen Moderne* (Stuttgart: Gerd Hatje, 1997); Klaus Kinold and Wolfgang Jean Stock, *Rudolf Schwarz: Church Architecture* (Munich: Hirmer Verlag, 2018); Wolfgang Voigt and Ingeborg Flagge, *Dominikus Böhm, 1880-1955* (Tübingen: Wasmuth, 2005); and Werner Durth, Wolfgang Pehnt and Sandra Wagner-Conzelmann, *Otto Bartning. Architekt einer sozialien Moderne* (Berlin: Akademie der Künste and the Wüstenrot Stiftung, 2017).

7. Detlef Mertins, *Mies* (London: Phaidon, 2014), 155. See also Fritz Neumeyer, *The Artless Word: Mies van der Rohe on the Building Art* (Cambridge, MA: MIT Press, 1994).

8. Peter Carl, 'The Godless Temple: Organon of the Infinite', *Journal of Architecture* 10, no. 1 (2005): 63–90.

9. Charles Taylor, *A Secular Age* (Cambridge, MA: The Belknap Press of Harvard University Press, 2007).

10. Iain Boyd Whyte, ed., *Bruno Taut and the Architecture of Activism* (Cambridge: Cambridge University Press, 1982), 226–8.

11. See Karl Löwith, *Meaning in History: The Theological Implications of a Philosophy of History* (London: University of Chicago Press and Cambridge University Press, 1949); and Hans Blumberg, *The Legitimacy of the Modern Age* (Cambridge, MA: MIT Press, 1983) for critical engagements with theories of secularization.

12. While most of the buildings discussed in the other chapters of the book are mainly situated at some historical distance from today, this chapter identifies ways in which thematic and formal continuities and reinterpretations are present in contemporary sacred architecture. For a work in a similar vein, which also discusses Peter Zumthor's *Bruder Klaus Field Chapel*, see James Pallister, *Sacred Spaces: Contemporary Religious Architecture* (London: Phaidon, 2015). See also Karla Britton, ed., *Constructing the Ineffable: Contemporary Sacred Architecture* (New Haven: Yale University Press, 2010).

13. See also James-Chakraborty's *German Architecture for a Mass Audience* (London: Routledge, 2000), particularly the chapter 'Spirituality', and Iain Boyd Whyte's edited book *Modernism and the Spirit of the City* (London: Routledge, 2003), particularly 'Part III: Faith'. Both of these books focus on the European context. For a recent collection of writings that address the North American context, see Anat Geva, ed., *Modernism and American Mid-20th Century Sacred Architecture* (London: Routledge, 2018).

14. Samarghandi's chapter also draws attention to the church's role as a significant patron of modern architecture in the years of urban reconstruction following the Second World War, and the consequences this patronage had for city and town planning. See also Sven Sterken, 'A House for God or a Home for His People? The Church-Building Activity of Domus Dei in the Belgian Archbishopric (1952-82)', *Architectural History* 56 (2013): 387–425; and Joks Janssen, 'Religiously Inspired Urbanism: Catholicism and the Planning of the Southern Dutch Provincial cities Eindhoven and Roermond, c. 1900 to 1960', *Urban History* 43, no. 1

(2016): 135–57. Furthermore, Samarghandi recognizes that church attendance among the general population remained high during the period under consideration. See also Callum G. Brown, *The Death of Christian Britain: Understanding Secularisation, 1800-2000* (London: Routledge, 2001).

15. The following are some of the spate of books on modern religious architecture published in the early 1960s – around the time of Vatican II: Joseph Picard, *Modern Church Architecture* (London: Orion Press, 1960); Reinhard Giebelmann and Werner Aebli, *Kirchenbau* (Zürich: Verlag Girsberger, 1960); George Everard Kidder Smith, *The New Churches of Europe, an Illustrated Guidebook and Appraisal* (Cleveland: World Publishing Company, 1961); Albert Christ-Janer and Mary Mix Foley, *Modern Church Architecture: A Guide to the Form and Spirit of 20th Century Religious Buildings* (New York: McGraw Hill, 1962).

16. Two other works that similarly thematize issues of sacrality in the context of museums are the following: Gretchen Townsend Buggeln and Barbara Franco, eds, *Interpreting Religion at Museums and Historic Sites* (Lanham: Rowman & Littlefield Publishers, 2018); and Buggeln Townsend, Crispin Paine and S. Brent Plate, eds, *Religion in Museums: Global and Multidisciplinary Perspectives* (London: Bloomsbury Academic, 2017).

17. See Hans-Georg Gadamer, *Truth and Method*, trans. Garrett Barding and John Cumming (London: Sheed and Ward, 1975).

18. For an anthology of key texts on religious themes written both by architects themselves and by others, and that similarly reinforces the view that issues of sacrality have occupied the thoughts of modern and contemporary architects to a greater extent than has been generally acknowledged, see Renata Hejduk and Jim Williamson, eds, *The Religious Imagination in Modern and Contemporary Architecture: A Reader* (New York: Routledge, 2011).

PART ONE
BEGINNINGS AND TRANSFORMATIONS
OF THE MODERN SACRED

CHAPTER 1
ARCHITECTURE AND THE QUESTION OF 'THE' SACRED
Peter Carl

The virtue of rendering sacrality as a concept – 'the' sacred – is its generosity: it proposes to accommodate all religious practices and beliefs. This is also its principal defect, since it has authorized deconstructing these beliefs and practices into attributes, analogies, patterns, behaviours and themes liberated from any actual religion or people and cast into a domain of speculation qualified by the methods of philosophy, literary criticism, semiotics, anthropology, psychology, social theory and art history, among others.

By the mid-twentieth century, 'the' sacred was least at home in actual religious practice, with its obligations to seasonal ritual cycles, to marriage customs or food symbolism, to modes of worship and theology. 'The' sacred became most credible to artists and architects as the compendia of motifs contained in such works as Gaston Bachelard's re-interpretations of the four elements (1938-48), Pierre Mabille's *Mirror of the Marvelous* [sic] (1940), Juan Eduardo Cirlot's Jungian *A Dictionary of Symbols* (1958) or Mircea Eliade's quasi-Structuralist *Patterns in Comparative Religion* (1958). Since then, conceptions of reality as the thermodynamics of embodied information suggest that received structures of reference might dissolve altogether. At the same time, established religions intermingle with adaptations[1] and ephemeral new cults. Under these conditions, 'the' sacred is more a question than an assured basis for inquiry or critique.

The implication of a conflict between 'the' sacred and 'the' conceptual is itself illuminating. In Europe, these two contexts for belief or truth might be said to mark the transition to the Enlightenment beginning in the fourteenth century. At a time when 'the' sacred seems to veer between dogmatic fundamentalism and a mere designation of importance (one hears toothbrushing or breakfast described as 'ritual'), it would be appropriate to try to clarify the architectural embodiment of 'the' sacred. A historical outline suggests that architecture's turn to perspectivism created fundamental ambiguities that came to a head in early Romanticism, when we were left with a conceptual 'space' oriented to human freedom, but also with the counter-understanding, recently resurrected, which acknowledges the claim of the fundamental conditions.

We may fruitfully begin with the alabaster cult pedestal, or altar, on which a relief depicts the Middle Assyrian 'king of kings' Tukulti-Ninurta I approaching and kneeling before a representation of itself (Figure 1.1).[2] The inscription dedicates the altar to a god associated with light, Nuska, who, however, is usually represented by a lamp; whereas it appears that the symbol atop the altar is actually a stylus and tablet, in which case the

Modern Architecture and the Sacred

Figure 1.1 Alabaster altar of Tukulti-Ninurta I, Assur, thirteenth century BCE.
Source: bpk-Bildagentur / Vorderasiatisches Museum, SMB.

deity invoked would be Nabu, associated with writing and the crafts.[3] Perhaps we can take the doubling of the king and of his altar to allow both Nuska and Nabu, anticipating Plato's much later use of the crafts, the *logos* and light in his rendering of participation in the World Soul.[4]

In any event, what is most important for present purposes is the base of the altar. The altar in the relief positions its base directly atop the base of the actual altar, whose upper surface provides the ground traversed by the king. There is no other indication of the setting, indoors or outdoors – the event takes place in the time-out-of-time that can be re-enacted in ritual, ceremony and, later, drama.[5] What is necessary is the base: its attachment to the boundless earth in a particular site enables the king to communicate with his deity. He traverses the 'ground' with humility, perhaps trepidation, barefoot, grasping his sceptre and extending his right index finger. In other words, the base establishes a condition between earth and the deities propitious for communication with humans.

This obviously recalls Heidegger's strife of earth and world,[6] although he emphasized the rift (*Riss*) in the earth, comparing it to the architectural ground plan (*Grundriss*).[7] Taking Heidegger's philosophical metaphor to indicate something like 'rupture', it is not difficult to see the stepped form of the altar base as a mini-ziggurat. By analogy the altar becomes a little temple, and this invocation of the cosmic mountain not only appears in countless ancient Near Eastern temples, statues and cylinder seals but also survives in the crepidoma of Greek temples and the humble earth altars of Aeneas in Virgil's *Aeneid*.

Architecture and the Question of 'the' Sacred

The arrangement presumes a temporality by which the earth precedes the base, which in turn precedes the altar, statue or temple. Conversely, reversing this sequence displays a stratification of dependency. The ephemeral rite can be re-enacted because the altar or temple resides upon its 'older', or more primordial, base which ruptures the even more primordial earth, giving it a horizon. Commitment to a particular place means the earth is always-already architecture.

The ceremonial architecture of the Bronze Age acknowledges this primordial claim and serves as the horizon or background for praxis in history, mediated by the rhythmic temporality of ornament, which appears on the architecture, the furniture and the regalia of the principal actors. Indeed, against Eliade's over-insistence upon a distinction between the sacred and the profane,[8] we find that rituals are rooted in what people do anyway (*praxis*), but attuned to rhythm: voices and words move towards song or poetry; noise is clarified into the music of drums, flutes, horns or strings; bodily movements become procession, dance or significant postures; temples acquire colonnades or buttresses scrupulous with their measure, as well as images, statuary and ornament suffused with rhythm. All this is arranged for the sake of communication with deities and their claims from the deep context manifest in the recurring iconography of animals, plants, earth, weather and heavens. The always-already-there of the primordial context collaborates in the myths with an elaborate thematization of origins, in which the ontologically primary conditions are deemed to inhabit a deep past, and with which initiatives in history strive to be reconciled. Indeed, the re-enactive temporality of the rites makes history accountable to these original, or foundational, conditions.

That architecture can convert temporal into spatial orientation is one aspect of architecture's participation in 'the' sacred. It is not restricted to ancient Near Eastern temple-palace compounds, but attains a distributed and more public character along the north side of the Athenian Acropolis, where all the cults important to the polis were located (Figure 1.2). This is the area now dominated by the restored remains of the Erechtheion, to which the archaic wooden statue of Athena Polias had been transferred after the original temple was destroyed by the Persians in 480 BCE. Gaps in the evidence, conflicts in the sources, the multivalent identities of the deities, destructions and rebuildings and the consequent breadth of scholarly debate necessitate a somewhat cursory treatment here.[9] However, for the purposes of grasping its temporal significance, two aspects may be noted. First, the several shrines were the subject of a group of ceremonies, processions and rites that took place at the turning of the year, of which the most important was the Panathenaea, when Athena Polias received her newly woven peplos. Secondly, the mythical corpus with which Athenians renewed their affiliation annually was situated in a period of archaic kings associated with the Mycenaean occupation of the site (from when the wooden statue was supposed to date, and surviving masonry recalls the 'strong-built house of Erechtheus' visited by Athena in Homer's *Odyssey* 7.81) and in particular the chthonic, fish-tailed Kekrops. His tomb was incorporated in the south-west corner of the Erechtheion and his daughters were commemorated in the Pandroseon and the House of the Arrhephoroi, as well as in the cave of Aphrodite and Eros, in the north face of the Acropolis, and the cave of Aglauros, on the north-east face, originally addressing

Figure 1.2 Diagrammatic reconstruction of area surrounding Erechtheion, Acropolis, Athens, fifth century BCE. Key: (1) shrine of Aphrodite and Eros, lower north slope of Acropolis; (2) Cave of Aglauros, in northeast face of Acropolis, facing pre-Classical agora; (3) stairs up from north slope to Acropolis plateau; (4) House of Arrhephoroi; (5) North Portico of Erechtheion; (6) western passage of Erechtheion; (7) Caryatid Portico; (8) Naos of Erechtheion; (9) Pandroseon; (10) Theatron; (11) foundations of archaic Athena Polias Temple; (12) great altar of Athena Polias; (13) precinct of Zeus Polieus.
Drawing by Peter Carl.

the pre-Classical agora.[10] To the time of Kekrops were attributed also the aetiological myths of the Acropolis, the contests of Athena versus Poseidon and Hephaistos; and the two male deities were respectively echoed in the doubled Erechtheus and Erichthonios. Poseidon was also the protagonist of the battle between Erechtheus and Eumolpos of Eleusis, another pairing (Athens-Eleusis) preserved in the annual cycle. To the east was the great altar of Athena Polias and further east lay the precinct of Zeus Polieus on the highest point of the Acropolis, which Pausanias attributed to the period of Erechtheus. Pausanias also recorded the cult's unusual ox-sacrifice (again part of the ceremonial cycle) in which the animal selected himself by eating grain; the priest fled after killing the ox, and the sacrificial axe was subjected to a judicial trial.[11]

The association of city-founding and violence committed by ancient hero-figures and their gods is not unusual – for example, Tiamat and Marduk, Cain and Abel, Romulus and Remus. We can detect here another modality of primordial earth and its temporality, whereby earth entombs the memory of the founding struggle; and the Greeks commemorated the *oikistes*, the city-founder of a colony-town, with a *heröon* (a commemorative tomb descended from Mycenaean practice). In this respect a city is like a symbol – it is a permanent locus of reinterpretation.

However, the myths associated with the Acropolis were not accomplished once in the past and then simply commemorated, or even annually re-enacted, as in the

Mesopotamian New Year's ritual.[12] It is quite likely there was never a single definitive reading of the tensions and reciprocities incorporated in these myths,[13] and the distributed character of the shrines and symbolic artefacts, with echoes well beyond the Acropolis itself, suggests an autonomy of the parts measured against a common ground of difference. For Athenian 'performance culture',[14] the drama of vulnerability and freedom in the context of divine forces was played out upon exposed ground in the agonic situations of Greek tragedy, of the bouleuterion, where laws were made, and of the law-courts, where the winner or the loser was less important than the affirmation of lawfulness. Under these conditions, 'the' sacred was not limited to the sacrifices, altars and temples, but rather pervaded the praxes of the polis with greater or lesser degrees of intensity, acknowledging claims from different deities, depending upon the topic. Indeed, the topic – what Hans-Georg Gadamer called 'the priority of the question'[15] – shares with the rupture or *Riss* the capacity to endow the common ground of difference with a direction, scope and horizon. In the performative, logos-culture of the democratic polis, the Heideggerian earth was latent with the Aristotelian *topoi*,[16] the 'common-places' or typical situations.

Encouraging a reading of the Periclean Erechtheion in terms of the conventions of tragedy was not only the theatron attached to the north facade (Figure 1.2, no. 10)[17] but also the east and west facades acted more like the fifth-century *skene*[18] than typical temple facades, if Alexandra Lesk is correct that the interior was a single room with its floor at the lower level.[19] Moreover, this might clarify the mysterious ascent from the Erechtheion's great north portico, along the inside of its west wall with its benches and central door to the Pandroseon, up a stair over the tomb of Kekrops within in the Caryatid portico (which rested on the foundations of the old Athena Polias temple), departing from the Caryatid portico's east door towards the altar of Athena Polias (Figure 1.2, nos. 3, 5–7, 12). Against the west-east orientation of all other movement on the Acropolis, this north-south ascent was deemed important enough to celebrate with the two remarkable porticoes, which significantly modified what otherwise could have been a simple box of a temple. One might speculate that the porticoes were intended to evoke a palace, specifically that of Erechtheus (certainly 'dwelling' is the fundamental metaphor of orientation, not just in ancient Greece); and the incorporation of Kekrops' tomb endows the building with the character of an heröon. However, the earth notably suffers in this precinct – the 'earth-born' Kekrops, Erectheus and Erichthonius all endure strife, the site is marked by Poseidon's sea-basin and trident-strike, and the building is positioned across a one-storey drop in the limestone. Accordingly, one suspects that this chthonic passage, unique on the Acropolis, incorporated the final segment of a Mycenean-era ritual ascent, reserved for a few celebrants: from the caves in the north face of the Acropolis, via the steps carved into the hill behind the House of the Arrhephoroi, traversing the cult sites of Athena Polias to arrive at her altar in the centre of the Acropolis plateau.

All this articulated the modalities of Athena, with whom the fractious polis found common identity. Athena's snake and owl, which inhabited the Pandroseon along with her olive tree, testify to archaic communication between the chthonic and celestial domains. Her Mycenaean character as mistress of the citadel was augmented by her command of the crafts (Hephaistos), of horse management (Poseidon), of agriculture (her olive tree) and of cunning intelligence (she was daughter of Metis, though ultimately born from the head of Zeus), which led Walter Burkert to call her a deity of 'disciplined civilisation'.[20]

With regard to the role of 'the' sacred in the possible architectural embodiment of 'disciplined civilisation', however, it is a profound irony that, except for classicists and archaeologists, this topography rich in practices and references, suffering and ambiguity – an earth deep in temporal symbolism – has been obscured by adulation of the bombastic, if carefully crafted, Parthenon. Without cultic significance and serving mostly as a treasury, this extravagant work of propaganda has nonetheless served generations of European architects since Cyriacus of Ancona in the fifteenth century as a paradigm of sacred architecture (alternating with the Gothic cathedral after Goethe). The pious sanctimony of Leo von Klenze's famous painting of 1846 became, twenty years later, the ecstatic *Prière sur l'Acropole*[21] of Ernest Renan, on which Le Corbusier drew for inspiration. Embodying the Enlightenment fascination with 'monuments', this misplaced adulation has distorted the expectations surrounding architecture's participation in 'the' sacred, and thereby of any architecture which aspires to incarnate the ancient Greek values supposedly captured in the innumerable views and obligatory architects' sketches of the Parthenon.

We might designate the area around the Erechtheion a topography of praxis, in virtue of the need for sustained and concrete involvement with its several distributed settings, as against the dominantly optical and didactic performance of the Parthenon. However, the Erechthion's *implicit* dialogue with the setting of tragic theatre became the *explicit* basis for representation in the theatrical perspectivism of the succeeding Hellenistic culture. The *skene* itself – demarcating a domain in which human and divine communicated in a time-out-of-time for the purposes of reflection[22] – became progressively more elaborate across the period and became the standard armature of architectural ornament (thus greatly influencing its Renaissance emulators). Additionally in the Hellenistic period, there developed a sensitivity to landscape composition, well known from wall frescoes and mosaics, but also deployed in the planning of significant ensembles, such as the Museion in Alexandria, where the practice originated,[23] the citadel at Pergamon,[24] the Macedonian development of Samothrace[25] and, in Rome, the Agrippan and Augustan installation of the Pantheon, Tomb of Augustus, the Horologium and Ara Pacis in the Campus Martius.[26] By incorporating Virgil's rewriting of the foundation of Rome (itself a characteristic Hellenistic play with genres), Augustus' *saeculum* of peace was made into the consequence of four temporalities: his own, the family *gens*, the symbolic history of Rome and celestial movements.[27] The ensemble was described by Strabo as 'presenting to the eye the appearance of stage-painting . . . so marvellous as to make the rest of the city its appendage . . . this most sacred part of Rome'.[28]

This conception of a landscape of didactic monuments, understood less through praxis than through views of relationships between edifices and artefacts bearing iconography and oriented to commemoration, lies at the heart of perspectivism.[29] Its evident debt to theatre will dominate Roman architecture and planning; it will be resurrected in the European Renaissance and will endure as the basis for architectural thinking into the present (as, for example, the subjective perception of 'forms' in 'space'). The Augustan operation exhibits the comprehensive ambitions of this style of thought by importing into European architecture the legacy of Alexander the Great, by which the polis is fused with Near Eastern and Central Asian styles of rulership: a more or less 'divine' king mediates earthly exigencies with the cosmic conditions. For the next thirteen and a half centuries, from Cordoba to Chang'an, there are no republican governments, only the hieratic thrones, domes and elaborate ornament of royal hierarchies and ceremony.[30]

In order for this to be effective, the literally 'visionary' architecture absorbed attributes of 'the' sacred, on the basis of the Stoic and then Neoplatonic conceptions of a continuum between divine and human. The late Roman imperial idiom, from which emerged Byzantine, Sassanid and Umayyad architectures, claimed the upper strata of this continuum, in which the personal and institutional aspects[31] of the princes and priests ensured that political, judicial or military exploits always carried an aura of 'the' sacred, even if, for Christian theology, Augustine had argued a distinct separation between the heavenly and earthly cities (*De civitate Dei*, 426 CE). For example, the niche addressing a communal room came to embody the divine authority of the ruler, priest, judge or teacher. All of these were combined in the figure of the enthroned Christ presiding over the Ecclesia set within the hemicycle behind Constantine's Anastasis Rotunda representing Heavenly Jerusalem at the end of time, in the fifth-century apse mosaic in Santa Pudenziana, Rome (Figure 1.3). The niche was a recurring presence in palaces,

Figure 1.3 Apse mosaic of Santa Pudenziana, Rome, fifth century CE (and sixteenth-century repairs).
Photograph by Welleschik, 2009. Wikimedia Commons (https://commons.wikimedia.org/wiki/File:Apsis_mosaic,_Santa_Pudenziana,_Rome_W2.JPG).

courts, churches and mosques (the *mihrab*), as well as in countless ivory reliefs, frescoes, mosaics and manuscript illuminations.

It is evidently another legacy of Hellenistic perspectivism and its preoccupation with the theatrical realm in-between gods and humans that attention shifted from the earth-oriented topography of praxis to elevational phenomena such as the niche, the triumphal arch, the *scenae frons* and the domed tetrapylon. A domed tetrapylon was the centre of al-Mu'tasim's (836 CE) vast palace and gardens at Samarra,[32] a mode of dwelling for royals favoured by divinities that can be traced from Babylon and Nineveh[33] via Tiberius' planetary villas on Capri and Nero's Domus Aurea to Versailles and the Yuangmingyuan (Old Summer Palace). Neither temples nor wholly secular, these configurations were exceedingly ambitious in their scope of reference,[34] and hosted the most sophisticated (and often dangerous) court protocol and artists – such as the famous Ziryab ('blackbird'), who, in the early ninth century, introduced to the court of Abd ar-Rahman II at Cordoba the manners, music, poetry, cuisine and the attire of the court at Baghdad.[35] These courts also managed education and scholarship, and the monasteries and madrassas were run as little courts.

Thus, all that mattered for situating oneself in the whole was framed by this culture, for whose stratification from heaven to earth the sixth-century Neoplatonic theologian Dionysius the Pseudo-Areopagite invented the term 'hierarchy'. The courts of both palace and temple expressed themselves in the manners and ceremonies of appearance, respect, judgement, obedience, propitiation, gratitude, gift-giving and elaborate hosting (or their equally formalized opposites, in the case of an enemy). For these purposes was imagined a fusion of actual and symbolic architecture, at once immanent and transcendent. A sixth-century ivory relief from Constantinople depicts the archangel Michael, looking like a young palace official holding an orb with cross and a staff, paused at the top step of an aedicula made of fluted Corinthian columns supporting an acanthus-ornamented arch and garland framing a cross inscribed within a victor's crown upon a scallop shell (Figure 1.4).[36] Since Michael was judge at the Garden of Eden and will be at the end of time, the festooned aedicula marks the alpha and omega of Christian temporal existence – a portal in both Eden and Heaven – and associates it with cosmic justice. There are three transformations in 'the' sacred represented here.

First, it is the assumption of traditional cosmologies that humans are ultimately obliged to the fundamental natural conditions in which they are embedded,[37] and that therefore errancy as freedom – from these conditions – lies at the heart of cosmic ethics. It is the significant attribute of being human to be both part of and potentially emancipated from these fundamental conditions (an insight present also in Aristotle's notion of humans as political animals or the phrase, 'human nature'). If the Assyrian and Greek examples exhibit an obvious obligation to the fundamental conditions, the Old Testament declared a purely ethical relation with JHWH, eschewing the media of participation of the Hebrews' Near Eastern neighbours (at least until Solomon's Temple and its cult). The New Testament doctrine of salvation went further, promising emancipation from human finitude to those who could negotiate the divinely created, historical world with faith, hope and love.[38]

Architecture and the Question of 'the' Sacred

Figure 1.4 Ivory half-diptych, Constantinople, mid-sixth century CE, depicting archangel Michael in a festooned portal.
Source: British Museum.

Secondly, this had a significant effect upon the experience of temporality. The Old Testament promised that deeds accomplished in history were potentially endowed with universal significance, as one sees in the cast of characters both named and anonymous that accompany saints and the Holy Family carved into Gothic Cathedral portals or frescoed on the walls of the Palazzo della Ragione, Padova. Festivals of saints and the Holy Family also marked the Christian year within a universal temporality oriented to the eschaton, when all historical time would be superseded and human finitude effaced. Similarly, the Christian ecumene transcended all actual empires, regions, cities, villages or houses. In a constant tension between Jesus the poor man of Nazareth and the Kingdom of Heaven, all true meaning resided in this transcendent condition: everything visible referred away from itself, it could only be an earthly allusion to the eternal state. The actual deferred to the real or true, following the incarnational principle of the iconodule John of Damascus (*On the Divine Images*, ca. 730 CE): things, images, architecture acted as the embodying vehicles for extravagant allegories (such as those of Maximus Confessor, *Mystagogia*, ca. 625 CE). These allegories fused the paradigmatic past and future; and in order to cope with the referential ambiguities – the ethical significance of the several temporalities in play – John Cassian (ca. 420 CE) was compelled to acknowledge four hermeneutic levels to account for the continuity between Jerusalem as history and as anagogic completion of Being.[39]

Thirdly, therefore, this temporal transformation deeply affected the embodying architecture. The most sumptuous church or palace evaporated into light and dense theology in a mood of constant preparation of one's soul – the invisible, essential part of one's identity (Figure 1.5).[40] If the modernist conception of 'space' received its experience of infinity from perspectivism's involvement with depth, extensity and the horizon, it received its expectation of spiritual intensity from the medieval metamorphosis of straightforward masonry architecture into its opposite: fields of colour, ornament and symbols.[41] The modernist concept of 'space' also expected abstract geometrical or mathematical relationships to refer to ideas or concepts, usually as fragments in a formally organized field. This too was prefigured, although within quite specific structures of reference, in the capacity of the rhythmic orders and patterns of the medieval coordination of architecture with ornament to embody a divine transcendence, as if the eschaton could be anticipated in an always-already time-out-of-time of the rites and ceremonies. When they were not eliminated altogether, as in Islamic sacred architecture, figures were reduced to faces, postures and garments, and they were extracted from the background scenography so important to perspective representation (and to later Persian miniatures). Instead, they were embedded directly in the highly articulate ornament,[42] alive with symbols actual and potential (such as the ubiquitous vine *rinceaux*, lying between geometric pattern and calligraphy). The rhythmic intensity of these configurations, re-enacted in the cycles of rites and ceremonies and embodied in the idiom of moral authority (which of course did not prevent wholesale slaughter and destruction in the name of justice), culminates the commitment to a temporality beyond history.

In the fourteenth century, this commitment began to dissolve and one can detect a turn to what might loosely be called 'humanism' in such phenomena as the development

Architecture and the Question of 'the' Sacred

Figure 1.5 Palatine Chapel of Roger II, Palermo, Sicily, twelfth century CE, combining Mediterranean Norman, Byzantine and Islamic ornamental practices.
Photograph by Fintan Corrigan, 2014. Wikimedia Commons.

of Persian narrative painting, the dramatic frescoes of the Chora Monastery (Kariye Camii), the Nasrid Alhambra after Muhammad V, the *Mudéjar* facade of the Parroquieta Chapel of La Seo de Zaragoza, Guillaume de Machaux's polyphonic *Messe de Notre Dame*, the works influenced by the Devotio Moderna anticipating the Lutheran reform and the rediscovery of both republican government and perspectivism in Northern Italy. Since the eventual outcome, with regard to 'the' sacred, was the secular culture of the European Enlightenment, the intervening centuries might be regarded the Great Transition,[43] if one follows Charles Taylor's long and detailed account of how we arrived to *A Secular Age*.[44] In particular, he argues a cluster of interwoven reciprocities: of theological reform with the advance of science, of disenchantment in the Christian dispensation with the courage to take responsibility for ourselves, of a transcendent Great Chain of Being with immanent chains of causation, of spiritual orientation with pathology and cure, and of hermeneutics with philosophically informed theory. The resulting 'society' of individuals acting reasonably for mutual benefit Taylor called 'exclusive humanism', and its evident debt to eighteenth-century economic theory allowed some thinkers to consider the equivalent of Adam Smith's hidden hand to be both the work of nature and, like nature, God-given.

The ambiguity of who or what was this God under such conditions – other than a symbol for the unity of Being – testifies to the interlacing of the European Enlightenment with post-medieval Christianity. For the visual arts, the result was 'space', achieved during Romanticism. Indeed, the first experiments with redefining the Christian God coincided with the first indications of what would be required for 'space'.[45] The French Revolutionary *Fêtes* of the late eighteenth century celebrated a Supreme Being embodied in didactic monuments set in a vast horizontal space (equality as indefinite extension) under the Creator God's[46] vault of heaven. The coercive scripting of spontaneous unity sought to suppress history or memories for the sake of new origins. This experience of temporality was the opposite of all conditions of 'the' sacred that we have considered. Even though both *arche* and *eschaton* can orient temporal interpretation – the first in terms of original conditions, the second in terms of final conditions – the historical unfolding of difference from the *arche* sustains a plurality of individual temporal characters, whereas the expectation that all diversity will add up to a Final Judgement leads to the notion of Time in the singular, conflated with pragmatic history. Accordingly, the Christian eschaton maintained an immanent presence in, for example, motifs of Progress (although open-ended and typically characterized by the death-and-replacement of technology) or Heidegger's lugubrious reflections on 'destiny'.[47]

However, it is the Romantic experience of Nature that seems to have contributed most significantly to 'space'. On the one hand, Nature was dissolving into the fields, forces and particles discovered by science, and described by an ever more sophisticated mathematics. K. F. W. Schelling's *Naturphilosophie* sought to rescue the situation, in particular the Kantian legacy of a separation, or need for a common ground, between 'Nature' and 'Mind'. *Naturphilosophie* is not a philosophy *of* nature, but rather nature philosophizing. Only seven years after Kant's *Critique of Judgement* appeared, he had argued in the *Ideas for a Philosophy of Nature*, 'Nature should be Mind made visible, Mind the invisible Nature. Here then, in the absolute identity of Mind *in us* and Nature *outside us*, the problem of the possibility of a Nature external to us must be resolved.'[48]

On the other hand, Baruch Spinoza's identification of God with Nature persisted, via concepts like the Absolute (philosophical) or the Sublime (psychological).[49] More precisely, Nature – as an object of contemplation – became a symbol of ethical commitment progressively more and more opposed to the Nature of science or technology.[50] Writing on 'landscape', a term which presumes natural processes are to be digested as a view, Carl Gustav Carus declared in 1831: 'Man had first to recognize the divinity of nature as the true bodily revelation or – in human terms – language of God.'[51] Samuel Taylor Coleridge, like Carus an avid student of Schelling, went even further in reprising a motif that originally appeared in the sixteenth century,[52] the identification of the artist-genius with *natura naturans* (the creative power of nature, usually accorded to God, as distinct from *natura naturata*, the things of created nature): 'Believe me, you must master the essence, the *natura naturans*, which presupposes a bond between nature in the higher sense and the human soul.'[53]

This intense negotiation between Mind, God[54] and Nature in Schelling's *Naturphilosophie* may have started with anxieties about Kantian dualism, but his *Ideas* strove to understand the mutual sympathy between life-processes and the then mysterious forces of, particularly, magnetism, but also electricity, heat and light as well as properties of air and matter and principles such as repulsion and attraction. Even if its philosophical importance declined in Schelling's lifetime, the aspiration to identify something like a World Soul (the topic of Schelling's publication immediately after the *Ideas*) immanent in Nature remained a stimulant, often indirect and unacknowledged, to scientists, artists and thinkers[55] well into the present, such as one finds in Le Corbusier's *Le Poème de l'angle droit*, or in Heidegger's commitment to Being and the pre-Socratics, or in Tim Morton's 'dark ecology'.[56]

Friedrich Schiller is usually left out of considerations surrounding *Naturphilosophie*, but his programme outlined in *The Aesthetic Education of Man*[57] to fuse Nature with morality and the 'sensuous instinct' (experience) with the 'formal instinct' (reason) in order to 'cherish triumphant truth in the sanctuary of your heart; give it incarnate form through beauty',[58] was deeply prescient as to how the new conditions would be understood. First, as a programme of education, it was a foundation-text for *Bildung* (literally, 'picturing'), and therefore for culture-as-project, the central motif of perspectivism.[59] Secondly, by effectively translating Immanuel Kant's critiques of judgement and pure reason into aesthetics, he made art – or, more generally, poesy – the principal domain in which the desired synthesis could take place. Certainly for architects, the dual legacy of Schelling and Schiller identified what the utopian aspects of 'space' were expected to achieve,[60] but as well the counterarguments from 'place'.[61]

And yet the artist- or poet-philosopher supposedly endowed with the creative powers of God never seemed able to escape a persistent melancholy, apparently cursed by a Faustian inability to turn human finitude into something genuinely creative – a mood now of course dominated by Anthropocene guilt – as if original sin too had been imported from Christianity. The transformation of the Great Chain of Being into things and fields with properties, attributes, forces, states of mind and so on, represented in equations, poetic stanzas, music or paintings – an ocean of possible affinities, conflicts and temporalities, governed alternately by necessity or chance – engendered another fundamental legacy of Romanticism: the fragment, 'complete in itself like a porcupine',[62] for which 'space' would become the receptacle.[63] Always permeated by the reciprocity of Schiller's sensuous and formal intuitions, as likely to be illuminated by wit as by logic, 'space' was a concept of infinity suspended between God and mathematical physics,[64] but which was determined to be apprehended by the emotive yet critical soul of the individual observer. Carus experienced landscape – still today mooted as a metaphorical 'ground' of 'space' – in these terms: 'you lose yourself in infinite space . . . your ego disappears. *You are nothing; God is all.*'[65]

In the paintings of Carus' good friend Caspar David Friedrich, the figures are lost in 'infinite space' in a particular way (Figure 1.6).[66] They are often seen from behind, as if sharing the view of the observer of the painting; and of course the view as critical contemplation is the mode of involvement here – literally world-as-picture. The great depth of his paintings, often following a path into the woods or towards a mountain or the sea, invites the viewer to join the figures on a journey to the horizon. This journey comes from the English Garden, which was designed not for the collective festivals of the Baroque Garden but for the critical observer, alone or accompanied by

Figure 1.6 Caspar David Friedrich, *Sunset (Brothers)*, oil on canvas, circa 1835.
Source: Hermitage, St Petersburg: ГЭ-10005. Public domain.

a few friends, who would roam a landscape and its monuments seeking insights for reflection – a *Petit Tour* through a 'natural' topography redolent of Culture and History recalling Strabo's description of the Campus Martius. This garden had been imported to France, where it became associated with the pre-social 'natural' order of Jean-Jacques Rousseau.[67] As if to replicate Schiller's sensuous and formal instincts, nature at this time became more 'organic', while architecture turned to introverted monuments obeying the geometric formalism of Claude Nicholas Durand's types disposed according to axial circulation routes – a reciprocity still alive in Le Corbusier's Ville Radieuse.[68] However, if the importance accorded to *la marche* as a succession of views was meant to embody something like a life-journey of *Bildung* (certainly expected of the characteristic Enlightenment institution, the museum), the wanderers in Friedrich's paintings found themselves claimed by an ensouled earth[69] whose horizon was frequently obscured by trees or by transitory atmospheric effects like moonlit fog. Often placed centrally, as if endowed with the status of Everyman, Friedrich's figures stared at temporalities marked by obscurity, death and sentimentality.

In other words, Coleridge's identification with the Godlike powers of *natura naturans* confronted its radical opposite, the abject Carus before the spectacle of God's *natura naturata*. The source of this dilemma was the Romantic inability to escape Cartesian-Kantian dualism (and therefore perspectivism) – positing existence as a problem of understanding, of accommodating Nature to Mind according to the latter's linguistic abilities, which required transposing everything concrete into concepts.

Once God, Nature, Mind and all reality are sublimated into concepts – Romanticism is the period from which 'the' sacred emerges along with the philosophical God – everything is essentially the same: fragments with their fields of reference, their debates and the people associated with them. Embodiment becomes an exotic topic, to be rediscovered after Heidegger[70] as a corrective to the noetic, anthropo-logo-centric Western project of domination. Even once acknowledged, 'embodiment' itself remains a concept, like 'the' body; and architects adhere to conceptual terminology – 'materiality' is preferred over 'wood' or 'plastic' or metaphors. The generalizations and options of conceptual thinking strive to control the freedom with a necessity made of internal consistency based upon formal coherence, of which style of thought architecture has become the paradigm. The Romantic framing of present aspirations is as insufficiently appreciated as is the degree to which 'space' has evacuated from architecture credible conditions for a living sacred.

It is quite possible that we do not need a living sacred; but the resulting vague sacrality inherited from Romanticism should be acknowledged for what it is. Temporally, modernist Romanticism sought to overcome the impasse of Coleridge and Carus by committing to an intramundane eschatology: the creation of new, inevitably better, futures, and typically through the motif of revolution. This included the Italian Fascists, who proclaimed an exhaustive iconography in their Exhibition of the Fascist Revolution, Rome, 1933. The succession of didactic rooms culminated in the lurid Sacrario celebrating 'sacred' martyrdom to the National Party of Fascism (PNF),[71] which installed the Romantic temporal dilemma at the heart of their enterprise.

Giuseppe Terragni's well-known Casa del Fascio in Como, 1936, presented itself as 'a House, a School, a Temple . . . the Houses of Fascism will be dedicated to the memory of the Fallen for the Revolution'.[72] As if to suppress Fascism's combination of culture and violence – a perverse rendering of Burkert's 'disciplined civilisation' – Terragni stressed the technical means by which the building achieved a symbolic synthesis. Respecting Mussolini's desideratum of reconciling Italic tradition with technological modernity, Terragni filtered a renaissance Florentine palazzo through prismatic geometry, clothing it in ancient marble articulated by steel, aluminium, glass and linoleum.[73] The visitor to the Como Casa del Fascio would be mesmerized by the gridded layers of whiteness, of opacity, translucency and reflections – a stereometric incarnation of Friedrich's luminous mists (Figure 1.7). Concentrated in the northwest corner of the building and facing the Duomo were the temple-like, commemorative settings.[74] Of these, the most significant was the Sacrario of the Martyrs of Como, a room 3.75 metres high and deep set on the ground floor directly opposite the polished black marble walls and glass block of the main stairs. Both Sacrario and stairs occupied a full structural bay marked by a reflective black ceiling, establishing between them a chthonic threshold to the central atrium. Terragni wrote of the Sacrario that it 'resolves . . . the surrounding geometry' and that its pink granite walls, black granite floor and black diorite memorial block 'can recall the primitive royal or religious constructions of ancient Mycenae or Egypt . . . a great sense of sepulchral religiosity'.[75] A Fascist dagger and revolver were fused in a block of crystal and immured partway in the floor. A crystal cabinet containing the squadron pennants was set into the west wall of the Sacrario, and its width was carried 3.75 metres across the

Figure 1.7 Casa del Fascio, Como, 1936, view south across atrium from conference room with reflection, as published in *Quadrante 35-36*, 1936, p. 16.

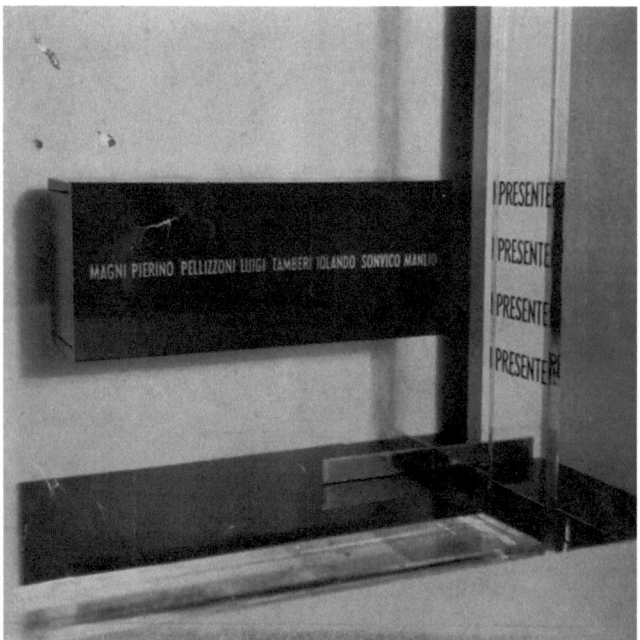

Figure 1.8 Casa del Fascio, Como, 1936, view of model of Sacrario; as published in *Quadrante 35-36*, 1936, p. 8.

floor in a slab of crystal, at whose end stood an isolated blade of crystal 70 millimetres thick rising to the ceiling (also 3.75 metres, making a square void framed by crystal), on which was inscribed 'PRESENTE' (the response at military roll call) four times, once for each martyr. Terragni passed over the possible Christian content of a stainless steel cross lying at the base of this stele in order to remark its role in the harmonic division of the floor (Figure 1.8).

Terragni called the Casa del Fascio's disturbingly beautiful fusion of resolute geometry and ecstasy 'the spiritual elements which stand at the base of all Fascist Mysticism'.[76] It would be hard to imagine a more intense, even poignant, manifestation of the Romantic dilemma of 'the' sacred than the isolated stele of crystal embodying the martyr's soul answering the call to muster in the posthumous army of the PNF. The massive granite blocks (the Romantic earth) of Terragni's Sacrario metaphorically compacted centuries of Italian culture into a pre-Italic origin that was released in the crystalline martyrdom. The Fascist transformation of the Christian *Ecclesia Militans* into a project for accomplishment in history conferred a bizarre sanctity upon the agents of violence.

The beauty of the Casa del Fascio disturbs because, unlike the ponderous monumentality usually associated with Fascist architecture (including Terragni's Danteum project), it exhibits characteristics of Romantic spatiality that draw 'orthodox' Modernism close to Fascism. The similarities and differences between Italian Fascist and other modernist utopias need not be argued here.[77] Comparisons with, for example, El Lisstizky's PROUN[78] room (1923) or Le Corbusier's notion of *l'espace indicible* or, for that matter, Leo von Klenze's *Befreiungshalle* (1842–63) would yield analogous aspirations to cope with the temporal anxiety of human finitude by resorting to Schiller's two intuitions: the expectation that a geometric arrangement of forms in space would anchor an emotional experience beyond pragmatic history. A consequence of attempting to arrange Being for the sake of human finitude, the persistent subject–object confrontation of our individual mortality with the infinite horizon leaves us always-already wanderers within a theatre of references and possibilities. 'Space' is the void between the mortal self and the horizon, potentially 'sacred' everywhere but nowhere actually; it makes the world available for our projects. The field depends upon the formal coherence of its fragments ('space') and will always remain introverted and hypothetical, whereas the universal arises from concrete involvements with particulars[79] (the topography of praxis) always reinterpreting the claims and affordances of the fundamental conditions.

The hypothetical character of Romantic spatiality might seem to preserve time-out-of-time coupled to a transcendence, even if one not recognized in any existing religion. This may have some truth for the architect's play with forms-in-space, always allegorical in varying degrees. However, the inhabitant is not a Nietzschean artist but a celebrant of PNF ceremonies such as those attached to the Sacrario. Terragni is reticent on the Casa's social remit and silent on God. Instead, he euphemizes Fascist violence by implying Christian martyrdom; but without the martyrs there is no 'Temple'. It is the sacrificial death which transcends the temporality of architectural history since Egypt and which makes the metamorphosis of granite into crystal (and therefore all the carefully judged glass in the building) more significant than a harmonious pattern of materials in light. It appears that the pathetic death for the PNF has been mobilized to save the architecture from dissolving into a useful, beautiful abstraction. The reverse is the case: this death, stranded within the horizons of history's great empirical process, is intrinsic to Romantic spatiality.

Could one extract the Sacrario and thereby remove the perfectly dignified, beautifully executed Casa del Fascio from the PNF *Gesamtkunstwerk*? There are considerable overlaps between sensible government and PNF policies, indicated by the ease with which most of the institutional buildings, stripped of their Fascist iconography, survived the fall of the party; and Fascist urban interventions were spatially less 'totalitarian' than their CIAM equivalents. Nonetheless, the Fascist, Nazi and communist regimes have confirmed the view that collective life organized by hierarchical government for 'spiritual' purposes suppresses individual freedom. Let us replace the Casa's emphasis upon martyrdom with an emphasis upon the situations of negotiation (therefore, more like Terragni's school – the Asilo Infantile Sant'Elia, Como, 1934–7). On this basis, we could admire the dignity of the elements rooted in Italian urban custom and decorum, such as the basic arrangement, the offices and the *sportelli* (the windows where propitiations by the populace are made), allowing the Casa to echo the medieval Broletto (meeting hall for civic assemblies) just north of the Duomo. However, we might hesitate at the Casa's isolated monumentality or the need for everything to obey a universal rhythm. This last quality is generally regarded one of its salient features, particularly insofar as it transforms the building into shades of luminosity; but it also betrays an aspiration to be another Parthenon-like 'temple'.

Ostensibly conforming to a programme similar to that of Mussolini – Prime Minister Jawaharlal Nehru's reconciliation of tradition with technological innovation – Le Corbusier's Capitol Park at Chandigarh has survived stigmatization, even neo-colonialism. Whatever one's opinion of Le Corbusier's interjection of his own myths (including a Martyrs' Memorial) and vaguely Mughal precedents in the dominantly Hindu Punjab, the proposition is embodied in the iconography of the architecture and landscape. The similarity to the planning of the Augustan Campus Martius is obvious, although the Capitol Park is institutional rather than commemorative: isolated from the town of Chandigarh on its own plateau, it displaces political and legal life from the agora to a semi-sacred acropolis.

It may be that the perspective theatre supporting a civic dignity is the best we can do. If so, it is not the ancient Greek topography of praxis, in which accountability to the fundamental conditions permeated all praxes, as a measure of ethical deviation (tragedy) and ontological orientation (philosophy), and was embodied in the whole polis. This accountability does not require myths, gods, sacrifices or martyrs (or ancient Greeks); but it does require a constant interpretation of the tension between freedom and the conditions pertaining-to-all.

We seem to be stranded in a Nietzschean effort to identify a Dionysian-Apollonian mediation honest to life's existential struggle, not demeaned by transfiguration into illusory, decadent or nihilistic beauty (false hope).[80] Unlike all but a few of their modern equivalents, ancient temples and shrines still command a general respect, even though the gods have been declared as ridiculous[81] as the ways of life and styles of government those temples once supported. At the same time, gigantic cities and technological innovations have reduced the visceral claims of earth and horizon, further displacing their meaning, common-to-all, from ontological origins to historical possibilities. The generosity or promiscuity of what Siegfried Giedion called 'space conception'[82] – open to all references but requiring everything to be supplied for concreteness, relevance or coherence – has reduced any rupture or *Riss* to merely a more or less radical modulation of the infinite field of possible forms.

Taylor sees our possibilities within exclusive humanism to be bracketed between Nietzsche's 'exhilaration in a Dionysian world of the eternally self-creating, self-destroying, beyond good and evil' and the dignity of Albert Camus' Dr Rieux in *The Plague*, who self-authorizes the 'absurd' commitment to others in the face of the indifferent universe.[83] Neither an orientation in temporality nor an ethical commitment to the collective of people, nature, things and technology have yet emerged to provide the conditions for creating new sacred practices. The history of architecture's embodiment of 'the' sacred suggests that a proper development of the supposedly 'failed' side of Romanticism, Schelling's *Naturphilosophie*, offers a more creative restoration of our obligation to the fundamental natural conditions than does the side of Romanticism which has enjoyed prominence – the revolutionary spatiality of individual freedom fulfilled in conceptual 'space'. Similarly, architects might need ontotheology less than a practical wisdom respectful of the deep metabolism of particular circumstances.

Notes

1. And conflict – see Peter Burke, *Cultural Hybridity* (Cambridge: Polity Press, 2009).
2. P. O. Harper, E. Klengel-Brandt, J. Aruz and K. Benzel, *Discoveries at Ashur on the Tigris, Assyrian Origins* (New York: Metropolitan Museum of Art, 1995), cat. no. 75.
3. See the entry by Klaus Wagensonner, then head of the Cuneiform Digital Library Initiative at Oxford: http://cdli.ox.ac.uk/wiki/doku.php?id=pedestal_tukulti_ninurta.
4. *Republic* 505a-541b.
5. Hans-Georg Gadamer, *Truth and Method*, trans. W. Glen-Doepel (London: Sheed and Ward, 1979), Part One.II.1.c; and see his *The Relevance of the Beautiful* (Cambridge: University of Cambridge Press, 1986). For more material, Alessandro Falassi, ed., *Time Out of Time, Essays on the Festival* (Albuquerque: University of New Mexico Press, 1987).
6. Martin Heidegger, 'The Origin of the Work of Art' (1936), in *Basic Writings: Martin Heidegger*, ed. D. F. Krell (London: Routledge, 1993 edition), 139–212.
7. Martin Heidegger, 'Language', in *Poetry, Language, Thought*, ed. and trans. A. Hofstadter (New York: Harper & Row, 1975), 204.
8. Mircea Eliade, *The Sacred and the Profane: The Nature of Religion*, trans. W. R. Trask (New York: Harper Torchbooks, 1957). Eliade's leading concept of the hierophany or theophany seeks to have 'the' sacred presented to a worshipper like an object to a subject, suppressing the immanence of deities and the deference to sacred protocol throughout existence. It is a

more nuanced version of Rudolf Otto's *mysterium tremendum* (*The Idea of the Holy*) (1917), trans. J. W. Harvey (Oxford: Oxford University Press, 1923 and 1950).

9. My reading is largely based on Jeffrey M. Hurwitt, *The Athenian Acropolis: History, Mythology and Archaeology from the Neolithic Era to the Present* (Cambridge: Cambridge University Press, 1999).

10. Pandrosos was the good daughter of Kekrops who obeyed Athena's instruction not to peer into the basket containing Erichthonios, unlike her two sisters, Herse and Aglauros, who leapt to their deaths off the north face of the Acropolis upon discovering Erichthonios' chthonic nature. Walter Burkert, 'The Legend of Kekrop's Daughters and the Arrhephoria: From Initiation Ritual to Panathenaic Festival', in *Savage Energies: Lessons of Myth and Ritual in Ancient Greece*, trans. P. Bing (Chicago: University of Chicago Press, 2001), 37–63.

11. Pausanias, *Guide to Greece*, 1.28.10-11 and 1.24.4.

12. Still useful is Henri Frankfort, 'The New Year's Festival', in *Kingship and the Gods* (Chicago: Chicago University Press, 1978 edition), 313–33.

13. See the A side of the large fifth-century red-figure calyx krater showing, in the centre, Kekrops and Athena with the olive tree and the basket hiding Erichthonios, surrounded by Kekrops' daughters, Hephaistos and Poseidon at [with bibliography]: http://www.beazley.ox.ac.uk/record/EEDE3A09-B840-4A28-BE4F-453F29D16F6D.

14. The term is from Rush Rehm, *Understanding Greek Tragic Theatre* (London and New York: Routledge, 2017).

15. Gadamer, 'The Hermeneutical Priority of the Question', in *Truth and Method*, Part Two.II.3.c.

16. Aristotle's *Topics* stood between the logic of the Organon and the practical wisdom of the *Politics* and *Ethics*.

17. Mary B. Hollinshead, 'The North Court of the Erechtheion and the Ritual of the Plynteria', *American Journal of Archaeology*, Archaeological Institute of America, 19, no. 2 (2015): 177–90.

18. Rehm, 'The Theatre of Dionysos', in *Understanding Greek Tragic Theatre*, chapter 4, 34–50.

19. Alexandra Lesk, *A Diachronic Examination of the Erechtheion and Its Reception* (PhD Thesis, University of Cincinnati, 2004), 154–64.

20. Walter Burkert, *Greek Religion,* trans. J. Raffan (Oxford: Basil Blackwell, 1985), 139–43.

21. For Renan, Athena and her temple embodied the core of 'absolute truth' and beauty; available in English and French at https://www.lexilogos.com/document/renan/acropolis.htm.

22. According to Aristotle's *Poetics*, Greek tragedy was a *mimesis* of praxis (1449b.6.2), which in turn involved action and reflection. The operation of *katharsis* was an aspect of the self-understanding which his *Politics* deemed the purpose of the polis (1323b40, 1325b14-33). Vitruvius (V.6.8) makes a compact architectural symbol of the *scenae frons*: it is a palace facade, framed by the *periaktoi* for changes of setting, whose front panels represent entrances from the forum and from abroad.

23. Judith McKenzie, *The Architecture of Alexandria and Egypt 300BC – AD 700* (New Haven and London: Yale University Press, 2007).

24. J. J. Pollitt, *Art in the Hellenistic Age* (Cambridge: Cambridge University Press, 1986).

25. Olga Palagia and Bonna D. Wescoat, *Samothracian Connections, Essays in Honour of James R. McCredie* (Oxford: Oxbow Books, 2010).

26. Diane Favro, *The Urban Image of Augustan Rome* (Cambridge: Cambridge University Press, 1996).

27. Phillip Hardie, *Virgil's Aeneid, Cosmos and Imperium* (Oxford: Clarendon Press, 1986).
28. Strabo, *Geography*, 3.5.8.
29. Martin Heidegger, 'The Age of the World-Picture', trans. W. Lovitt in *The Question Concerning Technology and Other Essays* (New York: Harper & Row, 1977), 115–54.
30. Matthew Canepa, 'Distant Displays of Power: Understanding Cross-Cultural Interaction Among the Elites of Rome, Sasanian Iran, and Sui-Tang China', *Ars Orientalis* 38 (*Theorizing Cross-Cultural Interaction among the Ancient and Early Medieval Mediterranean, Near East and Asia*) (2010): 121–54.
31. Ernst Kantorowicz, *The King's Two Bodies* (Princeton: Princeton University Press, 1957).
32. Alistair Northedge, 'An Interpretation of the Palace of the Caliph at Samarra (Dar al-Khilafa or Jawsaq al-Khaqni)', *Ars Orientalis* 23 (Pre-Modern Islamic Palaces, Washington DC, Freer Gallery of Art, The Smithsonian Institution and Department of History of Art, University of Michigan) (1993): 143–70.
33. Stephanie Dalley, *The Mystery of the Hanging Garden of* Babylon (Oxford: Oxford University Press, 2013).
34. The *maqsura* and *mihrab* niche in the Great Mosque at Cordoba of al-Hakam II seems to display a decorum slightly more intense than what can be deduced from the remains of his father's Hall of 'Abd al-Rahman III at the Alcazar of Madinat al-Zahra, both commissioned in the tenth century. By contrast, the richness and elaboration of the fourteenth-century vault of the Sala de las Dos Hermanas at the Alhambra exceeds that of any mosque: it is 'the most complex ceiling in the Muslim world and the apogee of Islamic art on the [Iberian] peninsula', according to James Dickie, 'The Palaces of the Alhambra', in *Al-Andalus, the Art of Islamic Spain*, ed. Jerrilynn D. Dodds (New York: Metropolitan Museum of Art, 1992), 146.
35. Carl Davila, 'Fixing a Misbegotten Biography: Ziryab in the Mediterranean World', *Al-Masaq, Journal of the Medieval Mediterranean* 21, no. 2 (August 2009): 121–36.
36. British Museum number OA.9999. http://www.britishmuseum.org/research/collection_online/collection_object_details.aspx?objectId=62025&partId=1
37. Philippe Descola, *Beyond Nature and Culture* (Chicago: University of Chicago Press, 2013). Of his four types of ontology, three – Totemism, Animism and Analogy – express the claim of the natural order in religious terms, whereas the fourth – Naturalism – is associated with Western emancipation from, and domination over, the natural order.
38. 1 Corinthians:13.
39. Historical, Analogical, Tropological, Anagogical: John Cassian, *Conlationes*, XIV.8.
40. Hans Belting, *Likeness and Presence: A History of the Image before the Era of Art,* trans. Edmund Jephcott (Chicago: University of Chicago Press, 1994).
41. Fabio Barry, *Painting in Stone: Architecture and the Poetics of Marble from Antiquity to the Enlightenment* (New Haven: Yale University Press, 2020), chapters 6–9.
42. The hierarchical disposition of significant figures in Greek Orthodox Churches by Otto Demus, *Byzantine Mosaic Decoration* (New Rochelle: Caratzas Brothers, 1976), is also evident in Latin churches. Similarly, these literally 'oriented' buildings translate the temporalities of the celestial cycles and the eschaton into a spatial disposition. The orientation of mosques to Mecca defers to the Kaaba, whose corners are oriented to the four quarters (with the Black Stone on the eastern corner), characteristic of ancient Near Eastern temples, as is the Qur'anic designation of the building in terms of modalities of house.

43. This reading is not intended to denigrate the obvious creativity of the architecture from Filippo Brunelleschi to Balthasar Neumann so much as it is to suggest that its rootedness in perspectivity lies at the heart of its influence upon contemporary notions of 'the' sacred. What first appeared in the ateliers as the perspectival field organized for a viewer was subsequently generalized by René Descartes as the *res extensa* and the *res cogitans*, by way of Luther's notion of individual communion with God. The Counter-Reformation response to Luther stimulated the shift from religion to religious experience in, for example, the *Spiritual Exercises* of Ignatius Loyola (Rome, 1548).

44. Charles Taylor, *A Secular Age* (Cambridge, MA: Belknap Press of Harvard University Press, 2007); Louis Dupré, *Passage to Modernity, an Essay in the Hermeneutics of Nature and Culture* (New Haven: Yale University Press, 1993); Amos Funkenstein, *Theology and the Scientific Imagination from the Middle Ages to the Seventeenth Century* (Princeton: Princeton University Press, 1986). On Vico, Paulo Rossi, *The Dark Abyss of Time*, trans. L. G. Cochrane (Chicago: Chicago University Press, 1984).

45. Mona Ozuf, *Festivals and the French Revolution*, trans. Alan Sheridan (Cambridge, MA: Harvard University Press, 1988), chapter 6.

46. Another frequently invoked correlate of the Christian God, from Jean-Jacques Rousseau's *Émile ou de l'Éducation* (*Émile, or On Education*), 1762. Le Corbusier will 'give thanks to the Creator' in *Le Poème de l'angle droit* (Paris: Teriade, 1953), section C.3, 89–91.

47. *Hölderlin's Hymn 'The Ister'*, trans. W. McNeill and J. Davis (Bloomington: Indiana University Press, 1996).

48. K. F. W. Schelling, *Ideas for a Philosophy of Nature* (1797 and 1803), trans. E. E. Harris and P. Heath (Cambridge: Cambridge University Press, 1988), Introduction, 42. The *Ideas* was the first of many publications on this topic.

49. Baruch Spinoza, *Ethics*, ed. and trans. E. Curley (London: Penguin, 1996), Part I, 'Of God.'

50. For example, Leo Marx, *The Machine in the Garden: Technology and the Pastoral Ideal in America* (Oxford: Oxford University Press, 1964).

51. *Nine Letters on Landscape Painting*, trans. D. Britt (Los Angeles: Getty Publications, 2002), Letter V, 117.

52. Jan Bialostocki, 'The Renaissance Concept of Nature and Antiquity', in *The Renaissance and Mannerism, Studies in Western Art, Acts of the Twentieth International Congress of the History of Art*, Vol. II, ed. Millard Meiss (Princeton: Princeton University Press, 1963), 19–30.

53. Samuel Taylor Coleridge, 'On Poesy or Art' [originally notes for a lecture in 1818], in *Modern Criticism Theory and Practice*, ed. Walter Sutton and Richard Foster (New York: Irvington Publishers, 1988), 39. Compare Novalis, *Pollen and Fragments*, trans. A. Versluis (Grand Rapids, Phanes Press), number 9 of *Pollen*: 'isn't the cosmos then in ourselves?'

54. The *amor Dei intellectualis* (the intellectual love of God) of Spinoza inspired the Romantic philosophical or literary God which had been mostly Christian and approximately Lutheran since Leibniz. See, in general, George Gusdorf, *Du Néant à Dieu dans le Savoir Romantique* (1983), now collected in *Le Romantisme*, Vol. I (Paris: Payot, 1993), 465–878.

55. Iain Hamilton Grant, *Philosophies of Nature after Schelling* (London: Continuum, 2008) and, for the context, Robert J. Richards, *The Romantic Conception of Life: Science and Philosophy in the Age of Goethe* (Chicago: Chicago University Press, 2004). John Tresch, *The Romantic Machine, Utopian Science and Technology after Napoleon* (Chicago: University of Chicago Press, 2012), on the influence of *Naturphilosophie* in France.

56. Timothy Morton, *Dark Ecology* (New York: Columbia University Press, 2016).

57. Friedrich Schiller, *Letters on the Aesthetic Education of Man*, trans. Elizabeth M. Wilkinson and L. A. Willoughby (Oxford: Clarendon, 1982).
58. Ibid., 59.
59. Heidegger, 'Age of the World Picture'; and Gadamer, *Truth and Method*, Part One.I.
60. El Lissitzky veers between the social engineering of *Russia: An Architecture for World Revolution* and the mysticism of his PROUN or NASCI texts, all collected in El Lissitzky, *Russia: An Architecture for World Revolution*, trans. E. Dluhosch (Cambridge, MA: MIT Press, 1970).
61. Edward S. Casey, *The Fate of Place* (Berkley: University of California Press, 1997).
62. Friedrich Schlegel, 'Athanaeum Fragment 206', in Friedrich Schlegel, *Philosophical Fragments,* trans. by Peter Firchow (Minneapolis: Minnesota University Press, 1991), 78.
63. Self-consciously first in Stéphane Mallarmé, *A Throw of the Dice will not Abolish Chance* (Seattle: Wave Books, 2015) first published in a journal Cosmopolis in 1897.
64. A legacy of the seventeenth century; see Dalibor Vesely, 'Mathesis Universalis in the Jesuit Tradition', in *Bohemia Jesuitica 1556-2006*, VI Capitulum, ed. Petronilla Cemus (Prague: Univerzita Karlova v Praze, 2010), 701–15.
65. Carus, *Nine Letters on Landscape Painting*, 97, emphasis original.
66. Joseph L. Koerner, *Caspar David Friedrich and the Subject of Landscape* (London: Reaktion Books, 2009 edition), proposes the term 'theomimesis' for the phenomena addressed here, and offers a slightly different reading.
67. See Dora Wiebenson, *The Picturesque Garden in France* (Princeton: Princeton University Press, 1978). See also Rousseau's final text, *Reveries of the Solitary Walker,* (1782) trans. R. Goulbourne (Oxford: Oxford University Press, 2011).
68. In parallel with similar oppositions: science-humanities, necessity-freedom, nature-culture or nature-ethics and the aesthetics of natural-artificial, and so on, all symptoms of the Nature-Mind dilemma.
69. August K. Wiedmann, *The German Quest for Primal Origins in Art, Culture and Politics, 1900-1933* (Lampeter: The Edwin Mellen Press, 1995). The earth of Friedrich differs from the Athenian common ground of difference in being rural and presented to individual visual contemplation marked by mortality within the transient horizons of history.
70. Martin Heidegger, *Being and Time,* trans. J. Macquarrie and E. Robinson (Oxford: Basil Blackwell, 1980), section III, 'The Worldhood of the World', 91–148, where the movement away from subject–object perspectivism is developed in terms of embodied spatiality. Merleau-Ponty, *Phenomenology of Perception* (1945), trans. C. Smith (London: Routledge & Kegan Paul, 1962) prefers the Husserlian 'perception-of', whereas the Heideggerian position encourages 'involvement-with' or 'claim-of'.
71. Dino Alfieri and Luigi Freddi, *Mostra della Rivoluzione Fascista*, reprint (Milan: IGIS spa., 1983); for the Sacrario – Sala U – by A. Libera and A. Valente, 227–9.
72. P. M. Bardi et al., *Quadrante 35-36 Documentario sulla Casa del Fascio di Como* (Rome, 1936), reprint (Como: Tipographia Editrice Cesare Nani, 1989), 14–15, this text signed by Terragni, capital letters original, my translation. On the institution of the Casa del Fascio, which housed Black Shirts as well as leisure and charitable organizations and all of which were required to have a sacrario, see Lucy Maulsby, *Fascism, Architecture and the Claiming of Modern Milan, 1922-1943* (Toronto: Toronto University Press, 2014); and Paolo Portoghesi, Flavio Mangione and Andrea Soffitta, eds, *L'Architettura delle Case del Fascio* (Florence: Alinea Editrice, 2006).

73. The dialogue between tradition and modernity is a persistent theme in the 'Technical Notes', written by Terragni, in Bardi et al., *Quadrante 35-36 Documentario sulla Casa del Fascio di Como*, 38–54.
74. Bardi et al., *Quadrante 35-36 Documentario sulla Casa del Fascio di Como*, 8, 15, 25, 52 for the Sacrario (ground floor); 28 for the secretary's office containing the labarum of the local federation (first floor); 8 and 52 for the Gigi Maino shrine room (third floor).
75. Ibid., 52.
76. Ibid., capitals original.
77. Roger Griffin, *Modernism and Fascism* (Houndmills and New York: Palgrave Macmillan, 2007); and Richard A. Etlin, *Modernism in Italian Architecture, 1890-1940* (Cambridge, MA: MIT Press, 1991).
78. English transliteration of a Russian acronym for 'Project for the Affirmation of the New'.
79. Peter Carl, 'On Depth: Particular and Universal, Fragment and Field', in *Fragments, Architecture and the Unfinished, Essays Presented to Robin Middleton*, ed. B. Bergdoll and W. Oechslin (London: Thames and Hudson, 2006), 23–42. Bruno Latour's Actor Network Theory was devised in the mid-1980s to account for the processes of the deep background; but, because he insisted on chains of direct connections, disallowing cultural contexts, it has not flourished as it might have.
80. Discussion in Daniel Came, ed., *Nietzsche on Art and Life* (Oxford: Oxford University Press, 2014).
81. Schiller, *Letters on the Aesthetic Education of Man*, 57, although the philosophical God persisted. Schelling had allegorized the Roman gods as aesthetic principles in his *Philosophy of Art* (originally lectures of 1802-3, posthumously published 1859), trans. D. W. Stott (Minneapolis: University of Minnesota Press, 1989).
82. *Space, Time and Architecture* (Cambridge, MA: Harvard University Press, several editions from 1941).
83. Ibid., chapter 15, section 8.

CHAPTER 2
ROMANTIC *KUNSTRELIGION* AND THE SEARCH FOR THE SACRED IN MODERN ARCHITECTURE
FROM SCHINKEL'S ALTES MUSEUM AS 'AESTHETIC CHURCH' TO ZUMTHOR'S BRUDER KLAUS FIELD CHAPEL AS *GESAMTKUNSTWERK* AND 'HEAVENLY CAVE'
Gabriele Bryant

'The temples remained sacred to the eye, when the gods had long become ridiculous', Friedrich Schiller wrote in 1795.[1] Nearly a century later, Richard Wagner observed that 'one might say that where religion becomes aesthetic, it is down to art to preserve the core of religion'.[2] And in the twentieth century, Hugo Ball wrote that 'modern artists are gnostics who do things that the priests have long thought forgotten',[3] while the social philosopher Max Horkheimer asserted that 'art has preserved the utopia that has fled religion'.[4] Indeed, when we look at the history of art and architecture across the last two centuries, the prominence of 'sacred' themes and spaces outside of the traditional realms of religion is striking. This chapter explores the modern fusion of art and 'the spirit of religion', with art eventually replacing religion as the seat of modern 'sacrality'. Friedrich Nietzsche's verdict concerning the death of God might well have been accepted by many modern thinkers and artists alike, but that does not stop them from employing time-honoured forms and symbols of sacrality in their work, and from continuing the quest for new and original expressions of spirituality and sacredness in modern times.

The historical-intellectual foundations of modern *Kunstreligion* (Art-religion) can be identified in early German Romanticism and the philosophy of German Idealism around 1800. While the theoretical background was established in the writings of the circle of poets around the brothers Friedrich and August Wilhelm Schlegel, the first prominent and highly influential example in the realm of architecture is Karl Friedrich Schinkel's Altes Museum in Berlin (1823–30) - a museum built as a temple and aesthetic pantheon (Figure 2.1). Since that time, the creation of art and exhibition spaces as cathedrals, mausolea, baptistries and so forth, and the continued exploration of themes of 'sacrality' in modern private, cultural and political spaces, and even in industrial and commercial buildings, is a phenomenon in the history of Modernism that still requires further scholarly attention.

Figure 2.1 Karl Friedrich Schinkel, Altes Museum, Berlin (1823–30). Photograph by Tony Bryant, 2019.

The dynamic relationship between processes of secularization and sacralization in modern times – and the special role(s) played by art – needs to be emphasized. Against the linear readings of the history of modernity in terms of a progressive secularization and rationalization, an analysis of the various forms of engagement between the secular and the sacred in the last two centuries both enlarges our understanding of individual works and movements in the history of art and architecture and contributes to a more general reassessment of the role of the sacred in modern times.[5] In the Romantic notion of *Kunstreligion* and in Schinkel's Altes Museum, we see the results of a process that can be characterized as a 'sacralization of art', or vice versa, an 'aestheticization of the sacred'. This development culminated later in the nineteenth century in Wagner's conception of the *Gesamtkunstwerk* (total work of art) and Nietzsche's 'sacralization of the artist' – as exemplified in the early-twentieth-century *Jugendstil* artists' homes that are artistic manifestoes and 'temples of the self'.[6] And in the crystal cathedrals of German Expressionsim and their 'Gothic of the Murdered God',[7] sociopolitical utopias were formulated in the language of *Kunstreligion*, thus embodying the faith in an art that has inherited the power not just to provide a *representation*, but the very *foundation* of a higher order of reality. We also encounter in the history of modern art and architecture many (in)famous examples of art in the service of a 'sacralization of power', which is inseparable from what Walter Benjamin famously characterized as the 'aestheticization of politics'[8] in fascism – a topic discussed in other chapters of this book. But while we have rightly become suspicious of such examples of aesthetic sacralization, the search for more 'authentic' forms and interpretations of the sacred continues in modern architecture in our own time, both within and outside of the traditional realms of organized religion. As an example of this ongoing concern, I will conclude this chapter with a discussion of Peter Zumthor's Bruder Klaus Field Chapel of 2007 – a 'heavenly cave' or 'sacred grotto' in which a great variety of religious and *kunstreligiös* artistic forms and traditions are fused, making for a striking reinterpretation of the *Gesamtkunstwerk* in the twenty-first century.

But before engaging in a study of individual works of architecture, some historical-conceptual background and terminological clarification is required. When using the term *Kunstreligion*, it is important to distinguish between two different – though inherently related – meanings and phenomena. One is the modern idea of an artistic/artificial creation of a new religion, as exemplified in the Romantic quest for a new mythology that Friedrich Schlegel described as the 'most artificial of all artworks'.[9] The other phenomenon, with which we are more concerned here, is the elevation of the status of art to the level of religion, and which might be called the 'sacralization of art'. In the artistic theory and practice of the last two centuries, art is often fused with, and subsequently replaces, religion as 'the absolute'. The transfer of the forms and functions of religion into the realm of Art, or to put it another way, the metaphysical charge of art signifies an absorption of the role and potential of religion to give meaning to the world, leading eventually to Nietzsche's characterization of art as 'the original metaphysical activity of man'.[10] Beyond providing a mere 'Ersatzverzauberung des Ästhetischen'[11] (aesthetic *Ersatz*-enchantment) as a compensation for what Max Weber has called the 'Entzauberung der Welt'[12] (disenchantment of the world), Romantic *Kunstreligion* thus marks a paradigmatic shift from the traditional understanding of art in the service of religion to art *as* religion/religion *as* art, which eventually culminates in Modernism's twin myths of the aesthetic creatability of the absolute and absolute creativity.

The philosophical precondition for the Romantic concept of *Kunstreligion* lies in the declaration of the aesthetic as a separate sphere of reality in the eighteenth century. Only once art has been declared autonomous can its status be elevated to such an extent that it can be considered an 'emanation of the absolute', as the philosopher Friedrich W. J. Schelling characterized it in 1802–03.[13] And while Friedrich Schleiermacher is credited with being the first to employ the term *Kunstreligion* in his 'Über die Religion: Reden an die Gebildeten unter ihren Verächtern' (Speeches concerning religion) (1799), he still did not posit a full analogy between them.[14] It is only in the writings of the Schlegel brothers and their circle that art actually replaces religion, in the sense that art is charged with a spiritual significance previously ascribed only to religion. From the Schlegels' time on, artistic practice becomes the equivalent of religious service, and the artist is seen as a kind of aesthetic medium and innerworldly *Heiland* (messias). In this context, aesthetic contemplation replaces prayer, as made explicit in Wilhelm Heinrich Wackenroder's 'Herzergießungen eines Klosterbruders' (Outpourings of an Art-Loving Friar) (1797), when he declares that 'I compare the aesthetic enjoyment of the noble work of art to prayer'.[15] The *kunstreligiös* creative artist thus finds his or her necessary counterpart in the *kunstfromm* (art pious) beholder, and this religious charge of both art production and art reception is the intellectual background against which the conception of the modern museum as temple of the arts or 'aesthetic church' has to be seen.

While today the term *Kunstreligion* is sometimes used in a pejorative way, its actuality is regularly asserted, and the origins and development of the concept have been extensively researched. The most comprehensive three-volume publication of a recent international research project on this multifaceted phenomenon generally divides its development into three stages: (1) the origins of *Kunstreligion* around 1800, (2) its radicalization after 1850, and (3) the diversification of the concept around 2000.[16] We can also follow this general chronology for *Kunstreligion*'s different manifestations in modern architectural history. Tracing the development from Schinkel's museum-temple and his declaration that 'art itself is religion'[17] to the pantheon-like artists' residences of the late nineteenth and early twentieth centuries and Peter Behrens's characterization of architecture as a 'precursor of redemption',[18] it is indeed justifiable to speak of a radicalization of the *kunstreliös* ambitions of the modern artist-architect from the nineteenth century onwards. Architectural historians have also convincingly shown that the seemingly 'sober' and *sachlich* language of the *Neues Bauen* often only masks some of its more Romantic and *kunstreligiös* aspirations. And while the unholy alliances of artistic avant-garde movements with various political religions and ideologies of the twentieth century are also increasingly well researched and understood, leading to a widespread rejection of the messianic programmes of many early- and mid-twentieth-century artists and movements, the more cautious re-engagements with Romantic aesthetic categories like the sublime, the numinous, *Stimmung* (mood), atmosphere and so forth still point to a desire to engage with the *All* and absolute among artists in our time.

Where art assumes the role of religion, the art museum becomes the focal point and the seat of the new cult of *Kunstreligion*. Johann Wolfgang von Goethe retrospectively describes his visit to the Schlossgalerie in Dresden in 1768 in terms of entering a *Heiligtum* (holy space), and Wackenroder's *Klosterbruder* demands that 'picture halls [. . .] should be temples'.[19] Such poetic readings and proposals for a sacralization of art and its spaces are turned into a museological programme in Schinkel's Altes Museum. This temple for the arts, built directly opposite the old Berliner Stadtschloss (City Palace), is really more a temple to Art, a grandiose piece of *Ideenarchitektur* in which the individual works of art are subordinated to the general effect of the building. This aspect becomes particularly apparent in the building's large, double-storey central space – the pantheon-like cupola room (Figure 2.2). Although this room is lined with antique sculptures, it serves not primarily as an exhibition room, but rather as a symbolic space and *Einstimmungsraum* (initiation room). Here, in Schinkel's own words, 'the aspect of a beautiful and *erhaben* (elevated/sublime) space must make receptive and provide a *Stimmung* (mood) for the enjoyment and understanding of that which the building preserves'.[20] The cupola room thus marks a boundary and place of transition between the outer profane world and the separate realm of art within; it constitutes a physical and mental-emotional preparation space for the spiritual discipline of an aesthetic contemplation, the anticipated *unio mystica* with the works of art on display in the rest of the building. And a similar spiritual hierarchy of spaces with separate areas and rites of passage for an initiation into the

Figure 2.2 Schinkel, Altes Museum, view of the cupola room. Photograph by Tony Bryant, 2019.

art-religious experience will become the hallmark of many modern museum spaces in the *kunstreligiös* tradition.

While it is generally held that the modern museum stands for a decontextualization and thus desacralization of the traditional work of art, the Romantic *kunstreligiös* museum – only seemingly paradoxically – turns the whole exhibition space and the building itself into a religious sphere and thus endows not just religious artefacts, but all of the other works of art displayed here with the aura of the sacred, which the visitor to this space is to contemplate in a state of *kunstreligiös* 'Gestimmtheit' (mood/attunement). As Schinkel echoes the aesthetic creed of early Romanticism and German Idealism, the role of providing spiritual and moral guidance shifts from religion to art, from the priest to the artist as the guide of the people not just in matters of taste.

Romantic *Kunstreligion* and its artistic heritage remain ambivalent phenomena in the history of Modernism, and their assessment tends to be guided by the different perspectives from which the complex relationship between modern art and the sacred is viewed. From the point of view of traditional religion, the 'sacralization of art' and the corresponding 'aestheticization of the sacred' are sometimes regarded as an irritation and/or a profound misunderstanding, if not to say: a denigration of the true divine. And the (ab)use of time-honoured artistic formulae for the purpose of an apotheosis of the modern subject might appear as a sacrilegious or at the very least devaluing practice. However, the readings that emphasize only a 'loss' and 'reduction' or 'devaluation' of religious truth are perhaps in themselves reductive and denigratory in their – often nostalgic and *kulturpessimistisch* – focus on the 'true' content of religion in former times and their dismissal of other types of religious experience as facile spiritualism and so on. Perhaps it is particularly in our time – one in which the absolute insistence on the one and only religious truth has once again shown its ugly and destructive side – that we should rejoice in the richness and diversity, the coexistence of a multitude of expressions and experiences of what Rudolf Otto has called the 'numinous'.[21] This by no means implies an uncritical stance towards artistic platitudes dressed in the language of divinity, for example the cathedrals of commerce or the 'secular sacred' stagings of lifestyle events, and especially the unholy alliance of sacralized art with politics, but it suggests instead an openness to differing manifestations of the search for spiritual meaning and 'the sacred' both within and outside the traditional realm(s) of religion. And in this context, we might also find that the Romantic idea of the *Gesamtkunstwerk* still lends itself to meaningful reinterpretations and adaptations by contemporary architects.

The quest for a modern *Gesamtkunstwerk*, the total work of art that aims not just at a unification of different artforms in one work, but also at creating artistic counter-models to a modern world increasingly seen to be characterized by sociopolitical fragmentation and existential alienation, has been a central concern of artists, theorists and critics for over two centuries. Famously hailed by Wagner in the mid-nineteenth century as a 'means to bring salvation from this unfortunate time',[22] the *Gesamtkunstwerk* is characterized as a 'fata morgana', that is, a mirage by the early-twentieth-century art and architecture critic Adolf Behne.[23] While references to the *Gesamtkunstwerk* abound in the discourse on modern art and architecture, we have also been told that the *Gesamtkunstwerk* idea has become obsolete, or, worse, that the mere mention of the term should inspire suspicion, and that it is forever tainted with the stain of aesthetic manipulation and totalitarianism.[24] A recent study of modern *Gesamtkunstwerk* conceptions in the theatre even concludes with a 'requiem to the *Gesamtkunstwerk*', claiming that 'the *Gesamtkunstwerk* does not work any longer, the spiritual world that created it has been drained of blood'.[25]

Despite these assertions of the potential dangers and the general demise of the modern *Gesamtkunstwerk* idea, contemporary artists and architects have continued to explore the aesthetic potential of an artistic programme that has its roots in the Early Romantic quest for a reconciliation of not only different artforms, but of all the senses, of the faculties of sensuality and reason, of the world of spirit and matter. And we shall explore the legacy of the *Gesamtkunstwerk* idea in our time here by taking a closer look at the Bruder Klaus Field Chapel (2005–07) in the German village of Mechernich-Wachendorf, designed by the Swiss architect Peter Zumthor. As Zumthor himself explicitly acknowledges being inspired by the idea of the *Gesamtkunstwerk*,[26] I argue that central aspects of the original conception of the *Gesamtkunstwerk* are still relevant today. However, in our time the ideologically charged avant-garde programme of the total artwork as 'precursor of redemption' has given way to a phenomenological understanding of a building as a multilayered receptacle and space with an 'atmosphere' that powerfully engages its users on a physical-sensual, spiritual-intellectual and emotional level. As Zumthor writes: 'The reality of architecture lies in its concreteness, its form, mass, space, and body. There is no idea, except in the things themselves.'[27]

The notion of 'atmosphere', which is closely linked to 'aura' as well as to the German *Stimmung*, plays a central role in the context of a redefinition of the modern *Gesamtkunstwerk*, and for Zumthor it holds the key to the creation of 'presence' in architecture.[28] The German philosopher Gottfried Böhme, who considers the role of 'atmosphere' as the foundation of a new aesthetic, also refers to 'spheres of presence' and to 'the ecstasy of the thing [. . .] the power of its presence in space [. . .] (as) the form of an object resonates outside. It radiates into its environment, takes away the homogeneity of the space around it and fills it with energies'.[29] Böhme thus defines 'atmosphere' as an aesthetic quality that is not restricted to the sphere of the object, but which is so significant for modern aesthetics precisely because it only exists in a space-continuum that includes, or rather, envelops both subject and object. Furthermore, for the modern *Gesamtkunstwerk* idea the concept of 'atmosphere' is of great importance as it also abolishes old distinctions between fine and applied arts and leads to a revaluation of *Handwerk* (crafts).

The Romantic idea of a unification of all the senses and human faculties, and of the creation of an artistic realm in which the visitor is fully immersed in an aesthetic world of universal order and harmony, continues to exert a powerful influence on modern artists. And it is no coincidence that it is frequently buildings or works of art that stand in marked isolation from their immediate surroundings, or rather, which establish their very connection with their context through their apparent separate- and solitariness, their 'insularity' and introvertedness, that best illustrate the continued appeal of the *Gesamtkunstwerk* idea. In Zumthor's Bruder Klaus Chapel, the idea of the primitive cave is reinterpreted as just such a *Gesamtkunstwerk*. In the history of modern architecture, the cave prototype alludes to a primitivist return to origins in addition to providing the starting point for highly sophisticated explorations of the restorative power of art in the modern world. The cave is invoked by modern and contemporary architects in various projects to provide a retreat or refuge – not just from one's immediate physical surroundings, but also from some aspects of 'reality' and modern life as such. However, this is not to be understood, I argue, as escapism, nostalgia or straightforward regression, but rather as a kind of going back to one's roots in order to restore oneself. The 'artificial cave' provides a space for restitution and spiritual renewal, irrespective of whether this spirituality is of a religious or a more individual and secular kind.

The Bruder Klaus Field Chapel (Figure 2.3) is situated in the German countryside around thirty miles outside of Cologne, and it appears in this landscape as a perfect illustration of Zumthor's assertion that 'there are buildings that fit themselves into a given situation, and there are other buildings that have to make a place. And this is a building that makes a place'.[30] Elsewhere he remarks that 'if a piece of architecture is just about something worldly or visionary, without making its concrete place resonate, I miss the sensual anchoring of the building, the specific weight of the locality'.[31] The *genius loci* is thus both embraced and created in architecture – the building as land-mark both interprets and *makes* its topography.

The Bruder Klaus Chapel sits in a landscape of rolling hills, fields and forests, and it is approached via a small footpath. From a distance the chapel appears as a simple

Modern Architecture and the Sacred

Figure 2.3 Peter Zumthor, Bruder Klaus Field Chapel, Mechernich, Germany (2007), in its landscape of rolling hills, fields and forests.
Photograph by Gabriele Bryant, 2019.

sandy-coloured vertical concrete block or *stele*, reminiscent of an ancient castle-keep or modern sentinel tower. What at first seems to be a simple rectangular monolith reveals itself to in fact be an irregular pentagonal shape in plan as one walks around the building. The chapel is entered via a heavy 3-metre-high chromed steel door in the shape of an acute isosceles triangle, which is not hinged directly from the body of the chapel, but rather swivels around a post anchored in the earth (Figure 2.4). And on crossing the threshold, it soon becomes apparent that the stark and austere chapel exterior is in marked contrast to its haunting, mystical interior.

Passing through the triangular opening, one enters a dark, low and narrow curved passage, formed by rough-textured blackened walls that lean asymmetrically inwards (Figure 2.5). This short passage then leads to the central space – a dark elliptical room that is 12 metres high, where one's gaze is immediately drawn upwards towards a teardrop-shaped oculus at the top of the building (Figure 2.6). This 'skylight' is left open to the elements, that is, it is not covered by glass, meaning that it not only allows in the light, but, depending on the weather, also admits the rain, which then trickles down the inner face of the walls and transforms their colour from a matte dark grey into a glistening black. The verticality of the central space is emphasized not just by the perspectival effect of the walls that taper towards the top like an inverted funnel, with shafts of light illuminating the space from the top downwards, but also by the shape and texture of the blackened concrete walls that have deep semicircular mouldings and ragged ridges.

Figure 2.4 Zumthor, Bruder Klaus Field Chapel, on approach.
Photograph by Gabriele Bryant, 2019.

The floor of the chapel is made of lead, which was melted on site and manually ladled onto the floor, resulting in an uneven and matte grey surface. The teardrop shape of the oculus is subtly echoed in the floor, in the form of the small pool of rainwater that collects on the ground before evaporating again. Apart from the opening at the top, a small amount of light also enters the chapel via 350 small cylindrical holes pushed

Figure 2.5 Zumthor, Bruder Klaus Field Chapel, entrance passage. Photograph by Gabriele Bryant, 2019.

Figure 2.6 Zumthor, Bruder Klaus Field Chapel, the teardrop-shaped oculus. Photograph by Gabriele Bryant, 2019.

into the walls and closed on the inside with mouth-blown glass plugs that protrude from the walls in the shape of semi-spheres, appearing as small crystal balls. There is no electricity or plumbing in the chapel, and the furnishing and decoration is kept to a minimum.

One of Zumthor's early drawings for the chapel depicts a uterus-like shape inscribed in the pentagonal ground plan (Figure 2.7), and it reveals much about the original conception of the chapel. This womb shape that is both literally and metaphorically central to the building is a primordial image of safe enclosure, birth and origins. It also recalls the shape of Zumthor's timber-framed Sogn Benedetg Chapel in Switzerland (1985–8), which the architect has characterized as 'a simple vessel [. . .] a soft, maternal form'.[32] The idea of the interior of the Bruder Klaus Chapel as a space of conception, the nucleus of a new life, is further emphasized in Zumthor's early drawing by its inner seed-/sperm-shaped core. The guiding image of the womb and the hermit's cell as primitive cave very much provide the foundation for the whole structure of this small chapel.

We have already noted the stark contrast between the tower-like exterior of the chapel – geometric and austere – and the cave-like, 'organic' and enclosing receptacle or sanctuary that is its interior. And the creation of this deliberate duality can be followed through in the construction process. The Bruder Klaus Chapel was constructed from the inside out. Its core was first formed by an elongated tentlike configuration comprising 112 locally felled slender spruce tree trunks (Figure 2.8). Over the top of this structure,

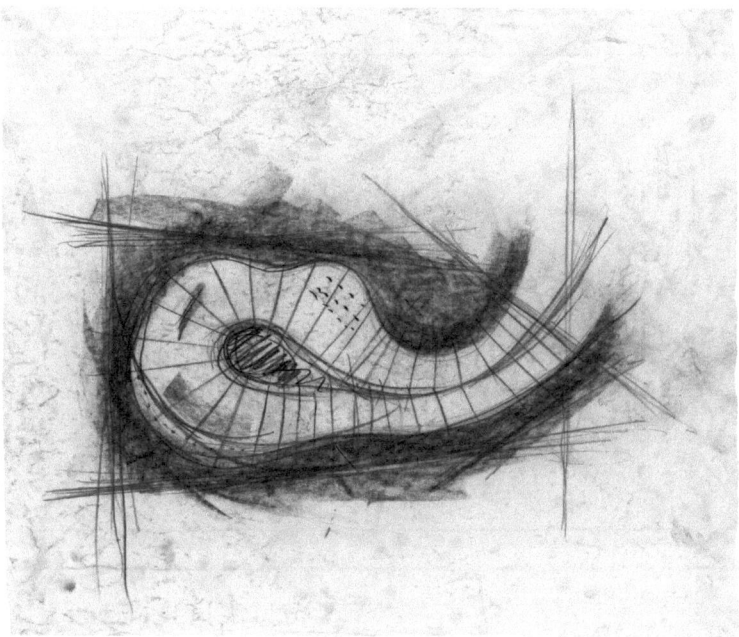

Figure 2.7 Zumthor, Bruder Klaus Field Chapel, an early sketch drawing.
Source: Atelier Peter Zumthor and Partner, Haldenstein.

Figure 2.8 Zumthor, Bruder Klaus Field Chapel, under construction.
Source: Atelier Peter Zumthor and Partner, Haldenstein.

which was erected on a concrete base, layer after layer of rammed concrete – with an amount of local, reddish sand mixed into it – was progressively built up. This was achieved by pouring the concrete between the timber formwork and the inner 'wooden tent' over a period of twenty-four working days, in layers of 50 centimetres at a time. Steel tubes were inserted between the inner and outer concrete shell, which would later also provide the small light tunnels that were subsequently closed with the spherical glass plugs. The different strata of the concrete layers show up on the outside of the building, reminiscent at once of the rings that mark the growth of a tree and the processes of geological sedimentation – the material memory of the history of the earth.

The next, most radical stage in the process of construction was the firing of the interior. A carefully controlled smouldering fire was kept alive for three weeks, after which the dried, charred and shrunken tree trunks were carefully extracted from the concrete shell. This left behind what is perhaps the most striking aspect of the interior: the imprint of the tree trunks, the negative of the original inner tent structure, the traces of the now-absent core of the whole, the presence but absence – both physical and symbolic – of that which originally carried and held together the whole. The smoky smell and black soot that has impregnated the porous, ribbed concrete walls remains an integral part of the whole structure, like a fresco. The memory of the fire, fire as the origin of human culture, evocative of ancient rituals and ceremonial burning, all speaking of primitive beginnings, of the hearth, of open fires in simple shelters, is triggered through all one's senses. And as the smell of woodsmoke, charcoal and ash lingers in the space, the whole body of the building seems to resonate with symbolic allusions to personal and collective beginnings – individual birth and cultural origins – which converge in the image of the womb and the cave.

The Bruder Klaus Chapel is an atmospherically charged space. Not only are different artforms united, as they are in the modern idea of the *Gesamtkunstwerk*, but Zumthor has also integrated a multitude of physical and sensory experiences, of sound, smell and touch, thereby achieving a sensuality that might ultimately lead the visitor towards a spiritual, transcendental dimension, which of course does not necessarily have to be of a conventionally religious nature. Beyond his creation of such a multisensory, synaesthetic experience in the chapel, what also becomes clear is Zumthor's understanding of and sensitivity for cultural history, tradition and symbolism. He explores the materiality of memory – where history is represented not in words and narratives, but is made 'present' in physical form – in this small chapel, which sensitively incorporates local materials and customs and is at the same time saturated with references and allusions to ancient rituals and to universal human situations, individual and collective memory.

The design of the Bruder Klaus Chapel as a cave or primitive hut is based on a process of extreme reduction – a reduction not just of formal means, but a (re)turn to primary elements. The materials can be seen to represent the four original elements of fire and water, earth and air, in their various states of interaction and transformation. Zumthor shares an interest 'in the mythology and sensuousness of materials'[33] with the German artist Joseph Beuys. And this mythology of materials, materials as repositories of memory, is also explored, if not to say embodied, in the Mechernich chapel. Encapsulated in the original shelter of the womb hut, in the transitory (nomad's) tent – a tent that is, however, secured and anchored or 'frozen' here inside the solid and immovable concrete tower – the visitor experiences the eternal light as it enters the building not just via the quasi-baroque effect of the open skylight and the crystalline glass beads, but also in the striking illumination or 'aura' of the chapel door that is seen from the darkness inside as a triangle that floats in space.

One of the most powerful themes embodied in the chapel, I would suggest, is the constant play between presence and absence. The original fire and the forest, for example, are represented *in absentia*, as their memory is kept alive in the physical-sensual/(material) traces they have left behind. And I hold that when labels like minimalism or asceticism are used to characterize Zumthor's work, what is being neglected is the strongly symbolic dimension of his particular take on the modern maxim that 'less is more', that is, a reduction to an essence that is not just functional or formal/aesthetic, but deeply symbolic and at the same time literally, physically tangible. Peter Rüedi has characterized Zumthor as an 'essentialist of the sensual',[34] and others have referred to him as a 'Proustian sensualist', for in his buildings and in his writing he explores the essential sensuality of memories, both personal and cultural. But I argue that beyond this, the symbolic and *kunstreligiös* dimension of his very sensualist approach still warrants increased emphasis.

Since a more detailed analysis of the symbolism of the Bruder Klaus Chapel would go beyond the scope of this chapter, attention will only be drawn here to a few of the most significant elements, the first of which is the number symbolism in the chapel. There is the obvious link between the triangle of the door and the Christian Trinity, but also to the number three as the ultimate image of unity and synthesis. There is the pentagon of the ground plan, which, according to Pythagoras, stands for the microcosm man and also, like the circle, appears as a symbol of unity. In other contexts, the number five is symbolic of the five senses, which appears very fitting for this building as a master exercise in synaesthesia, and in the Bible there are also the five points of the cross and the five wounds of Christ. Then we find the twenty-four days of manual labour that it took to create the outer concrete layer of the chapel, with the obvious reference to the natural cycle of the day. The teardrop shape of the oculus can be seen as the aureole, that is, the sacred aura of the invisible divine, while in terms of architectural history the open skylight establishes an interesting link between the Bruder Klaus Chapel and the Pantheon in Rome. The shape of the oculus might also be interpreted as the all-seeing eye of God, with the eye over the triangle belonging to ancient religious as well as masonic imagery. And finally, the multitude of luminous glass beads that stand out in the darkness conjure an image of a starry night sky, of light penetrating the dark as well as establishing a link to the symbol of the crystal, which played such a central role in nineteenth-century Romanticism and early-twentieth-century German Expressionism.

A central symbolic theme in the Bruder Klaus Chapel is that of a dualism of forces, forms and elements: of darkness and light, organic and nonorganic forms, spirit and matter, earth and sky, that is, chthonic and celestial forces, of separation and resolution, transfiguration and reconciliation, the ephemeral and the permanent. And throughout the whole building and its process of construction we find striking symbolic references to the ancient tradition of alchemy with its strong links to hermeticism and gnosticism. From the poured lead of the chapel floor to the role of fire in alchemical processes of purification and the transmutation of matter, the many links to the tradition of alchemy are about the time-honoured exploration of the link between the worlds of matter and spirit. The alchemical aspiration of the transmutation of lead into gold is seen as an analogy to processes of spiritual transformation and transubstantiation. In fact, the whole of the central interior space of the Bruder Klaus Chapel with its funnel-shaped wall construction, the tent structure with its opening at the top can be seen as a kind of (smoking) cauldron. Especially as one imagines the building as it was during the construction phase when the fire was still burning inside, the chapel appears a sacred vessel that one enters, body and soul, and where it is one's inner Self that is the beginning and end point in the elusive process of spiritual transformation. Furthermore, the shape of the ground plan of the internal cavity, which we have already understood as a womb/cave, also bears a strong resemblance to the alchemical vessel that artists for centuries have depicted as a bulbous open flask. In modern times, alchemy has also become a symbol of the processes of artistic creation as such. The German artist Anselm Kiefer, for example, states that 'as an artist I don't do anything different (from the alchemist). I just accelerate the process of transformation that is inherent in the things. That is magic, as I understand it.'[35] This sentiment appears to be shared by Zumthor, whose work also explores the link between matter or materials and more elusive, spiritual qualities. He in fact explicitly refers to alchemical processes when talking about his approach to architecture: 'The Magic of the Real for me is the "alchemy" of transforming real substances into human emotions, that special moment of an emotional appropriation or transformation of matter, of materials and form in an architectural space.'[36]

The tree-core interior and small reservoir of water in Zumthor's Bruder Klaus Chapel is also reminiscent of sacred groves with holy springs at their centre. A strong link exists in Western art between the grove and the cave as a place of retreat and healing, a return to sources, sanctuary, seat of an oracle and, above all, a metaphor of the cosmos and a place of passage between worlds, of which Naomi Miller has written:

> Withdrawal into this illusory realm [. . .] implies a communion, not with the outside world of nature still dominant in the garden, but here within the enclosed orbit of the grotto with the inner world of man.[37]

The introverted nature of the Bruder Klaus Chapel, the cave/womblike interior with its small pool of water at the centre – water itself being another symbol of the soul/psyche – situates it firmly in this Western architectural tradition of the grotto or artificial cavern. John Shearman has characterized the grotto as 'architecture overlaid with the dense accretions of time',[38] which explains its appeal to modern architects who endeavour to link their work to history and tradition without resorting to overtly historicizing building styles. Being in the darkness of the cave, however, does not just allude to the primitive beginnings of our existence, that is, our historical origins. It is also one of the most ancient philosophical metaphors for the human condition in our cultural heritage. From Plato's cave that served as a metaphor for the limits of human knowledge to the cave in which Nietzsche's prophet Zarathustra resides before going out into the world to spread his philosophy of 'inverted Platonism',[39] the cave is the mythical place to which the civilized imagination from Greek antiquity to modern times retreats in search of original answers – be they about the nature of truth (Plato), the exposure of the very idea of such a truth as myth (Nietzsche), or simply about the state of one's own soul.

In the reading of the Swiss psychoanalyst Carl Gustav Jung, the cave appears as an archetype of the collective unconscious, about which he writes: 'The cave is the place of rebirth, the secret hollow/cavity in which one is enclosed in order to be incubated and renewed.'[40] And the architects of *Jugendstil* and German Expressionism, for whom the image of the cave was an important inspiration, explored this idea not just in the way they created large central spaces as womblike enclosures, as for example in Hans Poelzig's famous interior of the Großes Schauspielhaus (1919), but also in the way they designed entrances and gateways that appear to mirror acts of sexual penetration and (reversed) birth processes,[41] a preoccupation echoed in the design of the narrow entry passage of Zumthor's Bruder Klaus Chapel.

In the creation of 'atmospheres', the allusive and emotional power of cultural references, collective memories and images plays a key role. And in the case of the Bruder Klaus Chapel, another important link to mention here is the frequent association visitors have inside this building with Gothic architecture. In Western Europe, the Gothic has for centuries been considered as the quintessential building style for sacred buildings. And standing in a space that was originally formed by trees that were bound together at the top also brings to mind the German Romantic accounts of the 'natural' origin of the Gothic, as well as the many *kunstreligiös* paintings of Gothic cathedrals – often in deep forest settings and in various states of ruination – by Caspar David Friedrich and Schinkel. Furthermore, there are more than a few thematic analogies between the Bruder Klaus Chapel and German Expressionist architecture, and it is worth keeping in mind here that in the early twentieth century the Gothic was shorn of its overtly religious overtones, and what was celebrated as the 'Spirit of the Gothic' by Karl Scheffler and Wilhelm Worringer was linked to a Nietzschean philosophy of individual self-transcendence.[42]

However, while formal and thematic connections can be established between German Expressionist architecture and the Bruder Klaus Chapel, it is also important to emphasize once again that one of the many ways in which Zumthor differs substantially from the *Gesamtkunstwerk* conceptions of early-twentieth-century architects is that he does not share their missionary zeal to educate or change people and/or society through architecture. Zumthor's approach to a multisensory architecture is thus both related to and yet fundamentally different from many earlier architectural *Gesamtkunstwerk* conceptions. The early modernist dream of the *Gesamtkunstwerk* was strongly linked to art assuming the place of politics, and of providing an – often overwhelming – artistic counter-world, of staging art, in the Romantic-Idealist philosophical tradition and the words of Schiller, as 'a moral institution'. Perhaps Zumthor, who has professed to be inspired by the idea of the *Gesamtkunstwerk*, but who is not interested in guiding the users of his buildings in a particular spiritual, political or social direction, has created with the Bruder Klaus Chapel an architecture that provides us instead with what Nietzsche – whose prophet Zarathustra, after all, also dwelt in a cave before coming down from the mountains to bring to the world his new wisdom – called more than a century ago an *Architektur der Erkennenden* (*Architecture of the Enlightened Ones*):

> What is missing most of all in our big cities: Quiet [. . .] spaces for thought [. . .] where no outside noise reaches us, where a higher sensibility would even forbid the priests their loud prayers: Buildings and complexes which as a whole express the higher state of meditation *(Sich-Besinnen)* and withdrawal *(Bei-Seitetreten)*. The time is past when the church had the monopoly of thought. As houses of God and seats of the cult of metaphysical traffic, those buildings speak a language of too much constraint for us [. . .] We want to have *ourselves* translated into stone; we want to amble *inside ourselves* as we walk through these halls.[43]

In the Bruder Klaus Chapel, the primitive cave is interpreted – with more than fleeting references to the Gothic – as a 'sacred grotto' and modern *Gesamtkunstwerk* which can, in the hustle and bustle of modern life, provide an artistic-spiritual retreat and serve as a beacon of (re)orientation. The visitor to this 'heavenly cave' assumes the role – albeit briefly – of the modern hermit; twenty-first-century man/woman retreats from the business of the world in order to temporarily dwell in an artfully created 'primitive' sanctuary. Entering and (re)connecting with an original space and state of being, the visitor is fully immersed and *aufgehoben* (at once enclosed, sheltered and elevated) in a sensual-spiritual world that is deeply rooted in our cultural history and mythology.

Peter Zumthor's buildings as *Gesamtkunstwerke* have been characterized as 'insular utopias',[44] and the architect has also been accused by some of being 'apolitical' or even 'unpolitical'. These critics claim, for example, that his work 'however thoughtfully and exquisitely crafted, exists in a decided vacuum [. . .] and is architecture for architecture's sake'.[45] However, the coupling of insular utopias with social disengagement or even escapism is founded on a misunderstanding of the original category of utopia, which is based on dialectical thinking and is political through and through.[46] Besides, an important question remains: Does every work of art, every poem, every building, really have to be driven by social activism and a quasi-missionary zeal to educate and edify, to 'better', 'correct', 'transform' and 'direct' life, to change individuals and society, or is it not perhaps also a profoundly political and ethical stance to give people space to think their own thoughts, to reconnect them with their own, individual and collective memories, in order to fully let them *be*?

Notes

1. Friedrich Schiller, 'Über die ästhetische Erziehung des Menschen in einer Reihe von Briefen' (1795), in Schiller, *Werke in vier Bänden* (Vienna: Caesar, 1980), 523.
2. Richard Wagner, 'Religion und Kunst', in Wagner, *Dichtungen und Schriften: Kommentierte Jubiläumsausgabe in zehn Bänden,* ed. Dieter Borchmeyer (Frankfurt/M: Insel, 1983), vol. 10, 117.
3. Hugo Ball, *Flight Out of Time*, ed. John Elderfield, trans. Ann Raimes (Berkeley and Los Angeles: University of California Press, 1996), 103.
4. Max Horkheimer, 'Neue Kunst und Massenkultur' (1941), in Horkheimer, *Gesammelte Schriften*, 19 vols (Frankfurt am Main: Fischer, 1988), vol. 4, 421.
5. Compare Hans Joas, *Die Macht des Heiligen: Eine Alternative zur Geschichte von der Entzauberung* (Berlin: Suhrkamp, 2017).
6. Margot Th. Brandlhuber and Michael Buhrs, eds, *Im Tempel des Ich: Das Künstlerhaus als Gesamtkunstwerk* (Ostfildern: Hatje Cantz, 2013).
7. Gabriele Bryant, 'Gothic of the Murdered God: From the Crystal Creed to the Spirit of Abstraction in Modern German Architecture', in *Phenomenologies of the City: Studies in History and Philosophy of Architecture,* ed. Maximilian Sternberg and Henriette Steiner (London: Ashgate, 2015), 181–93.
8. Walter Benjamin, *Das Kunstwerk im Zeitalter seiner technischen Reproduzierbarkeit* (1936) (Frankfurt am Main: Suhrkamp, 2003), 44.
9. Friedrich Schlegel, 'Gespräch über die Poesie', in Schlegel, *'Athenäums'-Fragmente und andere Schriften* (Stuttgart: Reclam, 2005), 190.
10. Friedrich Nietzsche, *Kritische Studienausgabe*, ed. Giorgio Colli and Mazzino Montinari, 15 vols (Munich: dtv, 1988), vol. 1, 24.
11. Cornelia Klinger, *Flucht–Trost–Revolte: Die Moderne und ihre ästhetischen Gegenwelten* (Munich: Hanser, 1995), 19.

12. Max Weber, *Wissenschaft als Beruf* (Munich: von Duncker & Humblot, 1919), 36.
13. Friedrich Wilhelm Joseph Schelling, 'Philosophie der Kunst', in Schelling, *Sämmtliche Werke*, ed. K. F. A. Schelling, 14 vols (Stuttgart/Augsburg: Cotta, 1856-61), vol. 5, 372.
14. See Annette Gilbert, 'Die "ästhetische Kirche": Zur Entstehung des Museums am Schnittpunkt von Kunstautonomie und –religion', *Athenäum* 19 (2009): 45–85.
15. Quoted in Ibid., 51.
16. Albert Meier, Alessandro Costazza and Gerard Laudin, eds, *Kunstreligion: Der Ursprung des Konzepts um 1800 (vol.1), Kunstreligion: Die Radikalisierung des Konzepts nach 1850 (vol. 2), Kunstreligion: Diversifizierung des Konzepts um 2000 (vol. 3)* (Berlin: DeGruyter, 2010–2014).
17. Quoted in Gilbert, 'Kirche', 79.
18. Peter Behrens, 'Zeitloses und Zeitbewegtes' (1932), reprinted in *Peter Behrens. Zeitloses und Zeitbewegtes. Aufsätze, Vorträge, Gespräche 1900-1938*, ed. Hartmut Frank and Karin Lelolek (Munich/Hamburg: Dölling & Galitz, 2015), 1042.
19. Quoted in Gilbert, 'Kirche', 45, 51.
20. Quoted in Ibid., 75.
21. Rudolf Otto, *Das Heilige: Über das Irrationale in der Idee des Göttlichen und sein Verhältnis zum Rationalen* (Munich: Beck, 2014).
22. Wagner, 'Das Kunstwerk der Zukunft' (1849), in Wagner, *Schriften,* vol. 6, 17.
23. Adolf Behne 1927. 'Von der Sachlichkeit' (1927), reprinted in Adolf Behne, *Eine Stunde Architektur* (Berlin: Archibook-Verlag 1984), 29.
24. Boris Groys, *Gesamtkunstwerk Stalin: Die gespaltene Kultur in der Sowjetunion* (Munich/Vienna: Hanser, 1988).
25. Guido Hiß, *Synthetische Visionen: Theater als Gesamtkunstwerk von 1800 bis 2000* (Munich: Epodium, 2005), 308.
26. Peter Zumthor, *Key Projects by Peter Zumthor*, de zeen magazine, 2009, accessed 29 June 2020, https://www.dezeen.com/2009/04/18/key-projects-by-peter-zumthor/; and Peter Zumthor, *Wir Schweitzer sind nicht so änfällig für Moden*. Spiegel online, May 2009, accessed 29 June 2020, http://www.spiegel.de/kultur/gesellschaft/stararchitekt-zumthor-wir-schweizer-sind-nicht-so-anfaellig-fuer-moden-a-627167.html.
27. Zumthor, *Architektur Denken* (Basel: Birkhäuser, 2010), 37.
28. See Zumthor, *Atmosphären* (Basel: Birkhäuser, 2006), and Zumthor, *On Presence in Architecture*, Royal Gold Medal Lecture at the RIBA in London, 2013.
29. Gottfried Böhme, *Atmosphäre: Essays zur neuen Ästhetik* (Frankfurt am Main: Suhrkamp, 2013), 33.
30. Zumthor, '"Sie stehen auf der Erde, aber Sie spüren die Öffnung zum Himmel": Peter Zumthor über seine Arbeit an der Bruder-Klaus-Kapelle in Mechernich'. Interview with Dina Netz. *kulturwest*, July 2007, http://www.kulturwest.de/architektur/detailseite/artikel/sie-stehen-auf-der-erde-aber-sie-spueren-die-oeffnung-zum-himmel/.
31. Quoted in Peter Rüedi, 'Peter Zumthor: Architekt'. *Neue Zürcher Zeitung*, February 2001.
32. Zumthor, *Peter Zumthor 1985-2013: Buildings and Projects.* 5 vols, ed. T. Durisch (Zurich: Scheidegger & Spiess, 2014), vol. 1, 63.
33. Quoted in Michael Kimmelman, 'The Ascension of Peter Zumthor'. *New York Times*, 11 March 2011, https://www.nytimes.com/2011/03/13/magazine/mag-13zumthor-t.html.

34. Rüedi, 'Zumthor'.
35. Quoted in Monika Wagner, Dietmar Rübel and Sebastian Hackenschmidt, eds, *Lexikon des künstlerischen Materials: Werkstoffe der modernen Kunst von Abfall bis Zinn* (Munich: Beck, 2010), 44.
36. Zumthor, *Architektur Denken*, 85.
37. Naomi Miller, *Heavenly Caves: Reflections on the Garden Grotto* (New York: Braziller, 1982), 11.
38. John Shearman, *Mannerism* (Harmondsworth: Penguin, 1967), 126.
39. Nietzsche, *Studienausgabe*, vol. 7, 199.
40. Carl G. Jung, 'Die Archetypen und das kollektive Unbewusste' (1934), in Carl G. Jung, *Gesammelte Werke* (Olten: Walter, 1976), vol. 9.1, 149.
41. Wolfgang Pehnt, 'Turm und Höhle', in *Moderne Architektur in Deutschland 1900–1950: Expressionismus und Neue Sachlichkeit,* ed. Vittorio Lampugnani and Romana Schneider (Stuttgart: Hatje, 1994), 51–67.
42. See Magdalena Bushart, *Der Geist der Gotik und die expressionistische Kunst* (Munich: Schreiber, 1990), and Bryant, 'Gothic'.
43. Nietzsche, *Studienausgabe*, vol. 3, 524–5.
44. Ole W. Fischer, 'Insular Utopias? Henry van de Velde, Peter Zumthor, and the Gesamtkunstwerk', in *The Death and Life of the Total Work of Art: Henry van de Velde and the Legacy of a Modern Concept,* ed. Carsten Ruhl, Chris Dähne and Rixt Hoekstra (Berlin: Jovis, 2015), 146–63.
45. Christopher Hawthorne, 'Swiss architect Peter Zumthor, 65, is 2009 Pritzker laureate'. *Los Angeles Times*, 12 April 2009, https://latimesblogs.latimes.com/culturemonster/2009/04/swiss-architect-peter-zumthor-65-is-2009-pritzker-laureate.html.
46. See Wilhelm Voßkamp, ed., *Utopieforschung: Interdisziplinäre Studien zur neuzeitlichen Utopie*, 3 vols (Frankfurt am Main: Suhrkamp, 1985).

CHAPTER 3
THE ORDINARY AS THE EXTRAORDINARY
MODERN SACRED ARCHITECTURE IN GERMANY, THE UNITED STATES AND JAPAN
Kathleen James-Chakraborty

The importance of sacred architecture to the story of modern architecture is typically acknowledged only when churches (and more rarely synagogues or other buildings designed for worship) are the work of the most celebrated architects of the twentieth century.[1] In large part this marginalization is part of an overly narrow definition of modern architecture that ignores much of the way that those who did not espouse an industrial aesthetic or socialist politics, but did employ abstract form and new materials, changed the mainstream of architectural practice across the course of the twentieth century. Extremely talented architects, in many cases themselves devout, and in others simply proud to belong to communities defined by faith, designed many outstanding modern churches, synagogues, mosques and other buildings for religious purposes. If we broaden our definition of modern architecture to include those who were neither members of the *Congrès Internationaux d'Architecture Moderne* (CIAM) or affiliated with the Bauhaus, and acknowledge that what has often been dismissed (or praised) as regionalist alternatives to these were in fact equally international in their orientation, then the design of churches, in particular, moves to the centre of the story of the modern architecture of the 1920s through at least the 1950s.[2]

There are at least three reasons that, while individual examples of modern sacred architecture have scarcely escaped the attention of scholars or the affection of the public, their collective importance has been discounted. The first is that religious devotion has too often been understood to be less than modern. Certainly, many fewer Western European Christians now attend Sunday services than was the case a century ago, but the great fall-off came not in the 1920s, when the new style of architecture was forged, but in the 1970s. Following the Second World War, religious observance remained high among West German Christians, for instance, and actually increased among American Jews. The first have often been accused of not being able yet to remember what they had perpetrated upon the relatives of the second, but both may have, in the immediate aftermath of the war, in fact chosen a different means to address both guilt and suffering than the commemorative approaches now esteemed by our own more secular society.[3]

A second reason that this architecture has been overlooked is the emphasis that historians of modern architecture have placed on a body of theory that insists on the functionality of its forms. The 1920s through the 1960s also witnessed the creation of a substantial body of literature about how to create spiritually meaningful places.[4]

Much of this, however, was targeted at theologians and congregations, rather than at the mainstream of the architectural profession. It thus remains outside of the history and theory that has been taught in architectural schools, especially since the importance of church construction began to wane across much of Europe and the English-speaking world at the end of the 1960s. The function of a church, a synagogue, or for that matter a mosque or temple, cannot be easily equated with the emphasis on the efficient use of space that might appeal to the client for a factory or an office block, even if inexpensive construction might be equally prized by a congregation of modest means. In the context of sacred architecture, functionalism almost always requires creating an alternative to the spaces of daily life. This might be achieved through the use of expensive materials and the extensive application of ornament but in the twentieth century was more likely to be realized through unusual forms carefully designed to create a sense of a place apart, often through the time-tested means of a low, dark transitional space followed by carefully placed windows high enough to prevent views of the surrounding city or landscape. Especially once the impact of empathy theory receded in the 1920s, the lack of textual attention paid to the means that made these buildings effective helped veil what was in fact their highly innovative character.[5]

Finally, unlike Le Corbusier's Chapel of Notre-Dame du Haut at Ronchamp, for instance, many of the twentieth century's greatest and most influential churches whisper rather than shout. In a domain previously noted for magnificent scale and lavish detail, subtlety now often mattered enormously, with the ineffable means of space and light at least as consequential as physically palpable brick or steel. Moreover, few examples of modern sacred architecture were located in city centres; instead, they clustered in suburban locations and often served congregations of relatively modest means.

And yet architects such as Dominikus Böhm and Eliel Saarinen, who in their day numbered among the most widely respected and influential members of their profession, deployed abstraction and modern technology in churches and other religious buildings that were entirely of their own rather than any earlier time. Their deft use of light and of both natural and new materials created understated and inexpensive spaces that many continue to find more conducive to spiritual contemplation and communal worship than more conventional predecessors. Leaving structures like Böhm's Christ the King in Bischofsheim (1926), Erich Mendelsohn's Jewish Cemetery in Königsberg (1929), Otto Bartning's Gustav Adolf Church in Berlin (1934), Eliel Saarinen's Christ Church in Minneapolis (1949) and Togo Murano's Memorial Cathedral for World Peace in Hiroshima (1954) out of the history of modern architecture diminishes our understanding of its original range and of important sources of its continued effectiveness.[6]

Nowhere did a modern approach to sacred architecture make earlier and deeper inroads than in Germany, where already during the Weimar Republic (1919–33) very few churches or synagogues resembled anything that had been erected just a few years earlier.[7] Many of these buildings were of extraordinarily high quality, but almost none are examples of the canonical International Style. The story of the efforts made by Dominikus Böhm, Rudolf Schwarz and Otto Bartning to reform Catholic Church design in the case of Böhm and Schwartz and that of Protestants in that of Bartning has been well told elsewhere. It need not be reviewed in great detail here as it can be found particularly in the scholarship of the German architectural historian Wolfgang Pehnt.[8] What instead merits emphasis in these pages is the degree to which these architects broke as definitively with the past as did their more celebrated counterparts such as Walter Gropius, Ernst May, Ludwig Mies van der Rohe and Bruno Taut, whose engagement with spirituality remained during these years independent of designing actual places for worship. In the adoption of radically simplified forms, stripped entirely bare of ornament, and in many cases employing new materials and the engineering that accompanied them, as well as new approaches to the organization of space, Böhm, Schwartz and Bartning were nothing if not modern.

Böhm, the founder of a dynasty that continues to this day, was the most senior and arguably the most influential of the three. Born in 1880 in the small Schwabian town of Jettingen, he was among the architects who in the years before the First World War were inspired by the work of Theodor Fischer, who taught first in Stuttgart and then in Munich and whose vaguely medieval reinforced concrete Garrison Church of 1910 in Ulm provided an important point of departure for the brick-faced concrete churches built in interwar Germany.[9] An early adherent of the Liturgical Movement, which emphasized the importance of the communal celebration of the mass over private devotion to the Virgin and saints, Böhm found an early champion in the theologian Johannes van Acken, who singled him out for praise in his book on Christ-centred church art, first published in 1922.[10] In 1926, Böhm became professor of sacred art in Cologne and, with the exception of the war years, continued to live there until his death in 1955. Here he initially exerted a strong influence on the career of Schwarz, a fellow supporter of the Liturgical Movement whom he had met already in 1924, and eventually garnered the strong support of Josef Cardinal Frings, the city's archbishop from 1942 to 1969, and one of the greatest church builders in German history.[11]

Consecrated in 1926, Böhm's Church of Christ the King was the first entirely new church building he designed completely independently, and it was as bold as any that had yet been erected in Germany (Figure 3.1).[12] The façade is more conventional than the interior, but it is absolutely impossible to mistake it for anything built before 1920 anywhere in the world, even if a debt to Josef Marie Olbrich's secular Wedding Tower in Darmstadt is certainly discernible.[13] Clad mostly in brick, with a tower that projects far forward of the entrance to the nave, it plays the modest arched openings seen on three sides of each tier of the tower against the multiplication, now in concrete rather than brick, of that motif at its top. They also echo the single much larger pointed arch that marks the entrance into the building, which is not only set back from the street but also elevated above it by a short flight of stairs opening onto a small terrace in front of the main door. The stepped arch allows Böhm to display the skill of his bricklayers without reverting to applied ornament; it is a lesson initiated by Olbrich, which contemporaries such as Michel de Klerk and Fritz Höger had also absorbed.[14] It also ensures that, although no one in 1926 had ever seen anything before that looked quite like this, there was no confusing the purpose of the structure, which was clearly identifiable as a church.

Figure 3.1 Dominikus Böhm, Church of Christ the King, Bischofsheim, Germany, 1926. Photograph by Elke Wetzig, 2009, Wikimedia Commons (https://commons.wikimedia.org/wiki/File:Christkoenig_bischofsheim_aussenseite_dominikus_boehm.jpg).

This preparation was perhaps necessary, because the interior broke far more radically with precedent. The nave, choir and sanctuary are sheltered under a single parabolic vault executed in exposed concrete. Into its length Böhm inserted a series of bays, also defined by parabolic arches and set perpendicular to the main vault. Böhm's decision could be considered to be a modern version of Romanesque barrel vaulting, but such a description does not fully capture how innovative it was to adapt forms pioneered in the context of market halls and airplane hangars to the design of sacred structures.[15] Alfred Fischer had already developed a similar solution for the much larger Antonius Church in Ickern (now a suburb of Castrop-Rauxel), but he had clearly separated the nave from the choir and sanctuary, something Böhm refused to do, although Böhm did set the sanctuary above the level of the nave.[16] In this he was following the Christ-centred liturgical theology of his mentor and advocate van Acken. Böhm's was the first church dedicated to Christ the King consecrated in Germany.[17] It was thus strongly associated with a progressive Catholicism, although only when Frings was appointed Archbishop of Cologne did Böhm gain strong support from the highest levels of the Catholic Church.

Böhm's impact was not limited to fellow Catholics; the German-Jewish architect Erich Mendelsohn also voiced appreciation for his work, which clearly influenced the synagogues Mendelsohn built in the United States, to which he immigrated in 1941, having fled Germany already in 1933.[18] During the Weimar Republic, Mendelsohn was Germany's leading commercial architect; his imposing office buildings, elegant shops, practical department stores and single cinema set the standard in these domains.[19] His dynamic yet functional approach fused an appreciation for the energy of the contemporary metropolis with a no-nonsense attitude towards adapting the American daylight factory, in particular, for new uses with dramatic night lighting substituting for conventional ornament.

Mendelsohn's design for the chapel of the Jewish cemetery in his wife's native Königsburg (today Kalingrad, Russia) avoided the flashiness that characterized much of his fashionable work, although in several of the handful of surviving photographs it appears almost ready to spring forward.[20] Designed in 1927 and completed two years later, this structure was destroyed in 1938 in *Kristallnacht*. The most dynamic views were taken from the rear of the complex. The view of the model and the surviving flower shop, gardener's cottage and administrative space at the entrance, as well as the plan, show a much less assertive arrangement which prioritized something close to symmetry on an awkwardly shaped site.

Mendelsohn derived the basic composition for the steel-framed cemetery chapel from his design of the far more celebrated Universum Cinema in Berlin of 1928, where a ventilation stack emerges from a curved structure whose ribbon windows one critic likened to strips of film.[21] The conversion, however, to a religious purpose entailed squaring off the volumes. Well aware of how badly the stuccoed masses favoured by many of his colleagues committed to what was often at the time termed the New Building weathered, Mendelsohn instead employed a roughly textured brick, which he accentuated through recessed bands, whose more protected surfaces he plastered.[22] These bands, and the contrast between the two materials, help anchor the building as well as establish a rich sense of texture that helps compensate for the absence of conventional ornament. The projecting cornices energize the result. In an arrangement that he would repeat in his Mount Zion synagogue in St Paul, Minnesota, completed posthumously in 1954, the central volume contained a chapel, which featured a tall stained-glass window facing towards the entrance to the complex (Figure 3.2).[23]

A modest space panelled in wood, the chapel had a much warmer and intimate character than was typical of contemporary German churches and indeed also of the Oberstrasse Synagogue in Hamburg, completed in 1930 to the designs of Felix Ascher and Robert Friedmann.[24] Clearly, it was intended, despite its simplicity, to provide a space that would shelter rather than alienate the mourners gathered within it, even if it lacked the ornament that bestowed conventional dignity upon Mendelsohn's first such commission, completed in 1913 in his native town of Allenstein (now Olsztyn, Poland), which has been restored and now serves as a location for intercultural dialogue.[25]

Mendelsohn's cemetery complex stands to the side of the revolution that was underway in church architecture in Germany at the time because of the cleanness of the lines and the energy that that animated the composition. The play of horizontals against verticals substitutes for the not usually oblique references made to Romanesque and Gothic traditions in churches that nonetheless often share the same material palette, with brick being the favoured material in part because stone was now too expensive for

Figure 3.2 Erich Mendelsohn, Jewish Cemetery Chapel, Königsberg, 1927. Photograph by Abraham Pisarek. Bildarchiv Pisarek / akg-images.

most congregations. Mendelsohn entirely rejected historic and historicist architecture, but he was scarcely the only architect to forsake all but the most abstract citation of the past.

The German Protestant church architect most committed to change was Otto Bartning.[26] Like Mendelsohn, he occupies a somewhat liminal position between the adherents of the *Neues Bauen* (New Building) and those who favoured change but remained sceptical of blank white boxes. Also like Mendelsohn, he was a founding member of the Ring, a group of architects initially established to pressure Berlin building authorities into accepting more experimental designs (Böhm, who never practised in the largely Protestant city, never joined).[27] In 1925, Bartning became the founding director of the architecture school in Weimar that took over the quarters occupied by the recently evicted Bauhaus, and he also contributed to Siemenstadt, a workers' housing estate in Berlin executed by a team that included Gropius, who was also a member of the Ring.[28] And yet Bartning was motivated above all by his strong Protestant faith. His projects, publications and churches eventually garnered a degree of international attention paid to no other interwar European churches, save Auguste Perret's Notre Dame in Raincy and the œuvre of his compatriot Böhm.[29]

The Gustav Adolf Church in the northern reaches of the suburban Berlin district of Charlottenburg was conceived in 1932 and consecrated in 1934. Bartning also supervised its provisional reconstruction after the war; it was altered again in the early 1960s to bring it back as much as possible to his original design.[30] Because it was completed during the Third Reich and then damaged during the war, it is not as well-known as his church for the 1928 Pressa exhibition in Cologne or his Resurrection Church in Essen, dedicated in 1930, but it is an even clearer statement of the clear break Bartning, like Mendelsohn, was willing to make with the past, and of the degree to which, unlike most designers of modern churches, he was willing to embrace an industrial aesthetic in the process. Bartning joined Böhm in being motivated by what he saw as the correlation between the new clear-spans made possible by reinforced concrete and steel construction and an approach to worship that stressed the creation of community across class lines. Having experimented in his renowned Resurrection Church with a circular form, he returned in the Gustav Adolf Church to a more conventional placement of the altar at the southeast end of the site, with the nave fanning out from it.

Bartning made the most of the corner lot, terminating his building in a bell tower that rises forty-seven metres above the street (Figure 3.3). Its stepped profile echoes the wedge-shaped volumes, three on each side of the central triangular volume, that together provide the seating for worshippers. Except for the powerful tower motif, which clearly identifies the building's purpose, the real story lies inside. The entrance façade, easily accessed from either of the flanking side streets, is unusually unassuming for an interwar church, although such restraint would become relatively common after 1945, if not in Bartning's own far more modest emergency churches (the Gustav Adolf Church is almost on the scale of a cathedral). As Böhm had in Bischofsheim, Bartning made creative use of reinforced concrete engineering, although panels of brick infill warm

Figure 3.3 Otto Bartning, Gustav Adolf Church, Berlin, 1934.
Photograph by Andreas Praefcke, 2009. Wikimedia Commons (https://de.wikipedia.org/wiki/Gustav-Adolf-Kirche_(Berlin)#/media/File:Berlin-Charlottenburg_Gustav-Adolf-Kirche2.jpg).

the rendered concrete frame on both the interior and exterior of the building, as do the timber roof structure and the stained-glass windows. These feature a warm gold along the side walls and cool blues at the altar end. The entire interior is designed to focus attention on the central pulpit and the altar behind it (Figure 3.4). The lines of the concrete structure converge on a vanishing point just beyond the altar. There is a curved, tiered sanctuary with the pulpit placed at the centre but several steps below the altar. Originally five sets of stained-glass windows above it faced the altar; the flanking pair on each side were filled-in after the war in a restoration entailing clear glass but have, like the rest of the original glazing, since been restored. The back wall is of blue-black brick with the mortar gilded to catch the light and to further mark the importance of this end of the building.

The stark simplicity of the Gustav Adolf Church, temporarily heightened by its initial post-war reconstruction, remained controversial after the war, even as it provided inspiration for buildings around the world. Its extreme spatial and structural clarity, despite the gold glow originally (and now once again) created by light pouring through the nave windows and the bands of glass tucked between the tiered roof, retained an appropriately Protestant distance from any sense of religious experience as something possibly mysterious, even as countless details subtly distinguish it from other buildings that share its basic concrete frame with brick infill arrangement.

Figure 3.4 Bartning, Gustav Adolf Church, interior.
Photograph by Algensan, 2016. Wikimedia Commons (https://commons.wikimedia.org/wiki/Category:Gustav-Adolf-Kirche_(Berlin-Charlottenburg)?uselang=de#/media/File:Gustav-Adolf-Kirche_Bartning-Otto_02.jpg).

Modern Architecture and the Sacred

Even greater austerity of means could produce, however, even in a Lutheran context, a sense, if not of mystery, then certainly of light at least as something potentially transcendent. The final work of the Finnish-born architect Eliel Saarinen, Christ Lutheran Church has stood since 1949 in a modest neighbourhood in Minneapolis, Minnesota.[31] A masterpiece of understatement, it was almost certainly designed with an awareness of Böhm's achievements and possibly also of Mendelsohn's, as well as the work of Schwarz and of Saarinen's younger countryman Alvar Aalto. In the way that it transforms cold winter light, often reflected off winter snow, Christ Lutheran is paradoxically both closer to the mainstream of the Modern Movement as it existed at mid-century and yet in its immeasurably richer subtle adjustment of geometry further from it, than the far more schematic and often busier work of Böhm, Mendelsohn and Bartning.

Eliel Saarinen is today best remembered as the father of the remarkable Eero, whose short, but significant career placed him at the centre of modern American architecture during the 1950s. During the first half of the twentieth century, however, Eliel was one of the world's most celebrated architects.[32] Christ Lutheran demonstrates why, although this is not immediately apparent when one approaches the building. On the exterior, in an arrangement that reprises on a smaller scale that of his earlier First Christian Church in Columbus, Indiana, completed in 1942, the Minneapolis church appears to be little more than a simple rectangular box with an appended bell tower on one corner (Figure 3.5).[33]

Figure 3.5 Eliel Saarinen, Christ Lutheran Church, Minneapolis, 1949.
Photograph by Carol M. Highsmith. Wikimedia Commons (https://en.wikipedia.org/wiki/Christ_Church_Lutheran_(Minneapolis,_Minnesota)#/media/File:Christ_Lutheran_Church,_Minneapolis,_Minnesota_LCCN2011631332.tif).

Both towers are modelled on Böhm's St Engelbert of 1932 in the Cologne suburb of Riehl, one of the most celebrated Catholic Churches of its day.[34] Such borrowings are an early nod towards the ecumenicalism that would become more commonplace in the post-war period, when for the first time Protestant authors routinely published Catholic Churches and vice versa.

Nor does one find any obvious drama once inside (Figure 3.6). In Columbus, Saarinen had clearly turned for inspiration to another recent German Catholic Church, Schwarz and Hans Schwippert's Corpus Christi in Aachen of 1930.[35] These buildings both have a relatively unusual arrangement featuring a single side aisle, which Saarinen places to the left of the altar and Schwarz to the right. In Minneapolis, however, Saarinen appears to have taken a leaf from Mendelsohn in the way in which two unusually narrow side aisles, a rejection of the literal emphasis on undivided space characteristic of Böhm and Bartning's search for community, find release in a relatively tall rectangular central space. The use of ribbon windows at ground level in place of the more common clerestory lighting inverts the usual means of closing the building off from its surroundings and thus buffering worship from daily life. At the same time, the resulting sense of compression this spatial arrangement creates probably does even more than Böhm and Bartning's churches to encourage parishioners, including those seated just outside the central volume to feel that they are gathered together in a relatively tight embrace that pushes their attention forward and upwards.

Figure 3.6 Saarinen, Christ Lutheran Church, interior.
Photograph by Carol M. Highsmith. Wikimedia Commons (https://upload.wikimedia.org/wikipedia/commons/e/e2/Christ_Church_Lutheran_Minneapolis_Highsmith.jpg).

It takes time to discern the many slight alterations Saarinen made to a formula he may have adopted from Mendelsohn, whom he had first met during the German architect's first visit to America in 1924 (his son Eero would later find significant inspiration in Mendelsohn's early sketches for his Dulles Airport, outside Washington, D.C.).[36] Together these account for the extraordinary effectiveness of this as sacred space. They include the careful illumination of the chancel, as well as the subtle curve of the wall behind the altar, the ripple of the right-hand wall defining the nave, and the slight tilting of the ceiling. It is these gestures, along with an equally restrained but sophisticated use of artificial as well as natural light, rather than expensive material finishes, that set this building apart from contemporary American churches and make it, along with Saarinen's decidedly less luminous steel-framed First Christian Church, the most radically new house of worship erected in the United States since Frank Lloyd Wright's Unity Temple, dedicated more than four decades earlier.[37]

The success of the interior may also bear the imprint of the elder Saarinen's admiration for Böhm, which spanned the historical divide between Protestants and Catholics, in a second way.[38] In St Engelbert Böhm accentuated the way that light coming into the chancel from the left washed across the crucifix. Saarinen intensifies the effectiveness of such side lighting, which now glints off a much larger and simpler metal cross, set at the end of a much longer and (as also in Cologne) somewhat darker space for the congregation. Somewhat paradoxically the altar's role as a destination is more alive here than in the Catholic models upon which Saarinen drew, while the pulpit that can rival it in some Protestant churches is a less forceful presence here than in Cologne.

All the examples discussed thus far emerged out of a northern European design sensibility that included the lingering impact of the attention that National Romanticist reformers, including Saarinen himself, had long paid to the tactility of their materials, very much including brick.[39] And while the National Romanticists themselves were not necessarily known for their use of natural light, Scandinavian architects of the next generation as diverse as Gunnar Asplund and Alvar Aalto famously were.[40] The link to Aalto, who himself only turned to brick once he came to the Massachusetts Institute of Technology, where he built Baker House between 1946 and 1948, reinforces the elasticity of the modernist canon (since 1955, Eero Saarinen's cylindrical red-brick chapel has faced out into the open space fronting Aalto's Baker House Dormitory).[41]

Although often labelled regionalist, this approach to architecture was never exclusive to northern Europe and the United States, nor was it confined to sacred architecture, although that is the subject here. Böhm, Schwarz, Mendelsohn, Bartning and both Saarinens were clearly all aware of one another's work, even if only that of Aalto and the younger Saarinen was lauded in seminal, widely circulated texts such as Sigfried Giedion's *Space Time and Architecture*.[42] The work of the elder generation did much to sanction the greater experimentation with both materials and plasticity that characterized aspects of the International Style as it was practised around the world in the 1950s. In the case of religious architecture, however, it often continued to operate at a slight distance from what was by this time orthodox Modernism. This is evident in Togo Murano's Cathedral for World Peace of Hiroshima, Japan, consecrated in 1954, which draws in particular upon the example of Eliel Saarinen and of Böhm.⁴³

Born in 1891, Murano was one of Japan's most important architects of his generation. Already in the 1920s, he travelled abroad and familiarized himself first-hand with contemporary developments in both Europe and the United States. Although his cathedral attracted less attention abroad than the much younger Kenzo Tange's Peace Center, also in Hiroshima, completed one year later, it was designed in a similar spirit.⁴⁴ Modernism provided an alternative here to nationalism, and, although aspects of it had been adopted in Japan already across the course of the twentieth century, communicated a desire to be reintegrated into a peaceful community of nations, who, however, needed to be reminded of the futility of war.

The composition of the street façade of the Cathedral of Peace clearly adheres closely to the precedent recently established by Saarinen in Minneapolis, although this was a Catholic cathedral (Figure 3.7). Saarinen used a steel frame for Christ Lutheran, which, he entirely covered in bricks of varying hues. Murano, however, chose concrete, which was undoubtedly less expensive and more widely available in post-war Japan. He furthermore chose to emphasize the nature of the frame by leaving it exposed, using brick only as infill. Murano was not entirely content, with such pragmatic understatement. Projecting from two sides of the base of his bell tower and from just to the right of the opposite end of the narthex are a baptistery and two chapels that slightly recall the 'light

Figure 3.7 Togo Murano, Cathedral for World Peace, Hiroshima, 1954.
Photograph by Wiiii. Wikimedia Commons (https://commons.wikimedia.org/wiki/File:Hiroshima_World_Peace_Memorial_Cathedral.jpg).

turbines' that Böhm appended in the early 1920s to his Church of St John the Baptist in Neu-Ulm.[45] That Murano's patron, the Jesuit Hugo Lassalle, was German, may have helped prod him in this direction (Lassalle later authored a number of books on Zen Buddhism).[46]

Murano's (and perhaps also Lassalle's) reluctance to experiment as boldly as Tange, whose Peace Center was widely hailed as one of the most original as well as culturally important buildings of its day, is nonetheless demonstrated on the Cathedral's interior. With its simple arcade at ground level, and its plain timber roof, it recalls the understated reserve characteristic of the reconstructions then being completed of German Romanesque churches like St Pantaleon in Cologne or St Michael's in Hildesheim, albeit now with a single passageway on each side of the nave rather than real aisles. This arrangement, although less dynamic, was not dissimilar from what Böhm had done in Bischofsheim. Interestingly, the actual source was likely Albert Bosslet's St Salvator, a Benedictine Abbey Church completed in Münsterschwarzach, in Germany, of 1938, while Murano quite possibly borrowed the shallow dome over the raised chancel culminating in a large figural painting from Bosslet's earlier Christ the King Church in Hauenstein, dedicated in 1932. These are churches that Holger Brülls has interpreted as examples of the cultural conservatism of the late Weimar and of the Third Reich.[47] Although clearly less radical than the work of the European-born architects discussed in this chapter, as reinterpreted by Murano nearly halfway around the world from their original early medieval sources, these arrangements certainly appear modern rather than Romanesque. Moreover, his use of an architecture viewed as appropriate by the Third Reich reminds us that neither German nor Japanese fascism was inherently anti-modern; if less overtly engaged with modern engineering than many German churches of the 1920s, this level of austerity found here was nonetheless entirely absent from the churches built by established German architects before the establishment of the Weimar Republic.[48]

By the time the Cathedral of Peace was dedicated in 1954, however, many of the buildings discussed in this chapter no longer looked so new. Novel engineering, of the kind Murano employed only in the parasol roofs over his chapels, was the wave of the future. The difference between two churches employing parabolic arches, Böhm's Christ the King, and Oscar Niemeyer's Saint Francis of Assisi completed in 1943 in the Pampulha district of the Brazilian city of Belo Horizonte, points towards the less monumental approach to sacred architecture that represented the cutting edge around the world in the first two post-war decades. In a complete rejection of Böhm's emphasis on solidity, Niemeyer played with the lightness of thin shell construction and of the slab that runs from in front of the church to the unstable inverted triangle of the bell tower. Decorative tiles designed by Candido Portinari provide a decorative and clearly non-structural alternative to the brick facing favoured by Böhm. In the face of a design by an architect who had collaborated with Le Corbusier on the Ministry of Education in Rio de Janeiro, those authors writing about this building typically fail to situate it in terms of the less obviously avant-garde German churches that clearly helped inspire it.[49]

By the end of the 1960s, there had been yet another shift, this time away from buildings that seemed almost weightless to those that were clearly monumental. Dominikus Böhm's son Gottfried designed a number of such churches. These looked back towards

German Expressionism at the same time that they participated in what was often termed 'brutalism'.[50] The most imposing of these is the Mariendom completed in the village of Neviges, now a part of Velbert, in 1968.[51] This immense church, built in accordance with the strictures of Vatican II, is, even when nearly empty of the thousands of pilgrims it was built to house, one of the most memorable of all twentieth-century sacred structures. The complex folds of its faceted roof create a vessel for light and for community as evocative as almost any Gothic cathedral. Van Acken had advised Gottfried Böhm's father's generation of church designers to learn from innovations in theatre, including Richard Wagner's staging of operas; despite the presence of balconies whose projections recall the loges of nineteenth-century opera houses, the Mariendom belongs to the same family of objects as Hans Scharoun's Philharmonie, which opened in Berlin in 1963.[52]

The many other creative experiments with structure in churches built in the 1950s and 1960s lie beyond the purview of this chapter, although they include others of equal aesthetic significance. The phenomenon, although once again widespread, was also relatively short-lived and quickly forgotten. The last three decades of the twentieth century witnessed a precipitous drop off in the number and the quality of new churches in most places. Poland, where the church embodied resistance to the communist government, provides a significant exception.[53] At the same time, the rise of postmodernism reduced appreciation of the many significant modern church buildings of the recent past as well in Catholic contexts of the sources of the architectural reforms mandated by Vatican II since these broke so definitively with historical precedent. Finally, the reaction against postmodernism by figures such as Kenneth Frampton stressed Modernism's 'critical' character in a way that left little room for an appreciation of the continuity in function that necessarily characterizes sacred architecture, even as its forms change.[54] Modern religious architecture was designed to support the status quo by demonstrating its relevance to the twentieth century, which was very different from championing architectural innovation as part of revolutionary overhauls of established institutions.

The history of modern architecture no longer needs to be written as a defence or, for that matter, an attack upon religious architecture. Instead, we need to reconstruct who adopted modern architecture and for what purpose. Such a history would include sacred buildings at its core. Modern churches, mosques and other religious buildings were important examples of how new ideas about style, structure and space were manifested in edifices that were at times controversial, as the new often is, but that also fulfilled the task of inspiring contemporary faith in ways that continue to be meaningful and influential today. Moreover, they were the means through which the exceptional entered the weekly – if not necessarily the daily – lives of millions of people, especially those who worshipped outside of historic urban centres in the many suburban communities erected across the course of the twentieth century. Far from being banal or indeed merely efficient, these were places successfully designed to evoke a strong sense that there was still room for spirituality in twentieth-century life, but that this no longer required material display but instead could be created through the deft transformation of ordinary materials into spaces suitable for sheltering the presence of the divine.

Notes

1. Karla Britton, ed., *Constructing the Ineffable: Contemporary Sacred Architecture* (New Haven: Yale School of Architecture, 2011), and Wolfgang Jean Stock, ed., *European Church Architecture 1900-1950: Towards Modernity* (Munich: Prestel, 2003). See also Wolfgang Pehnt and Hilde Strohl, *Rudolf Schwarz, 1897-1961: Architekt einer anderen Moderne* (Stuttgart: Gerd Hatje, 1997), and Wolfgang Pehnt, *Deutsche Architektur seit 1900* (Ludwigsburg: Wüstenrot Stiftung, 2005).
2. Eric Mumford, *The CIAM Discourse on Urbanism, 1928-1960* (Cambridge, MA: MIT Press, 2000). Walter Gropius was very involved in CIAM, but Ludwig Mies van der Rohe was not.
3. Frederic Spotts, *The Churches and Politics in Germany* (Middletown: Wesleyan University Press, date?); Edward S. Shapiro, *A Time for Healing: American Jewry since World War II* (Baltimore: The Johns Hopkins University Press, 1992), 147–51.
4. Christ-Janer and Mary Mix Foley, *Modern Church Architecture: A Guide to the Form and Spirit of 20th Century Religious Buildings* (New York: McGraw Hill, 1962); Joseph Picard, *Modern Church Architecture* (London: Orion Press, 1960); and G. E. Kidder Smith, *The New Churches of Europe, an Illustrated Guidebook and Appraisal* (Cleveland: World Publishing Company, 1961).
5. Kathleen James-Chakraborty, *German Architecture for a Mass Audience* (London: Routledge, 2000); and Richard Kieckhefer, *Theology in Stone: Church Architecture from Byzantium to Berkeley* (Oxford: Oxford University Press, 2008), 229–64.
6. Niall McLaughlin, 'Incarnation: Bishop Edward King Chapel Cuddesdon', in *Modern Religious Architecture in Germany, Ireland and Beyond: Influence, Process and Afterlife since 1945*, ed. Lisa Godson and Kathleen James-Chakraborty (New York: Bloomsbury Academic, 2018) acknowledges the importance of Rudolf Schwarz to his own church designs; James-Chakraborty, 'Modern German Church Architecture', in *The Cambridge History of Religious Architecture of the World*, ed. Richard Etlin (Cambridge: Cambridge University Press, forthcoming) for Schwarz's impact upon Peter Zumthor.
7. Pehnt, *Deutsche Architektur seit 1900*; and Hugo Schnell, *Twentieth Century Church Architecture in Germany* (Regensburg: Schnell & Steiner, 1974).
8. Werner Durth, Wolfgang Pehnt and Sandra Wagner-Conzelmann, *Otto Bartning: Architekt einer sozialien Moderne* (Berlin: Akademie der Künste and Wüstenrot Stiftung, 2017); Pehnt and Strohl, *Rudolf Schwarz, 1897-1961*; and Wolfgang Voigt and Ingeborg Flagge, *Dominikus Böhm, 1880-1955* (Tübingen: Wasmuth, 2005).
9. Maite Kröger, *Theodor Fischers architektonisches Prinzip am Beispiel der Ulmer evangelischen Garnisonkirche* (Munich: Grin Publishing, 2012); and Winfried Nerdinger, *Theodor Fischer: Architekt und Städtebauer 1862-1938* (Berlin: Ernst, 1988).
10. Johannes van Acken, *Christozentrische Kirchenkunst: Ein Entwurf zum Liturgischen-Gesamtkunstwerk* (1922. Gladbeck i. W.: A. Theben, 1923, 2nd edn).
11. Frings wrote the introduction to August Hoff, Herbert Muck and Raimund Thoma, *Dominikus Böhm* (Munich: Verlag Schnell & Steiner, 1962).
12. Voigt and Flagge, *Dominikus Böhm*, 131.
13. Ralf Beil and Regina Stephan, eds, *Joseph Maria Olbrich 1867-1908. Architekt und Gestalter der frühen Moderne* (Ostfildern: Hatje Cantz, 2010), and Olaf Gisbertz, 'Experiment, Utopie und Wirklichkeit: Die Mathildenhöhe und das Neue Bauen in der Weimarer Republik', in Landesamt für Denkmalpflege-Hessen, and so on, *'Eine Stadt müssen wir erbauen, eine ganze Stadt!': Die Künstlerkolonie Darmstadt auf der Matildenhöhe* (Stuttgart: Theiss, 2017), 251–60.

14. Manfred Bock, Vladimir Stissi and Sigrid Johanisse, *Michel de Klerk: Architect and Artist of the Amsterdam School, 1884-1923* (Rotterdam: NAi Publishers, 1997); Piergiacomo Bucciarelli, *Fritz Höger: Hanseatischer Baumeister 1877-1949* (Berlin: Vice Versa, 1992), and Niels Lehmann and Christoph Rauhut, *Fragments of Metropolis Rhein & Ruhr: Das Expressionistische Erbe an Rhein und Ruhr* (Munich: Hirmer, 2016).

15. Heinrich Küster, 'Die städtischen Markthallen in Breslau', *Zentralblatt der Bauverwaltung* 29 (1909): 74–8; and José Fernandez Ordoñez, *Eugène Freyssinet* (Paris: Éditions du Linteau, 2013).

16. Jörn-Hanno Hendrich, 'Alfred Fischer-Essen. 1881-1950. Ein Architekt für die Industrie', (PhD diss., RWTH Aachen, 2010), 166–75, viewed at http://publications.rwth-aachen.de/record/52244/files/3972.pdf on 5 December 2017.

17. Voigt and Flagge, *Dominikus Böhm*, 131.

18. Hoff, Muck and Thoma, *Dominikus Böhm*, 14.

19. James-Chakraborty, *Erich Mendelsohn and the Architecture of German Modernism* (Cambridge: Cambridge University Press, 1997), and Regina Stephan, ed., *Erich Mendelsohn: Architect, 1887-1953* (New York: Monacelli, 1999).

20. Bruno Zevi, *Erich Mendelsohn: The Complete Works* (Basel: Birkhäuser, 1999), 128–9, and James-Chakraborty, 'Kleinere Bauten für die jüdische Gemeinschaft in Tilsit, Königsberg and Essen', in Stephan, *Erich Mendelsohn*, 146–50.

21. James-Chakraborty, *Erich Mendelsohn*, 157–67.

22. Norbert Huse, *'Neues Bauen' 1918 bis 1933. Moderne Architektur in der Weimarer Republik* (Munich: Heinz Moos Verlag, 1975).

23. Zevi, *Erich Mendelsohn*, 364–83.

24. Carol Herselle Krinsky, *Synagogues of Europe: Architecture, History, Meaning* (Cambridge, MA: MIT Press, 1985), 97–9.

25. Michele Stavagna, 'Begräbniskapelle auf jüdischem Friedhof: Den Erstling wiederentdeckt', *Bauwelt* 23 (2014): 24–7.

26. Durth, Pehnt and Wagner-Conzelmann, *Otto Bartning*, and Helmut Lerch and Jürgen Bredow, *Otto Bartning. Materialen zum Werk des Architekten* (Darmstadt: Das Beispiel, 1983).

27. James, *Erich Mendelsohn*, 115.

28. Dörte Nicolisen, *Das andere Bauhaus: Otto Bartning und die Staatliche Bauhochschule Weimars* (Berlin: Kupfergraben, 1996).

29. Otto Bartning, *Vom neuen Kirchenbau* (Berlin: Verlag Bruno Cassirer, 1919); Lerch and Bredow, *Materialien zum Werk*; and Karla Britton, *Auguste Perret* (London: Phaidon, 2001).

30. Caterina Freundenberg, Christa Thorau and Immo Wittig, *Die Gustav-Adolf-Kirche in Berlin-Charlottenburg und ihr Architekt Otto Bartning* (Gifhorn: Balthauser Verlag, 2009); and Durth, Pehnt and Wagner-Conzelmann, *Otto Bartning*, 72–5, 104–5.

31. Albert Christ-Janer, *Eliel Saarinen: Finnish-American Architect and Educator* (Chicago: University of Chicago Press, 1979), 117–21.

32. Saarinen won the Royal Institute of British Architects Gold Medal in 1950; for his standing in Germany at the time of his death see R. P. 'Eliel Saarinen', *Baumeister* 47 (1950): 569.

33. 'Christ Church', *Architectural Forum* 93 (1950): 80–5.

34. Flagge and Voigt, eds, *Dominikus Böhm*, 145–7.

35. For Corpus Christi see Kieckhefer, *Theology in Stone*, 229–64; and 'Eliel Saarinens leztes Werk; Die Kirche in Minneapolis, USA', *Neue Bauwelt* 5, no. 45 (1950): 186–7.

36. Wolf von Eckardt, *Eric Mendelsohn* (New York: George Braziller, 1960), 13–14.
37. Joseph Siry, *Unity Temple: Frank Lloyd Wright and Architecture for Liberal Religion* (Cambridge: Cambridge University Press, 1998); and Jay M. Price, *Temples for a Modern God: Religious Architecture in Postwar America* (Oxford: Oxford University Press, 2012).
38. Kathleen James-Chakraborty, 'Dominikus Böhm in Amerika', in Voigt and Flagge, *Dominikus Böhm*, 88–91.
39. Barbara Miller Lane, *National Romanticism and Modern Architecture in German and the Scandinavian Countries* (Cambridge: Cambridge University Press, 2000).
40. Nicholas Adams, *Gunnar Asplund's Gothenburg: The Transformation of Public Architecture in Interwar Europe* (State College: Penn State University Press, 2014), and Eeva-Liisa Pelkonen, *Alvar Aalto: Architecture, Modernity, and Geopolitics* (New Haven: Yale University Press, 2009).
41. Stanford Anderson and Gail Fenske, eds, *Aalto and America* (New Haven: Yale University Press, 2012). For Böhm's influence upon Saarinen's chapel see James-Chakraborty, 'Dominikus Böhm in Amerika', 99–100, and for a German appreciation of it, Frei Otto, 'Eero Saarinens jüngste Arbeiten', *Bauwelt* 46, no. 6 (1955): 104–7.
42. They appeared only in later editions. Sigfried Giedion, *Space Time and Architecture* (1941. Cambridge, MA: Harvard University Press, 1967), 618–67.
43. Botond Bognar, *Togo Murano: Master Architect of Japan* (New York: Rizzoli, 1996).
44. David B. Stewart, *The Making of a Modern Japanese Architecture: 1868 to the Present* (Tokyo: Kodansha International, 1987), 172–7.
45. Voigt and Flagge, *Dominikus Böhm*, 128–9.
46. Hugo M. Enomiya-Lassalle, *Zen Meditation for Christians* (La Salle: Open Court, 1974); and Ursula Baatz, *H. M. Enomiya-Lassalle: Jesuit und Zen-Lehrer: Brückenbauer zwischen Ost und West* (Freiburg im Breisgau: Herder, 2004).
47. Holger Brülls, *Neue Dome: Wiederaufnahme romanischer Bauformen und antimoderne Kulturkritik im Kirchenbau der Weimarer Republik und der NS-Zeit* (Berlin/Munich: Verlag für Bauwesen, 1994), 86–8 and 92–6; and Frank-Bertholt Raith, *Der Heroische Stil: Studien zu Architektur am Ende der Weimarer Republik* (Berlin: Verlag für Bauwesen, 1997).
48. A point made already for Germany in Barbara Miller Lane, *Architecture and Politics in Germany, 1918-1945* (Cambridge, MA: Harvard University Press, 1968).
49. Stamo Papadaki, *Oscar Niemeyer* (New York: George Braziller, 1960), 22–4; and David Underwood, *Oscar Niemeyer and Brazilians Free-form Modernism* (New York: George Braziller, 1994), 56.
50. Wolfgang Voigt, ed., *Gottfried Böhm* (Berlin: Jovis, 2006).
51. Karl Keim, 'The Multi-layered Concrete Rock: The Pilgrimage Church in Neviges', in Voigt and Flagge, *Dominikus Böhm*, 60–79.
52. Wilfried Wang and Daniel E. Sylvester, eds, *Hans Scharoun: Philharmonie Berlin, 1956-1962* (Berlin: Wasmuth, 2013).
53. Vladimir Gintoff, 'These Churches Are the Unrecognized Architecture of Poland's Anti-Communist "Solidarity" Movement', *ArchDaily*, posted 7 March 2016, accessed 16 December 2017, https://www.archdaily.com/782902/these-churches-are-the-unrecognized-architecture-of-polands-anti-communist-solidarity-movement.
54. Kenneth Frampton, *Modern Architecture: A Critical History* (London: Thames and Hudson, 1980).

CHAPTER 4
CITTÀ DEI MORTI
ALVAR AALTO'S FUNERARY ARCHITECTURE
Sofia Singler

In a poem that he wrote in 1958, the Finnish modernist poet Pertti Nieminen remarked: 'Few read / the epitaph engraved in the wind.'[1] Like epitaphs engraved in the wind, Alvar Aalto's four funerary projects never assumed built form, likely explaining their relative obscurity in architectural history. Irrespective of their unrealized status, they illuminate Aalto's engagement with burial as an architectural theme and programme and help to situate his approach in relation to the funerary architecture of others during the twentieth century. If not quite epitaphs, his funerary projects might be considered epigraphs to an enquiry into modern architecture, death and its associated rituals – and, by extension, the sacred.

Having founded his atelier in 1923, which he directed together with Aino Aalto, Alvar Aalto designed his first funerary commission, the Jyväskylä Funerary Chapel, in 1925. This historicist proposal references the Renaissance buildings the Aaltos had admired on their honeymoon in Tuscany the year before.[2] The chapel adjoins a mortuary tumulus and its entrance is announced by a cloistered forecourt. After a five-year delay due to lack of funding, the project was rekindled in 1930, this time as a determined functionalist design.[3] The church council rejected Aalto's new version, however, and decided to award the commission to Pauli Blomstedt instead. Completed in 1931, the chapel became one of Blomstedt's last classical works before he, like Aalto a mere few years before him, 'converted' to functionalism.[4]

In 1934, Aalto took part in a competition for an extension to the Malmi Cemetery in Helsinki. The key feature of the design is a zig-zagged spine of greenery that divides the burial land into irregular zones for individual, family and urn burials. The scheme also demarcates potential sites for funerary chapels, although they were not required by the competition programme. Unacknowledged by the jury, the project was the last of a series of unsuccessful ecclesiastical competition entries submitted by Aalto in the 1920s and 1930s. An intermission of seventeen years followed, during which he designed no ecclesiastical projects.

Aalto's return to sacred architecture in the post-war era yielded more fruit. The churches and parish centres of the 1950s and 1960s in Finland, Germany and Italy are counted among his most significant projects. Parallel to his first major churches, Aalto designed two funerary complexes. In 1950, he took part in a competition to design the funeral chapels at Malmi, where he had been unsuccessful in the cemetery extension competition eleven years earlier. This time, his proposal *Trinitas* won first prize. The scheme consists of three red-brick, flat-roofed chapels clustered around a service core. Aalto also designed a bell tower and matrix of monumental columns atop the ridge next to the chapels.

In the following year, 1951, the Danish municipality of Lyngby-Taarbaek announced a competition with two separate categories, one for a cemetery and the other for funerary chapels. Aalto and his assistant Jean-Jacques Baruël's cemetery failed to rate a mention, but their chapel won second prize. Later, the chapel was elevated to first prize, as the jury decided Henrik Iversen and Harald Plum's winning proposal was 'too conventional' after all.[5] Aalto and Baruël's scheme consists of two chapels, a crematorium and a mortuary, all set together in a rectangular white-brick enclosure. The cemetery encompasses two amphitheatre-form burial zones laid out along ravine slopes.

Had Aalto's four projects been realized, he would have been counted among the most prolific funerary designers in Finland.[6] His designs engage with themes and motifs common in his contemporaries' funerary work, underscoring Aalto's close involvement in modernist circles. The projects also support claims made of the rest of Aalto's portfolio, particularly his interest in detail and sensitivity to scale. Nevertheless, the schemes also encompass qualities specific to or especially heightened in the burial context. Above all, attributes such as an ambiguous relationship to nature, sense of separation from the outside world, and decidedly anti-technological servicing shed light on the kind of 'urban primitivism' Aalto adopted and adapted in his architecture of death.

Ancient typologies and topographies

Aalto's proposal for the Malmi cemetery extension does not quite fulfil the expectations of sylvan density promised by its title *Lehto* (Finnish for 'grove'). Its central spine of trees reads more as a formal, albeit twisting, boulevard than it does a verdant thicket. As was also the case in many of the civic and public commissions he designed throughout his career, Aalto seems to have been frustrated with the flatness of the site. He devoted one entire drawing to illustrating how much the northern and eastern edges of the land should be raised. Such topographic surgery would allow for the stepped splaying of each burial sector along a decline of its own, making the existing cemetery, laid out in a strict square grid, an orthogonal basin down below. In Aalto's vision, the funerary chapel on site – completed in 1923 to the design of Selim A. Lindqvist – sits at the hem of the new inclines, standing both as the terminus point of the old cemetery's main axis and as the boundary marker for the ascending gradients of the new add-ons.[7] Aalto's scheme was left partially unfinished, but his sketches document the exploration of wavy, radial and zig-zagged layouts for the new graves, providing varying degrees of contrast to the orthogonal order of the existing cemetery.

Aalto fervently satisfied his impulse to lay a burial ground down a slope two decades later, at Lyngby-Taarbaek. There, Aalto and Baruël's cemetery surrenders to the landscape completely, its grave rows following the contours of the slopes like a draftsman's topographic lines. The plots flow down the slopes of two grassy bowls, forming a set of

Città dei Morti

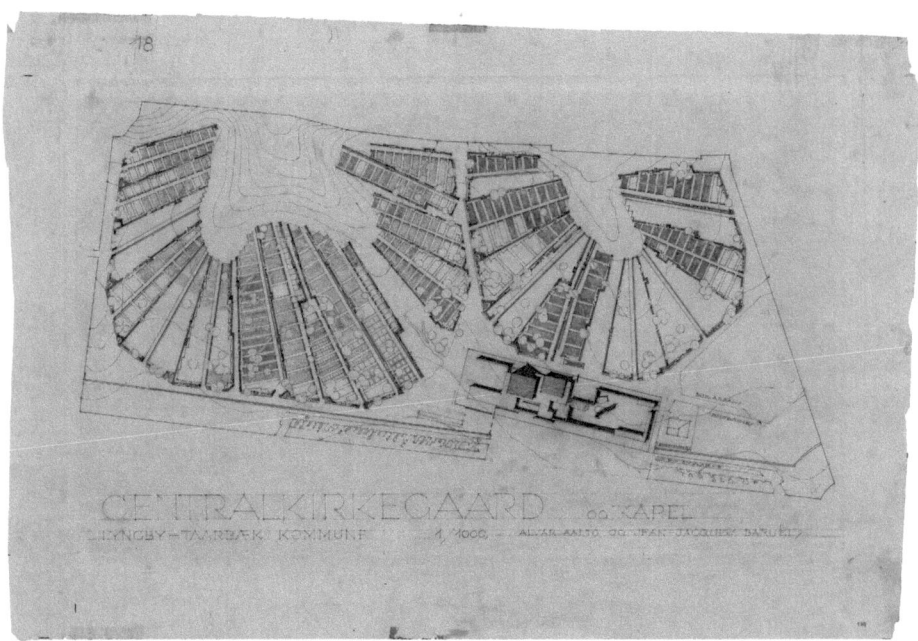

Figure 4.1 Alvar Aalto, *Città dei morti*, Lyngby-Taarbaek Funerary Chapels and Cemetery, Denmark, competition entry (1951). Site plan.
Source: Courtesy of the Alvar Aalto Museum Archives, Jyväskylä, Finland.

twin amphitheatres in plan. Sectors for different types of burial are divided by low brick walls that emphasize the radial layout. Within each amphitheatre, a single sector is left devoid of graves, leaving a walkway to the plateaus at the bottom. The drama of the burial valleys is premised more on a romanticized vision of the site than a serious survey of its topography, however: Aalto liberally exaggerated the inclines of the site (Figure 4.1).[8]

Aalto's admiration of Southern Europe, including but not limited to its classical architecture and culture, is well known; his own definition of a voyage to Italy as the *conditio sine qua non* of his creative endeavours hardly seems an overstatement.[9] Both of his cemeteries at Malmi and Lyngby-Taarbaek evoke Italianate hillsides more than the unremarkable Nordic flatlands they were planned for. Aalto's ever-present references to stoas, agoras, piazze and the like – typically as abstracted, collaged, fragmented or even ruinous spatio-formal motifs executed with contemporary construction techniques – are widely acknowledged. In his funerary projects, elements such as the colonnades guiding mourners into the chapels count as typical examples. At Malmi, however, Aalto also engages in a surprisingly literal reference to the classical: caryatids look down the main façade of the largest chapel.[10] It is difficult not to be reminded of the Erechtheion on the Athenian Acropolis. Given his propensity for architectural references simultaneously serious and playful, it may be relevant that the Erechtheion's caryatids held up one of three porches: Aalto's maidens peer down the elevation of one of three chapels. Even

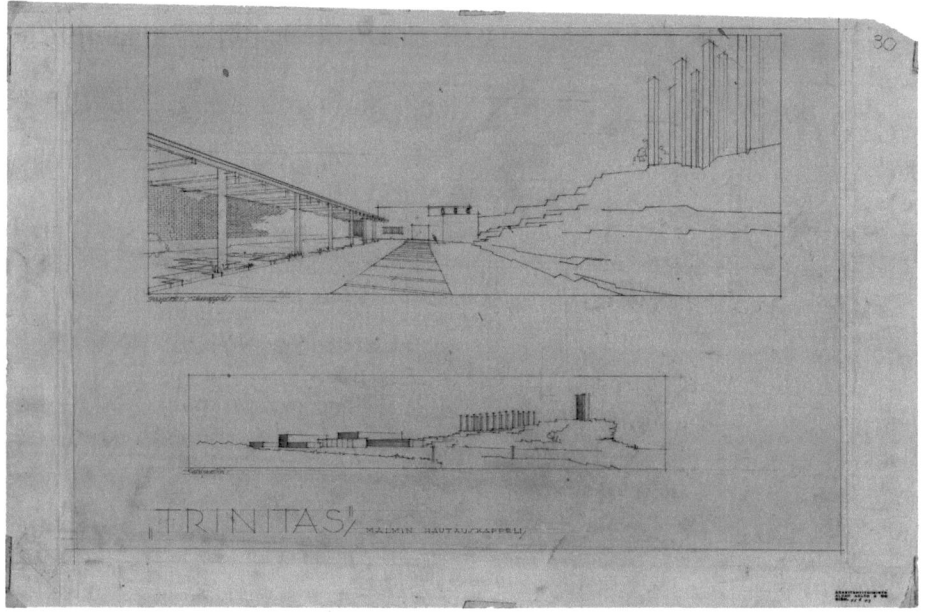

Figure 4.2 Alvar Aalto, *Trinitas, Malmi Funerary Chapels, Finland, competition entry* (1950). Exterior perspectives.
Source: Courtesy of the Alvar Aalto Museum Archives, Jyväskylä, Finland.

in the otherwise dogmatically functionalist final version of his Jyväskylä project, Aalto included classical reliefs in the chapel interior and main façade.

Many of the architectural history quotations in Aalto's funerary projects are not purely classical, but more ambiguously ancient or even prehistoric. The eight truncated columns that he designed on the ridge at Malmi can be interpreted as pre-Christian elements insofar as they evoke connotations of ancient menhirs and classical pillars. The columns denote the section of the cemetery dedicated to urn burials and serve to create an ambience of immutability coupled with tender melancholy. Their monumentality obscures traditional boundaries of function, elevating emotive expression to a worthy purpose of its own. The classical interludes and abstracted ancient monumentality of the scheme are indicative of neither a straightforwardly functionalist rejection of ornament nor a recourse to traditional religious iconography (Figure 4.2).

Aalto's two cemeteries illustrate that his appreciation and appropriation of the ancient encompassed not just typologies but also topographies. In many projects like the Maison Louis Carré (1959), Aalto aggrandized sites' existing inclines or arranged them into stepped banks so as to produce richly layered and levelled flows of spaces inside and outside. His cemetery designs show how the drive to step the ground plane serves not only to desirably complicate the spatial syntax of a building but also to complement or even compose a landscape. Particularly considering how often he filled his travel journals with sketches of steep hills and rocky ridges, one might consider Aalto's stepping of sites a classical reference in itself, a topographical nod to the landscapes of Greek poleis and

Italian villages.[11] The richness of the archaeological evidence of Western burial rites accumulated in the Greek islands and Italian peninsula – from prehistoric paganism to classical antiquity – would make the Mediterranean a particularly pertinent natural landscape to reference in the funerary context.

Aalto's classicizing topographical tendencies stand in contrast to the 'naturalism' of most Nordic cemetery designers. For the first half of the twentieth century, the Nordic cemetery ideal was the 'natural cemetery', rooted in traditional woodland burials. As a rejection of the Romantic churchyards and grand urban cemeteries of Britain and France, it strove to honour the existing nature of a site 'as found'. Sigurd Lewerentz, for example, designed his Malmö Eastern Cemetery around a natural mound and meadow in deliberate evocation of the typical Scanian landscape.[12] Rather than accepting natural features as given in their existing state, Aalto amplified, manipulated and exaggerated them to resemble faraway, aspirational landscapes. In invoking places where the Western city matured, and in blurring the boundary between typology and topography – as illustrated by the amphitheatric slopes of Lyngby-Taarbaek – Aalto's disposition might be considered 'urban'. It seems that for Aalto, the city – understood not as a densely populated metropolis but as a cultivated and cultured context that harks back to the origins of man – informed both the landscape and the architecture of his funerary works.

Walled enclosures

The characterization of Aalto as an architect of intimate connections to 'nature' is so common that it has become a scarcely questioned truism. Curiously, however, his funerary chapels stand apart from this appreciation, in that they stand unusually separate from their settings. Even the stepping of landscape, a technique Aalto used to complement the architecture of many of his other commissions, serves in his funerary proposals to shape cemetery land as distinct from, rather than intertwined with, crematoria and chapels. In contrast to his secular buildings, Aalto's funerary works never really invite nature inside, but rather separate themselves from it.[13] Where the natural appears to meet the man-made – primarily in the planting and overgrowth Aalto drew on the chapels' exterior walls – the interface seems more a confrontation than fluent connection.

At Malmi, the *Trinitas* chapels sit at the foot of a steep ridge. The hill's vegetation provides a counterbalance to the strictly rectangular massing of the chapel complex, with some trees and shrubbery spilling into the forecourts. Similarly, the walls at Lyngby-Taarbaek are boldly solid, but impending disintegration is implied by the vines that crawl along them. Contrasting the cycles of nature with the sturdy permanence of built form hints at the shared fate of eventual decay. The autumnal withering and vernal reinvigoration of nature aptly conveys themes of decay and rebirth – and, in the Lutheran context, Christ's resurrection. Joel Robinson's analysis of Aalto's tombstones can be extended to his funerary chapels: '[T]hey harbour an inbuilt consciousness of the deleterious effects of nature', seeking to mirror 'human transience and mortality through an image of architecture's own frailty or finiteness, given how architecture rises and falls in time, not unlike life itself'.[14] The tension between man-made and natural is underscored by the suggestion of eventual overgrowth: the chapel enclosures' resistance to nature is subject to inevitable failure with time.

Complementing the way that raw nature serves as a foreboding of architecture's – and by association, human life's – temporal limits, the more cultivated genre of the garden becomes an anchor of sepulchral connotations extending both backwards and forwards in time. The walled garden, either as a memorial garden for urn burials or as a walled forecourt, is the typological core of Aalto's funerary œuvre; it features in all of his funerary projects. The garden has long been part of a Nordic iconography of death. In the Middle Ages, the dead were said to 'sleep in a flowery garden'.[15] Nordic Christian art of the late nineteenth and early twentieth centuries portrayed gardens as loci of rich, paradisiacal – if unkempt and forest-like – vegetation in allusion to a Northern Eden. National romantics complemented garden imagery with depictions of forests and fells in their drive to valorize Finnish nature; Albert Edelfelt's painting *Christ and Magdalene* (1890) is set in a birch-tree grove by a lake.[16]

In contrast, Aalto's gardens are not lusciously vegetated, but empty, or at most, sparsely populated by a handful of bare trees and shrubs. Aalto's funerary gardens acquire memento mori status by articulating emptiness in lieu of heavenliness. After all, Eden may have been a lavishly vegetated cradle of perfection, but it was also the backdrop for the Fall of Man. Interpreted as metaphors extending not just backwards to the prelapsarian past but also forwards in time – recalling the eschatological orientation of medieval cloisters – the emptiness of Aalto's gardens suggests an uncertainty concerning the afterlife. Stripping the garden of its main attribute, flora, implies that paradisiacal growth is a potential but not a promise; the goods of the heavenly garden are suspended. If empty niches and apses in funerary interiors are considered metaphors of sorrow or uncertainty, empty gardens might be interpreted as exterior expressions of the same (Figure 4.3).[17]

Aalto's funerary projects do not just contain walled gardens but read as walled complexes in themselves. The walled forecourt appears first in the Jyväskylä Funerary Chapel and is further developed at Malmi, emerging ultimately in its most urban form at Lyngby-Taarbaek. Aalto and Baruël referred to their design for Lyngby-Taarbaek as a '*città dei morti*', a necropolis. Aalto was referring once more to his beloved Italy, where the walled perimeter is the defining characteristic not just of monumental cemeteries but of small village burial grounds as well. Furthermore, the conscious evocation of the image of a walled complex anchors Aalto's chapel projects to the iconographic history of heavenly cities. One of the most salient attributes of a heavenly city is its bounding wall; so too Aalto's cities of the dead hint at sacred enclosure, setting them apart from the everyday.[18] In cemeteries and funerary architecture, boundary walls serve to 'strengthen the impression of a microcosm of death, separate from the rest of the world'.[19] The massiveness and solidity of Aalto's walls emphasizes the feeling of enclosure. His schemes prefigure the emergence of walls as the prime 'functional and architectural' theme in Finnish funerary chapels in the 1960s, exemplified in projects like Osmo

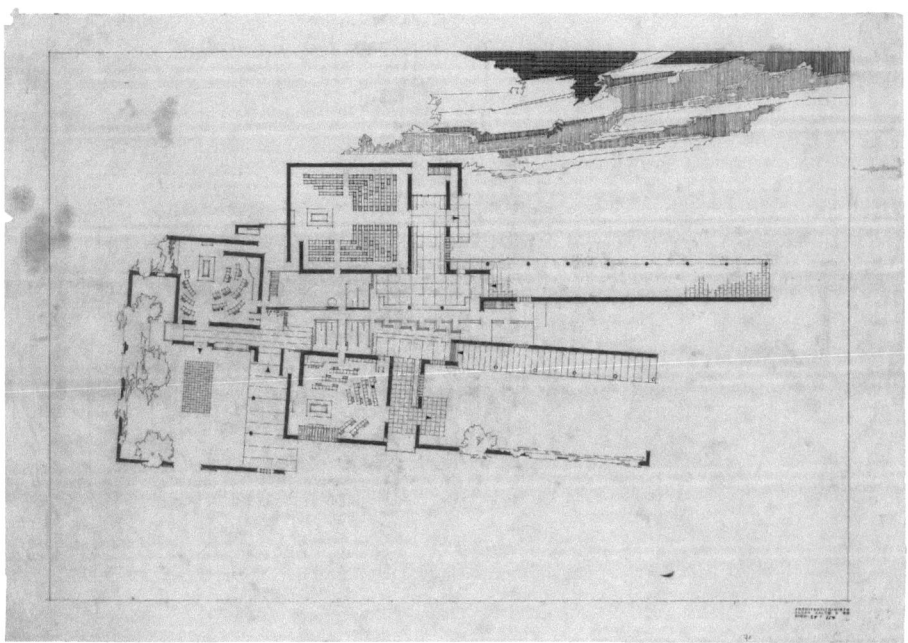

Figure 4.3 Alvar Aalto, *Trinitas, Malmi Funerary Chapels, Finland, competition entry* (1950). Ground floor plan.
Source: Courtesy of the Alvar Aalto Museum Archives, Jyväskylä, Finland.

Sipari's Paattionlehto Chapel (1960), where uninterrupted walls flow from the interior all the way to the cemetery.[20]

The curved forms Aalto is famous for – the undulating ceiling of the Viipuri library or the glass of the Savoy vase, for instance – are entirely absent from his funerary architecture at any scale, even that of the furnishing. The projects' rigid orthogonality serves to strengthen the contrast between building and nature, and also to forge connotations to ancient enclosures for both the living and the dead. Mastabas come to mind. It is as if an architecture of death requires determined solidity and rectilinearity. Perhaps the burial setting demanded particularly 'pure' geometries in Aalto's hand; there, the techniques of collaging, overlaying and fragmenting he used so often in other commissions are notably absent.[21] His funerary chapels do not deny 'the dominance of a singular visual image' to the extent that his civic or residential projects do, but rather consist of spatial sequences more coherent and less permutable than his typical 'episodic' and 'separate architectural scenes'.[22]

Within their walled perimeters, the designs for Malmi and Lyngby-Taarbaek are divided into sets of chapels arranged such that mourners attending different funerals being held at the same time would not come in contact. In both complexes, each chapel is entered via its own forecourt. The separation of circulation routes and sight-lines between the different chapels, and their acoustic isolation, ensures that each funeral party enjoys privacy. Aalto wrote of his ambition to ensure that 'the impact of the public

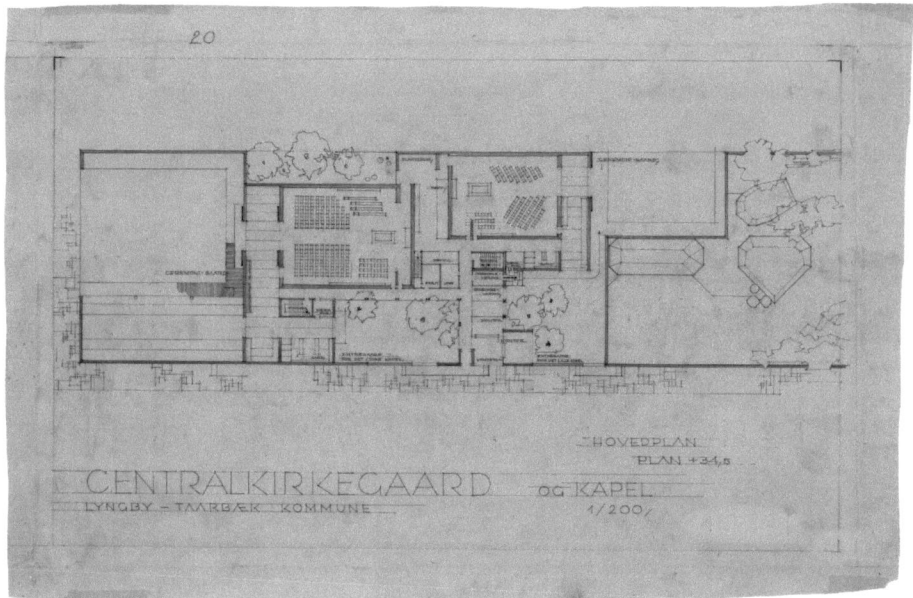

Figure 4.4 Alvar Aalto, *Città dei morti*, Lyngby-Taarbaek Funerary Chapels and Cemetery, Denmark, competition entry (1951). Ground floor plan.
Source: Courtesy of the Alvar Aalto Museum Archives, Jyväskylä, Finland.

does not create a psychologically distressing factor'.[23] It is likely that he turned to Gunnar Asplund's Chapel of the Holy Cross (1940) as a precedent, to the extent that it uses separate entrances for different chapels in a shared funerary complex.[24] While Aalto's funerary projects certainly illustrate his commitment to mitigating the undesired effects of quasi-industrialized funeral operations, many forget that the competition programme already suggested three different chapels at Malmi. Similarly, the Lyngby-Taarbaek competition programme called for two separate 'funeral halls' within a unifying complex (Figure 4.4).[25]

Modulating a common template slightly to create distinctive characters for each of the chapels highlights their intimacy and particularity – each is a meaningful place of its own, rather than an anonymous component in a series. The chapels at Lyngby-Taarbaek are both square in plan but acquire individual identities thanks to different types and arrangements of pews and the unique materials with which each forecourt is paved. At Malmi, Aalto's design was praised by the jury for having 'given, by simple means, each chapel a different character'.[26] There, too, the chapels acquire sensibilities of their own through unique materials, furniture and lighting systems. Aalto, like his contemporaries, was interested in the possibilities of mass production, and spent much of his career developing standardized furniture, building components and even self-build homes for war veterans. He never uncritically embraced the method, but gravitated towards a stance he himself labelled 'flexible standardisation', a term which might well be used to describe his treatment of the chapels at Malmi and Lyngby-Taarbaek.[27] Indeed, 'particularity of place' is often considered an attribute of sacred space.[28]

In addition to ensuring the privacy of different parties attending services at the same time, Aalto's works allow and even demand moments of individual solitude. The scale and configuration of the plans of Malmi and Lyngby-Taarbaek define suites of spaces unsuited to large groups. Their entrances are too narrow to permit all of the funeral party to enter at once: each person must enter alone. Many Finnish poets contemporary with Aalto referred to the inevitable aloneness forced upon each individual at the time of their death, explicating ideas related to the self. V. A. Koskenniemi's *Elegy to Loneliness* famously begins: 'Alone you are, man, alone among all, / alone you are born and alone will you depart.'[29] By directing mourners through narrow loggias, and even narrower interior corridors that have twists and turns along the way, Aalto issues moments of individual solitude along the path of an otherwise collective ritual. John Gamble's term 'degrees of retreat [from the communal]', from his analysis of Aalto's University of Jyväskylä Main Building, might also be applied to the modulation of individual and communal moments in Aalto's funerary projects.[30] Deep inside enclosures walled off from their surroundings, the junctures of individual solitude mark the most isolated moments of Aalto's architecture of death and recall the projects' core theme of separation from the outside world.

Ritual and representation

The storyboard for Aalto and Baruël's submission to the Lyngby-Taarbaek competition includes – in addition to the plans, sections, elevations and perspectives demanded of all participants – thumbnails for two supplementary drawings. They describe what appear to have been the two main rituals the designers had in mind: 'watering' and 'catafalques'. A system of terracotta chutes channels water down from the hilltop chapels to the lowest dips of the burial sectors. Clay pots are integrated into the cemetery walls for visitors to fetch water for the graves' flowers. References to the pleasant practices of gardening alleviate the anxiety related to burials. In one of the most famous Finnish frescoes *Kuoleman puutarha* ('The Garden of Death'), painted by the symbolist Hugo Simberg in 1906 in Tampere Cathedral, robed skeletons water plants in their garden, evoking a sense of death treating man with tender care. Perhaps in conscious counterpoint, the water in the cemetery walls also recalls connotations of descent to the underworld. In Nordic folklore, aquatic zones are evoked as places of crossing over to, and then travelling within the land of the dead. Tuonela, the Finnish equivalent of Hades, is described in the national epic Kalevala as having a wide river running through it.[31] Archaeological evidence has shown that clay pots were used in burial rituals throughout ancient Greece; like the ambiguous menhir-cum-pillars at Malmi, the water channels at Lyngby-Taarbaek collapse centuries of historical and cultural references into one.

One might also consider the water to be an element that balances the fire of the crematorium furnaces; Aalto and Baruël specified in their drawings that the water

Figure 4.5 Alvar Aalto, *Città dei morti*, Lyngby-Taarbaek Funerary Chapels and Cemetery, Denmark, competition entry (1951). Basswood model.
Photograph by Valokuva Oy Kolmio, 1952. Courtesy of the Alvar Aalto Museum Archives, Jyväskylä, Finland.

basin was to follow 'along the cremation route'. The project takes on cremation with expressive lucidity. Its three crematorium chimneys rise from the memorial garden as humble giants next to some trees, as though they were a species of trees themselves. The image of a tree that 'dies' each autumn mirrors the concept central to cremation: 'For dust thou art, and unto dust shalt thou return.'[32] In Lutheranism, corporeal decay is reality – the physical body disintegrates, and only the soul is awoken at the Resurrection.[33] Lyngby-Taarbaek does not sequester the chimneys from sight; they balance between the extremes of being on the one hand morbidly perfunctory monoliths, and on the other ostentatiously decorated stacks designed to divert attention from the origins of the smoke. The most idiosyncratic elements of the project, the polyhedral blocks in the larger memorial garden, also relate to cremation. Shaped like step-cut diamonds in plan, the frusta protrude from the basement to just above eye level, capping three spaces below: the coffin reception room, the mortuary and the furnace. They stand as uncanny forms whose sole purpose is to articulate the stages of cremation (Figure 4.5).

Despite the directness with which Aalto's projects confront cremation, the technology demanded by the process remains subservient to manual ritual. Aalto's self-professed and much-researched antipathy to totalizing mechanization is evident in his funerary designs. Allowing mourners to perform rituals themselves entitles them to catharsis, helping them engage as involved participants rather than passive spectators to a machine-led process.[34] At Malmi, a mechanical catafalque connects the basement mortuary to the chapels above. But at Lyngby-Taarbaek, Aalto defied the competition brief's requirement for a mechanical catafalque: mourners carry the deceased to the grave themselves or, in the case of urn burials, lift the coffin to the crematorium by hand rather than watch a hydraulic device push it into the flames. In a drawing of the catafalques at Lyngby-Taarbaek, Aalto wrote: 'The author accepts no mechanical processes associated with the ritual (sinking or vanishing coffins, mechanically closing doors, etc. (That is Hollywood)).'

Neither Aalto's rejection of mechanization nor the straightforwardness with which he treats cremation is entirely unique among Nordic modernists. Before Aalto, Asplund had written of his dislike of mechanical systems in the funerary context, although he still included them in his Woodland Cemetery chapels.[35] The Vatican forbade cremation until 1964, leading Protestants to create architectures of cremation and urn burial long before Catholics. It has been suggested that Protestants' radically different conception of embodiment and early acceptance of cremation resulted in the characteristic lack of theatre in their funerary design.[36] Indeed, Finland's first crematorium in Hietaniemi, designed by Bertel Liljequist in 1926, makes no attempt to hide the flues of the crematorium. Pronouncing the building's purpose architecturally was a key motivation given that the project was financed by the Finnish Cremation Association (*Polttohautausyhdistys*) in order to convince sceptical church officials and the public of the method's virtues.[37] In contrast, many contemporaneous English and American counterparts disguised their chimneys as bell or clock towers.[38]

Aalto's designs treat cremation as candidly as most of his contemporaries, but they stand apart in terms of pictorial representation. All other entries to the Malmi chapel competition of 1950 contained bold crucifixes or murals depicting Biblical scenes. Even in a group of modernist proposals, Aalto's was the only one devoid of traditional Christian ornament. Two very early croquis for the project contain crosses, the first a single cross on the main façade of the biggest chapel and the second a group of three in the urn burial grove as free-standing sculptures; the latter anticipates Aalto's Church of The Three Crosses in Vuoksenniska (1958) and its eponymous altarpiece. Aalto seems to have discarded these sketches immediately, however, and abandoned legible Christian iconography in favour of floral reliefs and frescoes. Nature is kept strictly outside the walled enclosures of his chapel complexes but is the main theme of their internal decoration. The interiors of both Malmi and Lyngby-Taarbaek are painted with quasi-abstract plant motifs. Although a nature-inspired representational register could be linked to sacral themes such as Christ's description of himself as the true vine and his Father as the gardener (Jn 15.1), it also possesses pantheist tones common to Nordic modernists.

Artists, authors and musicians alike, whom Aalto was well connected to, took to pre-Christian themes to express the idea of nature being sacred, in and of itself. Indebted to Romanticism, modernists found holiness not in an anthropomorphized image of God but in nature itself. Helvi Juvonen's poem, beginning with a line from the Gospel of Luke (17.21), became an unofficial slogan for Finnish modernists' pantheistic agnosticism: 'Nor will people say, "Here it is", or "There it is", because the kingdom of God is in your midst.'[39] Aalto's employment of classical caryatids was exceptional, but the abstracted, organic motifs present at Malmi and Lyngby-Taarbaek are typical of the time. Erik Bryggman's Resurrection Chapel in Turku (1939), for example, was widely admired for the naïvist floral ornamentation of its wall screens and the generosity of light flowing in from an entirely glazed southern façade; the project became known as Finland's 'first true nature church'.[40] By the 1950s, pantheist tones had become common not just in the funerary but the ecclesiastical context more generally, notable examples including Kaija and Heikki Sirén's Otaniemi University Chapel (1956) and Raili and Reima Pietilä's Kaleva Church (1966).

The pantheist qualities of the chapels' ornamentation are complemented by the treatment of light. Natural light was considered important in communicating the consolation promised by belief in the Resurrection and a Christian afterlife.[41] Side-light from clerestory windows and top-light from Aalto's trademark round skylights would have enlivened the floral reliefs of the altar walls at Jyväskylä, Malmi and Lyngby-Taarbaek. Still, the light in all of Aalto's funerary schemes is indirect, and mourners are never granted direct views outside, in contrast to most contemporaneous chapels. The indirectness of the light emphasizes the chapels' separation from the outside, even evoking connotations of cave myths both in a pagan and Christian sense, and indirectly anticipating or engaging with themes pertinent to Le Corbusier's Notre-Dame du Haut (1955).

Conclusion

Aalto's funerary works support interpretations of his so-called humanism, typically understood as the promotion of that which 'makes human beings human' in contrast to the rationalist tenets of International Style Modernism.[42] Particularly in terms of their detailing, material qualities and sensitivity to scale, the projects conform to what one has come to expect from Aalto. Notwithstanding the kinship between Aalto's funerary works and his secular ones, however, the former differ in seemingly subtle but ultimately significant ways. They imply that, for Aalto, the burial ritual demanded an architecture of its own, and they also point to themes salient in his ecclesiastical architecture more generally.

What distinguishes the funerary projects is their heightened sense of separation from the outside, a commanding inward-looking character. Nature is represented abstractly in ornament but otherwise austerely subdued or entirely absent, even in gardens where one might assume plentiful vegetation; there are no views from the interiors to the outside; and the bounding walls are unwaveringly rectilinear and solid. Of course, questions of outside and inside were central to architectural Modernism since the advent of the free plan and elevation. Aalto paid attention to the skin and the entrance of all of his buildings, but his religious œuvre suggests that the dynamic between interior and exterior was of particular importance in the ecclesiastical realm.[43] In the funerary projects, the dynamic becomes almost forbidding in its separateness.

This separateness is not, however, related to a sense of isolation from culture, society and history, nor a withdrawal from the man-made to 'unspoilt' nature. Rather, as Aalto's predilection for *cities* of the dead suggests, urbanity – or the evocation of an impression of urbanity, visually and spatially – constituted the basis for Aalto's architectural treatment of the burial ritual. The 'urban', in this case, refers not to industrialized cities along with their technological development and population sizes but to elementary, ancient conceptions of living together in a community. It might be considered an 'urban primitivism', an evocation of humanity's social history, crystallized in the notion of living together. Considering the extent to which Aalto's *Città dei morti* contrast to contemporaneous natural cemeteries, it is worth noting that the latter's focus is on 'the deceased resting in the forest as individuals', as illustrated by the lack of unified grave rows or tombstones, whereas 'in necropoleis, the dead form a community'.[44]

The city was a key consideration in twentieth-century, particularly post-war, religious architecture, both in Aalto's portfolio and in Europe at large.[45] In his funerary projects, Aalto's allusion to the city serves to underscore how collective life, and indeed collective ritual, defines human existence in the world. Although the entrance sequences of his funerary chapels impose moments of aloneness on the mourner, the exits – arriving and leaving happen through different doors – are wide enough to allow for multiple persons at once. The steadfast commitment to manual rather than machine-led ritual also encourages collective activity; a coffin is too heavy to carry alone. Aalto's references to the ancient sites and rites of the Mediterranean attain special gravitas in the burial context. He explained: 'For me Italy represents a certain primitivism, characterized to an astonishing degree by attractive forms on a human scale [. . .] Every culture, like every religion or ideology, has an original, pure simplicity about it.'[46] In his funerary œuvre, Aalto aimed to grasp the 'pure simplicity' of the urban, communal human condition at its most primitive. There, more than anywhere else, the comfort of the collective is needed to console the individual.

Acknowledgements

Nicholas Ray deserves profoundest thanks for his role in shaping and inspiring this research. Thanks are also due to Katariina Pakoma, Merja Vainio, Mia Hipeli, Antti Heino, Risto Raittila and the late Arne Hästesko at the Alvar Aalto Museum, Jyväskylä, Finland. The symposium *Modern Architecture and the Sacred* at Pembroke College, Cambridge, in April 2017 enriched my thinking and questioning. I am grateful to Drs Ross Anderson, Karla Britton, Gabriele Bryant, Kathleen James-Chakraborty, Hannah Malone, Matthew Mindrup and Maximilian Sternberg for their insights and criticism.

Archival sources

The corpus of archival material at the Alvar Aalto Museum in Jyväskylä, Finland, consulted in 2012–13 and 2016, consists of one basswood scale model and 228 original drawings filed in the folders 'Jyväskylän siunauskappeli', 'Lyngby-Taarbaek, Tanska', 'Malmin hautausmaa' and 'Malmin siunauskappeli'.

Notes

1. Pertti Nieminen, *Uurnat. Runoja* (Helsinki: Otava, 1958), 39.
2. The design resembles Brunelleschi's Ospedale degli Innocenti. See Eeva-Liisa Pelkonen, *Alvar Aalto: Architecture, Modernity, and Geopolitics* (New Haven and London: Yale University Press, 2009), 40–2.
3. Aalto received a Beaux-Arts-derived training at the Helsinki University of Technology (1916–21). Before he designed the Viipuri Library and Paimio Sanatorium in the late 1920s – which catapulted him to international fame – his portfolio comprised classical residential commissions, church renovations and competition entries in Central Finland and Ostrobothnia.
4. Simo Paavilainen, ed., *Nordic Classicism, 1910–1930* (Helsinki: Finnish Museum of Architecture, Helsinki, 1982), 92–3.
5. Lyngby-Taarbaek Kommune, *Konkurrence om Centralkirkegård med tilhørende kapelanlæg for Lyngby-Taarbaek kommune* (Jyväskylä: Alvar Aalto Museum Archives, 1952). Although the committee justified the change of opinion with architectural merit – Aalto and Baruël's chapel is deemed 'the clearest and best' – it is possible that the revelation of the participants' identities would have played a role. Aalto was at the height of his international fame at the time.
6. The most prolific was Mikael Nordenswan, designer of seven funeral chapels and crematoria. For an overview of the history of Finnish funerary architecture, see Terhi Lehtimäki and Hanna Lyytinen, *Siunauskappeli rakennustyyppinä: Evankelis-luterilaisten seurakuntien siunauskappelit 1917–2000* (Tampere: Arkkitehtitoimisto Hanna Lyytinen Oy, 2015).
7. Soon after the competition, the Malmi parish decided against new builds and divided Lindqvist's cross-plan chapel into three small chapels instead. In 1966, the parish added a crematorium next to Lindqvist's building.
8. Rob Howard and Ernst Petersen, 'Visualisation of Unbuilt Buildings in their Landscape', *Proceedings of the IEEE International Conference on Information Visualization* (July 1999): 110–15.
9. Alvar Aalto, 'Viaggio in Italia', *Casabella Continuità*, no. 200 (1954): 5. Quoted in *Alvar Aalto in His Own Words*, ed. Göran Schildt, trans. Timothy Binham (New York: Rizzoli, 1997), 38–9.
10. Aalto also used classical motifs like column capitals and acanthus leaves in his tombstones. For a list of his grave designs, see Göran Schildt, *Alvar Aalto: The Complete Catalogue of Architecture, Design and Art* (New York: Rizzoli, 1994), 62–4.
11. Aalto first visited Italy in 1924 and Greece in 1933. Vittorio Golia considers the Lyngby-Taarbaek chapels 'crowns on an Acropolis'. Vittorio Golia, 'La città dei morti, un cimitero di Alvar Aalto', *ArtWort*, accessed 6 April 2019 https://www.artwort.com/2014/04/12/architettura/citta-dei-morti-cimitero-alvar-aalto/.
12. Ingrid Campo-Ruiz, 'Equality in Death: Sigurd Lewerentz and the Planning of Malmö Eastern Cemetery 1916–1973', *Planning Perspectives* 30, no. 4 (2015): 639–57.
13. Aalto is known for drawing 'light, sun and greenery into the heart of interior space'. Sarah Menin and Flora Samuel, *Nature and Space: Aalto and Le Corbusier* (London and New York: Routledge, 2003), 3.
14. Joel Robinson, 'Death and the Cultural Landscape (On the Cemetery as a Monument to Nature)', *Proceedings of the Forum UNESCO University and Heritage 10th International Seminar 'Cultural Landscapes in the 21st Century'* (April 2005): 2.

15. Paula Kivinen, *Tampereen Tuomiokirkko* (Porvoo: WSOY, 1986), 122.
16. Given that his own interest in the Middle Ages was limited, Aalto's knowledge of medieval traditions came primarily through the work of the National Romantic architects and artists of the late nineteenth century, including his teachers at the Helsinki University of Technology.
17. Kalevi Pöykkö, 'Kuolema ja arkkitehtuuri', in *Synty ja kuolema*, ed. Simo Lahtinen, Tapani Pennanen, Rostislav Holthoer and Roger Luke (Tampere: SKSK, 1989), 89.
18. Othmar Keel, *The Symbolism of the Biblical World: Ancient Near Eastern Iconography and the Book of Psalms*, trans. Timothy J. Hallett (Winona Lake: Eisenbrauns, 1997).
19. Juhani Pallasmaa, 'Kuoleman kuvat arkkitehtuurissa', in *Mikään ei häviä. Kirjoituksia kuolemankulttuurista*, ed. Huttunen et al. (Helsinki: WSOY, 2006), 116–17.
20. Lehtimäki and Lyytinen, *Siunauskappeli rakennustyyppinä*, 59.
21. Antony Radford and Tarkko Oksala, 'Alvar Aalto and the Expression of Discontinuity', *The Journal of Architecture* 12, no. 3 (2007): 257–80.
22. Juhani Pallasmaa, 'Hapticity and Time: Notes on Fragile Architecture', *Architectural Review* 207 (2000): 78–84.
23. Katariina Pakoma, 'Cemetery and Chapel of Rest, Lyngby-Taarbaek', in *Drawn in Sand – Unrealised Visions by Alvar Aalto*, ed. Aila Kolehmainen and Esa Laaksonen (Helsinki: Alvar Aalto Museum and Alvar Aalto Academy), 48–9.
24. Schildt, *The Complete Catalogue*, 59.
25. Lyngby-Taarbaek Kommune, *Program for en offentlig skitsekonkurrence om en Centralkirkegård med tilhørende kapelanlæg* (Jyväskylä: Alvar Aalto Museum Archives, 1951).
26. 'Tävlan om begravningskapellet i Malm', *Arkkitehti*, no. 1 (1951): 15.
27. See, for example, Schildt, *Alvar Aalto in His Own Words*, 271.
28. Marja Laine, 'Siunauskappeli arkkitehtuurina ja tilakokemuksena' (MA thesis, University of Jyväskylä, 2011), 45.
29. V. A. Koskenniemi, *Elegioja ynnä muita runoja* (Porvoo: WSOY, 1917), 11–12.
30. John Gamble, 'Alvar Aalto: Formal Structure and a Methodical Development of an Inclusive Architecture' (PhD diss., University of New South Wales, 2014), 249.
31. Aalto's alma mater, the Jyväskylä Lyceum, was founded in 1858 as the first Finnish-speaking school in the autonomous Grand Duchy of Finland. The curriculum, a product of the Fennophile movement that aimed to elevate the status of Finnish culture and language in the Russian Empire, emphasized knowledge of both classical antiquity and Finnish mythology and folklore. See Erkki Fredrikson, *Lyseotalon vuosisata – Jyväskylän Lyseon päärakennuksen ja opinkäynnin vaiheita 1900-luvulla* (Jyväskylä: JYLY ry, 2002).
32. In the funeral service order of the Finnish Lutheran church, these words, from 1 Moses 3.19, are said by the pastor as the coffin is blessed. Wooden boards painted with this verse are found above the entrances of some nineteenth-century mortuaries. Outi Orhanen, 'Siunauksen tilat: Pohjalaiset siunauskappelit ja hautaushuoneet' (MA thesis, University of Jyväskylä, 2015), 47.
33. Eero Huovinen, *Kuolemattomuudesta osallinen: Martti Lutherin kuoleman teologian ekumeeninen perusongelma* (Helsinki: Suomalainen Teologinen Kirjallisuusseura, 1981).
34. Juha Pentikäinen, adapting French social historian Philippe Ariés's thought to the Nordic context, postulates that in the modern era Finnish culture became 'death-denying' partially

as a consequence of technological optimism. If belief in technology is associated with a denial of mortality, persistent commitment to pre-industrial, manual rituals in the funerary context might be considered, conversely, accepting of death. See Juha Pentikäinen, *Suomalaisen lähtö. Kirjoituksia pohjoisesta kuolemankulttuurista* (Pieksämäki: Suomalaisen Kirjallisuuden Seuran toimituksia, 1990), 194–7.

35. Carl-Axel Acking, 'Artist and Professional: Glimpses of Asplund's Last Years', in *Erik Gunnar Asplud: Architect,* ed. Claes Caldenby and Olof Hultin (Stockholm: Arkitektur Förlag, 1985), 20–1.

36. Edwin Heathcote, *Monument Builders: Modern Architecture and Death* (Chichester: Academy Editions, 1999), 37; Michel Ragon, *The Space of Death: A Study of Funerary Architecture, Decoration, and Urbanism* (Charlottesville: University Press of Virginia, 1983), 259.

37. Tuomo Lahtinen, *Polttohautaus Suomessa. Aatehistoria ja kehitys* (Åbo: Åbo Akademi, 1989), 63–4.

38. James Stevens Curl, *A Celebration of Death: An Introduction to Some of the Buildings, Monuments, and Settings of Funerary Architecture in the Western European Tradition* (London: Constable, 1980), 310.

39. Helvi Juvonen, 'Pikarijäkälä', in *Pohjajäätä* (Porvoo: WSOY, 1952), 60.

40. Lehtimäki and Lyytinen, *Siunauskappeli rakennustyyppinä*, 47.

41. Tuula Airio, *Lappeen hautausmaa Lepola. Ilmari Wirkkalan 1930-luvun hautausmaaideaali* (Tallinn: Lappeen kotiseutuyhdistys, 2010), 72.

42. Schildt, *The Complete Catalogue,* 81.

43. Sofia Singler and Maximilian Sternberg, 'The Civic and the Sacred: Alvar Aalto's Churches and Parish Centres in Wolfsburg (1960–68)', *Architectural History* 62 (2019): 205–36.

44. Pallasmaa, 'Kuoleman kuvat arkkitehtuurissa', 117.

45. Sofia Singler, 'Constructing Country, Community and City: Alvar Aalto's Cross of the Plains', in *Territories of Faith: Religion, Urban Planning and Demographic Change in Post-War Europe, 1945–75,* ed. Sven Sterken and Eva Weyns (Leuven: Leuven University Press, forthcoming, 2019).

46. Aalto, 'Viaggio in Italia', 5.

PART TWO
BUILDINGS FOR MODERN WORSHIP

CHAPTER 5
LIGHT, FORM AND *FORMACIÓN*
DAYLIGHTING, CHURCH BUILDING AND THE WORK OF THE VALPARAÍSO SCHOOL
Mary Ann Steane

This chapter explores the significance of light not to form but to *formación* (literally 'forming', typically translated as 'training' but more akin to *Bildung*, self-education) at the Valparaíso School of Architecture. Church building has remained a significant, not unusual, task for Chilean architects since the Second World War. At Valparaíso this has shaped a pedagogical outlook which gives emphasis to the theatre of architecture, the sense in which architecture is enacted collaboratively rather than produced, and one whose primary ambitions include the proper architectural expression of community and locality. The chapter concludes that a different perspective on natural light is made possible when architecture is treated as Gadamerian event, and design as the playful navigation of a game, in that this avoids the engagement with spectacle that has transformed so much recent architecture into a form of egregious conspicuous consumption.

The existence of a spiritual void at the heart of the modernist project is often still assumed, one associated with the decline of religion as a cultural institution across much of the global north. But this is not the case everywhere. In modern Chile, Christianity has remained central to everyday life and continues to find vivid expression in the religious settings around which its communal life unfolds.

The distinctive pedagogical approach of the Valparaíso School has been the subject of a number of studies over recent decades, most notably Ann Pendleton-Jullian's 1996 *The Road That Is Not a Road and The Open City, Ritoque, Chile*.[1] Influenced by the rich dialogue inaugurated by the architect Alberto Cruz and the poet Godofredo Iommi, following their arrival in 1951, design practice at Valparaíso starts from the particular conditions of a site so that context is not assumed but discovered through the making of architecture. As the large body of work built over the subsequent decades exemplifies, the school's emphasis on the architectural act rather than the architectonic artefact has anticipated a wider shift in educational priorities – a greater focus on learning through collaborative making – that is only now being more fully acknowledged and implemented elsewhere.

Framing its teaching as a quest to establish the relationship of architecture to poetry, the Valparaíso School has adopted a curriculum that engages with post-colonial issues of identity in wrestling with how life in Chile can be fostered and celebrated tellingly through design. This has not only prioritized informal engagement with the enactment of city life as a proper form of urban and architectural research but also allowed the time and place of festival to be given special emphasis. I argue here that Catholicism has not only influenced this rethinking of the delivery and goals of architectural education but revealed light's role in design as a cue for inhabitation, an important index of and response to locality. Priests are respected members of staff at PUCV, the Catholic University to which the Valparaíso School belongs, saints' days are celebrated with festive design challenges and church design has remained a critical source of inspiration for the school's design philosophy. These related threads have had a major impact on pedagogy, with focus given to how design practice can emerge from the reinterpretation of familiar spatial settings in making architecture that stems from intense and direct engagement with the local.

In a talk given towards the end of his life, Hans-Georg Gadamer called for education to be seen differently, identifying its ultimate goal as the nurturing of 'lived understanding'.[2] For Gadamer, understanding consists in a circular tension between the familiar and the strange, between feeling at home and feeling alienated. He was questioning how – beyond the direct acquisition of knowledge – proper self-education or *Bildung* could be fostered. For Gadamer *Bildung*[3] is not just the 'culture' one has acquired, but also action, a cultivation or forging of oneself in a never-ending 'living process of becoming'. In exploring this possibility, he stressed the necessity for students to live through experiences that affirm and shake up their orientation, suggesting that *Bildung* happens through an accumulative mode of learning that depends on the presence of others, and that 'lived understanding' must itself be an experience of limitation.[4]

Until now the Valparaíso School is probably most well-known for its coastal settlement/experimental building laboratory at the Open City and its collective approach to design through drawing and hands-on making. This chapter will reframe these achievements by considering the influence of Roman Catholicism on the teaching of 'lived understanding' at Valparaíso. In particular it reviews whether the school's advocacy of enterprise, resourcefulness and improvisation involves students in 'experience of limitation' and how a nuanced concern for light as a local phenomenon impacts on the *Bildung/formación* it provides.

In exploring these questions, two phases that mark the school's evolving understanding of pedagogical principle are important. Two projects, a text and a building, exemplify the first phase: the 1953 presentation by Alberto Cruz of the design process for a chapel near Santiago, and the 1961 reconstruction of the small church at Corral near Valdívia. A built project and a teaching method exemplify the second phase: the 1976 – ongoing oratory/cemetery at the Open City, and the *travesía*, a design journey/collective project undertaken annually since 1984 by students and staff at the school.

As will be argued here, and in tune with the 'Catholicity' the school embraces (but does not impose on its students), the Valparaíso approach to design education can be considered a training in ethics, one which recognizes a communal basis for practical wisdom in which students discover the rewards of austerity and of sacrifice in a common cause. Beyond creating a powerful esprit de corps, its inarguable strength is that it builds trust in the city, trust in what is seen and heard, not trust in abstractions like form or space, a recognition that 'humane capabilities' are nurtured when design education is treated like a game whose players must remain alert to its limits and opportunities as they unfold.

Renewing architectural education: The first two decades at Valparaíso

From 1951 onwards, the architect Alberto Cruz and the poet Godofredo Iommi instigated an alternative approach to the teaching of design whose emphasis on observational drawing, and learning through making, sought to demonstrate the relation of poetry to architecture. In questioning assumptions about the priorities of design education, they challenged the autonomy of the individual architect by exploring how collaborative practice can unfold, giving particular attention to staging architecture as a conversation between different voices. Pursued against the background of tumultuous national politics, particularly during the last four decades of the twentieth century, the engagement with how people interact, combined with a desire to dissolve the boundaries between art and everyday life, led to the emergence of two modes of common life. Summarizing this stance, Cruz himself wrote of these early years, 'The university thus becomes a way of working. And what has been the experience of this way of working? Before everything else: a collective life.'[5]

The first short-lived experiment took place close to the school in a group of adjacent houses on a street on Cerro Castillo, Viña del Mar shortly after Cruz's arrival in Valparaíso. Forswearing the stifling autonomy of typical domesticity, these dwellings whose doors were never closed supported intense companionship and spontaneous debate. Their white walls, simple furnishings and windows without curtains reflected the effort to reduce life to essentials. If the focus of the German *Existenzminimum* of the 1920s had been minimum spatial and environmental standards for individual families, the embrace of austerity at Valparaíso signalled rather interest in the shared fate of the larger community. Given wider social uncertainties in post-war Chile, its explicit rejection of conformist bourgeois values lent this voluntary poverty a Franciscan character, as David Jolly, a former Head of Architecture at the school acknowledges in his remark, 'In the salon one needs many kinds of clothing, in the monastery only one.'[6] Emptiness was reinterpreted in relation to action: as a gulf to cross, a cleared field on which to do battle. Seen in this light the serene yet serious poverty of whiteness became an opening between compatriots, a white table around which to gather, a new sheet of paper on which to draw.

During or just after this period, the school engaged in a number of projects for religious institutions of particular significance to its developing ethos. These included the 1953 Los Pajaritos Chapel, which stimulated Cruz's first major theoretical tract, discussed later, and the Las Condes Monastery and Santa Clara Chapel in Greater Santiago of the years 1954 to 1960, all unbuilt. The reconfiguration or replacement of earthquake-damaged churches in the south of Chile followed in 1960 to 1963.[7] These projects enabled theory to influence practice, particularly as far as light was concerned, as exemplified by the church of Nuestro Señora del Tránsito at Corral.

The 1953 Los Pajaritos chapel project: A 'battle for the cube of light'

Alberto Cruz's text 'Project for a chapel in the estate of Los Pajaritos'[8] analyses his own design process for a small chapel on an agricultural estate outside the Chilean capital Santiago (Figures 5.1, 5.2, 5.3 and 5.4). Gnomic in character, with the structured density of poetry, Cruz's insights are delivered in circular fashion and punctuated by provocative plays on words. Written in the first person in stream of consciousness mode, it places great emphasis on the active process of finding words to distil design ambitions. For Cruz, poetry is an architecture of words. He is seeking to demonstrate how through its making and inhabitation architecture is a poetry of acts.

Design, he argues, rewards intellectual 'nakedness' and should invoke a 'return to not knowing'. That is, it should be discovery, not the unfolding of a set of rules. He repeatedly underlines the need to abandon *a priori* thinking. The modernist idea that an efficient marriage of technics and aesthetics is all that is required of architecture is ridiculed. Rather than choosing from a spectrum of already-established forms, or naively assuming form equals function, a designer should identify a direction worth following through direct observation of human settings. Design is thus not logic-unfolded or history-fulfilled but empathetic wayfaring.

In placing his focus on human settings Cruz rejects totally the idea that architecture should make a spectacle of itself. What architecture itself looks like is not the end but the means of whatever life it accommodates. In this case, Cruz decides that the architecture of his chapel should construct a light conducive to prayer, an ambition triggered by personal experience of how indirect natural light had transformed an ordinary living room into a temporary oratory.[9] To illustrate his assertion that 'architecture is the exterior circumstance supporting the possibility of the interior act',[10] he declares, 'The light is the sand that enables being near to the sea of our praying ... The rest doesn't matter, it is not at all interesting, let it be what it wants.'[11] Cruz treats light as circumstance not prospect – not what you look at but where you find yourself. References to previous experience suggest the way in which light gathers, supports and orients a collective act of prayer.

Figure 5.1 Model of the Los Pajaritos chapel interior illustrating its 'equal' light.
Photograph by Mary Ann Steane.

Figure 5.2 Model of the Los Pajaritos chapel exterior.
Photograph by Mary Ann Steane.

Light, Form and *Formación*

Figure 5.3 Sketch of the liturgical celebration envisaged at the Los Pajaritos chapel.
Source: Archivo Histórico José Vial Armstrong, Escuela de Arquitectura y Diseño, PUCV.

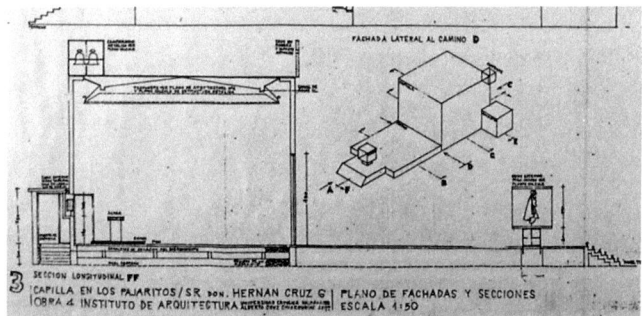

Figure 5.4 Section of the Los Pajaritos chapel project, looking south-east. A statue of Mary framed within an aedicule commands a topography of steps and platforms at one end of an axially arranged plan.
Source: Archivo Histórico José Vial Armstrong, Escuela de Arquitectura y Diseño, PUCV.

In this fashion he implies that light is a more fundamental aspiration than form. An aspiration for a particular quality of light is born of looking; it is not the consequence of form or geometry but rather its origin.

The structuring power of light has always been fundamental to orientation in religious settings. In the chapel project, white walls washed indirectly with natural light from above create a calm airy interior whose orientation is given by the route of entry from the main doors towards the altar and its glowing tabernacle niche, which is also top lit (Figure 5.2). Cruz describes his aim as a soft homogenous 'equal' light, and this leads to the adoption of a cubic form for the building. Ultimately, he declares that his 'cube of light' will constitute 'a church of the form of absence'. Why this framing of ambitions? Beyond allowing him to imply once more that architecture should be the stage not the protagonist, it underlines Cruz's assertion that the architecture which makes a church present does not concern form/the formal. As he adds, an already-established style or a formal fantasy about what may one day come will not guarantee an eloquent staging of either prayer or liturgical gestures and choreography. In making architecture, in enacting theatre, designers should neither look backwards nor forwards, but be alert to present possibilities. Thus, a church that is present has the power to displace those at prayer within. This paying attention to the present is the primary ambition of the annotated observational sketches with which every design challenge begins at the Valparaíso School.

The changes to the liturgy that had been promoted by the Liturgical Reform Movement since the beginning of the twentieth century were not widely shared in Chile. Fernando Perez et al. argue however that in the post-war years Cruz and others at Valparaíso (José Vial, Arturo Baeza and Jaime Bellalta) were initially more aware of the impact of the reforms on recent church architecture in Europe than those in clerical circles.[12] In treating the congregation as co-protagonist in the liturgy, the Valparaíso church designs from the late 1950s and early 1960s predated the guidance of Vatican II by replacing a more processional arrangement with one that enables more of the congregation to surround the main altar. In these works, an enlarged presbytery houses a larger-than-normal platform for the altar, although this arrangement is not monofocal. The design of the platform allows it to organize a series of secondary elements. As elsewhere, the asceticism adopted in Chile reflected wider ambitions among reformers to recover the spirituality associated with the Early Christian Church.

On the face of it the whiteness and horizontality of the chapel seem unquestionably modern. There are no Gothic pointed windows, no classical elements stripped of their details. Instead, a set of subtly modulated white cubes – or almost cubes – structure a journey away from the road and across a raised platform into the building. Hence, a cubic aedicule with a votive statue of Mary marks the chapel's location on the road and frames the tall doorway into the chapel itself, and the altar and tabernacle within. Two points concerning this overall arrangement are worth making that back up the motif of humility. First, roadside shrines are everywhere in Chile. Some boast significant buildings that attract well-attended pilgrimages, but many are more modest. Made by ordinary people to commemorate the violent death of friends or relatives *animitas* are white house-form shelters for candles and mementoes of the deceased. They mark the spot where body and soul were separated, and where it is believed the soul (*anima*) may linger. On the one hand, in discussing the siting and civic role of his chapel, Cruz likens his project to these 'dispersed cities of candles'. On the other hand, the emphasis on the structured interplay of light, liturgy and enclosure, recalls Appia's minimalist stagesets. (Entitled *L'œuvre d'art Vivant*, Adophe Appia's 1921 summary of the significance of the manipulation of light and shadow to the mise en scène of theatre had a major influence on modernist staging of promenades/ascents to light like those of Le Corbusier's early houses or Terragni's Danteum.)

Is half-light or austerity the more important goal of this design? Cruz's commentary on this point takes the form of a parable about a white table that denigrates Modernism's fixation on formal issues, its concern for self-referential coherence. In alluding to the way white surfaces acquire a patina in recording what happens across them, Cruz locates architecture within everyday life, not beyond it, as the page on which life gets written.[13] Architecture he argues is not about constructing idealized forms divorced from their context, but devising the framework for a play of occupation that does not draw attention to itself. In this context, the 'quality of space' that whiteness delivers is both the presence and persistence of light and an openness to local colour. It is the self-negation of backdrop or foil. To back up this assertion, Cruz goes out of his way to describe the glittering spectacle of flowers and devotional images his church will accommodate. Unlike many a modernist *Gesamtkunstwerk*, the church of Los Pajaritos is conceived as a humble setting for popular devotionalism. It overtly recognizes the potential nobility of all materials for such a task, however prosaic they may be.

Cruz's detailed analysis of this project reflects the change of approach he sought to introduce to the curriculum at Valparaíso: a new attention to experience, a new attentiveness to observation as a means of reframing the questions architecture should address. In this framing of architecture's task, empathetic observation is a goal not an assumption, and what it demands by way of an engaged eye and ear is at stake. His subsequent 1959 paper, entitled 'Improvisation of the architect Alberto Cruz'[14] expands on this pedagogy, elaborating its ethical underpinning that makes openness to others fundamental rather than formal or technical knowledge.

Cruz underlines that young architects must learn to see. Their seeing requires not passive reception but active interpretation. He urges a focus on people and their activities, asking students to consider the informality of everyday exchanges and their circumstances, not formal concerns like axis, surface or materiality. The inhabited world is actively interrogated in walking, drawing, thinking and writing – an order to events that helps recording become 'seeing' and design a matter of shrewd arbitration rather than formal dexterity. The ethical basis for this approach is revealed when Cruz suggests that teaching designers is a matter of developing resilience, empathy, nous – a trust in seeing, a trust in engaging with others. Hence, according to Cruz, an architect's education should actively develop character, civic responsibility and an ethical imagination.

The unique character of Valparaíso drawing is worth underlining. Many schools pay close attention to the craft of drawing. At Valparaíso, annotated hand-sketching is considered the critical method for understanding the world and its inhabitation. It therefore always complements photography and other less grounded forms of cartographic and statistical analysis. Unusually however, a common line/hand is encouraged. Student sketchbooks do not begin with an eclectic collage of personal fragments but annotated line drawings completed on site whose authorship is not easy to identify such is the discipline imposed. This subsuming of individual eyes within the collective both constructs and gives limits to the school's common life.

Reconstruction of the church of Corral, 1961

Whereas the school's religious projects in Santiago (Santa Clara, the Las Condes Monastery) had encouraged experimentation with light as a way of reconciling poetry and science,[15] their 1961–2 church reconstruction projects fostered architecture that is responsive to the locality and its climate of light. This approach is particularly well documented for the project at Corral,[16] a small coastal hamlet not far from Valdívia whose tin church of Nuestra Señora del Tránsito suffered serious damage in the 1960 Chilean earthquake. Perched above the shoreline, the partially destroyed building had been a simple shed divided lengthways into a rectangular nave/presbytery and ancillary classroom accommodation. Given these remote and humble surroundings, the Valparaíso architects treated the project as a chance to work with and reinterpret the existing building, framing their task as making a more dignified place of prayer from the shed they were presented with, using whatever materials and craftsmanship that were at hand:

> The sacredness established by the hand of another is reflected in a nobility of endeavour that transcends the modesty or luxury of the construction, and is something not tradeable, i.e. without economic or pragmatic impetus. The church must persist as a hub of the community.[17]

In accepting this role they nonetheless sought to coordinate new ambitions for the church's space and structure with those concerning light. As their words make clear, they were keen to take forward the insights of the Los Pajaritos project: 'The architectonic form is founded in the act of praying, the withdrawal of the presence of form, and in the light of prayer.'[18]

But what was the local light like? They knew the chapel would primarily be seen by daylight and so its local pattern of change became an important point of departure for the design of both the interior and exterior of the building. In broad terms, the concern was to make the most of the frequently diffuse, relatively dim light created by Corral's situation at the base of several deep valleys beside the sea, one which makes looking through open windows hard because of glare. Their close engagement with the critical phenomena is illustrated in their summary of the village's situation:

> The light of the city matters for the exterior constantly and for the interior at the hours of mass. It varies in intensity in winter and summer . . . in the evening the height of neighbouring hills and their position make the direct sun disappear very early. So for many hours the light reflected by the sky reaches the city – which is very intense because the sun is still at a good height. That is, there is a long twilight of zenithal light reflection so that it remains almost constant. The hills, at that hour, full of trees, are very absorbent, and appear shady while the sea and buildings and sky have reflected light.[19]

They termed their pragmatic marriage of old and new 'reconstructive surgery'.[20] It was surgery driven by a concern to support communal gathering by restructuring space with respect to light. Removal of the classrooms and the insertion of a longitudinal rather than a crosswise structure enhanced the building's capacity to withstand earthquakes and allowed the nave to be widened, and its central barrel-vault to be retained. The new structure – large triangular beams, supported by two pairs of cross-braced towers at either end – also permitted a new side altar, a small sacristy and a more generous chancel

(Figures 5.5 and 5.6). Within a lower overall volume, this created a new relationship between nave and presbytery, by differentiating them more obviously through light. The original high barrel-vaulted space still led the eye to the altar, but the wider asymmetric nave – no longer crowded with columns – became a more generous place of assembly whose inner skin of diagonal timber boarding led the eye around a less axial space.

Importantly, the 'presence of form' was weakened by introducing new sources of light that challenge the building's four-square order. While the high windows in the gables at each end still signal the main orientation, unaligned lower windows bring light on both sides. The space is further enriched by indirect lighting from above in three corners. A painted white line encircling the interior creates a horizon above which windows are fully open but below which they are veiled with delicate light-filtering screens. Hence, the position of the two lateral towers that stiffen the structure and form part of these screens is determined by the lighting strategy, not structural considerations.

On the exterior, owing to the conditions of salinity and humidity at the coast, it was decided that the building's metal sidings and roof should be painted. As the architects themselves note, their colour scheme of silver (roof and upper walls) and red (lower walls) establishes a violent difference between interior and exterior in which these planes that camouflage the external volume – while still implying its internal horizon – are subsequently supplanted by the warmth of the timber within. Alluding to their earlier light studies, the architects justify these decisions in relation to the local climate,

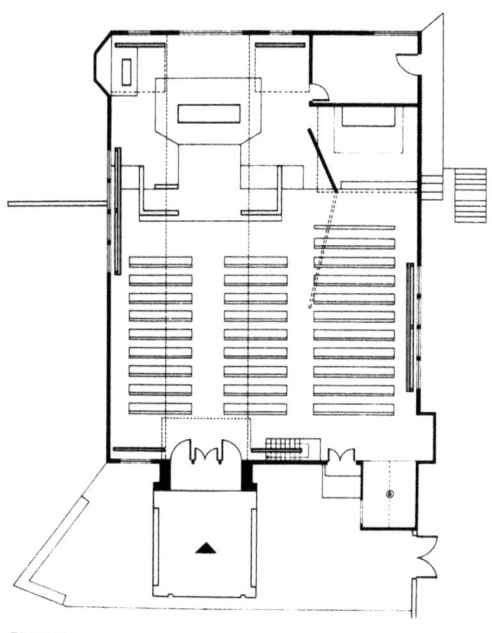

Figure 5.5 Plan of the reconfigured church of Nuestra Señora del Tránsito, Corral.
Source: Archivo Histórico José Vial Armstrong, Escuela de Arquitectura y Diseño, PUCV.

Figure 5.6 Diagonal view across the nave of the Corral church after reconstruction.
Source: Archivo Histórico José Vial Armstrong, Escuela de Arquitectura y Diseño, PUCV.

explaining their impact 'as a form of presence that corresponds to the external light prevailing in Corral: in both winter, when there is a constant drizzle with bright clouds; and in summer, when Corral becomes a spa with moments of splendid sun in which the mass of the sea dominates'.[21]

At Corral, the design team lived on site for a considerable period while the building was constructed. Unusually, this enabled not only acquisition of the on-site collaboration skills by which the school continues to set great store, but a greater awareness of local light conditions and their implications for the staging of worship and community.

The Open City's co-operative life, 1971–present

The second mode of communal life adopted by the school arose with its foundation of *La Ciudad Abierta*, the Open City, in 1971. This settlement lies nineteen kilometres north of Valparaíso/Viña del Mar at Punta de Piedra. Sited on ground that was once considered wasteland but recently given the Chilean equivalent of 'Site of special scientific interest' (SSSI) status, the experimental architecture, mostly houses but also shared public spaces, interior and exterior, is not only 'open' to the natural conditions, but frequently reworked. It involves collaboration among teachers and students in which design is treated as a journey navigated by and between participants. Hence, the initial catalyst for each project is a collective poetic act, *la phalène*, whose background is the work of Parisian urban poets like the surrealists. Requiring participants to enact a collective journey to a site in the spontaneous creation of a *poesía del ha lugar* (poetry of place),[22] the 'words of origin' spoken on site foster insights on – and thus a design response to – the site's specific conditions. Natural light is treated as an important aspect of the local conditions that helps forge architectural identity. Whiteness is again at issue.

As a co-operative entitled 'Corporación Amereida', many teachers from the school now live at the Open City in dwellings known as *hospederías* (guesthouses). They live separately from one another, but with the aim of fostering hospitality, each *hospedería* contains an interior capacious enough for the whole community to gather for decision-making meetings. Likewise the external *agoras* of the Open City form clearings in the landscape whose location and character allow them to stage the regular meetings of the community also termed *agoras*, at which the founding principles of the settlement concerning the common life it seeks to foster are an important topic. These outside spaces also support the less formal events and festival days[23] that sustain the political/social life of both settlement and school.

The Open City oratory[24]

Perhaps the most open of all of the projects at the Open City is its oratory (Figures 5.7 and 5.8). Forming part of a larger complex of gardens that include the settlement's cemetery, it is a study in how assembly can be grounded and oriented out of doors; what accounts for both a sense of movement and a sense of arrival; and how, through light, enclosure can be implied rather than imposed.

With its ground of brick pavers encompassing not only steps but also seats, the oratory interconnects a series of terraces that modify the upper part of a natural gully in low cliffs behind high sand dunes. Located about halfway up, its broad terrace demarcates a pause in the journey. It is literally a crux or crossing place where several paths meet. It has no walls, though the gully itself helps contain the space. The enclosure is ultimately provided by the surrounding ground and the lush vegetation sustained by the gully. Views onto the flanks of the gully are therefore permitted when you sit 'inside' the oratory. More important to the sense of enclosure is the roof. A series of L-shaped white mesh sails seventy-five centimetres deep are held taut by a metal and timber structure whose twelve slender posts create the church's aisles. In its condensed lightness, this 'roof' both is and is not enclosure. The rain may come in, but the roof's capture of sunlight creates the shade necessary for an open-air service; the glow of the sails against the dark trees attracts the eye and provides a sufficient horizon of containment.

Also worth noting is the 'antechamber' just below the oratory which juxtaposes the lightweight architecture just described with its dark natural counterpoint. Here in another wall-less 'interior', circular concrete steps edged with brick ascend the gently sloping ground between pine trees landscaped by Jorge Sanchez and Juan Purcell. The dense foliage above, echoing the roof beyond, contains the space by defining its upper horizon. A sculpture *pozo* (well) by Claudio Girola, whose bent path slices into the hill

Modern Architecture and the Sacred

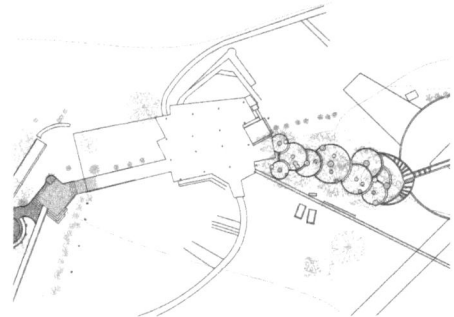

Figure 5.7 Site plan of open-air oratory at the Open City, 2003.
Source: Archivo Histórico José Vial Armstrong, Escuela de Arquitectura y Diseño, PUCV.

Figure 5.8 The Open City oratory looking west from the path that ascends towards it through a group of pine trees.
Photograph by Mary Ann Steane.

nearby, presents a second antithesis to the church that also concerns light. Here a narrow architecture of increasingly high brick walls slices a piece of sky in defining a small unroofed chamber deep inside the hill.

Despite its lack of built walls, and therefore explicit interiority, the oratory's surprising capacity to capture sound is as significant as its capture of light. It is a milieu that cannot be anticipated. Hence, this sketch of a building, in material terms *une fleur ephemère*, is a rule-breaking *capriccio* whose skeletal glowing roof makes an oratory present by invoking its absence.

The *travesías*, 1984–present

The *travesía* (journey, crossing) is a form of poetic action adopted at Valparaíso as a teaching/learning exercise, seeking to acknowledge the reciprocity between the literal and metaphysical dimensions of building as a collective act.[25] The Spanish term for pilgrimage, *peregrinación*, has a religious meaning no longer so evident in English, so its use for the *travesía* is inappropriate. The *travesía* does not exclude religious issues if they arise, but in character it is active rather than contemplative. The American continent is its horizon, and building a new relation with this land – one of gratitude not exploitation – is its goal. Reverie may be encouraged at the start of the journey but subsequently it involves the expenditure of considerable energy. At Valparaíso participants use the phrase *salir de travesía* (going out for *travesía*), hinting that such journeys also help illuminate their learning in and from Valparaíso.

Like the *phalène*, it is a 'live project' in that architecture is designed, built, and then gifted by its builders – a group of staff and students – to those who host them. Most of these journeys have been to sites on the South American continent and have a duration of two to three weeks. Unusually for architectural education, the school acknowledges that the life in common that the *travesía* requires offers design students several key lessons. Achievement of an architectural work by fostering self-discipline and mutual respect among participants – the giving room to one another necessary among pilgrims – is understood as a positive educational outcome. Such a consequence presupposes that during their time together the members of the group occupy a common space, share a common way of working and keep to a common timetable.

Typically, the work built during a *travesía* is lightweight – an ephemerality linked to the nature of the enterprise.[26] The project must be able to be completed within the time limits of the exercise. As it is a gift, such lightweightness also allows its hosts to accept or reject it. Depending on the task identified, close consideration of lighting issues may or may not be significant, but students will always be asked to observe the locality and its character, and record this in annotated sketches, before they embark on a design.

Importantly, during the *travesía* a subgroup of the students are charged with maintaining its poetic trajectory by devising a series of quasi-ritual events that dramatize the significance of concerted action, manifesting the group's collectivity of purpose and the 'liveness' of its enterprise. While there is no script for this theatre, the 'poetic acts' staged to mark each phase of the project keep the multiple ambitions of the journey in view while building strong group morale and a shared grasp of timing. They always involve readings, and the drama is often intensified through the use of candlelight. In particular, by giving the journey a recognizable rhythm, these events underline the strict 'limits' of the *travesía*'s 'festival time'.

Sacred architecture, light and *formación/Bildung*

So what is the significance of sacred architecture for a design programme that actively fosters enterprise, self-education – a learning how to learn? Arguably three modes of 'lived understanding' accrue as a result of the Valparaíso approach to design and its enactment.

First, self-education is promoted at Valparaíso through interaction with others, self-education being understood as a keeping oneself open to what is other. As Gadamer says of practice in *Reason in the Age of Science*: 'the normative character of practice and hence the efficacy of practical reason is "in practice" still a lot greater than theory thinks it is'[27] – that is, one cannot conduct practice according to a recipe or rules, one must 'be practised'. And, 'in contrast to all other goods it is not diminished by being shared but actually gains through participation,'[28] and 'practice is conducting oneself and acting in solidarity'.[29] In this understanding, successful architecture depends on a capacity for empathy best developed through 'live projects'. Critically, design is considered both 'a road that is not a road' and a form of disciplined play. The boundaries/limits in the game-playing exercises staged at Valparaíso are significant – whether they are of place or time – because they are experienced by students as spurs to creation, rather than difficulties to be overcome. In a game you have to take risks to test possibilities. Moreover, winning/losing is inherent to game-playing. The realization among students that in forging a design path playfully, failure is always intrinsic to success, is a crucial lesson of Valparaíso teaching. At the same time, game-playing aids esprit de corps – a collective ethos – and builds the capacity to adapt to new situations and to make sound judgements and act on them. Such openness to discovery through *shared* observation and conversation reflects a Franciscan engagement with the everyday, the humble, rather than the formalism of high art. It therefore echoes Gadamer's turning away from a *Bildung* oriented to high culture – *Kultur* – and towards one oriented to the praxis of civic life. Importantly, participants are encouraged to have both the courage to speak and the patience to listen. Like an arduous journey, a *travesía* demands accommodation to circumstance and enacts learning through negotiation in which the mutual difference raised by debate is ultimately seen not as a difficulty but as an opportunity for growth and enrichment.

Secondly, Valparaíso practices design as a common life within which common sense emerges. Festive celebratory events actively create community through their profound presentation of our own reality. As Gadamer notes, the artwork *festivises* – it makes participants alive to the present.[30] It reveals our personal indebtedness to past and future communities of meaning, thereby building faith in the city. An open city may be undefended but it recognizes its common life. In the school, traditions and a 'common sense' develop, risk-taking is supported and a strong group ethos is developed by an insistence on common words, a common style of drawing, and more or less intensely, depending on the location of the work, a common life. In manifesting the Franciscan belief that austerity can provoke eloquence and support a focus on the essential, this life demands discipline from participants but rewards them with lively camaraderie and depth of understanding.

Thirdly, the persistent focus on light and lightweightness means that art/architecture is treated primarily as an open-ended event neither completable nor oriented to a completed object. This concern with presence over permanence, and potential dynamics, reflects the school's desire, echoing Gadamer, to 'bring things out into the open'. Hence, the *travesía* projects, like those in the Open City, seek to enact a playful response to local conditions and 'the lightweight' emerges as a serious – because playful – proposition. Issues of inhabitation always take precedence over form and formal matters in such work, reflecting the oft-stated Valparaíso engagement with 'reticent form'. In particular, a nuanced concern for inhabited light is evident in the design of church buildings where beyond its role in orientation, light is treated not primarily as something to be looked at, but a milieu within which inhabitants find themselves, that is, not as a spectacle but a setting. Critically, light is treated as a specific phenomenon rather than one that is general, and one whose localization in the settings of the churches invokes a participation of those worshippers and their histories in the divine dispensation.

Establishing core skills is always an important goal in schools of architecture, but it is rare in the West to give the emphasis to sketching that Valparaíso recommends. It is likely that their shared discipline of sketchbook production would also be controversial, as both a teaching method that is old-fashioned in the extreme and one assumed to act as a barrier to innovation. What justifies the Valparaíso emphasis on collective expression, and by extension the idea that a diversity (or individuality) of design approach is not a priority?

At Valparaíso an ethical outlook on design teaching is implicitly shaped by Roman Catholicism. This is absolutely not a matter of indoctrination – of students either going to church or declaring their faith – but an approach open to being sermonized. Architecture's 'calling' is presented as a discipline involving mutual respect and the renunciation of a degree of autonomy, and establishment of the kind of group ethos which belonging to a church – or an army – entails. Teaching architecture at Valparaíso involves establishing appropriate conduct through example and in the process architectural education becomes not only a discovery but also a kind of ordeal. That is, *formación* – a test of a group's mettle, as well as its creativity. In the work of the school, *formación/Bildung* is a more important ambition than form. It is as if the focus on inhabitation and light, inhabited light – architecture as event – when linked to the open-endedness of design as play, supports the attention given to 'lived understanding' and its necessarily collective unfolding at a specific locality and among a cohort of students.

Notes

1. Ann M. Pendleton-Jullian, *The Road that Is Not a Road and The Open City, Ritoque, Chile* (Cambridge, MA: MIT Press, 1996). See also Fernando Pérez Oyarzun and Rodrigo Pérez de Arce, *Valparaíso School Open City Group* (Basel: Birkhäuser, 2003).
2. Hans-Georg Gadamer, 'Education is Self-Education', *Journal of the Philosophy of Education* 35, no. 4 (2001): 529–38.
3. For a detailed examination of *Bildung* as a concept see Hans-Georg Gadamer, *Truth and Method*, chapter 1, trans. Garrett Barding and John Cumming (London: Sheed and Ward, 1975).
4. See Deborah Kerdeman, 'Hermeneutics and Education: Understanding, Control and Agency', *Educational Theory* 48, no. 2 (Spring 1998): 241–66, for further discussion on the significance but also the difficulties of responding to Gadamer's call for a re-evaluation of educational goals when planning curricula in tertiary education. https://education.uw.edu/sites/default/files/u261/Kerdeman%20ET%201998.pdf.
5. Alberto Cruz, 'Improvisación del Arquitecto Alberto Cruz', *Proceedings of the First Conference of Latin American Faculties of Architecture*, Universidad Católica de Chile, Santiago, Doc.27/12 November 1959, appendix to Doc. 26 of November 1959, from http://www.ead.pucv.cl/1959/improvisacion-del-arquitecto-alberto-cruz/ (Retrieved 20 November 2017).

See also Mary Ann Steane, *The Architecture of Light, Recent Approaches to Designing with Natural Light* (Abingdon and New York: Routledge, 2012), 109–12, for further discussion of this text and its impact on other projects at the Open City.

6. David Jolly, personal communication, November 2013.
7. These renovation projects in southern Chile included the parish churches at Curanilahue, Arauco, Puerto Montt, Corral, Lebu, Florida and the chapel of Nuestra Señora de la Candelaria at San Pedro outside Concepción.
8. Alberto Cruz, 'Projecto para una capilla, en el fundo Pajaritos', *Anales de la UCV* 1 (1954): 219–34, trans. author, published on the web at https://www.ead.pucv.cl/1954/proyecto-pajaritos/ (accessed November 2017).
9. Ibid.
10. Ibid.
11. Ibid.
12. Fernando Pérez Oyarzun, Pedro Bannen Lanata, Hernan Riesco Grez and Maria del Pilar Urrejola Dittborn, *Iglesisas de la modernidad en Chile, precedentes europeos y americanos*, Escuela de Arquitectura, PUC (Santiago: Ediciones ARQ, 1997), 115–16.
13. Ibid., 97–9.
14. Cruz, 'Improvisación del Arquitecto Alberto Cruz'.
15. Steane, *The Architecture of Light*, 112–14.
16. The project is by José Vial, Jorge Sanchez and Alberto Cruz with the collaboration of other Valparaíso tutors, structural engineer, Sergio Rojo; construction adviser, Alberto Vives; environmental adviser, Reinhold Klubstchko. José Vial Armstrong, Jorge Sanchez and Alberto Cruz, 'Reconstrucción Parroquia de Corral', *CA, Ciudad y Arquitectura*, no. 32 (1982): 28–33, published online at http://wiki.ead.pucv.cl/index.php/Reconstrucción_Parroquia_de_Corral (accessed November 2017). See also Fernando Pérez Oyarzun, Rodrigo Pérez de Arce, Horacio Torrent and Malcom Quantrill, eds, *Chilean Modern Architecture since 1950* (College Station: Texas A &M University Press, 2010), 67–70; Pérez, et al., *Iglesisas de la modernidad en Chile*, 142, 150–3. Sketches and documents concerning the project are published at: https://docs.google.com/file/d/0BxuJ5FxWMboMd3lhSG96ZTN0dVE/edit (accessed November 2017).
17. Vial et al., 'Reconstrucción Parroquia de Corral'.
18. Ibid.
19. See Jose Vial Armstrong, 'La Luz de Corral', 1961, published online at https://drive.google.com/file/d/0BxuJ5FxWMboMVlZVMVdSRzJ3Sjg/view
20. Vial et al., 'Reconstrucción Parroquia de Corral'.
21. See Vial et al., 'Reconstrucción Parroquia de Corral'.
22. For detailed commentary on Valparaíso's poetry of place see Mary Ann Steane, 'The Origins of City: Paseo', *arq: Architectural Research Quarterly* 16, no. 4 (2012): 330.
23. October 4th, the feast day of the School's patron, Saint Francis, is celebrated each year with a major theatrical event. A Franciscan spiritual outlook, a giving honour to the beauty of creation while fostering collective creativity, remains an important tacit source of inspiration. Consciously or not, his encampment outside Assisi, with its small church and houses for each of the brethren, anticipates the Open City.
24. The original project project is by Alberto Cruz, Mastrantonio, Juan Baixas with students; built version: Jorge Sanchez, Juan Purcell, Patricio Cáraves (1976–present). Although

sometimes referred to as a *capella* (chapel) by its users, the Open City 'church' is an oratory in canon law since as an open space it cannot be consecrated.

25. For further discussion of the *travesía* as wayfaring, see Mary Ann Steane, 'Found in Translation? Reconfiguring the River Edge of Cochrane, Patagonia, a travesía project of the Valparaíso School led by David Jolly and David Luza, November 2013', *Brookes e-journal of Learning and Teaching* 8, Issues 1 and 2 (April 2016), published online at http://hejlt.org/article/found-in-translation-reconfiguring-the-river-edge-of-cochrane-patagonia-a-travesia-project-of-the-valparaiso-school/
26. David Jolly, trans. author, 'Arquitectura Effimera', 2010, unpublished essay.
27. Hans-Georg Gadamer, trans. Frederick G. Lawrence, *Reason in the Age of Science* (Cambridge, MA: MIT Press, 1981), chapter entitled 'What Is Practice? The Conditions of Social Reason', 69–87, 83.
28. Ibid., 77.
29. Ibid., 87.
30. See Hans-Georg Gadamer, *The Relevance of the Beautiful and Other Essays* (Cambridge: Cambridge University Press, 1986), chapter 1 (57–65) and chapter 8 (123–30).

CHAPTER 6
READING, STORING AND PARADING THE BOOK
BETWEEN TRADITION AND MODERNITY IN THE SYNAGOGUE
Gerald Adler

Introduction

The church, as a building type, has enjoyed a privileged position among places of worship in architectural histories dominated by Western thinking for so long that 'spiritual space' has come to be associated with Christian tropes of contemplation, religious service and community. The spirit of Modernism touched ecclesiastical architecture profoundly, going far beyond the superficialities of style that have been the major preoccupation with the design of synagogues, mosques and other denominations' places of worship and prayer.[1] This chapter focuses on one aspect of synagogue design, namely that of the *bimah* (the large desk set in its raised enclosure, upon which the Torah scrolls are unfurled and read) and its spatial relationship with the sanctuary as a whole. It examines the changing position of the *bimah*, and ponders the significance this has for the function and expression of the Jewish liturgy, as well as questioning what this implies about the identity of Jews, in nineteenth- and twentieth-century Britain. In broader terms, it represents a chapter in the story of architecture and ritual, presenting developments in synagogue layout in terms of anthropology as well as architectural history, in its strict and conventional sense.[2] In general anthropological terms, Clifford Geertz's concept of 'thick description' comes into play here, as does Victor Turner's work on ritual.[3] His namesake Harold Turner provides an anthropological and phenomenological bridge to Jewish sacred spaces, while contemporary scholarship has been greatly enhanced by the research and publications emanating from the *Bet Tfila* (Hebrew: 'House of Prayer') project hosted by the Research Institute for Jewish Architecture in Braunschweig and Jerusalem, and the Institute for the History of German Jews, Hamburg.[4]

The history of synagogue design since the Enlightenment offers a gloss on the oftentimes competing claims of tradition and modernity, and their respective expressions in architecture. The paradox to be explored in this chapter is the tendency towards architectural expression that mimics Christian forms within more reform-minded Jewish communities, as opposed to the continuation of traditional layouts that communicate a specific Jewish identity. Two historic moments are recalled: the late-nineteenth-century heyday of the synagogue reflecting the eclecticism and stately presence of contemporaneous church buildings and the mid-twentieth century, when Modernism in the guise of Brutalism produced two completely different synagogues at opposite ends of the tradition/modernity debate.

In this chapter I question the dominance of Western, Christian concepts that put the church building at the centre of architectural analysis. One only has to look at Banister Fletcher's *A History of Architecture*, or Nikolaus Pevsner's *The Buildings of England*, to see the pervasiveness of this way of thinking. Pevsner, in particular, maintained a strict hierarchy in describing towns and villages, beginning with the parish church (invariably Church of England), then proceeding to other Anglican establishments, before itemizing other denominations, and ending on non-Christian places of gathering. These buildings were prime, preceding other municipal ones such as libraries, hospitals, fire stations and schools, which were then followed by his wonderful perambulations. Such an approach has coloured our perceptions of towns, for better or worse: we start at the geographical centre, a place always represented by structures of political and/or religious power. I believe it has ingrained in us an assumption of what constitutes the religious building per se, and with this chapter I am challenging us to consider afresh architectural and spatial concepts of gathering, community and worship. This is, then, essentially a work of architectural hermeneutics, of interpretation and of finding meaning in buildings; as Lindsay Jones, put it in *The Hermeneutics of Sacred Architecture*:

> Where sacred architecture 'works' . . . devotees do not stand over, above, or outside the elements of the built context in which they worship. Rather, where architecture succeeds, ritual participants and built forms are engaged as partners in a hermeneutical conversation or as players in a hermeneutical game.[5]

The purpose of this chapter is to judge the architectural success of just such a quest for meaning.

Synagogue characteristics

The synagogue building essentially comprises a meeting hall – a place of congregation. This lies at the root of the Greek-origin word *sunagōgē*: a gathering, from *sunagein*, to bring together. It is not a sacred space as such; indeed, the early synagogue would have been regarded as sacrilegious had claims for any sanctity rivalling that of the Temple in Jerusalem been asserted. It is the claims to mooted sacredness, or indeed what actually constitutes the sacred, that makes this a relevant topic for discussion here. Harold Turner, the ethnographer who has contributed so much to the cultural understanding of religious space wrote that the synagogue

> represents a radically new development in the history of places of worship. As against a building for a sacrificing priesthood, it served a non-sacrificing laity; in place of a cult that was largely individual, apart from the great seasonal festivals,

it provided for worship that was entirely corporate; instead of being a *domus dei* with multicell plan and graded degrees of sanctity, it was a house for the assembly of the people of God, equivalent to a *domus ecclesiae,* and consisted essentially of a single cell or room.[6]

The distinction between the *domus dei* and *domus ecclesiae* is absolutely crucial if we are to understand the development of church architecture. And it is largely through the all-pervasive transference of Christian liturgical concepts onto the architectural manifestations of the other (monotheistic) religions' places of worship, prayer and gathering that has led to misunderstandings and muddles regarding synagogue architectonics.

* * *

The synagogue began life in Palestine, during the time of the second Temple, as well as in the Jewish diaspora around the eastern Mediterranean. The prime locus of Jewish communal life was then still focused on the Temple itself, the place of sacrifice and of pilgrimage, particularly during the New Year celebrations and the subsequent Day of Atonement, and the three 'foot' (so-called because one would walk to the Temple Mount in Jerusalem from the surrounding regions of Judea and Israel) festivals of Tabernacles, Passover and Pentecost. At this time, the synagogue existed solely as a focus for specific local communities, serving settlements that were too distant from the Jerusalem Temple and allowing individuals to meet on a daily and weekly basis. It served purely practical ends, as Turner explains:

> So long as the two centres for worship [the Jerusalem Temple and the synagogue] existed together the synagogue building could remain primarily a utilitarian structure without any sacred character or temple features; the very little rabbinic legislation in the Mishnah [the Jewish oral law] concerning the synagogue ignores such matters as site, position, orientation and architecture.[7]

One might therefore suppose that the position and status of the synagogue would undergo a radical change with the destruction of the (second) Temple at the start of the Christian era and that it would attach to itself the sacred aura that the Temple possessed. However, this was not to be the case, although a certain aura of holiness did accrue to the synagogue. It was only with the advent of Western Jewish emancipation in the eighteenth century that synagogues and a limited number of them, at that, would start to take on the single-focus, sacred aspect that the Temple had commanded two millennia earlier.

The first Christians, let us not forget, had met in cryptic spaces of private houses and subterranean urban hideaways. These were essentially meeting places of the faithful, and the church as building was originally a *domus ecclesiae.* However, as the church assumed a more official presence, the church building as *domus dei* began to be in the ascendancy, a position it only began to shed with the rise of Protestantism in the seventeenth century.

This tendency gathered pace with the subsequent waves of nonconformism in the following centuries. As regards the synagogue, throughout the medieval period until early modernity, it was always a bastion of orthodoxy, and could be nothing but a house of assembly, the Hebrew *Beit HaKnesset* being a literal translation of this. It was believed that the coming Messiah would re-establish the Temple in Jerusalem, and so the idea of imbuing the synagogue with an aura of the sacred – vying with the Temple Mount, in effect – could not be entertained.

And yet it would be going too far to assert that the synagogue is completely devoid of sacredness. The architectural historian Harman Thies's luminous essay 'Idea and Image of the Synagogue' suggests as a common ancestor of the synagogue, church and mosque the Temple in Jerusalem, culminating in Le Corbusier's honouring of it – in plan and isometric – in his classic 1923 tract *Vers une architecture*.[8]

Varieties of modern Judaism, and their respective synagogues

According to Carol Herselle Krinsky, '[t]he bimah is the principal influence on the synagogue's plan'.[9] But what is the synagogue for, if it is deficient in the sacred by not housing God? It is the place where individuals might come to pray, at one of the morning, afternoon or evening services, or the place where they would come to hear the Torah read. Over the course of the year, the entire Torah scroll comprising the Pentateuch (Five Books of Moses) and corresponding additional writings (Prophets, etc.) are read, or chanted, on three days (Monday, Thursday and Saturday) of the week.[10] If the Jews are the People of the Book, then the synagogue is where the book is kept, carefully conserving the parchment scrolls of the Torah (the Pentateuch), and more conventional prayer books (*siddurim*) and handy printed versions of the Scriptures (*chumashim*). Any 'public' Jewish service, in a synagogue or elsewhere, requires the presence of a *minyan* (the tradition calls for a minimum of ten adult males); the synagogue was never the equivalent of a church or chapel with its invitation to private devotion and prayer.[11] In addition, the most significant prayer is that which 'stands in' for the Temple sacrifices that could no longer take place; they did indeed require the sacred space of the Temple for their enactment.[12] The high points of the Sabbath service on Saturday (and of the other two days' Torah readings) are the removal of the Torah scrolls from the cupboard in which they are stored (the Ark, or *Aron HaKodesh*) and their parading around the synagogue and delivery to the Reading Desk (the *bimah*, or *almemor* as Sephardi Jews refer to it). Lars Lerup links the peripatetic nature of Jewish existence in the Diaspora to the 'mobility' of its liturgy in synagogues, such that 'existence in [the] Diaspora does not lend itself to form but to spirit and imagination. [L]uggage had at all times to be packed. All important objects had to be small and portable.'[13] Synagogue architecture – building layout, furnishings and fittings – still carries the memory of this unsettled history, even in contemporary Diaspora (and Israeli) places of relative safety.

In all synagogues, up until the modern period these two structures of *bimah* and Ark formed twin poles, or focal points, within the synagogue. The only real difference lay in the degree of polarity: in Sephardi synagogues, they tended to be further apart, with the *bimah* closer to the west (entrance) end, while in the Ashkenazi tradition they were closer, with the *bimah* positioned centrally within the sanctuary.[14]

Parading the Torah scrolls entails removing them from the Ark, then forming an orderly procession around the synagogue, 'presenting' the Scrolls to the entire congregation who will come forward and crowd round them, eager to establish physical contact with them. They finally get taken up to the *bimah*, where they are unwrapped, unrolled and finally read from. At the end of the readings, the parade is reversed, so that scrolls end up back in the Ark. The whole process entails a kind of ritual dance, a '*Reigen*' in the philosopher Susanne Langer's terms,

> [that] has nothing to do with spontaneous prancing; it fulfils a holy office, perhaps the *first* holy office of the dance – it divides the sphere of holiness from that of profane existence. In this way it creates the stage of the dance, which centres naturally in the altar or its equivalent – the totem, the priest, the fire – or perhaps the slain bear, or the dead chieftain to be consecrated.[15]

There are several points to note here: first, the holy is not quite cognate with the sacred; in Judaism, it denotes a distinction or separation, and operates at many levels in Jewish life, for instance the injunction to separate meat from milk, the Sabbath day from the other six days of the week, and so on. Secondly, since Judaism has no priests to intercede directly with the divine, nor sacrificial victims since the demise of the Temple, the Torah procession marks out a ring that is centred on the *bimah*, one whose centre of gravity needs to be within the community, and not relegated to the periphery of any liminal wall space. But this is not a static state of affairs; congregants distant from the procession will crowd towards it, a movement that is clearly aided by the central position of the *bimah*, but is not predicated by it.[16] Here Langer is clearly relating her focal spaces demarcated by ritual movement to her mentor Ernst Cassirer's symbolic forms.[17] A third point concerns movement per se. Clearly one has to move, generally to walk, from outside to within any building, so notions of architectural circulation come into play. In terms of the church, we are talking about the narthex, nave, aisles, pews and so on, architectural features deeply imbued with notions of circulation (or of stasis). Additionally, though, movement concerns actions that have liturgical significance: the prostrations in a mosque, the walking to the altar rail to receive Communion, and the parading of the Torah scrolls.

The general layout of the synagogue, regardless of its members' adherence to the Ashkenazi (German) or Sephardi (Spanish) rites, was similar: the Ark at the eastern end, against the rear wall, and the *bimah* in the centre, or towards the entrance front (or west) end. Most of the service, comprising the reading of the Torah and the leading of various prayers or Psalms, had a spatial focus on the *bimah*. This was where the lay readers stood, ordinary (historically, adult male) members of the congregation. The rabbi's task was largely to instruct; he (invariably a man until the advent of Reform gender equality in the twentieth century) was in no wise a priest (and hence a sacred figure) as was the case with Catholicism and Eastern Orthodoxy.[18] There existed then a perfect concordance of the liturgy of the synagogue – lay readers leading prayers and giving readings – and the architectural layout. The *bimah* was a raised rectangular platform, longitudinally aligned with the axis of the hall synagogue, and culminating in the Ark. The readers were of the people and among the people, and aligned with the people, seated behind the Ark in rows, or in the midst of those sitting on cross benches to either side. Proxemics come into play here: the *bimah* is a particularly crowded, even claustrophobic and bustling place during Torah readings. The layout in terms of plan is uncannily like that of the British House of Commons (although here the prime minister and her opposition counterpart fight it out at the bottom of a bearpit), while the raised box of the *bimah* reminds one of a boxing ring set at the centre of a packed and thronged gathering. Elevating the *bimah* means that the activities taking place there may be readily seen and heard, no matter how crowded and constricting the synagogue space is.[19]

The fact that the *bimah* is invariably a raised platform is both *halachic* (i.e. the rules regulating its form and location may be found – however fleetingly – in the Talmud), but also pragmatic. Unlike the floor of the British House of Commons, the synagogue aims to counter any sense of a dichotomy of performers and passive onlookers. Which is not to say that there is not clearly a heightened 'aura' associated with the *bimah*, Ark and indeed the synagogue *tout court*. As Seth Kunin, in his important phenomenological study of sacred spaces and places in Judaism, explained:

> The aspect of height, or raised areas, as a significant feature of positive sacred space is already indicated by the location of the synagogue, originally in the highest part of the city. Raised areas are also used to indicate the most sacred parts of the synagogue. The *bimah* is usually a raised platform. Thus the most important aspects of the service, especially the reading of the Torah, symbolic revelation, are always led from a symbolic mountain, that is, a positive liminal space. The positive, and significant, aspect of going up is emphasized by the term used to describe being called to participate in the Torah service: *aliyah*, that is, 'going up'. Like the *bimah*, the Ark is always built in a raised position, usually higher than the *bimah*.[20]

Nonetheless for Kunin the *bimah* is crucial – far more crucial than the Ark – in characterizing the Jewishness of synagogue space, through its apparently 'positive liminality' of occupying a raised, but central, position amidst the congregation.

To conclude this section, then, the synagogue, up until the nineteenth century, was most decidedly a *domus ecclesiae*, a point given acute historical emphasis if we observe Britain's oldest synagogue, Bevis Marks, in the City of London. Designed by the Quaker carpenter Joseph Avis and completed in 1761, Bevis Marks resembles nothing less than a (rather grand) nonconformist meeting house.[21] The general point here is that reformed Christianity was moving back to the earlier church form of the *domus ecclesiae* and meeting up with synagogue layout that had never 'lost faith' and departed from this tradition.

The nineteenth century: Upper Berkeley Street and South Hackney

From the mid-nineteenth century, British Judaism was becoming ever more accepted within the nation. Benjamin Disraeli, of Jewish descent, had risen to prominence and become prime minister in 1874. The long-established Sephardi communities (the principal groups that settled after Cromwell's readmission of the Jews in the 1650s) were augmented by smaller groups of Ashkenazim from Germany and Central Europe; all adhered to broadly orthodox and traditional interpretations of Jewish law and custom, with a concomitant approach to synagogue liturgy. Later, towards the end of the nineteenth century and at the start of the twentieth century, the texture of British Jewry would be significantly altered by the influx of great numbers of relatively poor, artisan Ashkenazi Jews, fleeing the pogroms of the Russian Empire. However, from the middle of the century assimilation was ongoing, as a result of both the growing acceptance of Jews within British society and, from a religious perspective, the influence of the 'Jewish Enlightenment' (the *Haskalah*) from continental Europe.[22] In terms of design, synagogues started to take on attributes of the dominant (state) religion: in England, those of the Church of England, in Germany, of the Lutheran Church.

Developments in Germany are particularly interesting for our story. Thies uses the examples of the synagogues at Halberstadt, Seesen, Wörlitz and Dresden to chart the progressive drift of the *bimah* from the centre of the sanctuary towards the Ark at the east end of the synagogue.[23] Two new, large synagogues that were built towards the end of Victoria's reign, and that bear witness to these developments as translated to late nineteenth-century London, will be examined.[24] They are from different parts of the spectrum of Anglo-Jewry, but nonetheless show converging attitudes in terms of layout, aesthetics and identity. The synagogue at Upper Berkeley Street, in London's West End, was (and remains) the 'Cathedral' of the British Reform movement, with a liturgy and architecture directly inspired by the *Haskalah*. It stood for an ecumenical coming together of the two main families of Judaism – the Ashkenazi and the Sephardi – and devised a liturgy that combined salient features from both traditions in a reforming spirit. It found a site in the West End, where many of the increasingly prosperous Sephardi Jewish families had relocated away from the insalubrious East End, and commissioned Davis and Emanuel to design what Pevsner called 'one of the finest of Victorian synagogues' (Figure 6.1).[25] An examination of this synagogue tells us a great deal about the relationship between liturgy and layout, even if it tells us little about architectural style, per se. Its general Moorishness in (what is visible of) its external form and interior decoration speaks of its 'otherness' – its Jewishness – and offers no index as to the 'brand' of Judaism practised there, as any contemporary Christian church undoubtedly would.[26] As Sharman Kadish explained:

> [w]hile Reform added nothing to the debate on style, it did alter the liturgical arrangement of the synagogue. The traditional dual focus on the ark, orientated towards Jerusalem, and the central *bimah* had become standard in *Ashkenazi Europe* . . . Nineteenth-century Reformers moved the *bimah* to the east,

creating a platform (stage) combining the ark, *bimah* and pulpit – an innovation based on church practice – all facing the congregation on the east wall. The seating was realigned to face the combined ark and *bimah* platform at the front of the hall, thus breaking with the tradition of men's seating generally surrounding the *bimah*. This reordering accentuated the eastern axis of the space.[27]

Completed in 1870, the synagogue was traditionally laid out with the central *bimah* on the longitudinal (east-west) axis, and a most unusual fretwork Ark through which the Torah scrolls could clearly be seen. The *bimah* was located towards the western (entrance) end, in common with Sephardi practice, and faced the Ark raised up on its dais across an expanse of marble-inlay flooring.[28] It had an uncanny resemblance to the Nożyk synagogue in Warsaw, as recounted by the architectural historian Joseph Rykwert, which 'was built in a homely Moorish manner considered by some nineteenth-century architects appropriate to synagogues, with a domed marble shrine fronting the curtained recess of the Torah scrolls. An elevated, nearly central *bimah* had a table for the cantillated Torah readings.'[29] The West London's fretwork Ark marked a break with tradition, since it revealed its contents even when the doors were shut. However, this feature did not attract any adverse criticism at the time. It sits within its Moorish aedicule, surmounted by its own little dome, and stands proud of the arcaded screen (with similar fretwork infill), which serves to close off the eastern apse housing the choir.

Figure 6.1 Upper Berkeley Street synagogue, as depicted in the *Illustrated London News* in 1872.
Source: © Illustrated London News Ltd/Mary Evans.

Figure 6.2 Upper Berkeley Street synagogue, present-day appearance. Note the new *bimah* installed in 1897, at the top of the steps leading to the Ark. The grandiose lectern is to the right and is never used today.
Photograph by Gerald Adler, 2019.

The apse contains a magnificent integrated pipe organ, the only one of its kind in any British synagogue. However, just twenty-four years after its completion the Synagogue Council undertook to move the *bimah* from its central location, adopting a scheme drawn up by 'Messrs Davis and Emanuel' in order to 'provid[e] for 107 additional seats' (Figure 6.2).[30] The works were carried out later that year, the old *bimah* duly demolished and a new forward-facing one built immediately in front of the Ark, nicely integrated with the sweeping staircase. What is fascinating, and ultimately revealing, about the lack of interest on the part of the Jewish community in architectural form, and its relationship with liturgy, are the reasons given for such a change: extra seating. As the anonymous correspondent ('S') to the *Jewish Chronicle* wrote:

> The reading-desk [*bimah*] has been turned around, so that the reader always faces the congregation. Now, except in the case of the Amidah [the 'standing prayer' at the heart of any Jewish service], there is no rule that a worshipper must face the East, but still I think that the change is a mistake, not so much ritually as aesthetically. What is the function of a Reader in a place of worship? Surely not to read prayers *to* his congregation, certainly not to read prayers *for* them, but to pray to God *with* them. It therefore seems to me that the ordinary position of the Reader in our synagogues [i.e. on a central *bimah*] is the more appropriate.

In Berkeley Street there is too much done for the worshipper. He is preached to as a matter of course, but he is also sung to. Everything should be done to induce him to sing with the choir, to join in heartily with the Reader, and all this can be done decorously. If this were effected, something of the hardness and coldness of the Reform service would be removed. In the 'Life of Dean Hook' we are told that when he became Vicar of Leeds he insisted upon reading the prayers with his face to the altar, so that the duty of the congregation to pray with the officiating minister should be more effectively taught.[31]

'S' was absolutely right, and his or her opinions might have been those of many Church of England, or Roman Catholic parishioners, at the time of the Liturgical Movement or Vatican II at mid-twentieth century.[32]

The next example is a new synagogue at South Hackney, London; the architect was Delissa Joseph. Although belonging to the Orthodox United Synagogue, it bore a striking resemblance to the West London at Upper Berkeley Street, and was inaugurated in 1897, the same year as the reordering of the West London. It was to have 'accommodation for 310 males [i.e. on the ground floor], the whole of the seats will be placed crossways; and the Ark, Pulpit and Reading Platform [the *bimah*] will be grouped together at the Eastern end of the building'.[33] In fact, the United Synagogue (a kind of Church of England for Anglo-Jewry: the British Chief Rabbi always comes from within its ranks) was not doctrinaire about synagogue layout and gave the impression, along with nascent Reform Judaism, that it tacitly approved of synagogues being laid out almost as if they were Protestant hall churches, with serried, and parallel, ranks of seating facing the east wall in front of which was a tight composition of raised Ark, *bimah* and pulpit.

The twentieth century: South Hampstead United and Belsize Square (Reform)

If the last two examples of synagogues are separated by the extent of the City of London, the pair of synagogues taken as exemplary at mid-twentieth century are near neighbours in Hampstead, North London. Both designs owe much in form and materials to the then-fashionable Brutalism, while expressing quite opposite attitudes to tradition and assimilation. Heinz Reifenberg's Belsize Square synagogue (1958), for an exiled German Reform community, has the *bimah* upfront, sharing its raised platform with the Ark, whereas South Hampstead, designed by Lyons Israel Ellis in 1962 for the Orthodox United Synagogue, maintains the tradition of the central *bimah*, embedded within the congregation.

Heinz Walter Reifenberg (1894–1968) had trained and practised as an architect in Berlin but left for Palestine in 1933 on the Nazis' taking power. By the time the Second World War had started, he was in London. His one major executed project, in partnership with the founder of Building Design Partnership (BDP), George Grenfell-Baines, was the Power and Production Pavilion at London's South Bank, for the Festival of Britain.[34]

The Belsize Square synagogue originally occupied the Vestry behind St Peter's church. It has an unusual shape, twice as wide as it is long: a two-square plan, deeply chamfered at the east end. This shallow, but broad, plan allowed for good acoustics, with the *bimah* and Ark sharing a raised platform at the east end, accessed from a pair of short staircases from the floor of the prayer hall. The effect was remarkably close to a utilitarian, postwar school assembly hall – an impression reinforced by the exposed concrete roof beams, fair-faced brick walls and vaguely industrial-looking steel windows with square opening frames counterposed by the central mullions of fixed lights above and below. The prominent beam structure delineates a square central section of the congregational seating flanked by three areas of similar polygons, comprising the raised *bimah*/Ark and the two side 'aisles', with seating cranked 45 degrees to face the Ark. In its original state it must have presented a rather uncomfortable mix of light-hearted Festival of Britain jollity, such as the jazzy glazing pattern and simple but bold Ark surround, with carved emblems of distinctly Jewish themes, for example a *Menorah* (a seven-branched candelabra), Star of David and ram's horn contrasted with its overtly utilitarian palette of materials (Figures 6.3 and 6.4).[35] Shortly afterwards much of the exposed brickwork was wood-panelled in an attempt to lend the synagogue greater warmth and intimacy. In 1992, the synagogue underwent its most recent renovation (by the architect, and congregant, Michael Brod). The 'stage' accommodating the *bimah* and Ark was lowered, the flanking walls plastered, with a suspended ceiling canopy added. The theatricality of the sanctuary was heightened, and the 'proscenium' converted into something approximating to a thrust stage. The new *bimah* was an interesting design that allowed for the reader to be in either of two positions – the traditional one facing the Ark, that is, in the same orientation as the congregation, or the new, 'Reform' position facing the congregation.[36] This ambivalence regarding the position and form of the *bimah* can be observed in many contemporary American synagogues (invariably styled 'Temples'),

Figure 6.3 Heinz Reifenberg, Belsize Square synagogue, London (1958). Interior view looking towards the Ark and the north window. Photograph courtesy of Belsize Square Synagogue.

Figure 6.4 Belsize Square synagogue, View of choir gallery. Photograph courtesy of Belsize Square Synagogue.

particularly those affiliated to the Conservative movement (a midway position between traditional Orthodox and Reform).

The new building for the United Synagogue at South Hampstead (1959–62) – a short walk from Belsize Square – is instructive for our discussion. Designed and built at exactly the same time as Belsize Square, it embodies the continuing tradition of an orthodox synagogue layout with its central *bimah*. The architect was Edward Lyons of the architectural practice Lyons Israel Ellis.[37] The practice (David Gray became a full partner in 1970) was one of the foremost forcing grounds of New Brutalism in Britain at mid-century, nurturing among others the young Jameses Gowan and Stirling.

The synagogue building does not figure prominently in Lyons Israel Ellis's œuvre. The one monograph on their work has one plan and three section drawings, with no description (and calls it a Liberal synagogue), while Pevsner misattributes the building completely.[38] Why should this be? Externally the building is undemonstrative, its scale a close fit with the early Victorian villas characterizing this North London suburb. The bulk of the building makes clever use of the sloping site, with the volume of the prayer hall disguised by the monopitch roof that rises up to the southern, entrance front. It is all receding planes of buff brickwork, offset by a great south-facing clerestory of vertical, white, concrete louvres and boldly expressed staircases 'framing' the main volume. The interior is a surprise, with an intimacy and warmth largely a result of the centrally placed *bimah*. The seating is almost all arranged in parallel banks along the length of the prayer hall – as though we were in the House of Commons debating chamber – apart, that is, from the 'Ladies' gallery above, taking up the west side with a larger portion facing the Ark, below the clerestory. The longitudinal axis, while symmetrical with the raked gallery seating opposite the Ark, is thrown off-centre by an imbalance in the numbers of rows of (men's) seating either side of the *bimah*, with five rows to the north and three to the south (Figure 6.5). The external massing, materials and the unexpected asymmetry of the interior make this project a fine and distinguished example of Lyons Israel Ellis's œuvre. The extant drawings of the scheme have a rare beauty and have a punctilious clarity with regard to indicating the layers of materials, and the geometric relationships

Figure 6.5 Lyons Israel Ellis, South Hampstead synagogue. View of the *bimah* from the Ladies' Gallery.
Photograph by Jono David.

governing layout. Lyons, the most 'Romantic' of the partners and chief designer of the synagogue, looked to Dutch and Scandinavian architects such as Willem Marinus Dudok and Erik Gunnar Asplund for inspiration, whereas his partner Tom Ellis brought more of an Alvar Aalto sensibility to the mix. All are evident at South Hampstead.[39]

Conclusion

'It's not the *binyan* [building] that's important, it's the *minyan* [community].'[40] These words of the unnamed Brighton rabbi cited by the British architectural historian Sharman Kadish characterize the difficulty an architectural historian has in dealing with the synagogue. The relative indifference to architectural form, born perhaps of an innate suspicion of aesthetic form for its own sake, or, more prosaically, gratitude for there being synagogues at all, means that the nicer points of architectural design, and the relationship of form and space to use and practice, have been largely absent from synagogue design. There has been precious little of the 'discourse' surrounding it that there has been in (Western) Christianity, and nothing to compare with the upsurge in thinking and doing that accompanied the Liturgical Reform Movement in the twentieth century.[41] Where is Judaism's Rudolf Schwarz, or indeed its Peter Hammond?[42] Given these lacunae, it is perhaps no surprise that progressive Judaism tends towards what is, in essence, a Christian layout, with the *bimah* associated with the east end and the Ark.[43] For some critics the synagogue's 'indifference' to architectural form is a boon to modern architects when it comes to designing, since if 'building form in Jewish culture is free, open to speculation, [then its] built fabric is symbolically soft, [and] the sacred objects are hard and unchangeable. Thus, buildings can take any form [of] pragmatism of a people on the move.'[44] Most architects, though, relish the opportunity of finding some ritual or cultural trait to relate to, some precedent of form and decor as a means of 'informing' their designs.

This chapter represents, I hope, a modest contribution to architectural and to Jewish studies. I share Barbara Mann's wish to bring the 'spatial turn' in the humanities and social sciences into a Jewish area, one that has seemed to be impervious to the allure of space.[45] My second, more focused and practical ambition is to allow the synagogue (among other Jewish sites) to play its proper role within architectural culture. Towards the end of the twentieth century, Kadish felt moved to complain about the invisibility of the Jewish contribution to architecture; my intention, with this chapter exploring the 'changing polarities' of the synagogue, is to begin to challenge this attitude, inviting architects to question, and Jewish communities to be more alive to form and space.[46]

Acknowledgements

I am particularly grateful to Alfred Jacoby, Seth Kunin and Rabbi Jonathan Romain for their helpful comments and advice, and to Rabbi David Mitchell and Micky Nathanson from the West London Synagogue for facilitating my research. Many thanks to Rabbi Shlomo Levin for warmly welcoming me to the South Hampstead Synagogue, and to Michael Brod for his insights into the Belsize Square synagogue. I am grateful to Maximilian Sternberg and to Ross Anderson for inviting me to participate in the 'Sacred' symposium at Pembroke College, Cambridge in 2017, and for the stimulating debates and discussions that ensued.

Notes

1. See Robert Proctor, *Building the Modern Church: Roman Catholic Church Architecture in Britain, 1955 to 1975* (Farnham: Ashgate, 2014), 15–29; and Gerald Adler, *Robert Maguire & Keith Murray* (London: RIBA Publishing, 2012), 68–105.
2. See Peter Blundell Jones, *Architecture and Ritual: How Buildings Shape Society* (London and New York: Bloomsbury, 2016).
3. Clifford Geertz, *The Interpretation of Cultures* [1973] (London: Fontana, 1993) and Victor Turner, *The Ritual Process: Structure and Anti-structure* (Chicago: Aldine, 1969).
4. See http://bet-tfila.org/indexen.html (accessed 23 January 2018).
5. Lindsay Jones, *The Hermeneutics of Sacred Architecture: Experience, Interpretation, Comparison, Volume One/Monumental Occasions: Reflections on the Eventfulness of Religious Architecture* (Harvard: Harvard University Press, 2000), 47.
6. Harold Turner, *From Temple to Meeting House: The Phenomenology and Theology of Places of Worship* (The Hague: Mouton Publishers, 1979), 100.
7. Ibid., 99.
8. Harman H. Thies, 'Idee und Bild der Synagoge', in *Synagogenarchitektur in Deutschland: Dokumentation zur Ausstellung*, ed. Aliza Cohen-Mushlin and Harmen H. Thies (Petersberg; Michael Imhof Verlag, 2008). Schriftenreihe der Bet Tfila-Forschungsstelle für jüdische Architektur in Europa, edited by Aliza Cohen-Mushlin und Harmen Thies, vol. 5, 21–40, here pages 22–5, citing Le Corbusier, *Vers une architecture* (Paris: G. Crès & Cie, 1923), 53–5.
9. Carol Herselle Krinsky, *Synagogues of Europe: Architecture, History, Meaning* (Mineola: Dover, 1996), 21. In Chapter Two: 'Ritual Arrangements' Krinsky gives a succinct overview of the *bimah* in the context of synagogue architecture.
10. See Katrin Kessler, *Ritus und Raum der Synagoge: liturgische und religionsgesetzliche Voraussetzungen für den Synagogenbau in Mitteleuropa* (Petersberg: Michael Imhof Verlag, 2007). Schriften der Bet Tfila-Forschungsstelle für jüdische Architektur in Europa, edited by Aliza Cohen-Mushlin und Harmen Thies, vol. 2, for an exhaustive account of the relationship between rite and space in the Central European synagogue.
11. See Jonathan A. Romain, *Faith and Practice: A Guide to Reform Judaism Today* (London: RSGB, 1991), 102–4 for an explanation of the traditional view governing minimum presence at a public service, in addition to present-day Reform practice.
12. This prayer, the *Amidah* ('standing', because one stands to recite it), is also called the *Shemoneh Esreh* ('Eighteen' [Benedictions]). It is expanded on the Sabbath and on holidays to include specific reference to the sacrificial offerings in the Temple. This lends further credence to the synagogue being 'a miniature of the lost sanctuary [of the Temple].' Alan

Mintz, 'Prayer and the Prayerbook', in *Back to the Sources: Reading the Classic Jewish Texts*, ed. Barry W. Holtz (New York: Summit, 1984), 406.

13. Lars Lerup, 'Architektur nach ihrer Zerstörung' ('Architecture after its Demise'), in *In einem Neuen Geiste/ In a New Spirit: Synagogen von/ The Synagogues of Alfred Jacoby* (Deutsches Architektur Museum: Frankfurt am Main, 2002), exhibition catalogue, 11 (trans. by Alfred Jacoby).

14. Krinsky gives a clear account of these typologies in *Synagogues of Europe*. See Chapter 3, 'Central Bimah and Twin-Nave Plan' (44–56) and Chapter Four, 'The Sephardi Two-Pole Pattern' (57–75).

15. Susanne Langer, *Feeling and Form* (London: Routledge & Kegan Paul, 1953), 191. Here Langer develops Ernst Cassirer's 'symbolic forms' into the realm of dance (she borrows from Curt Sachs, translated by Bessie Schonberg, *World History of the Dance* (London: Allen & Unwin, 1937).

16. See Tobias Lamey, 'Bimot in Polish Stone Synagogues until 1650: Forms, Functions, and Religious Aspects', in *Jewish Architecture in Europe*, ed. Aliza Cohen-Mushlin and Harmen H. Thies (Petersberg; Michael Imhof Verlag, 2010). Publications of Bet Tfila – Research Unit for Jewish Architecture in Europe edited by Aliza Cohen-Mushlin, Alexander von Kienlin and Harmen H. Thies, vol. 6, 109–16, here page 113. Lamey states that 'a *bimah* [. . .] erected at a wall and connected to it, is not permitted'.

17. Ernst Cassirer, *Die Philosophie der symbolischen Formen*, 3 vols (Berlin: B. Cassirer, 1923-29).

18. There was a general sense of equality among male members of the community in the orthodox synagogue. Women, on the other hand, if they attended, were consigned to a section of seating behind a curtain or screen or were banished upstairs to a gallery.

19. For an exhaustive description and discussion of the synagogue, in particular its interior layout, decoration and furnishing in respect of the liturgy, see Kessler, *Ritus und Raum der Synagoge*.

20. Seth Daniel Kunin, *God's Place in the World: Sacred Space and Sacred Place in Judaism* (London and New York: Cassell, 1998), 52.

21. Sharman Kadish, *Jewish Heritage in Britain and Ireland: An Architectural Guide* (Swindon: Historic England, 2015), 4–8; and Simon Bradley and Nikolaus Pevsner, *London 1: The City of London* (The Buildings of England) (New Haven and London: Yale University Press, 2002 [1997]), 272–3. The layout of Bevis Marks is an extreme instance of synagogue spatial polarity, with its *bimah* at the opposite end from the Ark, thus emphasizing the duality of focus. See also Rachel Wischnitzer-Bernstein, *The Architecture of the European Synagogue* (Philadelphia: Jewish Publication Society of America, 1964), 102–4 for a description of this casebook Sephardi twin-pole-cum-galleried-hall type.

22. Paul Johnson, *The History of the Jews* (London: Phoenix, 2001 [1987]), 298–300, and 335–6.

23. See Harmen H. Thies, 'Jewish Architecture in Europe: An Introduction', in Cohen-Mushlin and Thies (eds), *Jewish Architecture in Europe*, 31–40, here pages 31–3. Thies is unequivocal when he states that Gottfried Semper's placing of the *bimah* upon a platform immediately in front of the Ark 'resembles the arrangement in Protestant churches'. (p. 33). For the synagogue at Seesen, see Cohen-Mushlin and Thies, eds, *Synagogenarchitektur in Deutschland*, 155–8.

24. 'The large synagogue building itself was regarded as a tool of Anglicization.' Judy Hillman, 'Assimilation by Design: London Synagogues in the Nineteenth Century', in *The Jewish Heritage in British History: Englishness and Jewishness*, ed. Tony Kushner (London: Cass, 1992), 171–209, here page 173. 'The pulpit, which had come to dominate the synagogue

Reading, Storing and Parading the Book

interior and superseded even the Ark as the main focal point, was considered a tool of anglicisation.' Ibid., 196.

25. Bridget Cherry and Nikolaus Pevsner, *London 3: North West* (The Buildings of England) (New Haven and London: Yale University Press, 2002 [1991]), 606. See also Sharman Kadish, 'The Anglo-Jewish "Reformation"', in *Reform Judaism and Architecture*, ed. Andreas Brämer, Mirko Przystawik and Harmen H. Thies (Petersberg: Imhof, 2016), 79–96, especially pages 83–5. Henry David Davis (1839-1915) and Barrow Emanuel (1842-1904).

26. See, for instance, James Stevens Curl, *Victorian Churches* (London: Batsford, 1995).

27. Kadish, 'The Anglo-Jewish "Reformation"', 87.

28. See *The Building News*, 7 April 1871, 258, for an account of the design and a double-page perspective (n.p.) of the Sanctuary, together with a ground plan of the synagogue.

29. Joseph Rykwert, *Remembering Places: A Memoir* (Abingdon and New York: Routledge, 2017), 7.

30. West London Synagogue, Council Minutes, 28 March 1897. Resolution No. 1.

31. *Jewish Chronicle*, 3 December 1897 (Letter to the Editor), 8. Hook (1798–1875) was famous from his days as Vicar of Leeds when he campaigned for rented pews, the source of great social inequality in churches, to be abolished. See W. R. W. Stephens, *The Life and Letters of Walter Farquhar Hook*, 2 vols (London: Richard Bentley, 1878).

32. See Barbara Borts, 'Mouths Filled with Song: British Reform Judaism through the Lens of Its Music' (PhD Diss, Durham University, 2014). Available online at http://etheses.dur.ac.uk/10797/, Borts gives a good portrait of the West London Synagogue – its history and contemporary style of service – especially chapter four, 115–75. The parallels between received understandings of tradition in music and in architecture are clear. See also Krinsky, *Synagogues of Europe*, 299–302, for a succinct account of the West London Synagogue's debt to German Reform and its subsequent reordering.

33. *Jewish Chronicle*, 19 February 1897, 11. The pulpit would only be used for the Rabbi to give a sermon. The grand pulpit at the West London, accessed from the raised platform comprising *bimah* and Ark and directly in front of the choir screen, has not been used for many years, the *bimah* functioning as the sole place of readings.

34. See *Architects' Journal*, 12 June 2003, 'Unmasking "mysterious" architect H J Reifenberg' (Letters to the Editor), from Ursula Mercer and Charlotte Benton, *A Different World: émigré architects in Britain 1928-1958* (London: RIBA Heinz Gallery, 1995), with contributions by David Elliott and Elain Harwood, 198–9.

35. The angularity and generally utilitarian appearance of the Belsize Square synagogue puts one in mind of any number of Weimar German (and, indeed, post-war West German) public buildings. It is the Parisian Belleville synagogue, though (Germain Debré, 1931) with which it bears a striking resemblance when one considers the cranked aisles, that raised *bimah* immediately in front of the Ark, and wide expanses of geometrical glazing. (Dominique Jarrassé, *Guide du patrimoine juif parisien* (Paris: Parigramme, 2003), 100–4.)

36. Tamar Wang, ed., *The Synagogue at Sixty* (London: Belsize Square Synagogue, 1999).

37. South Hampstead Synagogue, 21–22 Eton Villas, London NW3 4SG. Heritage Assessment L B Camden application ref: 2013/7887/P j887 EBA Heritage Assmt v2a, Ettwein Bridges and others, 31 February 2014. See Bridget Cherry and Nikolaus Pevsner, *London 3: North West* (The Buildings of England) (New Haven and London: Yale University Press, 2002 [1991]), 209. Here the building is attributed to one H. J. Georghiou.

38. Neave Brown, Alan Colquhoun, James Gowan, Peter Smithson and others, *Lyons Israel Ellis Gray: Buildings and Projects 1932-1983* (London: Architectural Association, 1988), 30. Moreover, the synagogue is mistakenly attributed to the Liberal Jewish community.

39. Alvin Boyarsky with Neave Brown, Alan Colquhoun, Christopher Dean, Alan Forsyth, David Gray John Miller, Frank Newby and Ron Simpson, 'Conversation', in Neave Brown et al., *Lyons Israel Ellis Gray: Buildings and Projects 1932-1983* (London: Architectural Association, 1988), 106–9. Sad to report, but the South Hampstead Synagogue has now been demolished to make way for a new building as part of a mixed-use development. The prayer hall takes the form of concentric arcs of seating, focused on a *bimah* and Ark in close proximity at the east end. See http://www.southhampstead.org/new-building-project/#!/plans (accessed 11 December 2017).

40. Middle Street Rabbi, cited in Sharman Kadish, *The Synagogues of Britain and Ireland* (New Haven and London: Yale University Press, 2011), 296. Middle Street (Thomas Lainsman; 1874/75) is one of the great Victorian synagogues, located in Brighton, East Sussex. Nikolaus Pevsner and Ian Nairn did not include it in their *Buildings of England* volume on Sussex (1965).

41. See my book on the British Liturgical reform architects, *Robert Maguire & Keith Murray*. In this I present an overview of architectural (Christian) liturgical thinking, particularly from a mid-twentieth-century perspective.

42. See Rudolf Schwarz, *The Church Incarnate: The Sacred Function of Christian Architecture* (Chicago: Henry Regnery Company, 1958), and Peter Hammond, ed., *Towards a Church Architecture* (London: The Architectural Press, 1962); and *Liturgy and Architecture* (London: Barry and Rockcliff, 1960).

43. See Carol Herselle Krinsky, 'Is there a Jewish Architecture?' in Cohen-Mushlin and Thies (eds), *Jewish Architecture in Europe*, 353–64.

44. Lerup, 'Architektur nach ihrer Zerstörung' ('Architecture after its Demise'), 11–12.

45. Barbara E. Mann, *Space and Place in Jewish Studies* (New Brunswick and London: Rutgers University Press, 2012), 5.

46. Sharman Kadish, 'Squandered Heritage: Jewish Buildings in Britain', in Kushner (ed.), *The Jewish Heritage in British History*, 147–65. See also Sharman Kadish, 'Constructing Identity: Anglo-Jewry and Synagogue Architecture', *Architectural History, Journal of the Society of Architectural Historians of Great Britain* 45 (2002): 386–408.

CHAPTER 7
COMPACTING CIVIC AND SACRED
GOODHUE'S UNIVERSITY OF CHICAGO CHAPEL AND THE MODERN METROPOLIS
Stephen Gage

Writing in the *University of Chicago Magazine* in 1931, Hugh S. Morrison asserted that 'Modern criticism has been too insistently demanding that all our architecture should "express the Machine Age", without being quite sure in the first place that we are in it, and if we are, what it is . . . Fine architecture is too varied and elusive a thing to be judged by any such narrow formulae.'[1] In the 1920s and 1930s, the American metropolis was often seen as a signal of modernity, its automobiles and skyscrapers invoking a romanticized paean to the promise of technology. At the same time, both the architectural profession and the larger public continued to embrace historicist architecture, and despite its increasing prominence, many were sceptical of the avant-garde Modernism coming out of Europe. In this climate of contradictions and rapid change, architectural style was only one aspect of an emerging discourse on the role of architecture in modern society. From progressive politics to mass consumerism, architecture was enlisted as an important shaping force in the emergence of a new *urban* culture springing from the conditions of the American city.

What role did once-prominent sacred spaces play within the exciting glamour of the new metropolis, especially as churches receded before newly monumental commercial and civic buildings? Architects, community leaders and many other groups took this question seriously, and in the process gave new life to traditional styles associated with Christianity, especially the Gothic. Already passé in Europe, the Gothic revival in America remained popular into the 1940s, and was imbued with new meanings in the process.[2] For architects like Ralph Adams Cram, it formed the key to an antimodernist rhetoric calling for an all-encompassing revival of medieval spirituality.[3] For others, the soaring verticality of the Gothic cathedral was perfectly matched to both the form and cultural ambitions of the modern skyscraper, most famously in Raymond Hood's winning design for the Chicago Tribune Tower competition in 1924 (Figure 7.1).[4]

Imbued with sacred overtones and expressive of both tradition and aspiration, Gothic models were especially attractive to educational leaders. Unlike the piecemeal Victorian Gothic buildings of earlier decades, the Collegiate Gothic university architecture that emerged in the 1890s took inspiration from the academic traditions of medieval Oxford and Cambridge, most notably their quadrangle organization.[5] Founded in 1892 with a quadrangular master plan by Henry Ives Cobb, the University of Chicago was among the first examples of the Collegiate Gothic realized on a large scale. Receiving substantial

Figure 7.1 Chicago Tribune Tower.
Photograph by Stephen Gage.

support from oil tycoon John D Rockefeller and Chicago's business community, the new campus grew rapidly, and its national standing skyrocketed thanks to ground-breaking research and innovative educational reforms by its president, William Rainey Harper. The university thus became one of Chicago's leading cultural institutions, and Cobb's original plan was quickly superseded by an ever-expanding group of monumental Gothic structures.[6]

The most prominent of these was the University Chapel, designed by Bertram Grosvenor Goodhue and completed in 1928 (Figure 7.2). Goodhue was Cram's chief partner, but after they parted ways in 1913, he gained national recognition for his bold, eclectic designs, including the Nebraska State Capitol and the Los Angeles Central Library.[7] His work was particularly associated with the 'Modern Gothic', abstracting and repurposing traditional Gothic motifs for the twentieth century, and the Chicago Chapel was among his last works before his unexpected death in 1924. Its design encapsulates the synthesis of tradition and modernity that made Goodhue, as the university's chief architect Charles Coolidge argued, 'the greatest master of Gothic in America or England in this generation'.[8]

More broadly, Goodhue's chapel raises questions about the nature of sacred space in the modern city and was tied to the university's own quest to directly shape Chicago's larger cultural ambitions. This resulted in tensions over the extent to which the chapel was seen as a place of religious worship, a symbol of the university as an institution and a public monument representing all Chicago. The chapel's employment of traditional

Figure 7.2 The University (Rockefeller) Chapel, completed in 1928. Photographic Archive, University of Chicago Special Collections Resource Center.

Gothic forms was complicated by these larger intentions, especially in how it co-opted religious iconography for civic-secular purposes. This chapter will trace the history of the chapel's design, analysing how this civic/sacred synthesis was manifested in the selection and development of a site plan, in debates over the use of Gothic precedent and promotion of the chapel's urban role. If Goodhue saw the Modern Gothic as a new and distinctly American architecture, his work complimented the agenda of a university eager to assert civic leadership through its ability to look backwards and forwards simultaneously. Drawing heavily from established tradition, the Chicago Chapel stands in contrast to the modernist quest to erase the past; nevertheless, it reveals an acute exploration of modernity through a search to reinterpret and find a meaningful place for sacred space within the modern city.

Developing a site plan

Located seven miles south of Chicago's central business district, the University of Chicago was located in Hyde Park, a rapidly growing former suburban community annexed into the city limits in 1889. The site of the university was further distinguished by directly fronting the Midway Plaisance, a wide parkway connecting Washington and Jackson Parks.[9] All three were designed by Frederick Law Olmsted, part of an extensive park and boulevard system that ringed the city.[10] The university's location was thus characterized by

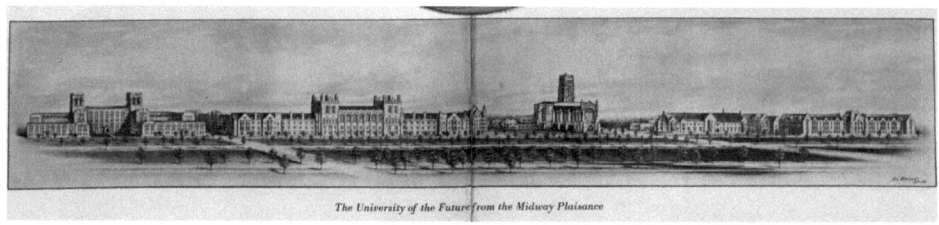

Figure 7.3 The University's Academic Avenue along the Midway. Rendering by A. L Bradley, 1925. Archival Buildings File, University of Chicago Special Collections Resource Center.

a striking combination of the urban and the rural, its rapidly urbanizing neighbourhood contrasted by the pastoral naturalism of Olmsted's parks and boulevards. As the campus expanded, it gradually abandoned Cobb's enclosed quadrangles and reoriented to the Midway, creating what its leaders termed an 'academic avenue', a linear procession of grey-stone Gothic buildings fronting the Midway's public green (Figure 7.3). While a new master plan reflecting the increased scope of the campus never materialized, university leaders nevertheless emphasized ordered growth and the symbolic weight of key buildings.

Central to these concerns was the chapel's location. Originally founded as the Baptist denomination's national university, a chapel was intended to form one of the campus' most prominent buildings from the earliest plans.[11] In Cobb's master plan, it was placed on axis with a library/administration building in the ceremonial central quadrangle. Located adjacent to the main entrance gate, the chapel would have been the first structure seen by visitors entering the campus.[12] In the 1890s, available funds were channelled to urgently needed teaching and laboratory spaces, but plans for the more monumental buildings still occupied the administrators and trustees. At the request of President Harper, Cobb completed several studies of the proposed chapel between 1896 and 1899.[13] Though unbuilt, the proposed chapel was frequently referred to in guidebooks as the 'most beautiful' design of all the campus' buildings.[14]

In 1900, Cobb was replaced by the Boston architects Shepley, Rutan and Coolidge, and a period of rapid expansion ensued as Rockefeller helped the university purchase all land on the north and south sides of the Midway.[15] As a result, the main library was reconceived to face the Midway, designed and built by Coolidge between 1906 and 1912 as a memorial to the late president Harper.[16] This left the chapel as the most conspicuous building from the original plan not yet realized, and when Rockefeller made his final $10 million gift to the university in 1910, he stipulated that $1.5 million be set aside for it. Further, he mandated that it 'ought to be the central and dominant feature of the University group' and should 'embody those architectural ideals from which the other buildings, now so beautifully harmonious, have taken their spirit, so that all the other buildings on the campus will seem to have caught their inspiration from the Chapel'.[17] With these stipulations, the chapel was destined to become the most prominent icon on the rapidly growing campus.[18]

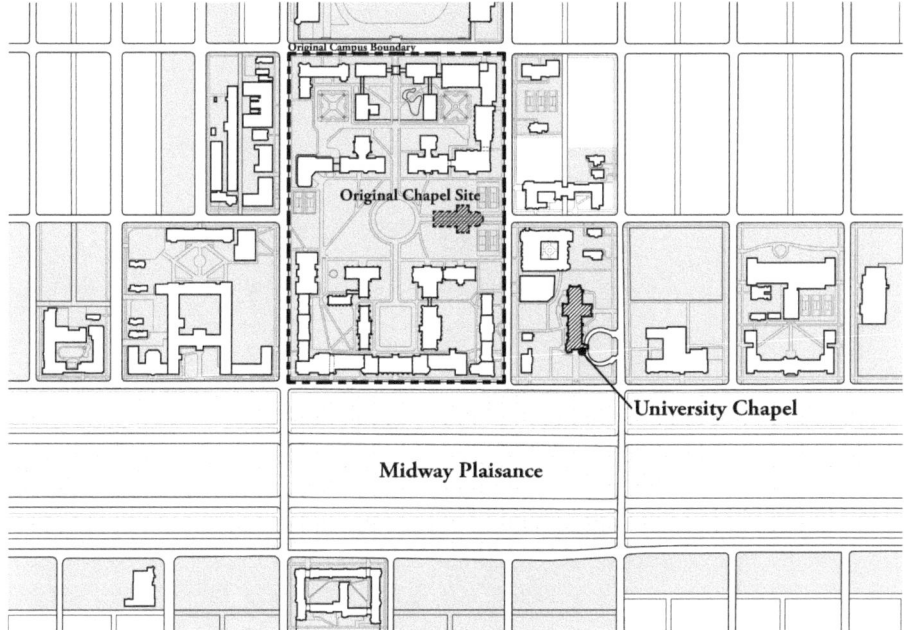

Figure 7.4 The University of Chicago Campus in the 1930s.
Drawing by Stephen Gage, based on Annual Register 1892–3 (Chicago: University of Chicago Press, 1893) and 'Plot Plan – The University of Chicago, Department of Buildings and Grounds'. 4 February 1930, map, from Architectural Drawing Collection, University of Chicago Special Collections Resource Center.

University officials took Rockefeller's conditions seriously and soon decided that, like the library, a Midway site was needed (Figure 7.4). As President Harry Pratt Judson described to Rockefeller's son in 1913:

> This location would be approximately central, and [the chapel] . . . would be more conspicuous . . . The Midway is the main line of travel for people in the city between the Parks, and ultimately will be the central artery for the University, its buildings being erected on both sides. The Chapel will obviously be the most impressive and beautiful building on the entire front.[19]

Judson not only references the university's future expansion plans but also calls attention to the Midway's public character and connection to the adjacent parks. Earlier statements had stressed the chapel as a primary gathering and assembly space for the student body, but now the chapel was increasingly positioned as a public monument.[20]

In 1916, the board of trustees officially confirmed the chapel would '[face] the Midway Plaisance, and that the entire block be devoted to the Chapel and buildings appertaining to it'.[21] Various problems delayed the project until 1918, when Goodhue was hired as architect.[22] The auxiliary uses for the chapel block were outlined in the summer of 1919,

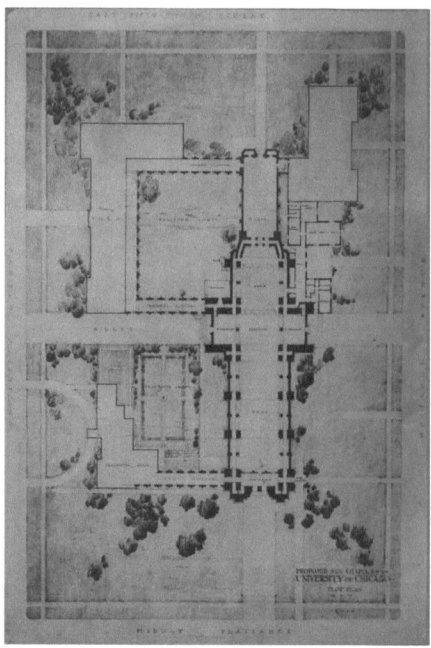

Figure 7.5 'Proposed New Chapel for the University of Chicago, Plot Plan'.
Drawing by B. G. Goodhue & Associates, 1919. Architectural Drawings Collection, University of Chicago Special Collections Resource Center.

including separate buildings for a YMCA and YWCA, a new president's house and an open-air court to be used for the university's convocation ceremonies.[23] Goodhue submitted his first site plan incorporating these features in August 1919 (Figure 7.5).

Goodhue's plan represents a decisive departure from the formal enclosed quadrangle Cobb envisioned as the setting for the chapel; instead, the block is left open at the perimeter, with interconnected gardens and cloisters surrounding the chapel and subsidiary buildings. This creates a dynamic interplay of scales: the chapel as monumental object when seen from a distance, but with a ground plan tightly integrated into the surrounding fabric. Most formal is the entry portal, set back 100 feet by an open lawn and a broad walkway leading from the Midway to the main entrance. Whereas most campus buildings went directly to the property line, here is a transitional space belonging to both Midway and campus, enabling a spacious public approach and more dramatic views of the building. The strong reciprocity between chapel and public green is further supported by relocating the more private president's house towards University Avenue, leaving the entire Midway frontage dedicated to this expansive 'forecourt'.[24]

The in-between nature of the Midway front suggests a spatial ambiguity replicated in other elements of Goodhue's plan. The convocation court, for example, adopts the form of a cloister garth. Flanking the chapel and the YMCA, a continuous open-air corridor surrounds it on three sides, mimicking the scale and rhythm of traditional monastic cloisters.[25] However, Goodhue inverts the cloister's usual role as a space of quiet contemplation and adapts it for large public gatherings, with a raised platform and speaking pulpit forming one corner. In a further break from precedent, open portals fronting public pathways establish multiple entry points, allowing direct connection to the surrounding gardens and streets. The roofs of the cloister also provide additional seating for large ceremonies.[26] Thus, unlike earlier campus buildings that emphasize interiority and closure, Goodhue freely adapts traditional religious typologies to create a setting characterized by spatial fluidity and urban integration.

The final version of the site plan, completed in 1924 just before Goodhue's death, shows further refinement, including greater integration between the more defined central area and the perimeter green spaces (Figure 7.6). The President's Garden is separated from the chapel to allow a public path directly connecting Midway and convocation court, now taking on a more open-ended arrangement. From there, a double-sided arcade leads to a new courtyard space to the north. Opening directly onto 58th Street, its transitional character is comparable to the Midway frontage, but treated more intimately in accordance with the residential character of its surroundings. Borrowing again from the cloister garth typology, this court is articulated through a four-square path, suggesting parallels to sacred tradition despite an open and irregular form. In the Middle Ages, this pattern was often associated with abstract representations of paradise, but here it assumes the more prosaic purpose of circulation route, directly connecting the YMCA, YWCA and convocation court with the street.[27]

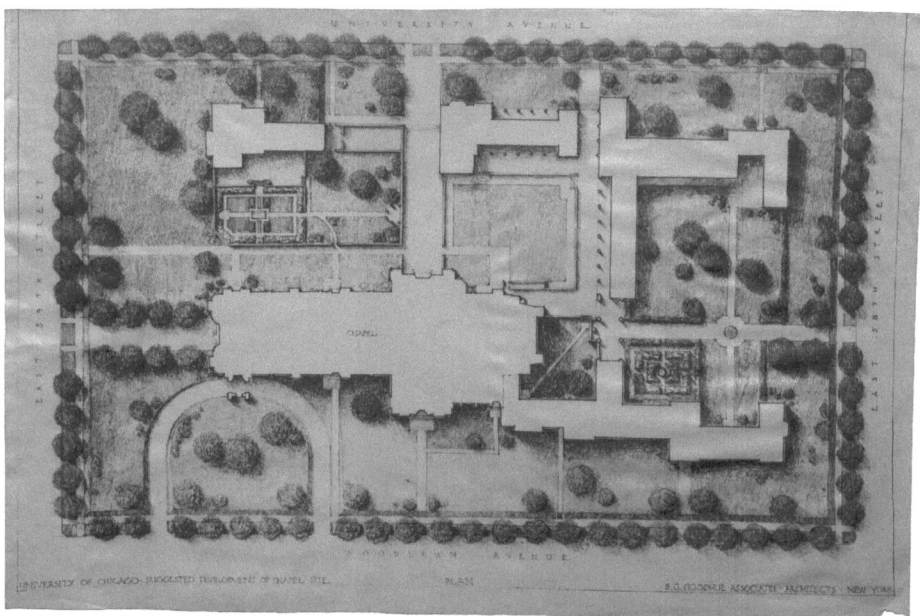

Figure 7.6 'Suggested Development of Chapel Site'.
Drawing by B. G. Goodhue & Associates, 1924. Architectural Drawings Collection, University of Chicago Special Collections Resource Center.

Goodhue's free adaptation of well-known Gothic typologies (the cloister in particular) occupies a place between the enclosed Oxbridge quadrangle and the openness of the typical American college. Apart from the creative adaptation of precedent, this degree of openness and informality also suggests intriguing parallels with more well-known examples of 1920s spatial planning, including the work of Le Corbusier, Mies van der Rohe and Frank Lloyd Wright. At the same time, the plan is a careful response to the site itself; taking equal inspiration from the intimacy of the courtyard and the civic scale of the linearly oriented Midway, it strikes a balance between spiritual calm and public celebration, between the serenity of the garden and the spectacle of the crowd.

Adapting Gothic precedent

In the design of the chapel itself, Gothic precedent played an even more prominent role. If Goodhue's site planning manipulated the courtyard/cloister typology to achieve a greater sense of public integration, debates over the chapel's form reveal tensions between accommodation of religious tradition and the desire to enhance the chapel's connections to the modern city.

Even before Goodhue began his plans, President Judson solicited the faculty for design suggestions. The scope and seating capacity of the project was still being determined, namely whether it should be used strictly for religious purposes or serve as a larger and more general assembly space. The faculty was strongly in favour of a larger building that would become a setting for public and secular events.[28] Of the various responses, James Roland Angell was most explicit:

> Although there is much to be gained from the . . . sentimental point of view by a building which should be used solely for religious exercises, I can but feel that under the conditions of contemporary American life, particularly in a great civic center like Chicago, such a procedure would be anachronistic . . . I should hope that the building when constructed would lend itself to many purposes of a positively ethical character connected with the social, moral, and religious interests of the University community . . . I should hope that the working out of this conception of the building would not be found incompatible with the erection of a very splendid type of the Gothic cathedral, which might suitably crown the beauties of our present group of buildings.[29]

The desire to accommodate contemporary needs while replicating the forms of a Gothic cathedral was a running theme in many of the responses.

The idea that the Gothic *cathedral* formed the most appropriate precedent, and not chapels or meeting halls, was a further affirmation of the public aspirations of the project. Just as the university viewed its larger mission as one of public service, the cathedral form connoted a landmark for the city, in service to the entire population. These ambitions set the Chicago project apart from most chapels at other universities.[30] In this regard,

Angell's invocation of Chicago's civic life is telling; for him and many others, a cathedral chapel could both recall the glories of the past and speak to the values of modern secular society.

Goodhue's original 1919 design envisioned a monumental structure with a dominating 200-foot central tower at the crossing of the nave and transepts, probably inspired by Giles Gilbert Scott's Liverpool Cathedral.[31] Goodhue also followed Scott's design with a strikingly wide bay width, forty feet, which gave the chapel a bold simplicity and allowed for greater daylighting. By the same logic, elaborate stained glass was rejected in favour of clear glass, compensated for by replacing traditional stone vaulting with coloured acoustic ceiling tiles.[32] The Committee on Building and Grounds was enthusiastic about the design, and working drawings proceeded swiftly. Interestingly, these more innovative features went unchallenged, and the chief debates through this period centred on the chapel's urban presence, including its positioning within the block and its elevation level and axial alignment judged in relation to adjacent buildings.[33] Official cost estimates in the summer of 1920 proved to be so overbudget, however, that the project was put on hold for several years.[34]

Between 1922 and 1924, Goodhue resumed work on the project with various efforts at reducing the cost. He soon suggested moving the tower to the west transept. This idea gained traction, and university officials agreed it would allow for a more soaring tower and a better overall proportion; by eliminating the heavy central crossing piers, it would also create an unbroken and lighter interior. The university did insist, however, on changing the tower to the east transept, which would 'present the more monumental aspect to the street', and not the subsidiary buildings.[35] Once again, the university prioritized the chapel's public urban presence.

New working drawings proceeded in 1924, but Goodhue's unexpected death in early May once again provided an obstacle, and the university deliberated for many months on how to proceed. President Ernest DeWitt Burton (who took over for President Judson in 1923) visited Coolidge in June, who strongly urged retaining the design. Coolidge noted that Goodhue had 'taken an historical style which is tried and proved, which has charm and historic association, and adapted it to modern conditions by modern methods . . . Such a building will have a great influence for good on all Western architects and architecture. It will elevate the style of the whole West.'[36] Coolidge's statement generously ascribes the project a definitive role as a regional icon while aptly summarizing the perceived advantages of the Modern Gothic.

Despite these assurances, some university officials were increasingly concerned about the 'correctness' of Goodhue's unconventional design. President Burton in particular took the idea of Gothic cathedral precedent seriously, and he toured England that summer to get a more in-depth perspective, including a meeting with Giles Gilbert Scott. As Burton described, his chief concern was to determine if Goodhue's wide bays were 'permissible', while secondary considerations included the design of the tower, the dimensions of the nave, and the character of the roof and windows.[37] While there was no precedent for the forty-foot bays apart from Liverpool, Burton notes that Scott stressed 'unqualifiedly and repeatedly' that this bay width was 'entire practicable and correct'.[38]

Modern Architecture and the Sacred

In his report, Burton also dwells at length on the example of King's College Chapel in Cambridge, noting that despite the absence of a tower or transepts, it was closest in overall dimensions and form to Goodhue's design.[39] As he wrote to board of trustees president Harold Swift, 'It is stunningly beautiful, & confirms my feeling that ours can be so also. This & Liverpool have been the *most suggestive* of all that I have seen.'[40] In hindsight it is fitting that Burton was inspired by two such disparate examples, one a recent cathedral undertaken for a rapidly growing commercial municipality, and the other a fifteenth-century collegiate chapel strongly associated with the history of higher education. From its founding, the University of Chicago's leaders were obsessed with the institution's place in the lineage of Western education, even as they developed its central mission to confront the problems of Chicago and, by extension, modern urban society.[41]

The final form of the chapel can be seen as an expression of these somewhat contradictory aims, inspired from the two English precedents that best expressed them. As witnessed by Burton's trip, university leaders gave enormous deference to precedent, to an extent that may seem perplexing today. Religious sentiment played little part in this. Rather, their anxieties and eventual approbation of Goodhue's Modern Gothic cathedral were more emblematic of the university's own conflicting desires to claim the mantle of academic tradition while boldly aiming to reform the industrial city through its own progressive agenda.

Symbolizing the modern city

Despite minor scruples, Burton's report concluded that 'the Goodhue plan is practicable and good in all its essential features and dimensions, and it would be unwise to abandon it'.[42] The trustees deferred to his judgement and the final plans proceeded unhindered, completed by Goodhue's former associates. Construction of the chapel began in August 1925, fifteen years after Rockefeller's gift, and the building was dedicated on 28 October 1928.[43] Because of budget limitations, the full site plan with subsidiary structures was abandoned, but nonetheless the chapel's completion was heralded as a capstone in the university's development (Figure 7.7).

The dedication was accompanied by extensive commentary on the chapel's larger meaning. The dean, Charles W. Gilkey, wrote that just as Goodhue used Gothic tradition as the starting point for new creativity, the activities associated with the chapel should explore experiments in reshaping religious thought based on the experience of modern life. Referencing the university's common moniker as the 'Gray City', he concluded that the chapel was more than a religious building, but symbol of the entire university, 'a spiritual Capitol for the "City Gray that ne'er shall die".'[44] Von Ogden Vogt echoed this idea in noting that the chapel represented neither 'the barrenness of evangelic piety' nor the 'dryness and partiality' of science; rather, he associated its modern Gothic aesthetic with a fusion of scientific and religious feeling: 'Let nobody make the mistake of thinking that a Gothic chapel is a backward turn to outworn ideas. On the contrary, it proclaims the validities of immediate experience and knowledge . . . It affords one of the noblest

Figure 7.7 The chapel entrance on the Midway as completed.
Photograph, 1937. Photographic Archive, University of Chicago Special Collections Resource Center.

settings so far achieved in the history of American culture."⁴⁵ In these statements, the chapel's design was enlisted to reject religious sectarianism for a more abstract conception that equated the sacred with the values of a democratic urban society.⁴⁶

These broad discussions of the chapel's spiritual meaning downplayed traditional religion and bolstered a more general sense of civic spirituality. In the promotional campaign that accompanied the construction and dedication period, the Midway location and the chapel's monumental scale drew widespread notice. Local newspapers took up the story with enthusiasm, dubbing the project the 'Cathedral of the Midway'.[47] Prone to journalistic exaggerations, the chapel was named as rival to 'the beauty of the great medieval cathedrals of Europe' and 'Chicago's greatest monumental religious structure'.[48] If a bit overblown, these statements do underscore the larger cultural meaning attached to the building.

This direct comparison to European cathedrals was encouraged by the university's press department:

> Modern methods have made possible the financing and construction of a structure with all the magnificence, mass and beauty of the great Gothic cathedrals of Europe, in a short span of time, and without the sacrifices which they required. This opportunity has been taken advantage of in the plans for the University of Chicago chapel, which, perhaps, might best be termed a cathedral.[49]

While this statement favourably compares the chapel's architectural beauty with the Gothic masterpieces of the past and directly co-opts the cathedral terminology, it equally celebrates the speed and ease made possible by modern construction and financing techniques. The fusion of tradition and modernity instrumental to the chapel's design over its long gestation period thus also became a running theme in commentaries on the project's completion. Tradition was rooted in Gothic imagery, the chapel's monumental scale and its masonry construction.[50] These elements were contrasted by structural and technological advances, its widely varied sculptural programme, and its bold geometric massing.[51]

Above all, though, it was the chapel's unique urban setting that drew comment. In September 1925, A. B. Jay wrote an editorial to the *Chicago Tribune* praising the chapel as 'one of the jewels of Chicago', but somewhat anomalously criticizing its siting; according to Jay, the design made the same mistake as the French cathedrals by being cramped along the street and surrounded by 'horrid shacks which cling to the cathedrals like leeches'.[52] J. Spencer Dickerson, secretary of the board of trustees, responded on behalf of the university:

> The chapel ... will have ample 'ground for a site' and not be 'jammed tightly against the street'. It will rejoice Jay's soul to see its great windows and imposing tower from the neighboring parks and the long stretch of the adjoining Midway ... There will be found in the neighborhood of the Cathedral on the Midway, a striking combination of beauty and architectural effectiveness seldom found in England or France."[53]

Dickerson draws attention to the chapel's relationship with the Midway and the nearby parks. This was another manifestation of the Modern Gothic – traditional models improved by the harmonious relationship with a picturesque setting of modern parks and a close communion with nature.

Compacting Civic and Sacred

In embracing the setting provided by Olmsted's parks, the chapel became directly associated with Chicago's extensive system of parks and boulevards (Figure 7.8). Planned in the 1860s during the heyday of the Parks Movement, they were predicated on nature as a sacred presence that could help combat the evils of the industrial city.[54] This idea was of particular relevance to the university because of its own Gothic buildings and the strong connections between the naturalistic legacy of Olmsted and the pastoral image of Oxbridge in popular imagination.[55] These ideas continued to be relevant into the twentieth century, as witnessed by the dramatic expansion of Chicago's parks.[56] The Special Park Commission of 1905 led to the establishment of parks and playgrounds in immigrant and working-class neighbourhoods, while the implementation of Burnham's *Plan of Chicago* after 1910 included the creation of new boulevards and lakefront parks through extensive shoreline infill.[57]

Chicago's park system also housed the city's primary cultural institutions, including the Art Institute, the Field Museum and the university itself. Thus, alongside the pastoral legacy, the parks were equally associated with cosmopolitan sophistication and cultural achievement.[58] In efforts to combat the city's entrenched reputation for crass commercialism, Chicago's leaders saw this unique fusion of parks and culture as proof of Chicago's civic destiny. In the words of the Chicago Plan Commission, this was a manifestation of a 'spirit of civic co-operation' that would make Chicago 'the world's largest, and most attractive, healthful and prosperous city'.[59]

Figure 7.8 The University Chapel as seen in relation to the Midway Plaisance. Photograph, c.1930. Photographic Archive, University of Chicago Special Collections Resource Center.

The university was heavily invested in promoting its own role in this wider civic vision. As its largest and most publicly oriented building, the chapel was the most direct manifestation of this link, and helps to account for the intense promotion and commentary surrounding its completion. Most direct, perhaps, was journalist Henry Justin Smith in describing the chapel's relation to Chicago:

> The University has never been a walled town, protecting itself against intrusion by the vulgar world. It has been a partner of the rest of the city, at every stage . . . Some day, no doubt, a . . . reverence . . . untarnished by superstition will be entertained by most Chicagoans toward the University Chapel . . . They will recognize it as a pure and perfect emblem of their own ideals . . . So much the better for their faith in this city, and their faith in the endeavors of men and women everywhere.[60]

Goodhue's Modern Gothic 'cathedral' was thus tied to more than a reinvention of tradition. While its use of Gothic motifs sought legitimacy from the past, its urban siting and the civic ambitions attached to it envisioned a very modern role.

The continued validity and relevance of medieval imagery to modern university leaders has puzzled many historians, with a tendency to view such attitudes as inherently reactionary. Some have tried to pit forward-thinking faculty against prestige-minded trustees, but as the positive testimony of Angell quoted earlier indicates, this is an oversimplification. It has also been common to make negative comparisons with the lineage of American progressive traditions, from the writings of the transcendentalists to the architectural work of Louis Sullivan and Frank Lloyd Wright, which all emphasize the close connection between democratic values and the natural American landscape.[61] They were in the minority, however; for many, progressive values could be incorporated within more established traditions, and for them the Gothic cathedral was an entirely appropriate image. Yet this reliance on precedent was only one of many simultaneous associations. Indeed, shorn of Gothic stylistic elements, the combination of Olmsted's naturalistic parks and Goodhue's open-ended site planning is not so far from Wright's own Prairie School ideals.

Looking beyond the well-worn dictates of Modernism which relegates the past entirely, this project can be seen as a subtler fusion of old and new, where the associations with morality and higher purpose central to traditional sacred imagery were rechannelled towards a new civic purpose. With a mission founded on using research and education to solve real problems in the modern city, the University of Chicago Chapel was seen by its creators and many observers as the crowning symbol of these ideals. Faced with the glamorous (or even morally questionable) image of the jazz age metropolis, buildings like this were meant to instil a greater sense of civic pride and communal belonging in face of an increasingly corporatized and mass consumer society that was still in the process of taking hold. While there are certainly elements of this vision to be critical of, the well-worn critique that a Gothic chapel built in the 1920s was anachronistic is far too simple an assumption.

In its subtle invocation of tradition and modernity, the University Chapel was both innovative and contradictory, an expression of the modern quest to define a meaningful civic culture among the chaotic and impersonal landscapes of the industrial-commercial metropolis. Seeing this task as a new kind of sacred mission, the university drew upon a complex rhetoric that invoked the spirt of medieval cathedrals, the moral purity of nature, and the dynamism of the Machine Age simultaneously. In this context, questions over the aesthetic merits of the late Gothic revival are not so important as the complex ways Goodhue and the university's leaders engaged with the subject of the modern city. They used Gothic tradition and its religious and educational associations as a starting point, but imbued them with a sense of public engagement and civic symbolism that were inseparable from the American industrial city in the twentieth century.

Notes

1. Hugh S. Morrison, 'Collegiate Gothic', *University of Chicago Magazine* 23, no. 9 (July–August 1931): 414.
2. Michael J. Lewis, *The Gothic Revival* (London: Thames & Hudson, 2002). Surveys typically give no more than a cursory glance.
3. See T. J. Jackson Lears, *No Place of Grace* (New York: Pantheon Books, 1981), and Michael D. Clark, 'Ralph Adams Cram', *Journal of American Studies* 23, no. 2 (August 1989): 195–213.
4. Katherine Solomonson, *Chicago Tribune Tower Competition* (Cambridge: Cambridge University Press, 2001).
5. Paul Venable Turner, *Campus: An American Planning Tradition* (New York: Architectural History Foundation, 1984), 215–47.
6. See Thomas Wakefield Goodspeed, *A History of the University of Chicago* (Chicago: University of Chicago Press, 1916); John W. Boyer, *The University of Chicago: A History* (Chicago: University of Chicago Press, 2015); Jean Block, *Uses of Gothic: Planning and Building the Campus of the University of Chicago, 1892-1932* (Chicago: University of Chicago Library, 1983).
7. Richard Oliver, *Bertram Grosvenor Goodhue* (Cambridge, MA: MIT Press, 1983), 51–94. With Cram, Goodhue completed pioneering projects like the Military Academy Chapel at West Point and the Saint Thomas Church in New York City.
8. Charles Coolidge, quoted Ernest D. Burton to Harold Swift, 19 June 1924, typescript letter in Swift, Harold H. Papers (HSP) [Box 210, Folder 4].
9. Jackson Park and the Midway were also the site of the World's Columbian Exposition in 1893; see James Gilbert, *Perfect Cities* (Chicago: University of Chicago Press, 1991).
10. Daniel Bluestone, *Constructing Chicago* (New Haven: Yale University Press, 1991), 20–61, and Victoria Post Ranney, *Olmsted in Chicago* (Chicago: RR Donnelley & Sons, 1972).
11. Goodspeed, *History,* 12–129 and Boyer, *University of Chicago,* 66–103. The university was founded under the American Baptist Education Society; President Harper and many of its early leaders worked in theological fields.
12. The history of the Cobb plan's development can be found in University of Chicago, Founders' Correspondence, Special Collections Research Center, University of Chicago Library (SCRC). See also Edward W. Wolner, *Henry Ives Cobb's Chicago* (Chicago: University of Chicago Press, 2011), 181–243.

13. Henry Ives Cobb to William Rainey, Harper, 24 June 1896, typescript letter in University of Chicago, Office of the President, Harper, Judson and Burton Administrations (HJB) [Box 14, Folder 3]; 'Mr Cobb's Preliminary Study for University Chapel', *Chicago Times-Herald*, 24 July 1896, newspaper clipping in Scrapbooks Collection [Box 2].
14. 'Buildings and Grounds of the University of Chicago: A Souvenir 1892-1899', *University of Chicago Weekly*, printed guidebook in Archival Buildings File (ABF) [Folder 25], n.p.
15. Minutes of the University of Chicago Board of Trustees ™, Vol. 4, 15 December 1903; 'Announcements', *University Record* 8, no. 8 (December 1903): 245–6; and 'Gift of $2,000,000 by John D. to U. of C', 27 April 1907 newspaper clipping, in Goodman Papers [Box 7].
16. Block, *Uses of Gothic*, 94–103 and Goodspeed, *History*, 422–9.
17. John D. Rockefeller to Board of Trustees, 13 December 1910, reprinted in TM, Vol. 7, 19 December 1910.
18. The chapel budget dwarfed the campus' other key buildings: The Tower Group ($400,000) and Harper Library ($800,000) (*William Rainey Harper Memorial Library*, dedication booklet (Chicago: University of Chicago Press, 1912)).
19. Harry Pratt Judson to Rockefeller Jr., 10 April 1913, typescript letter in HJB [Box 14, Folder 9].
20. 'The University of Chicago' 1892 fund-raising pamphlet, in HJB [Box 68, Folder 1].
21. TM, Vol. 9, 9 May 1916.
22. TM, Vol. 10, 9 April and 5 July 1918. The chief obstacle was approval for vacating semi-public alleys on the site. Judson was in correspondence with Goodhue since 1913, making it likely he was informally considered for the commission from this point (Bertram Grosvenor Goodhue to Judson, 19 August 1913, in Department of Buildings and Grounds Records (BGR) [Box 26, Folder 11]).
23. Wallace Heckman to Goodhue, 23 June 1919 and Goodhue to Martin Ryerson August 1919, typescript letters in BGR [Box 26, Folder 11]. The existing president's house was designed by Cobb in the 1890s and directly fronted the Midway on the proposed chapel block.
24. Highly aware of this public frontage, the university worked with city officials to rearrange the existing street lights in front of the chapel to improve visual harmony between the chapel and the Midway (Harold Swift to Lloyd R. Steere, 25 September 1928 and Steere to Swift, 23 October 1928, typescript letters in HSP [Box 210 Folder 6]).
25. Cloisters were also part of the Oxbridge legacy. Burton sent Swift a postcard of the Magdalen College cloister during his 1924 cathedral tour (see Note 40).
26. Goodhue to Ryerson, 4 August 1919, typescript letter in BGR [Box 26, Folder 11].
27. Mary W. Helms, 'Sacred Landscape and the Early Medieval European Cloister', *Anthropos* Bd. 97 H. 2 (2002): 435–53.
28. Eight of eleven responses in the archives favoured a more public building against a strictly religious one (HJB [Box 14, Folder 9]).
29. James Roland Angell to Judson, 10 July 1918, typescript letter in ibid. Shortly after, Angell assumed the presidency of Yale where he developed Sterling Memorial Library, another defining monument of the Modern Gothic (Oliver, *Bertram Grosvenor Goodhue*, 223–6 and Aaron Betsky, *James Gamble Rogers and the Architecture of Pragmatism* (Boston, MA: MIT Press, 1994), 118–26).
30. Cram's new chapel at Princeton came closest in scale to Goodhue's and also opened in 1928 (W. Barksdale Maynard, *Princeton: America's Campus* (University Park: Penn State Press, 2012), 138–49).

31. Goodhue to Heckman, 11 August 1919, typescript letter in BGR [Box 26, Folder 11]. Scott won the competition for Liverpool in 1902. Goodhue visited the project under construction in 1913 and was effusive in his praise (Oliver, *Bertram Grosvenor Goodhue*, 128–30).
32. Ibid., 139–41.
33. Working drawings were authorized 26 August 1919 (Ryerson to Goodhue, 26 August 1919, typescript letter, in BGR [Box 26, Folder 11]). See extended correspondence between Goodhue and Heckman, August 1919–October 1920 in BGR [Box 26, Folders 11–12].
34. Anglin-Norcross Limited to Goodhue, 18 August 1920, Heckman to Goodhue, 30 August 1920, and Goodhue to Heckman, 5 October 1920, in BGR [Box 26, Folder 12]. Original estimates came in at $2.8 million, later revised upward to $3.1 million.
35. Ryerson to Goodhue, 19 January 1923, in BGR [Box 26, Folder 13].
36. Charles Coolidge, quoted in Burton to Swift, 19 June 1924.
37. Ernest D. Burton, 'Report on the Cathedrals of England as Bearing on the Plans for the Chapel of the University of Chicago', 3 September 1924, typescript report in HJB [Box 14, Folder 10]:1.
38. Ibid., 2–4.
39. Ibid., 4–5.
40. Burton to Swift, 13 August 1924, postcard in HSP [Box 210, Folder 1] (emphasis Burton's). Burton wrote numerous postcards to Swift recording his impressions of the sites visited.
41. In the university's oft-quoted Alma Mater, the White City of the 1893 Fair is eclipsed by the university's lasting cultural impact: 'The city white hath fled the earth / But where the azure waters lie / A nobler city hath its birth / The city gray that ne'er shall die'.
42. Burton, 'Report on the Cathedrals', 9.
43. Frank Hurburt O'Hara, *The University of Chicago* (Chicago: University of Chicago Press, 1928), 18; 'Dedication of the University Chapel', event programme in HSP [Box 210, Folder 6].
44. Charles W. Gilkey, 'Response' in 'The Dedication of the University Chapel', souvenir booklet, in HSP [Box 210, Folder 6]: 21. Gilkey's use of the term 'Capitol' is notable, with its direct connotations of civic government and democratic processes.
45. Von Ogden Vogt, 'The University Chapel: Fabric and Idea', *University of Chicago Magazine* 21, no. 2 (December 1928): 68–72.
46. The university's connection to democracy and the modern city was discussed repeatedly: 'Chicago, the City; Chicago, the University', 1925 pamphlet, in Development Campaign and Anniversaries Record [Box 6 Folder 9]; Nicholas Butler Murray, 'Addresses at the Dedication of Emmons Blaine Hall', *University Record* 9, no. 1 (May 1904): 13–17; 'Why Chicago?' 20 May 1920 newspaper clipping, in Scrapbooks Collection [Box 13].
47. The University's first official press release on the Chapel described the building as 'A cathedral structure which will crown the group of university buildings and be a majestic feature on the Midway Plaisance . . .' (University Press Release, 26 August 1925, in ABF [Folder 161]).
48. 'Midway Chapel Nears Completion', *The Journal*, 12 January 1928, in ABF [Folder 161].
49. University Press Release for Chapel Cornerstone Laying, 10 June 1926, in ibid.
50. O'Hara, *University of Chicago*, 119–30. Many other contemporary Gothic buildings used steel framing as the primary structure (Betsky, *Rogers*, 53, 125–30).
51. The symbolic programme of the chapel, chosen by faculty committee, included representations of statesmen, philosophers, scientists, writers and architects; they aimed

'to embody their conviction that the chapel of a great university, built in the twentieth century, should be a symbol of how all these experiences and disciplines merge in a high type of religion'. Edgar J. Goodspeed et al. to Swift, 13 March 1926, typescript letter in HSP [Box 210, Folder 3].

52. A. B. Jay, 'The Cathedral on the Midway', *Chicago Tribune,* 3 September 1925, in HSP [Box 210, Folder 4]. Jay was probably referring to the existing residential dwellings on the chapel block which the university intended to demolish.

53. J. Spencer Dickerson, 'The Cathedral on the Midway', *Chicago Tribune,* 7 September 1925, in HSP [Box 210, Folder 4].

54. Thomas Bender, *Toward an Urban Vision* (Louisville: University of Kentucky Press, 1975) and James L. Machor, *Pastoral Cities: Urban Ideals and the Symbolic Landscape of America* (Madison: University of Wisconsin Press, 1987).

55. Olmsted's park designs and the popular American image of Oxbridge were indebted to English picturesque theory. See John Conron, *American Picturesque* (University Park: Penn State Press, 2000) and David Schuyler, *New Urban Landscape* (Baltimore: John Hopkins Press, 1986), 24–75.

56. William H. Tishler, ed., *Midwestern Landscape Architecture* (Champaign: University of Illinois Press, 2000). In Chicago, the picturesque tradition was carried on in the early twentieth-century work of Jens Jensen and Ossian C. Simmonds.

57. See Condit, *Chicago 1910-1929: Building, Planning and Urban Technology* (Chicago: University of Chicago Press, 1973).

58. Bluestone, *Constructing Chicago,* 22–6. This cosmopolitan imagery had been attached to Chicago's parks from their inception.

59. 'Chicago Plan Progress', published report (Chicago: Chicago Plan Commission, 1 July 1927), 8, and 'New Chicago', publicity pamphlet (Chicago: CC Mitchell & Co, 1920), n.p.

60. Henry Justin Smith, 'The University Chapel – Its Relations to Chicago', *University of Chicago Magazine* 20, no. 9 (July 1928): 480.

61. Bachin, *Building the South Side: Urban Space and Civic Culture in Chicago, 1890-1919* (Chicago: University of Chicago Press, 2004) and Haar, *The City As Campus* (Minneapolis: University of Minnesota Press, 2011). Wright's famed Robie House (1909) was completed across from the Chicago campus, within direct sight of where the chapel would be built.

CHAPTER 8
A DIASPORA OF MODERN SACRED FORM
AUGUSTE PERRET, LE CORBUSIER AND PAUL VALÉRY
Karla Cavarra Britton

Modern architecture and sacred language

Until recently, sacred form has been one of those areas of research that has been largely overlooked in the history of modern architecture. Yet as the theme of the current volume demonstrates, one can no longer ignore the fact that recent reassessments of the evolution of architecture over the last century have brought the idea of the sacred to the foreground. Its impact on twentieth-century architecture as an arena in which many major architects made innovative advances is only now being taken into account. Yet the concept of the sacred and its material expression was in various guises a major refrain in modern architecture long before its critical capacity was fully acknowledged by contemporary historians. As the Yale art historian, Vincent Scully, presciently observed in 2007, 'in fact the attainment of the sacred was one of the well-hidden agendas of canonical modern architecture as a whole'.[1] Scully was referring in part to what he termed the 'ferocity' of the defensiveness in regard to religious architecture that characterized many critical observers of modern architecture (and his observation was intended as a reproach to them). Yet by way of reinforcing Scully's contrary observation, one can point to examples such as Colin Rowe's adoption of biblical language in the late 1970s as a means of presenting a critique of modern architecture. Both Scully and Rowe, albeit using different registers, demonstrate how many of the protagonists of modern architecture shared a world view which developed into an understanding of the prophetic nature of modern architecture – the expression of which is echoed in the intensity and uniqueness of religious experience.[2]

Following this critical lead, the intent of this chapter is to draw out certain parameters of the attention given to sacred building and thought by two of the most prominent architectural protagonists of the twentieth century: Auguste Perret (1874–1954) and Le Corbusier (1887–1965), especially in relation to what they shared in common with their mutual intellectual mentor, Paul Valéry (1871–1945). The chapter is bracketed by two key moments. The first is Perret's concept of the 'sovereign shelter' (*l'abri souverain*) as it was expressed through a new religious architectural language as early as his 1923 skeletal frame design for Notre Dame du Raincy. This seminal building established a model of material economy and monumental character that was disseminated around the globe in ensuing decades, from the work of the Swiss architect Karl Moser in the late 1920s, to the later achievements in the 1950s of the Czech architect Antonin

Raymond and the Japanese modernist Tōgo Murano.[3] The second moment is Le Corbusier's phenomenological concept of 'ineffable space' (*espace indicible*), which he first published in an article in 1946 and then used again in numerous reprises. The idea of ineffable space perhaps found its most forceful expression in Le Corbusier's chapel of Ronchamp, which became a kind of theoretical statement about the nature of the spiritual for Le Corbusier, providing a model for future understandings of sacred space by any number of world architects. Both of these moments, coming out of the context of a uniquely modern French tradition of religious thought and expression (notably focalized in the journal *L'Art Sacré*), address the pursuit of the expression of religious thought beyond the predictable boundaries of architecture's material and technological concerns, demonstrating how religious buildings often became the locus of significant experimentation within the global diaspora of the modernist project.

Significantly, beyond Perret's and Le Corbusier's methods for constructing sacred form lay a distinct set of philosophical presumptions, many derived from the philosophical writings of the French poet and literary critic, Paul Valéry. He provided both architects with an underlying source for pursuing a modern understanding of architecture's spiritual concerns, especially in his extended meditation on architecture, *Eupalinos, or the Architect*.[4] Rooted in a French modern context, Valéry's writings provided the methodology for a progressive understanding of the nature of the spiritual. These ideas would resonate with the imaginative impulses of both architects: in particular, they both drew inspiration from Valéry's concept of the classical and the metaphorical significance of the ancient Greek temple. For Perret, this model of the temple was rooted in the idea of a heroic Hellenism conveyed in his idea of 'the sovereign shelter'. For Le Corbusier, on the other hand, the temple model meant a return to the power of his early personal encounter with the Parthenon itself. Building in the spirit of Paul Valéry, each architect conveyed a sense of the underlying philosophical impulses which would push forward new ideas about modernity and the power of sacred form.

Auguste Perret: The church as 'sovereign shelter'

The religious building type was an important focus in Perret's work, including some twenty-five projects in all.[5] It synthesized many of his lasting concerns, such as his reverence for the placement of monumental public buildings within the normative character of a residential urban fabric; the construction of buildings with a truthful character; and his determination to elevate the material of reinforced concrete from a maligned industrial building material to a medium that could be handled with the craftsmanship of precious stone. As such, he believed that concrete could be made appropriate to civic, religious and therefore monumental architecture. Hence, he saw in his meticulous treatment of reinforced concrete a particularly appropriate means of renewing the religious building type, and it was in part through this role as a 'pioneer' and 'precursor' of the Modern Movement in general, and concrete construction in particular, that Perret's reputation in architecture was established.

While it is difficult to define the spiritual dimension in relation to the architecture of Perret in an absolute sense, it is clear that at root it was related not only to the exploration of his use of reinforced concrete construction but also to the furthering of the typology of French ecclesiastical architecture. Perret saw the programme of the religious building type in relation to his idea of the 'sovereign shelter', or as he defined it, 'a vessel, a framework . . . capable of housing in its unity the variety of organs necessary to fulfil its function'.[6] In other words, a sovereign shelter is a building which utilizes a minimal structural skeleton, in a tectonic manner evocative of classical Greek monumental architecture, to provide for a building's successful realization of its programme. Perret's two most authoritative churches – Notre Dame du Raincy and the much later St Joseph (1951–4, built as part of the post–Second World War reconstruction of the city of Le Havre) – are decisive in this regard, from their tectonic strength to their economic ingenuity in handling of the basic volumetric arrangements. With a clear attention to typology, expressivity and referential detailing, these church buildings express a distilled sense of order derived from concepts of ideal geometry and mathematics that are the distinguishing characteristics of Perret's work.

Among the significant projects which shaped the vocabulary of Perret's architectural language was his first engagement with the construction of a modern ecclesiastical building, the Cathedral of Oran (1908), done in collaboration with Albert Ballu. (Interestingly, this was also a project that the very young Le Corbusier worked on during his apprenticeship at the Perret Frères office in Paris.) Perret's firm was called in to assist with the construction of the building based upon Ballu's design, and the North African context provided opportunity for experimentation with both new forms and constructional techniques. For instance, a glance at the Oran cathedral shows the ways in which Perret developed the precast concrete claustra panels which would inform his later pattern of fenestration, a usage that became a key element of his ecclesiastical designs.

More than a decade after the Oran project, when Perret was challenged with the task of memorializing the trauma of the First World War in the church at Le Raincy, he deployed elements such as the claustra screen and use of concrete, drawn from the Oran project, creating a new ecclesiastical idiom which was to become a modern prototype (Figure 8.1). The church was commissioned by the local priest, Abbé Félix Nègre, as a memorial to those who died in the war, especially the Battle of the Ourcq. At the time, Le Raincy was a working-class town with many wartime industrial workshops, situated northeast of Paris on the rail-line to Germany. In the aftermath of the war, there were few resources available for building a new church, so after finding that traditional ecclesiastical architects were unable to work within his meagre budget, Nègre sought out Perret as one who could construct economically, given his experience with industrial buildings and the new material of reinforced concrete. Perret built the church in a single year, from April 1922 to June 1923, and he indeed used it as the opportunity to 'reconsider the tradition of religious space in light of [his] industrial experience'.[7] Something of the aesthetic he thereby engendered was reflected in a *New York Times Magazine* article in 1926, which suggested a reading of the church as a 'sublimated workshop'.[8] In the asperities of the

Modern Architecture and the Sacred

Figure 8.1 Auguste Perret, Notre Dame du Raincy, Le Raincy, France, 1923. Interior. Photograph by Frank Yerbury. F. R.Yerbury/Architectural Association Photo Library.

church's design, inspired by the wartime workshops of the town, many aspects are evident which become important keys to Perret's particular concept of the religious architectural language – including that the methods and constraints of industrial construction are in no way inimical to an ecclesiastical architecture. So in addition to the tapered, slender columns holding up the barrel vault roof, Perret introduced aesthetic elements such as the stained glass that fills in the claustra that make up the church's exterior walls, designed by the painter Maurice Denis and executed by Marguerite Huré.

Ferdinand Pfammatter, in his 1948 study *Betonkirche*, treated Notre Dame du Raincy as a kind of fountainhead for a whole tradition of concrete church construction in the first half of the twentieth century. Calling the church an 'astonishing phenomenon' (*überraschende Erscheinung*), he emphasized its structural clarity as a model for the renewal of religious architecture through a reworking of the typology of the church cumulatively represented by a number of subsequent buildings.[9] Most notably, he pointed to St Antonius Church in Basel by the Swiss architect Karl Moser (1927), which overtly exemplifies Perret's concern for materiality and structure. Echoing Pfammatter, the English historian Peter Hammond described the church as 'the full accomplishment of the technical revolution that was begun at Le Raincy'.[10] Here the dominant motif of Le Raincy – the tall slender columns – is utilized in the form of square shafts that likewise hold up a barrel vault over the nave, yet the altar is more traditionally set apart from the nave, with a blank wall behind it concentrating visual attention in a way that Le Raincy does not. Pfammatter cites numerous extensions of this new building tradition, including such churches as Jean Combaz's St Suzanne in Brussels (1928); St Pierre à Roye, Somme (1931) by Duval and Gonse; and the University Chapel, Fribourg (1941) by Dumas and Honegger. Perret's influence has also been attributed to Cecil Burns' Christian Science Church, Tunbridge Wells (1933); and in the post–Second World War era, to Florentine Giovanni Michelluci's Church of the Madonna in Larderello (1956–7), and Karl Band's Church of Sainte-Elisabeth in Cologne-Mülheim (1951–2).

Extending on the idea of the 'sovereign shelter', Perret also contributed to a theological and sociopolitical history of the *église-tour* (tower church), a less-well-known typology for a church which nevertheless has its own place in the history of modern and post-war urban development. In particular, he contributed to reimagining the church as an *église-tour* through three specific projects: his extraordinarily ambitious entry for the Basilica of Saint-Jeanne-d'Arc de Paris, submitted for the 1926 competition sponsored by the Diocese of Paris; a project for the cathedral of Buenos Aires of 1936; and the construction of the St Joseph Church in Le Havre in 1954, which became the built fruition of his previous work. The St Joseph Church – with a centralized plan characterized by its dramatic reinterpretation of the tower church in relation to new construction technology and ideas of city planning – is a focal point for the community of the post-war rebuilt city. Following the destruction of the city's entire centre by Allied bombing, the destroyed area was completely rebuilt by a team led by Perret. In addition to the focal point of the St Joseph Church, a monumental Hôtel de Ville (the administrative centre of the city) functioned as the second focus in the overall city plan, emphasizing a balance in the urban scheme of both the religious and the civic realms. Perret evidently had a close relationship with the *curé* and the congregation of St Joseph, and in the dramatic interior (rising to a height of 394 feet, or 107 metres), he illuminated the interplay of architecture and theology, urbanism and religious symbolism in European post-war development. He thereby deployed the *église-tour* as a vehicle for readdressing the social vision of architecture and even the theological dimensions of urban community.

In examining the ecclesiastical work of Auguste Perret, one is reminded of the fact that as modern architecture grew beyond national and cultural boundaries, it provided a critical form of support for the parallel migration of the demographic centres of Christianity, especially to the Global South. In this context, one of the long-term consequences of Perret's components of the 'sovereign shelter' was the mark it left on architectural practices around the globe. In Le Raincy, Perret clearly demonstrated that 'Modern Art' could enter into the spiritual realm of the church, a position that earned him inclusion in 1948–9 in discussions with the circle that produced the journal *L'Art Sacré* around Matisse's Chapelle du Rosaire in Vence, anticipating the later close collaboration in the 1950s between Le Corbusier and Père Marie-Alain Couturier. Yet Perret's influence was not limited to the European context, and the technical revolution of his architectural vocabulary was reproduced in an astonishingly wide variety of contexts. Perret's designs for churches in France and North Africa, for instance, represent how the modern church became a normative component of Christian urban culture. Perret had an impact on several modern churches in the Middle East, including his own design in the 1930s for a Dominican house in Cairo. The Lebanese architect Antoine Tabet was a major proponent of Perret, and his own monastery and church of St François des Capusins (1955) in Beirut showed effects of this allegiance, especially the bell tower. A more indirect influence might be seen in St Mark's Coptic Cathedral in Cairo, built by engineer Michel Bakhoum, which evokes some formal correspondence in its use of concrete with the work Perret himself carried out in Egypt. Elsewhere in Africa, the Cathedral of Our Lady of the Immaculate Conception in the centre of Maputo, Mozambique, exhibits strong influence from Perret, built in 1936 and designed by the Portuguese civil engineer Marcial Simões de Freitas e Costa. In Asia, Antonin Raymond's Chapel for the Women's Christian College in Tokyo (1932) is often cited as having been strongly influenced by Le Raincy (though in form it is actually more akin to Perret's Chapel in Montmagny). Likewise, the Japanese architect Tōgo Murano's United Church of Christ in Osaka (1928) betrays Perret's influence.

Even before the rise of air travel and information technologies, therefore, we can see in the interchange between these various church buildings how the global circulation of ideas and images shaped localized developments. Local themes were assimilated into constructions built by the dominant power, which in turn flowed outward between colonizing nations (a reciprocity that the architectural historian Jean-Louis Cohen has aptly termed a 'carousel of hegemonies'[11]). To highlight but one particular case: the general plan of the Cathedral of Oran – initially entrusted to the Algerian-based architect, then to a Paris-based architectural firm – was informed by structural systems that were once perfected by Mamuk architecture, and then later informed by the innovation of French church architecture, only to be exported by a Czech architect building in Japan, as well as a Portuguese civil engineer in Mozambique. This is just one instance of the patterns of influence, convergence and divergence that are to be discovered by entering into a more detailed and historical examination of the evolution of modern church architecture in a global perspective, recognizing that the sacred has often been an engine of both innovation and dispersion far beyond its more familiar association with the traditional.

The unity of the architectural act: Perret and Valéry

Ironically, standing intellectually behind Perret's body of ecclesiastical work is not so much a theological tradition as a literary one. In 1921, Paul Valéry published his Socratic dialogue *Eupalinos, or the Architect*.[12] This text expands upon Valéry's fascination with the life of the mind and the creative process, and on the nature of building and construction. Architecture, as he understood it, is that intellectual practice which provides the most complete example in material form of the disciplined mental act of giving structure to ideas. His ambition was to comprehend the power of the creative process itself through the analysis of the artistic form, and so he returned again and again to the theme of architecture as the integral example of the constructive act: as T. S. Eliot observed, 'Valéry's analogy, in the matter of structure, is Architecture'.[13] Architecture is a theme that first appears, for example, in Valéry's essays comprising the Leonardo da Vinci cycle,[14] and then more extensively in *Eupalinos*. The latter dialogue also becomes Valéry's vehicle for expressing architecture's relationship to thought and language (specifically poetry), as well as for defining architectural form's potential to express complex meanings of human experience, such as those pertaining to the themes of permanence, space and time.

The essential point Valéry makes in the dialogue is that construction is the essence of architecture: the materiality of architecture, and the tectonic assembly of its parts, ultimately define architecture's distinct characteristics apart from any of the other arts. This distinction is for Valéry the heart of the creative impulse that is concerned with *exactitude*: not a particular vocabulary or style, but a precision in design that contributes to an essential clarity of form which for Valéry was a visual map of what one seeks in the intellectual life of the mind. It therefore achieves an ethical import, in that it becomes a governing structure within which the architect not only conceives, but creates the forms which he imagines. Valéry was interested throughout his work in how this lucidity of intention relates to the creation of precise form – and hence Eupalinos' summarial question on the nature of architecture: 'What is there more mysterious than clarity?'

Perret knew Valéry personally as a friend and colleague, and it is clear from Perret's writings that he aligned himself with Valéry's poetic approach to architecture as understood through an emphasis on the exactitude of creation.[15] As a participant in the Parisian intelligentsia, and member of the Institut de France, Perret held an authoritative cultural role from the early years of the twentieth century well into the 1950s.[16] Working in a family building practice unique for its ability both to design and to construct, he focused on developing a modern aesthetic for the material of reinforced concrete, aspiring to translate into this new idiom the French architectural tradition understood in Valérian terms and thus defined by its attention to clarity in construction and to the authentic use of materials. Perret also worked within a larger cultural circle – including Valéry, but also with such figures as André Gide, Maurice Denis and Antoine Bourdelle – who aspired to the cultivation of values of cultural continuity expressed through the idioms of a classical modernism. In this regard, Perret pursued an architecture that was based on the principles of technique, economy and the patterns established by the French ideal of the *constructeur*, understood in the largest sense of the term as one who maintained control over the whole of the constructional process – from initial design to final realization.

The result of Perret's determination was an architecture defined by its distillation of form in work such as Notre Dame du Raincy, which as we have seen is a building that inspired admiration for the clarity of its constructional and compositional methods. Remembering the working process of Perret in the construction of the church, for example, the critic Marie Dormoy wrote in her memoir of Perret that he was an architect who put into practice a formula set forth by Valéry in *Eupalinos*: 'In a work worthy of its name there are no details.'[17] Perret could scarcely have wished for a more appropriate tribute to his working intentions. Dormoy's association of Perret with the Valérian formula ('no details in construction') revealed something of this architect's identification with his own sense of vocation. As Dormoy expressed it, during the building process of this church Perret 'thought about it without ceasing' and was 'attentive to all, surveying all, verifying the work of each of the workers'.[18]

Perret's personal and intentional intellectual association with Valéry thus becomes the determinative context for understanding Perret's own critical thinking about sacred architecture, especially as it is expressed in his *Contribution à une théorie de l'architecture*, a collection of his laconic aphorisms published in 1952 two years before his death.[19] The basis of a Valérian poetic in Perret's architectural thought can be seen at work throughout Perret's numerous aphorisms, especially those collected in the *Contribution*. In his perhaps most often-quoted maxim, he combines in a single statement the notion of language with construction, and the architect with the poet: 'Construction is the maternal language of the architect. The architect is a poet who thinks and speaks in construction.'[20] Perret also echoes in his philosophy on architecture a Valérian theme from *Eupalinos* on the interrelatedness of form and language: 'There is no geometry without the word', which insists that even abstract form is the product of a linguistic operation.[21] In a collection of unpublished aphorisms found among his personal papers, Perret's fascination with poetic concepts is even more directly reflected in a number of his observations: 'The poet sees what others do not see – he reveals it to them, he is a *révélateur*'; or again with regard to the language of the poet: 'It is not sufficient to learn some poems in order to become a poet – It is first necessary to know how to speak one's language.'[22]

Most important, however, is the proclivity that Valéry's poetics shows towards the ideal of exactitude: in architectural terms, creative form must exhibit what the French literary critic Jean Hytier summarized as a 'lucidity of intent united with an exactitude of construction'.[23] Valéry's theoretical focus therefore turns towards the architect and the deliberateness of the maker, the *constructeur*, whose work is set apart through a disciplined method and mode of working, as well as the significance of architecture as the ultimate paradigm for 'the work of the spirit'. In his introduction to the 'mélodrame' *Amphion*, Valéry writes further of architecture's importance as a means of providing order: 'A finished building, gives us at a single glance, the sum of intentions, inventions, insights and forces that imply its existence; it brings to light humanity's combined work of desire, knowledge, and ability. Uniquely among the arts, and in an indivisible moment of vision, architecture changes our souls with the sense of human capacities as a whole.'[24] And its capacity to do so is determined by nothing less than the exactitude of both its conceptualization and its realization, united as a single continuum of creative effort.

In the end, the significance of Perret's contribution to modern architecture and the sacred is not simply an architectural achievement, but even more so his assiduous ambition to unite in the role of the *constructeur* a serious discourse about the nature of making, inspired by the example of Valéry and his poetics of the creative process. The categories, or discipline, within which Perret set out to do his work are thus in strong contrast to what Valéry described as the intoxication of the modern condition with sensation and novelty – what he derisively called 'the new'. This radical stance, not only in respect to the craft of architecture but also in respect to Perret's sense of place in the world, sought a permanence that could resist the transience of sensation with a sense of permanence. It was this idea which Perret described in terms of his paradoxical aspiration for an architectural 'banality', which he understood not as the prosaic quality of mediocrity, but as a sense of timelessness with respect to form. For it was acutely characteristic of Perret's Valérian intellectual discipline to try to hold in a single thought both the potential of the modern era and the inescapable presence of the past, perhaps imagining a future which would be able to regard the product of the present as intelligible.

Le Corbusier and ineffable space

It is difficult to overstate the significance Le Corbusier has had on shaping an understanding of the ineffable and spiritual in relationship to modern architecture and sacred form. This is in large part due to his unifying concept of 'Ineffable Space', an idea which supports an essentially phenomenological approach to the sacred within the expression of the mystical elements made possible through the practice of architecture. As Le Corbusier himself remarked, 'I am not conscious of the miracle of faith, but I often live that of ineffable space, the consummation of plastic emotion.'[25]

Le Corbusier's ecclesiastical buildings, all built late in his career during the 1950s (or posthumously in the case of St Pierre in Firminy), have struck some disillusioned critics as representing a marked rupture from his previous work, which focused more upon the rational functionalism of a machine aesthetic. The pilgrimage chapel at Ronchamp (1955), the monastery of La Tourette (1953–61) and the church of Firminy (completed in 2006) – each of these stands out for its evocative and even mystical conjuring of light and space. In these sacred structures, Le Corbusier turns towards a focus on developing concepts for the spiritual and sacred through the expression of an architectural language. Yet this focus was characterized by his own abiding concern for the mystical nature of things, combined with the wider cultural emergence in the post-war period of a number of French clergy who were intellectually committed to reform – including a long-awaited reconsideration of the nature of religious art.

The Dominican priest Marie-Alain Couturier was crucial to this endeavour– and the implications of his relationship with Le Corbusier are well known. Couturier's name was inextricably linked with the journal *L'Art Sacré*, and early in the 1950s he proposed that Le Corbusier be the architect for the new Ronchamp pilgrimage chapel. While the journal's nominal subject was modern liturgical arts, Couturier used it to penetrate deeply into the concept of the spiritual in relation to the work of modern artists, and to explore a concern for the potential of aesthetic abstraction and 'primitivism' as a primal and universal expression of human interactions with the divine. *L'Art Sacré* became the vehicle for Couturier's belief in the power of modern art to deepen concepts of faith in relation to modernization. It embraced figures such as Marc Chagall, Fernand Léger and Georges Braque, who were all famously influential in making inroads into a rethinking of the nature of sacred space. Le Corbusier's focus on 'ineffable space' must therefore be seen as part of this revolutionary rethinking of architecture's relationship to the sacred.

Perhaps no single text written by an architect is more evocative of the ontological dimension of architecture than Le Corbusier's tract 'L'Espace indicible', first published as 'Art' in January 1946 in a special issue of *L'Architecture d'aujourd'hui*, and then later republished in both *Modulor* (1950) and *Modulor 2* (1955), and then used yet again as the opening of Le Corbusier's 1948 book, *New World of Space*. Le Corbusier apparently also contemplated publishing a book on the topic of 'l'espace indicible', as evidenced by a cover sketch he made (which is now held in a private collection). Le Corbusier's existential attitude implied a willingness to confront, in a critical sense, the logic of his five points on architecture by holding them alongside his more primitive sense of ineffability. His investigation of this phenomenon continued throughout the 1940s and 1950s, building on a genealogy that addressed new concepts of space and ontological experience including the work of Edmund Husserl, Sigfried Giedion, Maurice Merleau-Ponty and Albert Einstein.[26]

In his essay on ineffable space, Le Corbusier wrote that it emerges out of two conditions: the first is an understanding of the living being's foundational need to control space; and the second is the 'aesthetic emotion' that is a potential outcome of this ordered control when it is perfectly achieved. Architecture, sculpture and painting, Le Corbusier asserts, are those disciplines that may be fully bound up with this fuller understanding of the fundamental need for spatial control and its ineffable potential. When perfected, the 'action of the work' of the architect, sculptor or painter produces a 'phenomenon of concordance' as carefully controlled as a mathematical *'fourth dimension'*, where the construction of such space is capable of providing an ineffable human experience beyond real time and space. As Le Corbusier describes it, 'In a complete and successful work there are hidden masses of implications, a veritable world which reveals itself to those whom it may concern, which means: to those who deserve it. Then a boundless depth opens up, effaces the walls, drives away contingent presences, accomplishes the miracle of *ineffable space*.'

Le Corbusier's phenomenological exposition of the idea of the ineffable connects him (perhaps more closely than he realized) with a prominent affirmation within the Judeo-Christian tradition: that which is most holy is also unspeakable – specifically the name of God, or tetragrammaton, often rendered as YAHWEH. Philo speaks of the Holy Name as ineffable, lawful to be spoken only by those whose tongues and ears have been purified by wisdom. Maimonides notes that it was spoken once daily, but only in the Temple, and only in the priestly benediction. Yet the idea that the closer one comes to the holy, the more unspeakable it is, is not simply a prohibition. It also refers to the idea that what is ineffable is not merely forbidden to be said, but also that it is impossible to say, for it lies beyond words. So, for example, the American Jewish theologian Abraham Heschel once remarked that

> to become aware of the ineffable is to part company with words . . . The tangent to the curve of human experience lies beyond the limits of language. The world of things we perceive is but a veil. Its flutter is music, its ornament science, but what it conceals is inscrutable. Its silence remains unbroken; no words can carry it away.[27]

It is this sensibility of the inexpressible that Le Corbusier seems to have been drawn to in his own evocation of the mystical through the manipulation of light and space.

The resulting body of religious architecture has tended to be narrowed in critical accounts to readings of four major religious works: the proposed basilica at La Sainte-Baume (1946–60); the pilgrimage chapel of Notre-Dame du Haut Ronchamp; the Monastery of Sainte-Marie de la Tourette; and the Parish Church of Saint-Pierre, Firminy-Vert. Yet there are other spiritual works by Le Corbusier with which we are mostly far less familiar – the project for a church in Le Tremblay of 1929; the 1951 Delgado Chapel project in Caracas; and a list of commissions cited by the historian Gilles Ragot, which lists 'nine chapels, a convent, two monasteries and seventeen churches, coming mostly from Switzerland, Germany, Belgium and France, but also from Italy, the Netherlands, the United States, Venezuela and Rwanda'.[28]

Le Corbusier had Calvinist origins in his native Switzerland, and he had lived through the violent political turmoil that Europe suffered between 1914 and 1945. Given this experience, he repeatedly expressed deep concerns regarding the human spirit, yet his spiritual sense of the world defied easy classifications. This is evident not only in his well-known assertion that 'some things are spiritual and others are not, whether or not they are religious', but also in the manner in which the ongoing vacillation between the sacred and the profane is evident in the labyrinthine nature of his work and in the dialogical movement of opposites evident in his writings, including in particular his formation of the principles of Purism; his philosophy of Le Modulor; and his maxims and iconography in *Le Poème de l'angle droit* (1947–53). While underscoring Le Corbusier's deep fascination with the Orphic, the symbolic and the arcane, recent attention has been drawn as well to his involvement with debates on liturgy and theology in France prior to the Second

Vatican Council, especially as they related to the themes of poverty, hierarchy, rite and ritual.[29] In this vein, Le Corbusier had links to a variety of interlocutors in the mid-century discussions in France on how to put the sacred arts to most use in transforming the church. Among these figures are Couturier, whom Le Corbusier first encountered in 1948; Father Régemey, co-editor of *L'Art Sacré*; and Maurice Denis and the Ateliers d'art sacré (founded in 1919).

By way of example, attention has recently been paid to the Sainte-Baume project by Le Corbusier, which draws attention to the architect's partnership with Edouard Trouin, who had a fascinating vision for an elaborate underground basilica at La Sainte-Baume in Provence, at the heart of a grotto dedicated to Mary Magdalene. The context for this project was a design by the writer and diplomat Paul Claudel for an underground church, which in turn influenced Couturier and his work with the architect Antonin Raymond. For Le Corbusier, the project was an opportunity to initiate a deeper appreciation of Orphic harmony in its many forms. In part due to its schematic nature, the project suggests many complex and syncretic layerings which informed Le Corbusier's approach to the spiritual. Le Corbusier's preoccupation with the feminine has also become a major theme in his work: historians have drawn connections not only with his interest in Mary Magdalene at Sainte-Baume but also with Mary the Mother of God at Ronchamp. They have also discussed the influence of Le Corbusier's own mother, Marie Charlotte Amélie Jeanneret-Perret, and that of his wife Yvonne. The chapel at Ronchamp, for instance, includes the fuchsia-coloured glass in praise of 'Marie'. Le Corbusier's attention to women in his church architecture is, as some recent historians have discussed, part of his overall achievement and one of the main lessons to be learnt from Le Corbusier's churches.

Eschewing the readings given in various tendentious accounts of Ronchamp by British historians of Le Corbusier's religious buildings, including such critics as Nikolaus Pevsner, James Stirling, Peter Hammond and Peter Smithson, more recent accounts have made much of the chapel's enduring complexity: they have emphasized the play between light and dark; the tension between rationality and irrationality; the split between the spiritual and economic forces of human life; and the contrast of the sacred and the profane – what Kenneth Frampton has called the influence of 'Albigensian dualism'. Ronchamp thereby serves to call attention to the interpretive implications of Le Corbusier's enigmatic statement, 'I often live [the miracle] of ineffable space, the consummation of plastic emotion.'

Architecture as pure creation of the spirit: Le Corbusier and Valéry

Like Perret, Le Corbusier was an avid reader of Valéry's writings. Copies of *Eupalinos* and other texts were in his library, and he made copious notes in them in the margins. About Valéry, Le Corbusier once remarked, 'he felt and beautifully translated the same deep and rare things an architect feels when creating'.[30] As the German historian and journalist Niklas Maak has made evident, the chapter from *Vers une Architecture*, entitled 'Architecture, pure création de l'esprit', especially reveals the influence Le Corbusier drew from the writings of Valéry.³¹ In addition, Maak notes that during the late 1940s, while developing his modulor theory of design and writing *Le Poème de l'angle droit*, Le Corbusier consulted Valéry's 'Une Vue de Descartes', 'Mémoires d'un poème', 'Pieces sur l'art' and 'L'Homme et la coquille'.³²

Most significantly, Le Corbusier's concept of ineffable space exhibits distinct Valérian overtones. Valéry's conception of the creative process focused upon the ways in which all human constructions are the product of the rational application of human thinking to the organization and arrangement of materials. The artistic significance of a work is entirely related to the way in which this artistic intent is realized within it – a *poeisis* of creative activity.³³ Le Corbusier's description of the experience of the ineffable is based in just this kind of rational *poeisis*: it is, as we have seen, the climactic perfection of the 'action of the work' of the creator, producing a 'phenomenon of concordance' that leads into a fourth dimension of space. So when he described 'an aesthetic, a work of art' as 'first of all systems' (including the sacred), Le Corbusier was alluding to Valéry's constructional concept of the creative process.

And it is here that we discover the connecting link between Le Corbusier's development of the functional basis of architecture for which he is best known, with the more mystical explorations in his sacred works which at first seem so divergent: both ultimately rely upon a rational application of the mind to the perfection of space in order to create the intended effect, albeit with differentiated intentions. So as Vincent Scully noted, Le Corbusier always expressed 'that special aura, and this may be one reason why the followers of Le Corbusier have normally been so fanatic, perhaps because the sense of sacredness is somehow always in his work, early and late'.³⁴ In the case of Ronchamp, the inspiration comes from the contemplation of biological forms, echoing Socrates' description to Phaedrus in *Eupalinos* of his arresting discovery on the beach of 'one of those objects released by the sea, a white object, of untainted whiteness', which stopped all the rest of his thoughts as he pondered by whom it had been made.³⁵ As Maak describes it, the design of the chapel of Ronchamp offered a formal model for architecture to engage with this type of biological form, recalling the open, fragmented shapes of Le Corbusier's own 'objets à reaction poétique', and in his application of a particular spatial thinking which is grounded in found objects.

Moreover, at Ronchamp Le Corbusier derived inspiration from the classic temple as a sacred building type, and specifically its relationship to the sacredness of nature and the landscape. As is often discussed by historians, the chapel is an echo of the Greek temple, with its sense of the building as a physical embodiment of the sacred. The Ronchamp chapel returned Le Corbusier to his early life experience of the drama of the Athenian Acropolis, and especially the strength of the Parthenon as its plan leads towards the topographical panoramas and horizons of its setting. These effects are echoed at Ronchamp – which in Valérian terms becomes what Le Corbusier himself said in reference to the Parthenon, that it is a 'machine for stirring emotions'.³⁶ This intentionally evocative language has in turn led to a wide array of later modernist and contemporary sacred buildings that extend Le Corbusier's idea of the ineffable, including Richard Meier's Jubilee Church in Rome (2003); the Chapel of St. Ignatius by Steven Holl in Seattle (1997); Álvaro Siza's Church of Santa

Maria, Porto (1996); and several concrete churches by Tadao Ando such as the chapel on Mount Rokko, Kobe, the Church on the Water, Hokkaido, and the Church of Light, Osaka, all built between 1985 and 1989.[37] An especially tight parallel may also be drawn between Le Corbusier and the American architect Paul Rudolph: Rudolph's powerful design for the university chapel in Tuskegee, Alabama (1960–9), is in many ways a homage to Le Corbusier and even an explicit reworking of his experimental design and appeal to acoustical form in the chapel at Ronchamp.[38]

Conclusion

Perret's Notre Dame du Raincy and Le Corbusier's Notre-Dame du Haut both represent a personal built manifesto. Yet each of these buildings demonstrates as well a series of ideas which expanded beyond their immediate geography and present circumstances – leading towards a diaspora of the sacred architectural language which they each developed. In the case of Perret, Notre Dame du Raincy was a building that inspired architects interested in sacred form as an expression of material economy realized through concrete construction, as well as the incorporation of the tectonic skeletal frame in what Kenneth Frampton called the 'asperities of the Greco-Gothic'.[39] In the case of Le Corbusier, the inspiration for sacred form was derived from the ideal of ineffability, whereby the sacred is not so much represented as evoked. Whereas for Perret sacred form was rooted in the idea of a distilled understanding of the 'sovereign shelter', which inevitably meant a setting of limits on the role of the architect, for Le Corbusier sacred form led more to the absorption of historical precedent, and grappling with a series of oppositions: light and dark, sacred and profane, the void and the volume. Yet both share in common the intense rationality they each drew from Valéry. From these strategies for sacred form radiated a distinct set of philosophical presumptions which have gone on to inspire a 'diaspora' of sacred language around the globe.

Notes

1. Vincent Scully, 'The Earth, the Temple, and Today', in *Constructing the Ineffable: Contemporary Sacred Architecture*, ed. Karla Britton (New Haven: Yale School of Architecture, 2010), 27.
2. See Karla Britton and Kyle Dugdale, 'Theoretical A/gnosticisms: Paul Tillich, Colin Rowe, and the Theology of Architecture', in *Routes of Knowledge: Journeys and Vehicles of Architectural Theory*, ed. Elke Couchez, Rajesh Heynickx and Ricardo Agarez (Bloomsbury Press, forthcoming).
3. 'Auguste Perret's Notre Dame du Raincy', in *The Cambridge History of Religious Architecture of the World*, ed. Richard Etlin (Cambridge: Cambridge University Press, forthcoming).
4. The relationship of Perret and Valéry was a theme of Britton's monograph, *Auguste Perret* (London: Phaidon, 2001; French edition 2003), especially Chapter 4: 'The Poetic Syntax of Space'.

5. Simon Texier, 'Églises', in Jean-Louis Cohen, et al., *Encyclopédie Perret* (Paris: Monum, 2002), 139–44.
6. Auguste Perret, *Contribution à une théorie de l'architecture* (Paris: Cercle d'études architecturales, 1952), n.p.
7. Jean-Pierre Cêtre and Franz Graf, 'Les hangars: un type pleinement ouvert à l'expérimentation technique', in Jean-Louis Cohen, *Encyclopédie Perret*, 96.
8. Muriel Harris, 'Concrete Takes a New Form in a French Church', *New York Times Magazine*, 18 April 1926.
9. Ferdinand Pfammatter, *Betonkirchen* (Zurich: Benziger Verlag, 1948), 38.
10. Peter Hammond, *Liturgy and Architecture* (New York: Columbia University Press, 1961), 54.
11. Jean-Louis Cohen, *The Future of Architecture Since 1889* (London: Phaidon, 2016).
12. Paul Valéry, 'Eupalinos, or the Architect', in *Dialogues*, Volume 4 of *Collected Works*, ed. Jackson Matthews (Princeton: Princeton University Press, 1962). Originally published as 'Eupalinos, ou l'Architecte', in *Architectures*, ed. Louis Süe and André Mare (Paris, 1921).
13. T. S. Eliot, 'Introduction to Paul Valéry', in *The Art of Poetry*, trans. Denise Folliot (Princeton: Princeton University Press, 1958), xiv.
14. Valéry, 'Introduction to the Method of Leonardo da Vinci', in *Collected Works of Paul Valéry*, ed. and trans. Malcom Cowley and James R. Lawler (Princeton: Princeton University Press, 2015). Originally published as 'Introduction à la méthode de Léonard da Vinci' (Paris, 1894).
15. See especially Perret's *Contribution*.
16. For a fuller discussion, see 'Introduction: Perret's Role', in Britton, *Auguste Perret*.
17. Marie Dormoy, *Souvenirs et portraits d'amis* (Paris: Mercure de France, 1963), 98.
18. Ibid.
19. Perret, *Contribution*, n.p.
20. Ibid.
21. Valéry, 'Eupalinos', 105.
22. Perret's papers are housed at the Archives d'Architecture du XXe Siècle, part of the Institut Français d'Architecture in Paris.
23. Jean Hytier, *The Poetics of Paul Valéry*, trans. Richard Howard (New York: Doubleday, 1952), 71–2.
24. Paul Valéry, *Amphion: Mélodrame* (Paris: Lerolle, 1931).
25. William J. Curtis, *Le Corbusier: Ideas and Forms* (London: Phaidon, 1986), 179.
26. See Roberto Gargiani and Anna Rossellini, *Le Corbusier: Béton Brut and Ineffable Space, 1940-1965: Surface Materials and Psychophysiology of Vision* (London: Routledge, 2011).
27. Abraham Joshua Heschel, *Man Is not Alone: A Philosophy of Religion* (New York: Farrar, Straus & Giroux, 1951), 16.
28. Gilles Ragot, 'Cette église elle existe. La construction de l'église Saint-Pierre de Firminy 1958-2006', in *Firminy, Le Corbusier en heritage* (St. Etienne: Publications de l'université de Saint-Etienne, 2008), 75, n. 2. Cited in Flora Samuel and Inge Lindner-Gaillard, *Sacred Concrete: The Churches of Le Corbusier* (Basel: Bikhaüser, 2013), 180.
29. See Samuel and Lindner-Gaillard, *Sacred Concrete*.

30. Quotation cited in the paper by Barbara Scapolo, '"Eupalinos o l'architetto," o del fare consistente', in *Paul Valéry Eupalinos o l'architetto* (Milano-Udine: Mimesis Edizioni, 2011), 89–117. See A. Mozzato, 'Le Corbusier and the "Lection of the *gondola*"', a paper given at Le Corbusier, 50 Years Later, Universitat Politècnica de València, 18–20 November 2015, n. 26, http://ocs.editorial.upv.es/index.php/LC2015/LC2015/paper/viewFile/794/1300.
31. Niklas Maak, *Le Corbusier: The Architect on the Beach* (Munich: Hirmer, 2011). Maak offers an extensive discussion of the Valérian themes in Le Corbusier in Chapter 5: 'Le Corbusier and Paul Valéry'.
32. Maak, *Le Corbusier*, 133.
33. Mozzato, 'Le Corbusier and the "Lection of the *gondola*"', 7.
34. Scully, 'The Earth, the Temple, and Today', 42.
35. Valéry, 'Eupalinos', 112.
36. Jean-Louis Cohen, 'Introduction to Le Corbusier', in *Toward an Architecture*, trans. John Goodman (Los Angeles: Getty Research Institute, 2007), 22.
37. Samuel and Lindner-Gaillard, 'The Legacy of Le Corbusier's Churches', in *Sacred Concrete*. For a discussion of many of these buildings, see Britton, *Constructing the Ineffable*.
38. See Karla Britton and Daniel Ledford, 'Paul Rudolph and the Psychology of Space: The Tuskegee and Emory University Chapels', *Journal of the Society of Architectural Historians*, 78, no. 3 (September 2019), 327–46.
39. Kenneth Frampton, *Studies in Tectonic Culture: The Poetics of Construction in Nineteenth and Twentieth Century Architecture* (Cambridge, MA: MIT Press, 2001), 133.

CHAPTER 9
STRUCTURE FOR SPIRIT IN *THE ARCHITECTURAL REVIEW* AND *THE ARCHITECTS' JOURNAL*, 1945–70
Sam Samarghandi

Writing for *The Architects' Journal* in 1957, an anonymous author asked rhetorically: 'What should a church look like? Well, it should be massive and heavy and anchored firmly to the earth – as if God Himself had hurled it, like a thunderbolt, into position. Or, of course, it could be light, elegant and inviting – a building of its time.'[1] This quip encapsulates a familiar contraposition that has typified popular and scholarly discourse on church architecture and its difficult relationship with the Modern Movement during the second half of the twentieth century. It is a narrative that is often characterized by a simplistic duality between the authority of traditionalism as the model for religious architecture on the one hand (supported by historical and political institutionalism) and technological and social reformation that propelled architectural modernism in the early part of the twentieth century on the other. This chapter will commence with an examination of the problem of church building through what was written about it in architectural discourse, with the intent of moving beyond the simple duality in order to explore the rediscovery of the modern spirit in the churches that emerged by late 1960s. This discussion will centre on two British professional journals – *The Architectural Review* and *The Architects' Journal*[2] – that played a central role in both shaping and reflecting the course of architectural modernism in Britain. Particularly the period between 1945 and 1970 witnessed a significant cultural and intellectual transformation that correlated with reformulations in the design of places for worship. My contention is that critical examination of architectural writing from this period has the capacity to both inform contemporary understandings of religious buildings and help reconfigure inherited historical conceptions, which are often problematic.

Introduction: Primacy of the machine and the functionalist canon

To frame a discussion around twentieth-century churches that might conveniently be described as *modern* is to presume a stable historiography of Modernism. As Cornelius Castroriadis writes, this is a fraught proposition – as 'it is hardly necessary to remind ourselves of the schematic character of all periodisations, at the risk of neglecting continuities and connections'.[3] Nonetheless, conceptions of Modernism in the twentieth century were closely connected to the pervasive notion of the *machine-age*[4] and the art historical theory of Zeitgeist.[5] Both these terms remained synonymous with Modernism well into the post-war period. Most of the influential accounts of modern architecture written in the 1930s, such as Henry-Russell Hitchcock's *The International Style: Architecture since 1922* (1932) and Nikolaus Pevsner's *Pioneers of Modern Architecture* (1936), were very selective, including only buildings that most closely aligned with each authors' own conception of the trajectory of the 'Modern Movement', accompanied by carefully curated photographs.[6] Common among these early 'histories' were representations of the triumphs of the industrial age, as embodied in buildings such as railway terminals and exhibition halls, or illustrated in manifestoes from the *Congrès internationaux d'architecture Moderne* (CIAM) and the Italian futurists. The potent metaphor of the machine appealed to historians and architects beyond the avant-garde, encompassing, as Sigfried Giedion asserted, a 'desire for universality'.[7] Together with the affordance for leading architects to disseminate ideas through the publication of their own texts and images, the so-called spirit of the machine as a trope of twentieth-century Modernism was reinforced.[8] As an emblem, the machines encapsulated many qualities that resonated with attempts to propel both industry and art. The notion of *technology* as such, which enabled industrialized production, and *functionalism*, which gave it direction, were fundamental. The former was scrutinized by historians of the nineteenth century who were preoccupied with the social and cultural repercussions of increasingly mechanized and urbanized labour.[9] Industrial manufacturing and construction techniques and the adoption of steel, concrete and glass in the building industry also challenged the academic tradition in architecture. The machine became emblematic for that which was modern, and crystallized the narrative underpinning a new doctrine of architecture. Religious architecture, which relied on very different terms of reference, naturally diminished.

An examination of the role that some of the more significant professional journals played in shaping the narrative of Modernism and promulgating its tents reveals the milieu in which architects and critics were engaging with religious architecture. These popular journals played a key role in disseminating the views of many important writers on architecture during the early twentieth century. Andrew Higgott has discussed the influence that these publications had within the British discourse during the formative years of Modernism.[10] The *Architectural Review*, which was published during the 1930s under the editorial lead of its figurehead, J. M. Richards, had far-reaching impact. It informed a generation of architects who, in-turn, 'accepted the existence of modernism as a given'.[11] Higgott goes on to point out that the editorial focus, particularly under Richards, was often guided by unequivocal social imperatives – conscious of the European political currents of Modernism. This was in contrast to other prominent publications, for instance, the less politicized 'International Style' Modernism of Henry Russel Hitchcock and Philip Johnson, which found favour in the United States.

Issuing from the compulsion of Victorian-era industrial innovation, the functionalist idiom emerged as the core maxim of early modernist historiography in Britain. The notion of functionalism admitted greater weight to the moral and social dimension expressed in new architectural forms. Rosemarie Haag Bletter has discussed three facets within the work of the German art and architecture historian Adolf Behne that were significant in Europe and Britain during the 1930s and 1940s, by way of Pevsner and Giedion.[12] The potency of technical progress evident through the machine, together with the sense of gradual evolution and maturation that suggested the organic began as a pre-twentieth-century inkling and through the rhetoric of functionalism became the dominant ethos of early Modernism.[13] Haag Bletter gives the example of Horatio Greenough, who in 1855 alluded to this when observing that

> if we compare the form of a newly invented machine with the perfected type of the same instrument, we observe, as we trace it through phases of improvement, how weight is shaken off where strength is less needed, how functions are made to approach without impeding each other, how straight becomes curved and curved is straightened, till the straggling and cumbersome machine becomes the compact, effective and beautiful engine.

Echoing Higgott, Haag Bletter points out that the third dimension, that of the social, was subdued in the Anglo-American conception. By 1945, the language of rational functionalism was deeply pervasive in the British architectural media. Richards' editorial vision was strongly guided by an ideology that upheld the 'virtues of machines'.[14] In search of a seductive metaphor, early critics and writers looked to the conditions of life where the machine embodied the achievements of the industrial age and the functionalist ethos represented a modern spirit. Subsequent contributors to *The Architectural Review*, such as Reyner Banham, went on to question the distortion of Victorian-era functionalism that, to a large degree, denied artistic or historic impulses. Within two decades of Richards' affirmation of the new spirit, John Voelcker wrote in *The Architects' Journal*:

> Today, when one is searching desperately for some sense of continuity and hoping for development and not destruction, some knowledge of our position in time, as well as in space, is essential . . . It probably seemed unimportant 25 years ago, in so far as the polemical desire of architects was to break free from the past: architectural history has become an impediment for those who were seeking the new architecture and a sanctuary for those who were not.[15]

Sentiments such as these provide a glimpse into the way that Modernism was being reshaped within popular media after 1945. Whether or not these writings opened the way for a reimagined spiritual dimension in religious architecture remains largely unaddressed. However, close investigation of *The Architectural Review* and *The Architects' Journal* suggest that the gradual dogmatizing of functionalism blinkered critics from considering the role of religious art and architecture in the immediate post-war years.

Post-war Modernism in Britain

Modernism in British architecture in the immediate post-war period 'was no longer an avant-garde movement but part of the mainstream of architectural culture'.[16] I propose that the year 1957 was a pivotal moment in regard to re-engagement with modern church building in Britain following a period of conspicuous absence.

Modern Architecture and the Sacred

In the years leading up to 1957, a number of new and reconfigured churches were discussed in *The Architectural Review* and *The Architects' Journal*, albeit to a very limited extent. These writings were either brief news pieces or short illustrated articles that lacked critical analysis.[17] Several years of post-war reconstruction and rationing had diverted attention from non-essential building works, including significant new churches.[18] Of those new churches that were realized – usually either in Germany or in France – only a small number that were built in the modern style were made known to British audiences in the pages of *The Architectural Review* and *The Architects' Journal*.[19] The annual 'Buildings of the Year' feature of *The Architects' Journal* included a sole religious building between the years 1945 and 1955. This was the church hall in Stevenage, praised for its 'charming'[20] use of the traditional smooth-faced flint on its façade. It is likely that it was only selected owing to its siting within one of the 'New-Town' projects that were completed under the celebrated New Towns Act of 1946. A 1956 retrospective exhibition titled *Ten Years of British Architecture: '45 to '55*, hosted by the Royal Institute of British Architects (RIBA), did not feature one single church.[21] Rather, the exhibition showcased large-scale housing projects and school, for example, Peter and Alison Smithson's Hunstanton school that had attracted a review in *The Architectural Review* by Philip Johnson.[22] The Roehampton Estate, which Pevsner had described as a grouping of good 'rationalist' buildings with an 'up-to-date sanity' in the English tradition, was also included.[23] The pre-eminence of these building typologies of projects in the journals coincided with the occlusion of churches. It registered the progression of Modernism in Britain by the mid-1950s, particularly in the field of public works (Figure 9.1).

Figure 9.1 C. Holliday and L. G. Vincent, *Church at Stevenage*. Published in 'Church Hall at Stevenage', *The Architectural Review* 115 (1954), 231.

In order to characterize the period leading up to 1957, it is apposite to describe a subgroup of journal writings that dealt with churches primarily as the subject of historical interest, and that often concerned themselves with the question of the most suitable manner of rehabilitating churches that had been damaged in the war. Alongside this central question there were other concerns, such as technical analyses of the building's function – preoccupied with construction issues, operational matters and cost. Although this discourse might well be symptomatic of the conditions in British culture more generally at the time more generally,[24] the outcome of circumstances in which the development of religious architecture was overlooked would have ramifications on the discourse in the years to follow.

The new cathedral projects

In spite of the limited coverage of small-scale religious buildings in *The Architectural Review* and *The Architects' Journal*, two large-scale projects were more thoroughly discussed, prompted by widespread public and professional interest during the 1950s – the Anglican Cathedral at Coventry and the Roman Catholic Cathedral at Liverpool. Both of them were procured by way of design competition, attracting many entries from across Britain. The competition to replace the seat of the fourteenth-century Gothic Saint Michael's at Coventry, which had stood in a state of ruination since wartime bombing, was announced in 1950. Large areas of the city had been devastated, inspiring many to call for the creation of 'a new city – a modern city'.[25] The extent of the level of enthusiasm to construct a new urban metropolis, emboldened by the prospect of progressive modernist buildings is attested to by the extent of coverage across the media, including architectural magazines. An editorial in *The Architectural Review* exclaimed that the new cathedral might 'be the first great church of the twentieth century to owe no allegiance to any earlier age, a fitting symbol of the faith and aspirations of the people of Coventry'.[26] A decade later at Liverpool, the terms of the architectural competition were also framed by the practical economies of modern architecture.[27] Frederick Gibberd's winning scheme promised to be realized for a mere £1 million, whereas the vast classical edifice originally planned for the site was forecast to exceed £27 million. Perhaps as a consequence of their protracted realization over a period of fifteen years, along with an incipient discourse on modern worship space in the preceding years, both projects failed to live up to their promise.

The following is an examination of the question of whether the critique, therefore, may have inadvertently reinforced the belief that the conception of a church building involved an inherent challenge to Modernism, despite some calls to maturate the discourse and catalyse new forms. At the time of the announcement of Basil Spence as winner of the Coventry Cathedral competition, willingness to accept Modernism in Britain was readily apparent within the profession. Britain had hosted two CIAM conferences following the war – 1947 at Bridgewater and 1951 at Hoddesdon – led by the British subsidiary of CIAM, the Modern Architecture Research Group (MARS). The purported benefits of modern architecture, particularly in respect to town planning, were indispensable to the public authorities, including the London County Council and the New Towns Commission. Both authorities were given the remit of providing high-density housing. Coinciding with sponsorship by government and planning departments, prominent critics had established a discourse that validated modern architecture. Recent scholarship has begun to argue that this was evinced by a campaign disseminated largely through journals that traced the roots of Modernism to premodern English traditions – displacing the narrative of continental avant-gardism (Figure 9.2).[28]

Figure 9.2 Coventry cathedral interior perspective during design development, from Basil Spence, *Phoenix at Coventry*.
Source: London: Butler & Tanner Ltd Frome, 1962.

The Architectural Review and *The Architects' Journal* played an active role through their editorial position and by way of sponsorships, including the much anticipated 1951 Festival of Britain.[29] The festival was promoted as an opportunity to showcase the progress of the home nations through an exhibition of 'live' permanent buildings at the Lansbury Estate (a series of temporary structures were erected on the South Bank exhibition ground). The themes of *genius loci* and the *picturesque* dominated the exhibition – particularly at Lansbury Estate. For some commentators, including Richards and Pevsner, Frederick Gibberd's Market Square and town centre were appropriately modern, having been designed 'in the contemporary idiom' – reassuringly in keeping with 'the principles of the picturesque'.[30] To others, including the young Banham, conceptions of Modernism associated with nostalgic English traditions were ill-founded.[31] Two churches that were built within the estate serve to reveal two differing approaches common among church building, within and beyond the festival. Trinity Congregational Church is composed in an architectural language of unconventional structural forms and modern materials, whereas the St Mary and Joseph Roman Catholic Church is a collection of eclectic historicism – contrary to the stated objectives of the festival.[32] Both churches experimented with new forms of liturgical arrangements in their seating layout within their *nave* and *cruciform* driven spatial disposition. The coverage of these two particular buildings in *The Architectural Review* and *The Architects' Journal* was sparing, despite widespread coverage of the 1951 festival itself. One *Building Illustrated* feature was published in *The Architects' Journal*, centring on the technical aspects of the Trinity church – its assembly, heating, lighting and so forth. A brief assessment of its merits as a place of worship is fleeting and simplistic, noting only that it offers a 'setting of quiet dignity',[33] free from the hindrances of traditional liturgy afforded by a building brief that was 'Non-Conformist' (Methodist). Richards' assessment in *The Architectural Review* mentions the 'difficult stylistic problem',[34] of church building. He assigns the root of the problem to the need to create an appropriate religious setting without reverting to the traditional forms of expression that the worshipping public would expect. The deficiencies of this over-complex design were 'presumably' due to this challenge, according to Richards. St Mary and Joseph was in fact completed shortly after the festival but was not published or reviewed in *The Architectural Review* or *The Architects' Journal*, despite the prominence of the architect – Adrian Gilbert Scott – or the publicity generated by the festival. A 1975 retrospective of the festival in *The Architectural Review* once again raised their failing as discreet buildings and as architecture worthy of the exhibition programme.[35] The festival signified the inclination of *The Architectural Review* and *The Architects' Journal* to continue to instil the modernist ideal, despite few noteworthy modern churches and hesitant critique (Figure 9.3).

While the 1951 festival agenda relegated the parish churches to the sidelines, two cathedral projects completed around a decade later ultimately forced critics to confront the problem of church building head-on. Despite general agreement that Coventry Cathedral skilfully balanced the requirements of the competition brief

Figure 9.3 Cecil D. Handisyde and D. Rogers Stark, Trinity Congregational Church, Lansbury (1951).
Source: Architectural Press Archive / RIBA Collections.

(preferencing a gothic outcome) without resorting to overt historicism, Spence's design had faced challenges from the outset.[36] Following its completion in 1962, the building exemplified to critics the profound problem with modern religious architecture and provided the necessary platform from which to challenge it. Richard's 1952 critique of the winning scheme set forth with a forewarning of the familiar 'dilemma'[37] facing anyone attempting the design of a cathedral in a secular age. By the time Coventry Cathedral was completed in 1962, a review in *The Architects' Journal* called the modern context for designing a cathedral a 'rather desperate setting',[38] and reiterated a call to find an architecture that could truly encapsulate the 'change over in our society to scientific method'.[39] Richards' account was pessimistic – suggesting that society lacked the collective imagination centred on the cathedral that had once permitted medieval cathedral buildings to be realized with a unified character and natural order.[40] This was echoed in a 1962 review in *The Architectural Review* in which R. Furneax Jordan proclaimed that 'to build a cathedral is to challenge a thousand years of history. It is, also, inevitably to fail.'[41]

Nevertheless, the younger generation of commentators and historians did not dissociate the church commission from the sphere of modern architecture. Banham's critique brought attention to the argument for an authentic expression of architecture to parallel developments in liturgical practice, and refuted what many regarded as a retrograde *picturesque* compulsion within *The Architectural Review*. Despite this, his assessment of Coventry was unsparingly negative:

> There can be little doubt that Coventry Cathedral is the worst set-back to English church architecture in a very long time. Its influence, unless sternly resisted, can only be confusing and diversionary . . . church architecture is part of the mainstream of the Modern Movement, not a picturesque backwater.[42]

This assessment was compelling, not so much for its originality as for having given a platform to the marginalized discourse on modern church design that was previously only the domain of less prominent historians, progressive theologians and professional church-architects. Banham was unambiguous in pointing out the two intellectual factors underlying Coventry's failure. First, the 'betrayal and abandonment' of post-war British historians and theorists to progress the modernist maxims established by the earlier generation – including Pevsner, Richards and others at *The Architectural Review*. Secondly, that the intervening years between the competition and completion of Coventry Cathedral marked a critical juncture between *pre-war* and *post-war* Modernism.[43] The clearest alternative to Spence's polite modern cathedral – Spence himself called it 'a quiet design in the English tradition'[44] – was that of the Smithsons. In stark contrast to the winning scheme and other commended entries to the competition, their scheme was a rationalist expression uncompromised by the hindrances of traditional church forms. Banham recognized the prominence of Coventry Cathedral as an icon of nation rebuilding and seized upon the symbolic resonance of a twentieth-century cathedral project to bring to light division in the ranks of *The Architectural Review* and *The Architects' Journal*. This would play out during the 1960s and early 1970s, mirroring shifting attitudes to Modernism more broadly – leading the way for closer consideration of churches (Figure 9.4).

The competition for the Christ the King Cathedral at Liverpool may well have been the opportunity for reform, however, its construction was well underway by 1962. The range of competition entries was distinct from those of Coventry. Recurring themes were centralized planning – some placing the altar with bi-axial precision within a circular plan; exaggerated structural design; and tent-inspired forms. Gibberd's winning design, coincidentally judged by a panel including Spence, was realized in only five years. It would appear that the assessors were drawn to its pragmatic qualities,[45] the legible symbolism of its feature 'crown', and were sufficiently convinced of the implementation of liturgically up-to-date centralized planning. Nevertheless, Nicholas Taylor's critique in *The Architectural Review* seems to suggest that Liverpool achieved specifically what Richards had argued seven years earlier would be folly. Richards claimed that Modernism's vocabulary was ill-equipped to convey via emotional response 'the religious idea'.[46] Taylor, perhaps unwittingly, praised Liverpool as the worthy symbol of the city for its civic gesture, its iconic potency and its counter-play with the Liverpool Anglican Cathedral – Giles Gilbert Scott's neo-gothic 'pile'. According to Taylor, 'the architect has

Figure 9.4 Peter and Alison Smithson, *Coventry Cathedral competition entry* (1952), model. Source: RIBA Library Drawings and Archives Collections.

transmitted high emotional frequencies, not by introspective subtlety but by putting what can only be called architectural clichés in an uncannily right relationship with their site and with their surroundings.'[47]

As Robert Proctor wrote in 'Building the Modern Church', Liverpool Cathedral prominently marked a 'turning point'[48] in the conception of Roman Catholic churches in Britain. The principal achievement at Liverpool seems to have been a willingness on the part of the competition committee to adopt a conspicuously modern form for the creation of an *iconic* cathedral, rather than as a vehicle for intellectual consideration of the setting for worship.[49] Despite the significance of this pronouncement of the modern language of architecture, it was through smaller parish churches that architects and historians were now able to reimagine sacred space with greater nuance (Figures 9.5 and 9.6).

Rediscovery 1957–

> It can hardly be too strongly emphasised that the fundamental problem is not one of style, of finding a 'contemporary idiom'. It is rather a matter of rethinking afresh the whole question of what a church is for . . . a vague religiousness can never be more than a very imperfect substitute for an informed understanding of the essential function of a church.[50]
>
> Peter Hammond, 'A Liturgical Brief', The Architectural Review, *1958*

Figure 9.5 Frederick Gibberd, Liverpool Cathedral.
Source: Architectural Press Archive / RIBA Collections.

Figure 9.6 Selection of commended entries in the Liverpool Cathedral competition.
Source: The Architects' Journal 132 (1960): 319–33.

Peter Hammond's books *Liturgy and Architecture* (1960)[51] and *Towards a Church Architecture* (1962)[52] came to be known as the treatises that galvanized the development of the discourse of religious architecture in Britain during the 1960s.[53] In early 1958, *The Architectural Review* had published a lengthy essay by Hammond that introduced the case for a new understanding of the function of churches based on renewed liturgical paradigm that gave primacy to the closeness of clergy and laity in the celebration of the Eucharist. These developments were pre-empted by theological reformation in Germany and France and were subsequently enacted by the Catholic Church as part of the constitution of the Second Vatican Council[54]. Coinciding with these developments was increased collaboration between architects and church leadership – resulting in the formation of associations promoting progressive church design. The New Church Research Group (NCRG), led by Hammond and other regular contributors to *The Architectural Review,* was foremost among these. The group was founded in 1957, a year coinciding with a number of milestones in the evolution of British Modernism including the disbanding of the MARS and the Establishment of the Victorian Society. The organization held conferences on church design, visited new buildings throughout Britain and abroad, and produced publications to assist architects and clergy to develop a mutual understanding of the liturgy, and its role in shaping church design. Ten years after its founding the group produced a series of thirty-six briefing guides, technical studies and information sheets which were published by *The Architects' Journal* as a supplement. By this stage, interest in church design was evident in the increasing numbers of local churches selected for publication in the journal. The text accompanying the churches began to assume part of the general body of architecture – subject to the theoretical and stylistic transformations of the age, rather than a marginalized subset. Alongside the British examples were European and American churches where a great multitude of possibilities were to be found.[55]

The Anglican parish church of St Paul at Bow Common London was acclaimed in an article published in *The Architectural Review* in 1960 as 'the first notable representative of liturgical planning in Britain'.[56] The article was prefaced by an editorial that was strongly supportive of the ideas of Hammond and the principles of the 'Liturgical Movement'. The movement, it summarized, promoted the convergence of a renewed functionalist understanding of the church brief that emanated from the same rationalist underpinnings that drove school or hospital design, and the symbolic imperative of an architecture to house the altar:

> The Liturgical Movement does not offer the architect forms, it sets him a double functional problem to be resolved in a single solution . . . The outcome is only architecture if the functional and symbolic are indissoluble.[57]

Robert Maguire, one of the principal members of the NCRG and architect of Bow Common with Keith Murray, later described the 'indissoluble' objective as the creation of a 'set-apart space as a need of the human psyche'.[58] The members of the NCRG and the Liturgical Movement, however, did not represent all aspects of the discourse on churches during this period. Maguire noted a profound disagreement between those who upheld the moral imperative of churches to create a place of sanctuary and those who developed new social agendas for church building, often accommodating a variety of functions in multipurpose spaces. Parish community centres and church halls were becoming prevalent. They emphasized the role of the church as a locus for social engagement within the urban environment. Despite differing perspectives, the rediscovery of an architecture that asserted the sacral qualities of the church began to be actively reaffirmed within the pages of *The Architectural Review* and *The Architects' Journal* during the late 1960s. In a time marked by considerable change within the culture of British architecture, churches offered an alternative mode of expression.

The most illuminating example of this turn is to be found in a polemical 1970 special edition of *The Architectural Review – Manplan 5: Religion*.[59] It is worth reflecting on the language of this edition insofar as it contrasts with the superficial dualities which defined much of the discourse in the preceding years. Through a catalogue of images illustrating the environmental disharmony of the cities and towns of Britain, *The Architectural Review* portrays a state of crisis. Lance Wright depicts 'an environment dominated by the machine' as a condition of 'the last phase' of Modern Architecture.[60] Wright urges the nation to 'turn to the medium of religion rather than the medium of science . . . the voice of religion leads us to pleasurable survival'. He goes on to assert that as a 'medium', religion offers 'the facts with which to live'.[61] It follows that churches – which elevate our humanity – profess the way in which to build. Similarly political and prophetic overtones characterized each of the eight *Manplan* editions.[62] It is clear that the authors of *Manplan* did not set out to romanticize the religious styles of past ages nor measure the contemporary churches against a rigid modernist ideology as some pioneering historians, including Banham, seemed to suggest.[63] Rather, the journal called for re-engagement with the visible signs of religiosity in society, turning naturally to the material tradition of the church. There is a marked difference of intent between *Manplan* and the texts addressing the Liturgical Movement, yet together they registered a shift towards a reappraisal of church building.

Over the course of the decades that followed, *The Architectural Review* and *The Architects' Journal* continued to publish 'rediscovered' British churches from the 1960s and 1970s, often pausing to reflect on their own omission as well as their formative role in the discourse. In one such article from the 1990s entitled 'Church Triumph', Alan Powers begins with a clear acknowledgement of the misplaced categorization of twentieth-century churches set apart from Modernism. It is revealing that an article featuring an unpublished religious building might choose to begin with a summary of developments in church architecture in Britain in the immediate post-war period, and conclude by reaffirming that the lessons to be found in the most successful religious buildings of that era continue to bear relevance on all forms of architecture in the present day (Figures 9.7 and 9.8).[64]

Modern Architecture and the Sacred

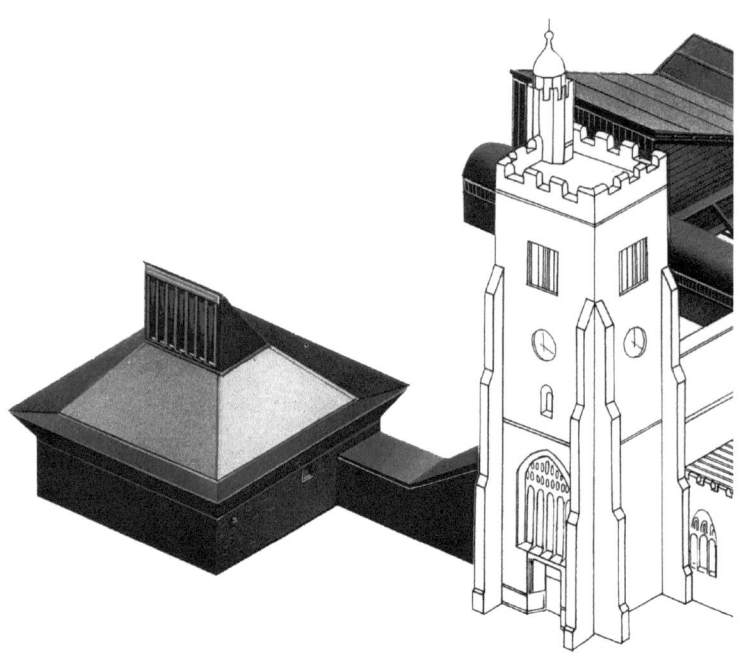

Figure 9.7 Illustration from special edition *MANPLAN 5: Religion*. Published in (Unattributed), 'Buildings for Cult', *The Architectural Review*, 147 (1970): 198.

Figure 9.8 Francis Pollen, *Church at Worth Abbey* (1964–75).
Photograph by Dennis Gilbert, in Alan Powers, 'Church Triumph', *The Architectural Review* 193 (1991): 30. Dennis Gilbert / VIEW Images.

Conclusion

In 1971, Richards retired after thirty-one years as editor of *The Architectural Review*, while Pevsner continued to redefine and republish histories in the tradition of his seminal *Pioneers of the Modern Movement*. As Modernism perpetuated and transfigured, the history of churches began to be situated within a broader discourse. Journals, as a vehicle for prominent voices speaking to a wide-ranging audience, played a significant role in framing religious architecture. The period 1945 to 1970, as seen through *The Architectural Review* and *The Architects' Journal,* reveals the extent to which the churches were overlooked, and subsequently remerged, in line with intellectual and cultural change in the discourse of architecture. The uncertain grasp of religion that characterizes the *Modern* identity explicit in early examples of the literature emanates from a functionalist rhetoric which struggled to articulate transcendent themes, whether they persisted or not. When played out through a persuasive agenda-driven media sphere such as was the case, the historiographic rift perpetuated was both significant and problematic. This rich period of church building was marginalized, if not excluded entirely, from the dominant architectural discourse. With much of this period of the built environment facing half a century of physical neglect, tracing the course of Modernism's shifting attitude to religion is pertinent to contemporary discussions of church design.

Notes

1. (Author unattributed), 'What Is Architecture, Daddy?' *The Architects Journal* 125 (1957): 688. The *Architectural Review*, and to a lesser extent *Architects' Journal*, often published articles and commentary without clear attribution of authorship, although its editors were well known. The publication details in this issue stated: 'To preserve freedom of criticism these editors, as leaders in their respective fields, remain anonymous.'
2. *The Architectural Review* was a monthly magazine published by the Architectural Press of London from 1896. *The Architects' Journal* was published weekly by the same publisher from 1919, with a focus on building industry news and technical resources. Providing both professional content and artistic critique, *The Architectural Review* gained prominence and became a leading platform for discussions by-and-for architects in Britain from the 1930s. Monthly circulation grew to approximately 11,500 by the early 1960s and this was sustained despite being briefly challenged in readership by *Architectural Design* in the early 1970s. Each issue comprised approximately seventy-five pages (not including advertisements). Typical content included photo-illustrated coverage of recent buildings, book reviews, correspondence and travel features. A selection of extended articles focused on issues of contemporary architectural thought were presented as a 'front-piece'. Internationally known architects and scholarly authors contributed alongside the editors and regular critics. As Steve Parnell recounts, the magazine's stated objective under long-serving editor Hubert de Cronin Hastings 'was to provide primarily "the raw material of architectural history" and secondly a "space for literary discussion of the visual arts."' Steve Parnell, 'AR's and AD's Post-war Editorial Policies: The Making of Modern Architecture in Britain', *The Journal of Architecture* 17 (2012): 763–75. Writing on the subject of J.M. Richards, a

prominent contributor and editor of *The Architectural Review* during the 1930s to 1970s, Jessica Kelly notes that it was 'part of the magazine's work to delineate what modernism in architecture was and promote it to their professional and layman readership. His work was part of a growing number of articles explaining and promoting architecture's relationship to the *Zeitgeist* or the "spirit of the age."' Jessica Kelly, 'Vulgar Modernism: J.M. Richards, Modernism and the Vernacular in British Architecture', *Architectural History* 58 (2015): 235. For discussion of the other key editorial staff see Jill Seddon, 'The Architect and the "Arch-Pedant": Sadie Speight, Nicolaus Pevsner and "Design Review,"' *Journal of Design History* 20 (2007): 29–41.

3. Castroriadis' discussion of modernity and the guidance for any attempt at periodization argues that, 'the individuality of a period is to be found in the specificity of the imaginary significations created by and dominating it.' Cornelius Castroriadis, 'The Retreat from Autonomy: Post-modernism as Generalised Conformism', *Democracy & Nature* 7 (2001): 17–26. The discourse of modernist architecture is arguably marked by the dominant imagery of *functionalism* and the *machine-age*.

4. See Chapter III, 'Architecture and Machinery', in J. M. Richards, *An Introduction to Modern Architecture* (Harmondsworth: Penguin, 1940), 30–44. For a point of view relevant to the period in question see Alan Colquhoun, 'The Modern Movement in Architecture', *British Journal of Aesthetics* 2 (1962): 59–65.

5. For a discussion of the philosophical motivations in Nikolaus Pevsner's 'Pioneers of the Modern Movement' (1936), see Colin Amery, 'Nikolaus Pevsner's "Pioneers of the Modern Movement," 1936', *The Burlington Magazine* 151 (2009): 617–19. Amery notes that 'Pevsner apparently wanted an end to individualism and independent artistic creativity; architecture had to conform to the *Zeitgeist* and to demonstrate rationality and unity within the social system', 618.

6. See Panayotis Tournikiotis, *The Historiography of Modern Architecture* (Cambridge, MA: MIT Press, 1999).

7. Sigfried Giedion, *Space, Time and Architecture* (Cambridge, MA: Harvard University Press, 1967), 8. The self-conscious character of the machine metaphor was compatible with the most influential texts of European Modernism, including those which were premised on an extended historical view, including *Space, Time and Architecture*.

8. An example of the impact of the machine metaphor can be found in Lionel Brett, *The Space Machine: An Evaluation of the Recent Work of Le Corbusier*, Brett writes: 'Le Corbusier's achievement lies not in any building but in his intuition of the power of the machine to enlarge the boundaries of human experience, and in his brilliant gift of communicating this intuition.' *Architectural Review* 102 (1947): 147–50.

9. One example which was influential in Britain was William Morris, 'Hopes and Fears', in *Hopes and Fears for Art* (Cambridge: University Press 1905), 169–217.

10. Andrew Higgott, *Mediating Modernism* (New York: Routledge, 2007).

11. Ibid., 39.

12. Rosemarie Haag Bletter, Introduction to *The Modern Functional Building* by Adolf Behne (Santa Monica: The Getty Research Institute, 1996), 183.

13. Horatio Greenough, 'American Architecture', *The Crayon* 2 (1855): 224–6.

14. J. M. Richards, 'Towards a Rational Aesthetic', *The Architectural Review* 78 (1935): 210–18.

15. John Voelcker, 'The Value of History to Students of Architecture', *The Architects' Journal* 129 (1959): 638.

16. Kelly, 'Vulgar Modernism: J.M. Richards, Modernism and the Vernacular in British Architecture', 246.
17. See, for instance, the coverage of the Church of Christ, The King and St. Peter by Lawrence Weston at Gloucestershire, which could foreseeably have attracted more thorough analysis had its programme been other than a church, in: (Author unattributed), 'Church', *The Architect's Journal* 112 (1950): 460-2.
18. See, for example, J. M Richards' introduction to the 1949 *Buildings of the Year* feature in which he states, 'It is still housing we chiefly think of when we consider present-day building activity, though schools and factories now come a good second.' The 1949 and 1950 lists comprise exclusively: housing, schools, transport and industrial buildings. J. M. Richards, 'Buildings of the Year: 1949', *The Architects' Journal* 111 (1950): 73.
19. See: (Author unattributed), 'Church in Nairobi, Kenya', *Architects' Journal* 118 (1953): 104–5, or (Author unattributed), 'Church at Dornach, near Basle', *The Architectural Review* 98 (1945): 43–4.
20. J. M. Richards, 'Buildings of the Year: 1954', *Architects' Journal* 121 (1955): 87–8.
21. The lack of church buildings was noted by historians who were supportive of church buildings forming part of the modernist discourse. Joseph Rykwert, for example, laments the state of church building at the time. He notes the categorical rejection of churches from the exhibition selection by the prominent curator-historian John Summerson, based on their exclusion of 'a programme capable of rational analysis.' Despite this, Rykwert goes on to discuss examples outside Britain that suggests a place for church building in the modernist paradigm.
    Joseph Rykwert, 'The Churches We Deserve?' *New Blackfriars* 37 (1956): 171–5.
22. Philip Johnson, 'School at Hunstanton', *The Architectural Review* 148 (1945): 152–3.
23. Nikolaus Pevsner, 'Roehampton: LCC Housing and the Picturesque Tradition', *The Architectural Review* 126 (1959): 21–35.
24. Jessica Kelly observed: 'The task of reconstructing British towns and cities after the war put architects at the centre of post-war British society and culture'. Kelly, 'Vulgar Modernism: J.M. Richards, Modernism and the Vernacular in British Architecture', 247.
25. (Author unattributed), 'Frontpiece: Coventry', *The Architectural Review* 108 (1950): 214.
26. Ibid.
27. Robert Proctor, *Building the Modern Church: Roman Catholic Church Architecture in Britain 1955 to 1975* (Farnham: Ashgate, 2014), 62.
28. For extensive discussion of this theme see William Whyte, 'The Englishness of English Architecture: Modernism and the Making of a National International Style: 1927-1957', *Journal of British Studies* 48 (2009): 441–65, and Michela Rosso, 'Between History, Criticism and Wit: Texts and Images of English Modern Architecture (1933-36)', *Journal of Art Historiography* 14 (2016): 1–22.
29. Harriet Atkinson, '"The First Modern townscape"? The Festival of Britain, Townscape and the Picturesque', in *Alternative Visions of Post-War Reconstruction: Creating the Modern Townscape*, ed. John Pendlebury et al. (Abingdon: Routledge), 82.
30. (Author unattributed), 'Special Issue on the South Bank Exhibition', *The Architectural Review* 110 (1951): 71.
31. For a recent extended examination see, John Macarthur, '"The revenge of the picturesque," Redux', *The Journal of Architecture* 17 (2012): 643–53.

32. Robert Proctor states that architect Adrian Gilbert Scott 'deliberately eschewed Lansbury's progressive modernism for an architecture that declared a conception of the parish church as a bastion of enduring values in a transient world.'
    Proctor, *Building the Modern Church*, 14.
33. (Author unattributed), 'A Symbol of Faith', *The Architects' Journal* 114 (1951): 274.
34. J. M. Richards, 'Old and New at Lansbury', *The Architectural Review* 110 (1951): 364.
35. (Author unattributed), 'Florid, Flash and Functional: 1950s', *The Architectural Review* 162 (1975): 231.
36. On Basil Spence' proposals, the editors of *The Architects' Journal* claimed that 'the architect has not attempted to express his Christian belief in any forms suggestive of the contemporary world. Rather, he has adjusted contemporary techniques to provide another, basically Gothic, conception of the form to be taken by a shrine to the glory of God.' See 'The editors', 'Twentieth Century Anachronism?', *The Architects' Journal* 115 (1951): 215–16.
37. J. M. Richards, 'Criticism: Coventry', *The Architectural Review* 111 (1952): 3.
38. (Author unattributed), 'Building Illustrated: Coventry Cathedral', *The Architects' Journal* 135 (1962): 1130.
39. Ibid.
40. 'The appreciation of architecture is no longer visual but literary – a matter of emotion being aroused by associations and by familiar symbols. We cannot therefore expect a building like a cathedral, whose role it is to create a particular atmosphere, to make successful use of an unfamiliar idiom, however much intrinsic beauty the architect puts into his design.' in Richards, 'Criticism: Coventry', 4.
41. R. Furneax Jordan, 'Criticism: Cathedral Church of St. Michael, Coventry', *The Architectural Review* 132 (1962): 25.
42. Reyner Banham, 'Coventry Cathedral – Strictly "Trad, Dad"', *Architectural Forum* 117 (1962): 118–19.
43. Ibid. Banham's assessment is revealing in that it suggests that the willingness of the architectural culture to accept a radically different scheme was imminent: 'If the Coventry competition had been postponed a mere ten years, the assessors would have been drawn from a different generation – a post-war gang instead of a pre-war gang- and the Smithsons would have won . . . In the context of the days of its conception – those unfortunate days that were neither pre-war nor post-war – Coventry was a perfectly sincere, heroic, though possibly doomed, attempt to set cathedral building for the first time in the modern era – the era of steel, concrete, austerity, mechanisation, universal agnosticism and post-war idealism.'
44. Basil Spence, *Phoenix at Coventry* (London: Butler & Tanner Ltd Frome, 1962), 35.
45. (Author unattributed), 'First Premiated Design by Frederick Gibberd: Assessors Report', *Architects' Journal* 132 (1960): 313. The assessors praised the design as one of 'logic and restraint.' The second-place design was judged as 'beautiful'.
46. Richards, 'Criticism: Coventry', 4.
47. Nicholas Taylor, 'Criticism: Metropolitan Cathedral, Liverpool', *The Architectural Review* 141 (1967): 437.
48. Proctor, *Building the Modern Church*, 56.
49. Thomas Markus reported in the *The Architects' Journal*: 'The central plan of the church was the almost inevitable outcome of the lead given in the Archbishop's brief to entrants in the competition, and listening to Gibberd, it was difficult to avoid the feeling that the good

qualities of his design were, liturgically, almost accidental, and not to wonder how well the building will work ... Much richness in thought and feeling may consequently be lost.' See Thomas Markus, 'Liturgical Conference – Church Worship and Its Setting', *The Architects' Journal* 136 (1962): 136.

50. Peter Hammond, 'A Liturgical Brief', *The Architectural Review* 423 (1958): 242.
51. Hammond, *Liturgy and Architecture* (New York: Columbia University Press, 1960).
52. Hammond, *Towards a Church Architecture* (London: The Architectural Press, 1962).
53. Mark A. Torgerson, ed., *An Architecture of Immanence* (Grand Rapids: WM. B. Eerdmans Publishing Co., 2007), 71.
54. Members of the Second Vatican Council convened between 1962 and 1965. A series of ecclesiastical directives were issued, the most unambiguous of which was the Constitution of the Sacred Liturgy in 1963. It sought to recodify the Catholic Church's official approach to church design and religious art in favour of increased participation in the liturgy. This led to a formal reordering of existing churches as well as a reconsideration of the physical relationships in the design of new spaces for worship. A liberated approach to artistic expression in religious representation and the shift towards vernacular language translated the architectural programme of the church, giving architects further impetus move away from tradition. A multitude of unfamiliar designs were realized in the years following, prompting renewed interest in the subject and leading to the publication of books such as G. E. Kidder Smith, *New Churches of Europe* (London: Architectural Press, 1964).
55. Some notable examples include: (Author unattributed), 'Church near Perugia', *The Architectural Review* 145 (1967): 221–3; and (Author unattributed), 'Pilgrim Church in the Rhineland: Church at Neviges, West Germany', *The Architectural Review* 145 (1969): 134–8.
56. (Author unattributed), 'Church at Bow Common – London', *The Architectural Review* 128 (1960): 400.
57. Ibid.
58. Robert Maguire, 'Church Design Since 1950', *Ecclesiology Today* 27 (2002): 2–14.
59. *The Architectural Review Manplan 5 Religion* 147 (1970): 169–230.
60. Lance Wright, 'Religion and Environment', *The Architectural Review* 147 (1970): 175–7.
61. Ibid., 229.
62. The 'Manplan' series was published as a series of eight special issues between September 1969 and September 1970. Their strongly worded text and images had a polemical tone, which was distinct from the typical format of the publication. Following the first issue, titled 'Frustration', the subjects covered in the following issues included transport, schools, health and welfare, local government and housing. See *The Architectural Review Manplan 1 Frustration* 146 (1969) - *The Architectural Review Manplan 8 Housing* 148 (1970).
63. See, for instance, Banham's 1960 article questioning attempts to critique Le Corbusier's Ronchamp chapel against a set of apparent modernist 'truisms': Banham, '1960: Stocktaking', *The Architectural Review* 127 (1960): 93–100.
64. 'Worth was a necessary confrontation of tradition and modernity in liturgy and architecture, integrating and reconciling apparently conflicting tendencies in a manner still relevant outside the specialist field of church building.' Alan Power, 'Church Triumph', *The Architects' Journal* 193 (1991): 30–7.

PART THREE
SEMI-SACRED SETTINGS IN THE CULTURAL TOPOGRAPHY OF MODERNITY

CHAPTER 10
REVELATORY EARTH
ADOLPHE APPIA AND THE PROSPECT OF A MODERN SACRED
Ross Anderson

This chapter provides an account of the important yet undervalued role that the modern Swiss scenographer Adolphe Appia (1862–1928) played in the development of twentieth-century aesthetics, particularly in regard to what might be spoken of as its spiritual ambitions, whether these remained covert or were made explicit. His contribution centres on the austere yet mysteriously atmospheric suite of drawings that he termed his *Espaces rythmiques*. The drawings – around thirty of them – frame a series of monumental yet minimal scenes taking in stairs, landings, platforms and terraces that might be the fragmentary remains of a past culture or the inauguration of one to come, offering a reading of modernity's simultaneous desire for radical newness coupled with a nostalgia for an ancient past (Figure 10.1).

The Romantic *Landschaftsseele* – a surrogate for the absconded god – is a constant, spectral presence in Appia's drawings, and they expose a certain paradox in the German romanticist view of art as the synthesis of the secular and sacred. Friedrich Schiller's brisk statement – 'the temples remained sacred to the eye, when the gods had long become ridiculous'[1] – identified a nascent modernist tendency of Romantic artists to retain the characteristics of traditional religions, including their architectural settings, without observing their spiritual obligations. Appia is similarly evasive; his settings are presented as the foundations for a temple to an unknown god, marrying an atavistic appeal to primordial experiences with removed perspectival clarity and precision.

Appia drew his remarkable *Espaces rythmiques* at a collapsible drawing board in his modest domestic lodgings – just a couple of sparsely furnished rented rooms – in the tower of the medieval *Château de Glérolles* that is lapped by the waters of Lake Geneva (Figure 10.2). While the scenographer gazed out of his room towards the snow-capped mountains rising above the stable horizon of the lake, the drawings gaze towards their own distant horizons, framing scenes that are all part hopeful and part melancholic. These drawings that now mostly nestle in plan drawers in an exceedingly modest archive in Bern – *The Schweizerische Theatersammlung* (Swiss Theatre Collection) – are generally described as monochrome, which is partly true – Appia only ever drew with charcoal, graphite and white pastel. But the subtle colour of the paper – always and only ever *Canson & Montgolfier*, and mostly hues of pale blue, green or beige – imbues each drawing with a distinctive ambient undertone. The reclusive scenographer might himself be thought of the same way – delivering to modern architecture an ambient and rhythmic undertone.[2]

Figure 10.1 Adolphe Appia, *Espace rythmique: The Diver* (1909).
Source: SAPA Foundation, Swiss Archive of the Performing Arts, Bern.

Appia himself was inspired by eurhythmics – the choreographed movement of bodies in space to music – invented by his Swiss compatriot and music pedagogue Émile Jaques-Dalcroze.[3] In 1908, Appia attended classes on eurhythmics at the Geneva Music Conservatory,[4] but it was twelve months later, in the Spring of 1909, that he was spurred on to create his *Espaces rythmiques* during a remarkably brief period of prodigious outpouring. He had seen a eurhythmic performance at the Conservatory for which Jaques-Dalcroze himself had prepared the staging, and Appia was dismayed by what he identified as a profound disconnect between the wonder of what he heard and saw of the performers themselves and the abjectness of their scenography. He later wrote: 'I took up paper and pencil and designed two or three *Espaces rythmiques* every day with feverish determination.'[5] He then parcelled them up and mailed the set to Jaques-Dalcroze, who was reciprocally impressed; as Appia later recalled, 'He was greatly enthused when he saw my drawings, and I was convinced that, both for his sake and for mine, I had brought

Figure 10.2 Château de Glérolles, Lake Geneva.
Source: Postcard c. 1911. Photographer unknown.

to realisation something convincing. The *Raumstil* (spatial style) for bodily movements had been found.'⁶

And so began their collaboration, one which attained its greatest realization at Hellerau, a modern garden city tucked away in the woodlands on the outskirts of Dresden. The garden city had been founded just a few years earlier by Karl Schmidt, the proprietor of a small furniture factory, and the philanthropist Wolf Dohrn, who would come to be referred to as Hellerau's *spiritus rector*. Their ambition was to create utopian community of social equality, universal education and the revival of art's relationship with labour.⁷ More particularly, it was intended to be an antidote to the arrhythmia that German economist Karl Bücher had identified in his 1896 *Arbeit und Rhythmus* (Work and Rhythm) as the primary affliction of urbanized modern industrial society.⁸ Having studied the rhymes, chants and songs of traditional craftspeople, as well as the physical movement each craft demanded, Bücher had determined that in ancient times work and art existed in harmony. This harmony, he argued, had been disrupted by the artificial, mechanized tempo of industrial machinery, and so he advocated for a rediscovery of traditional rhythm that would usher individuals back into healthy accord both with their original selves and with their community.

Schmidt and Dohrn came to share Bücher's vision, and they were both in the audience when Jaques-Dalcroze gave a demonstration of eurhythmics in Dresden in 1909. The two were so impressed with the music pedagogue's teaching methods that the very next day they made a proposal to him to set up a *Bildungsanstalt für rhythmischen Erziehung* (Institute for Rhythmic Education) that would in time become a beacon for a brand new bodily spiritual culture in Hellerau, and that would imbue the garden city with a semi-sacred atmosphere. As the art and architecture critic Karl Scheffler wrote, visiting Hellerau was 'like stumbling upon a secular monastic order of the youth'.[9]

Plans for the *Bildungsanstalt* were well underway by the spring of 1910 – a year after Appia had drawn his *Espaces rythmiques*. Heinrich Tessenow, a then 33-year-old architect and professor at the *Technische Hochschule* in Dresden, had been tasked with the design of the *Bildungsanstalt* that it was hoped would embody the elevated ambitions of the co-founder of the *Deutscher Werkbund* Theodor Fischer, who imagined 'not a school, nor a museum, nor a church, nor a concert hall, nor an auditorium! . . . something of these and also something more!'[10] Tessenow travelled down to Lausanne in April to discuss his preliminary plans for the Institute with Jaques-Dalcroze. The key reason the meeting was set up in Switzerland was because Jaques-Dalcroze had come to rely heavily on Appia for aesthetic guidance – having been beguiled by his *Espaces rythmiques* – and was adamant that the self-effacing and travel-shy scenographer should have a seat at the table.

Appia's drawings are cumbersome to transport; they are sizeable and subject to smudging. But Jaques-Dalcroze had a clever idea. He arranged for his friend, the Swiss photographer Frédéric Boissonnas – himself a remarkable and understudied figure – to photograph all Appia's drawings in his studio in Geneva. Jaques-Dalcroze then had copies printed off, which he could carry along to meetings – such as the one in Lausanne with Tessenow. These photographs by Boissonnas are excellent – the next best thing to being in the presence of the drawings themselves (Figure 10.3). However, they are of course monochrome, and this stripping of the ambient colour, coupled with the enhanced contrast, makes them more sharply profiled and, for want of a better word, more architectural.

The extent to which Appia's *Espaces rythmiques* impressed themselves on the young architect Tessenow is unknown, but it is certainly worth drawing attention to the uncanny resemblance between them and the configuration and proportions of the long shallow steps and heavy stone pilasters that greet visitors to the temple-like *Bildungsanstalt* (Figure 10.4). Inside, the building presents the pronounced nave, side aisle and transept

Figure 10.3 Photograph of *Appia's Espace rythmique: The Three Pillars*, taken by Frédéric Boissonnas in 1910.
Source: Bibliothèque de Genève.

Figure 10.4 Heinrich Tessenow, Jaques-Dalcroze Institute for Rhythmic Education, Hellerau (1912).
Photograph by Ross Anderson.

arrangement of a church, with the *Festsaal* at the heart of the composition (Figure 10.5). There is a syncretism of religious motifs at play – sometimes medieval, sometimes classical and sometimes oriental.

The *Festsaal*, in which eurhythmic performances would in the time to come be celebrated before enraptured audiences, was conceived as a kind of alchemical vessel, invoking a special temporality – the time-out-of-time of ritual and ceremony. This is the kind of temporality that the philosopher Hans-Georg Gadamer wrote about in *Über die Festlichkeit des Theaters* (On the Festive Character of the Theatre); one in which the meting-out of time in our everyday lives is suspended during festive celebration. For Gadamer, 'enactment is the festival's mode of being, and in the enactment, time becomes the *nunc stans* of an elevated presence in which past and present become one'.[11] And further, it is an 'intrinsic characteristic of every festival that it enjoys a specific, rhythmical recurrence that elevates it above the flow of time'.[12]

At Hellerau, it was in the luminous *Festsaal* that the rhythmical recurrence of festival performances was elevated above the flow of time, and was able to recall fundamental or original conditions – conditions embodied in the play between the dark metaphor of earth and of bright ethereal light (Figure 10.5). The design of the interior of the *Festsaal* was a collaboration between Appia and the Russian artist Alexander von Salzmann.[13] The two of them contrived an electric lighting apparatus that could regulate and temper the theatrical light – a 'luminous organ'. Both the walls and ceiling were made of taut canvas screens impregnated with cedar oil and illuminated from behind by thousands of electric

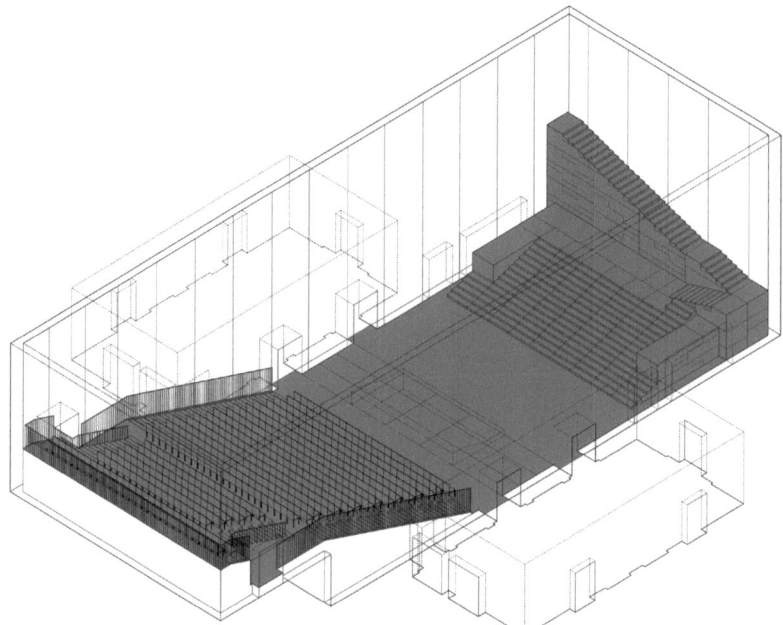

Figure 10.5 The *Festsaal* in the Jaques-Dalcroze Institute, Hellerau (1912).
Source: Cutaway oblique drawing by Sean Bryen.

globes, enveloping both the audience and the performers in the same mysteriously diffuse glow.

Appia had repeatedly outlined his ambition to diminish what he saw as the abyss between stage and seating, arguing that traditional theatres dulled their audiences, who only ever sat in semi-darkness in a state of total passivity. In *Die rhythmische Gymnastik und das Theater*, written at the Château de Glérolles in 1911, Appia boldly announced that 'Eurhythmics will overthrow this passivity. Musical rhythm will enter all of us, to say "you yourself are the work of art"!'[14] At the *Festsaal*, both the audience and performers entered the hall through twinned tripartite doors located in the middle of the long edges of the theatre, having mingled in the adjacent common areas. Stepping out onto the polished black floor, the audience then took their places in the 600 dark chairs banked in rows at the rear of the space, while the performers assumed their positions opposite. The uncanny reflection of the theatre's tiered seating implicated the audience in the performance. Appia, who placed exceptional importance on light as the carrier of moods and atmosphere, particularly when carefully calibrated with music, declared: 'The human bodies, bathed in this vital atmosphere will recognise it and salute *Music in Space*. For Apollo was not only the god of music; he was also the god of light!'[15]

The inaugural performance in the *Festsaal* was the highlight of the very first *Schulfest* that took place in the summer of 1912. It was a staging of the second act of Christoph Willibald Gluck's rendering of the story of *Orpheus and Eurydice*, and the minimal setting that Appia designed for the descent of Apollo's son Orpheus into the underworld in a doomed endeavour to retrieve his lover Eurydice from Hades was described at the time as being 'stripped of anecdote'.[16] It comprised a flight of dark stairs spanning from upstage right across the full width of the theatre to upstage left, a narrow centre-stage landing and a final dramatic run of full-width stairs down to the floor. The few existing photographs of the rehearsals and performance show choreographed figures in motion against the brilliant silky whiteness of the walls and ceiling (Figure 10.6).

None of these photographs were taken by Frédéric Boissonnas, who by that time had become Jaques-Dalcroze's photographer of choice. *His* earlier assignment had been to come up with an image that would serve as an emblem for the whole Hellerau-Eurhythmic endeavour – and it required a source of light both much stronger and more direct, one that would burn bright and fast on his photographic plates, capturing in freeze-frame agile youths in dynamic motion. In the frontispiece image to the inaugural volume of the Institute yearbook *Der Rhythmus* – printed in summer 1911, and as much a manifesto as a chronical – four lithe young women in flowing tunics spring aloft in unison over a brightly lit summer meadow. With their hands all clasped together and faces thrust skyward, they embody Jaques-Dalcroze's split dream of ecstatic abandonment and collective order (Figure 10.7).

The writings on the pages that follow are equally riven – between visions of a euphoric eurhythmic future and workaday accounts of the goings-on of the teaching activities at the *Institute* over the first year of its existence.[17] For example, Wolf Dohrn's mystically toned preface asserts at the outset that it is 'rhythm alone that gives form to life. So, for us, rhythm has become an almost metaphysical concept – it spiritualises the bodily and

Revelatory Earth

Figure 10.6 Rehearsals for Orpheus and Eurydice in the *Festsaal* (1912).
Source: Bibliothèque de Genève.

Figure 10.7 Frontispiece of *Der Rhythmus: Yearbook of the Jaques-Dalcroze Institute for Rhythmic Education* (1911).
Source: Bibliothèque de Genève.

embodies the spiritual'. At the other end, the yearbook is rounded-out with mostly dry facts and tallies, including the *Schülerliste*, an inventory of all 115 students who were enrolled in that first teaching year, and where they had come from. Each name is also furnished with a number: notable are number *9, Ada Bruhn, Berlin*, who Mies van der Rohe would marry two years later, having visited Bruhn in Hellerau on a number of occasions; and number *45, Albert Jeanneret, La Chaux-de-Fonds*, brother of Charles-Edouard Jeanneret – the future Le Corbusier.

The journeyman Swiss architect in fact visited his brother Albert in Hellerau on a number of occasions, and he also met with its founders Dohrn, Schmidt and Jaques-Dalcroze. Greatly enthused by what he encountered, Le Corbusier wrote that 'the greatest artists of Germany' were enjoying 'the most favourable circumstances so that genius might be manifest, so that artists can produce almost total works of art'.[18] And in another brief, unpublished text, *La salle, cathédrale de l'avenir?* (The Hall, Cathedral of the Future), Jeanneret wrote, 'Hellerau opened a reign of kindness with Jaques-Dalcroze, and an era of utility with Tessenow. A million people have gathered for these two men of rhythmic music . . . in this great and irreproachable room [the *Festsaal*] . . . in which city? Hellerau.'[19]

Le Corbusier was of course not the only modern architect to hold up the Gothic cathedral as an architectural paradigm that in its making gathered together all manner of arts and trades, providing the conditions for the creation of 'almost total works of art'. In his catalysing *Manifest und Programm* for the Staatliches Bauhaus in Weimar, printed in April 1919 and famously fronted by Lyonel Feininger's prismatic Expressionist woodcut *Kathedrale der Zukunft* (cathedral of the future), Walter Gropius pronounced 'the ultimate, if distant aim, of the Bauhaus is the *Einheitskunstwerk* – the great building'.[20]

Although clearly operating in separate social and artistic circles, Appia too shared Le Corbusier's and Gropius' ambition. For him too, it was the cathedral of the future – more as a glorious motif rather than anything actually buildable – that ignited the imagination. In a short text published in the same year as Gropius' manifesto, Appia wrote with great enthusiasm: 'Sooner or later we will arrive at what we shall call the *Saal* (hall) – the cathedral of the future – which will receive, in a free, large, transformable space, the most varied manifestations of our social and artistic life.'[21] And in the same year he finished the final draft for his *L'œuvre d'art Vivant* (The Work of Living Art), which was finally published in 1921. In it, he exclaims: 'We are, moreover, beginning to sense an ever more compelling need to unite with others, whether outdoors, or in a hall not restricted in advance to one or the other of our public activities to the exclusion of others.' Rather, 'one which, on the contrary, exists solely and simply to enable us to come together with one another, as once we did in our cathedrals . . . The term escapes me! I cannot recall it. Ah yes: it is in a cathedral of the future that we must take our vows!'[22]

The cathedral served Appia more as a grand abstract aspiration than it did as a historical model, and in fact the aesthetic that he was proposing was decidedly modern – a cohesive understanding of lightness and darkness, space and form, and their shaping of the body in movement. In *L'œuvre d'art Vivant*, he wrote, for example: 'The forms placed on [the stage] await light to render them visible. The stage therefore possesses a latent power, for space and light – the two primordial elements.'[23] And a couple of pages later: 'Now, we have seen that movement is the conciliatory principle that formally unites space with time. Architecture is therefore an art that contains – powerfully – time and space.'[24] And yet the manner of Appia's diffusion into European visual-spatial sensibilities, including architecture, remains something of a mystery. This is a fate that he predicted for himself, writing shortly before he died to a friend – whether in resignation or indignation – 'anonymity is the essence of my whole existence'.[25]

Two years after the release of Appia's *L'œuvre d'art Vivant*, Le Corbusier published his eminently quotable *Vers une architecture*, opening the first of his three reminders to architects with the memorable line, 'Architecture is the masterly, correct and magnificent play of forms brought together in light'.[26] He repeated the assertion word for word thirty years later, in the section of his *Œuvre complète* dedicated to the rooftop of the *Unité d'habitation in Marseille*, an architectural tableau that includes a nursery, kindergarten, swimming pool and gymnasium, all circumscribed by a running track that Le Corbusier termed the 'esplanade of physical culture'.[27] At its northernmost extremity, he composed an elemental open-air theatre in coarsely shuttered cast concrete, where festivals could be held in summer 'without any *mise-en-scène* or expense'.[28] As a monochromatic architectural proposition of perspectival clarity, the whole setting resonates deeply with Appia's drawings. It is paced with a rectangular grid impressed into the slab that Le Corbusier himself called, quote: 'a ruled surface',[29] and the perspective-like set-up is further emphasized by the long, closely grouped shuttering lines of the flanking wall as they converge towards the vanishing point on the horizon.

But as much as the rooftop and its stage can be spoken about in the same terms as a drawing, it was also the embodied setting for festive communal events that celebrated ancient cultural origins of the kind that Le Corbusier hoped to recuperate. In one of these performances, a young girl performed alone and barefoot on stage before an overcrowded jostling audience, wearing a coarse animal skin tethered around her waist by a length of cord.[30] Le Corbusier published a full-page reproduction of a photograph of this rooftop performance in his book *The Nursery Schools*, and paired it with a photograph of two children – one boy and one girl both around six years old – sitting quietly and facing each other on a large felled tree lying on a patch of stony ground dotted around by shrubs and cypresses. A fragment of the *Unité* nestles surprising well into the background.[31] The caption reads: 'Silence and beauty. Post-figuration of Daphnis and Chloë.' The cultural and topographical setting of both photographs considered together is at once classically Mediterranean and wholeheartedly modern.

The same can be said of the moody drawings that Appia made in the last few reclusive years of his life, which he lived out in a small chalet on the grounds of a psychiatric clinic near Nyon. The drawings are mostly solemn and religious-ceremonial, and yet they also emanate a promising luminosity. One of them was made for a staging of the ancient Greek playwright Euripides' mythical telling of Iphegenia's fate among the Taurians after she has been whisked away by the goddess Artermis to become a priestess at her temple, and where she is charged with the unenviable and gruesome duty of sacrificing on a bloody altar any and all wayfaring Greeks who happen upon the shores of Tauris.[32]

Modern Architecture and the Sacred

Appia's rendering of the set for the second act, *Interior of the Temple*, made in 1926 – two years before his own death – takes in a view towards the unyielding altar, seen from the side through a profoundly expectant ambient gloom (Figure 10.8).

In tenor and disposition, the drawing previews the more minimal strain of international modern architecture, embodied, for example, in the stripped-back interior of the diminutive brick chapel in Chicago that Mies van der Rohe – that other heroic modern architect who had wiled-away time at Hellerau – built in 1952, the same year that the *Unité* was completed back in Europe. On the interior of Mies' only ecclesiastical building, long uninterrupted side walls of squat buff-coloured bricks lead the eye towards the altar, which is backed by a lustrous deeply pleated altar curtain dividing the congregation from the cloistered chambers behind. The only other furnishings are two low oak-veneer benches, and a gleaming stainless-steel altar rail and cross.[33]

The plan of the chapel is divided in two – a lay area given over to the earthly and an area allied to the sacred – and the threshold between them is orchestrated by the most minimal of means: the floor of the nave rises up as a single very low step that reads rather as a wrinkle in the earth than an act of building. The solid travertine marble altar is the focus of the ascension and it is where the very substantial chthonic content of the chapel is founded (Figure 10.9). And here the client for the building, Bishop Wallace E. Conkling, shared and perhaps even exceeded, Mies' own estimation of the importance of the altar to the chapel: 'My dear Mies . . . Even though our funds be so limited, we *must* do the Altar right, above all else, for that is the thing for which we are building the

Figure 10.8 Adolphe Appia, *Iphigenie in Tauris. Act II: Interior of the Temple of Artemis* (1926). *Source:* SAPA Foundation, Swiss Archive of the Performing Arts, Bern.

Figure 10.9 Mies van der Rohe, Chapel of St. Savior, IIT, Chicago (1952). Photograph by Ross Anderson, 2013.

Chapel.'[34] Mies himself wrote little, and his words on the chapel are unsurprisingly few: 'I chose an intensive rather than an extensive form to express my conception, simply and honestly, of what a sacred building should be', and then, 'It was meant to be simple; and, in fact, it is simple. But in its simplicity it is not primitive, but noble, and in its smallness it is great – in fact, monumental.'[35]

Although for Mies architecture was ultimately a matter of building – as Ignasi de Solà-Morales wrote: 'This matter is abstract, general, geometrically cut, smooth, and polished, but it is also material that is substantial, tangible and solid'[36] – he was attentive to the importance of all of the ephemera that brings a building into being, and he gifted most of his drawings, letters and notes to the Museum of Modern Art (MOMA), who in 1968 dutifully established the Ludwig Mies van der Rohe Archive in Midtown Manhattan. This exceptional archive is matched by the Fondation Le Corbusier back in Paris, likewise established in 1968. Generously funded and comfortably accommodated in conjoined UNESCO World Heritage villas of the architect's own design, there is every indication that, as per its statutes, the Fondation Le Corbusier will be an institution of, quote, 'unlimited duration'.[37] The significance of these two archives to the consolidation of the reputations of the two canonical architects to whom they are devoted is inestimable. For example, the very first line of the acknowledgements in his widely read book *Mies van der Rohe: A Critical Biography*, Franz Schulze states, 'The greatest boon to Miesian scholarship in the past forty years has been the establishment in 1968 of the *Mies van der Rohe Archive* at the *Museum of Modern Art*.'[38]

Modern Architecture and the Sacred

The circumstances in which the major cache of Appia's drawings reside could not differ more from those of the Mies van der Rohe Archive in New York or the Fondation Le Corbusier in Paris, serving as a cipher for the scenographer's historiographical elusiveness, particularly when considered alongside the two famous architects. The *Schweizerische Theatersammlung* [Swiss Theatre Collection] is a modest cultural-philanthropic operation inconspicuously lodged in a repurposed corner of a carpark under the Bern courthouse in Switzerland. Having double-checked the address and opening times – Wednesday and Thursday afternoons – on an information board under the kind of triple-vaulted glaucomic fibreglass awning produced for suburban bus stops in the 1980s, you step inside and find that the reading room ceilings are low, the walls are windowless and the furniture is *sachlich* but comfortable; it feels like a small-town library. The staff are eager, capable and affable, and they are capably supported by enthusiast-volunteers and interns working away quietly on the grey laminate-topped tables in the reading room.[39]

Appia's drawing nestle in plan-chests in the room next door, and are delivered singly for white-gloved viewing. Up close, they are revelatory; the carefully considered details and faint evidence of the techniques used to achieve them are only evident at close range. At first it is the variety – of theme, composition and atmosphere – that is arresting, but after you settle into them, it is the constancies, whether born of habit or conviction, that impress themselves – for example, the sequence of faint drafting lines that Appia always used to set up his perspectives, or the realization that he only ever drew on *Canson & Montgolfier* papers, famed for their constancy of texture and colour that for Appia imbued each drawing with a distinctive ambient undertone.

Appia, the scenographer who was always distant yet also always enigmatically present, might himself be thought of the same way, and the extent of his influence – on architects including Heinrich Tessenow, Le Corbusier, Mies van der Rohe and others – is yet to properly register. The *Espaces rythmiques* that Appia drew and erased into being on the collapsible drawing board in front of him in his rented room in the medieval château on Lake Geneva not only brought to realization, in his own words, 'something convincing', the *Raumstil* (spatial style) for eurhythmics, but also visualized a profoundly modern sensibility that wanted things both ways: cultural rebirth and continuity with the depths of tradition.

For Appia, it was during the ecstatic time-out-of-time of theatrical performance that the time between antiquity and modernity collapses, when, to use Gadamer's words, 'time becomes the *nunc stans* of an elevated presence in which past and present become one'.[40] This was also Le Corbusier's claim for a successful work of architecture, in the presence of which 'a fathomless depth gapes open, all walls are broken down, every other presence is put to flight, and the miracle of *l'espace indicible* is achieved'.[41] While both of them were open to the prospect of the sacred, neither the scenographer nor the architect conceived of transcendence in terms of heaven, and one can imagine Appia agreeing with Le Corbusier's assertion that 'some things are sacred, others are not, regardless of whether or not they are religious'.[42]

Notes

1. Friedrich Schiller, 'Über die ästhetische Erziehung des Menschen in einer Reihe von Briefen', *Die Horen* (January 1795), Letter 9. Published in English as *Letters on the Aesthetic Education of Man*, trans. Elizabeth M. Wilkinson and L. A. Willoughby (Oxford: Clarendon, 1982).

2. The four-volume complete works of Adolphe Appia is the primary source of reference for scholarship on him, which to date has primarily been conducted in the discipline of theatre studies. See Adolphe Appia, *Œuvres Complètes*, ed. Marie L. Bablet-Hahn (Lausanne: L'Age d'homme): *Volume I: 1880-1894*, (1983); *Volume II: 1895-1905* (1986); *Volume III: 1906-1921* (1988); *Volume IV: 1921-1928* (1992). See also: Walter Volbach and Richard Beacham, eds, *Adolphe Appia: Essays and Scenarios and Designs* (London: UMI Research Press, 1989), 4; Beacham's *Adolphe Appia: Texts on Theatre* (London: Routledge, 1993), and his critical biography *Adolphe Appia: Artist and Visionary of the Modern Theatre* (Reading: Harwood Academic Publishers, 1994). My own essay, 'The Appian Way', *AA Files* 75 (December 2017): 163–82, was the first lengthy piece on Appia in architectural discourse.

3. For an early summary account of the theoretical underpinnings Émile Jaques-Dalcroze's Eurhythmics, including excerpts from his own lectures at Hellerau, alongside short essays by others, see Michael Ernest Sadler, ed., *The Eurhythmics of Jaques-Dalcroze* (Boston: Small Maynard and Company, 1913).

4. The classes on Eurhythmics that Appia attended at the Geneva Music Conservatory were taught by the Swiss dancer Suzanne Perrottet, who herself had been a pupil of Émile Jaques-Dalcroze and went on to become his teaching assistant at Hellerau.

5. Adolphe Appia, cited in Edmund Stadler, 'Jaques-Dalcroze et Adolphe Appia', in *Émile Jaques-Dalcroze*, ed. Frank Martin (Neuchatel: Eds de la Baconnière, 1965), 418.

6. Ibid.

7. On the founding of Hellerau, see the excerpts from Karl Schmidt's own undated and unpublished memoir that have been collated as 'Die Gründung von Hellerau', in *Hellerau leuchtete: Zeitzeugenberichte und Erinnerungen* (Dresden: Verlag der Kunst, 2007), 17–24. In one brief passage on page 22, Schmidt wrote of his invention of the name: 'The name Hellerau did not exist. But it was necessary to bestow a nice name on this new garden city. It was during a performance of "Don Juan" at the Dresden Opera that I came up with the idea (which I had heard from some farmers who spoke of the "*Au am Heller*"), to give it the name "Hellerau" . . .'.

8. See Karl Bücher, *Arbeit und Rhythmus* (Leipzig: Hirzel, 1896).

9. '. . . als weile man in einem weltlichen Mönchsorden der Jugend'. Karl Scheffler, 'Das Haus', in *Der Rhythmus Ein Jahrbuch* 2, no. 1 (Jena: Eugen Diederichs Verlag, 1913), 2–13.

10. Theodor Fischer, 'Was ich bauen möchte', *Hohe Warte*, no. 3 (1906–07): 327.

11. Hans-Georg Gadamer, 'The Festive Character of Theater', in *The Relevance of the Beautiful and Other Essays*, ed. Robert Bernasconi (Cambridge: Cambridge University Press, 1986), 58–9.

12. Ibid., 60.

13. For a recent collection of essays that address both the collaboration between Appia and Alexander von Salzmann and their individual contributions to Hellerau, see Dieter Jaenicke and Ralph Lindner, eds, *Rekonstruktion der Zukunft* (Leipzig: Spector Books, 2017).

14. Adolphe Appia, 'Die rhythmische Gymnastik und das Theater', in *Der Rhythmus, Ein Jahrbuch* (Jena: Eugen Diederichs, 1911). Cited in Adolphe Appia, *Œuvres Complètes, vol. III: 1906–21*, ed. Marie L. Bablet-Hahn (Lausanne: L'Age d'homme, 1988), 184.

15. Ibid., 188.
16. Ernst Ansermet, 'La Gymnastique Rythmique a Hellerau', *SIM* 97 (July–August 1913): 58.
17. Bildungsanstalt Jaques-Dalcroze, *Der Rhythmus: Ein Jahrbuch*, vol. 1 (Jena: Eugen Diederichs, 1911).
18. Le Corbusider, *Étude sur le movement d'art décoratif en Allemagne* (La Chaux-de-Fonds: Exole de L'Art, 1912), 42, 49. Note further that Le Corbusier sent Jaques-Dalcroze a copy of *Vers une architecture* on 12 January 1924 and wrote in his dedication: 'You are one of the personalities who has contributed most to the development of a true *esprit nouveau*.'
19. Unpublished, cited in Appia, *Œuvres Complètes*, 205. Appia was absent from these pronouncements, but the two had in fact met a couple of times in the garden city. In a letter to his parents, dated 28 October 1910, Jeanneret wrote: 'I found Appia here: an energetic *garçon* whom I had known as a dreamer and poet in Paris'. Le Corbusier, *Correspondance: Lettres à la famille, Tome 1: 1900-1925* (Paris: lnfolio, 2011), 326.
20. Walter Gropius, *Manifest und Programm des Staatlichen Bauhauses* (Weimar, April 1919).
21. Adolphe Appia, 'Darsteller, Raum, Licht, Malerei (1919)', in *Texte zur Theorie des Raums*, ed. Stephan Günzel (Stuttgart: Reclam, 2013), 121.
22. Adolphe Appia, *L'œuvre d'art Vivant* (Paris: Edition Atar, 1921), 101.
23. Ibid., 20.
24. Ibid., 25.
25. Adolphe Appia to Karl Reyle, 10 September 1926. Walter Volbach Collection on Adolphe Appia, Beinecke Rare Book and Manuscript Library, Yale University.
26. Le Corbusier, *Vers une architecture* (Paris: G Crès, 1923), 16.
27. Ibid., 219. The rooftop reveals an alliance with some of the deeper convictions of Eurhythmics in regards to the education and healthy physical development of children, incited by movement.
28. Willy Boesiger, ed., *Le Corbusier: Œuvre Complète 1946-1952* (Basel: Birkhäuser, 1953), 222.
29. Ibid., 221.
30. Ibid., 222.
31. Le Corbusier, *The Nursery Schools*, trans. Eleanor Levieux (New York: Orion Press, 1968), 82–3.
32. See Euripides, *Iphegenia Among the Taurians*, trans. Anne Carson (Chicago: University of Chicago Press, 2013).
33. For a close reading of the chapel, see my chapter 'Minimal Ritual: Mies van der Rohe's Chapel of St. Savior, 1952', in *Modernism and American Mid-20th Century Sacred Architecture*, ed. Anat Geva (London: Routledge, 2018), 15–30.
34. Wallace E. Conkling to Mies van der Rohe, 22 December, 1951. The word 'must' is underlined in the original letter.
35. Mies van der Rohe, 'A Chapel', *Arts and Architecture* 70, no. 1 (January 1953): 19. It should here be noted that Mies had a religious upbringing, and that his father was a stonemason. And further that his appreciation of the Gothic extended well beyond the anecdotal and might more accurately be described as unexpectedly studious – a surprisingly large number of the 150 books in his personal library that have been identified as being most important to him concern Gothic architecture. They include Erwin Panofsky, *Gothic Architecture and Scholasticism* (1951); John Fitchem, *The Construction of Gothic Cathedrals* (1961); and Otto

von Simson, *The Gothic Cathedral: Origins of Gothic Architecture and the Medieval Concept of Order* (1965). For the full selection, see Werner Blaeser, *Mies van der Rohe: The Art of Structure*, trans. D. Q. Stephenson (Basel: Birkhäuser, 1993), 228–31.

36. Ignasi de Solà-Morales, 'Mies van der Rohe and Minimalism', in *Differences: Topographies of Contemporary Architecture* (Cambridge, MA: MIT Press, 1997), 32–3.
37. Statutes of the *Fondation,* approved by Le Corbusier on 11 June 1965.
38. Franz Schulze, *Mies van der Rohe: A Critical Biography* (Chicago: The University of Chicago Press, 1985), xiii.
39. I would particularly like to thank Simone Gfeller for her gracious assistance during the week that I spent poring over Appia's drawings at the *Theatersammlung* in December 2015.
40. Gadamer, 'The Festive Character of Theater', 58–9.
41. Le Corbusier, *Modulor 2: Let the User Speak Next,* trans. Peter de Francia and Anna Bostock (London: Faber and Faber, 1958), 207.
42. Le Corbusier, cited in Jean Petit, ed., *Le Corbusier lui-même* (Geneva: Editions Rousseau, 1970), 183–4.

CHAPTER 11
ANAGOGICAL THEMES IN SCHWITTERS' *KATHEDRALE DES EROTISCHEN ELENDS*
Matthew Mindrup

Introduction

Begun in 1923, the German artist and amateur architect Kurt Schwitters' *Kathedrale des erotischen Elends* (The Cathedral of Erotic Misery) is an important contribution to the early-twentieth-century German avant-garde that provides a unique point of entry into a critical contact between the sacred and modern in architecture (Figure 11.1). Early musings about a conflation between these two concepts emerged from Bruno Taut during 1919 wherein he encouraged his fellow architects in his essay 'Eine Notwendigkeit' (A Necessity) to emulate German Expressionist painters' emphasis on the 'construction' of a painting in the construction of architecture.[1] As the Russian born, German Expressionist artist Wassily Kandinsky explained, this art was the result of the painter discovering an 'internal necessity' in the composition of forms and colours. For his abstract assemblies of found objects in two and three dimensions called Merz, Schwitters employed a similar interpretive strategy in his own selection and rejection of found materials depending upon how well they contribute to an ineffable *Ausdruck* (expression). Similar to Aristotle's hylomorphic conception of material and immaterial form, Schwitters' *Ausdruck* was contingent upon a process of transubstantiation by which a found object must be able to *Entmaterialisieren* (dematerialize) an immaterial identity or purpose he called its *Eigengift* (inner poison) and take on a new one in a work of Merz art or architecture. In this way, Schwitters' Merz came to embody the concept of modernity which Charles Baudelaire's posed in his 1864 essay 'The Painter of Modern Life' as an exploitation of the ephemeral, transitory nature of meanings in contemporary life in order to gauge and appreciate that which is perpetual – things themselves and a human imagination that continues to find meanings in them.[2] Like his peers in the Arbeitsrat für Kunst (Working Council for Art), the ideal paradigm for Schwitters' architecture was the Gothic cathedral not merely as a *Gesamtkunstwerk* (Total work of Art), but because of the anagogical function of its materials – leading the mind from the world of appearances to the contemplation of final causes. This chapter explores Schwitters' sublimation of anagogical themes into the construction of his *Kathedrale des erotischen Elends* (KdeE), as a model for a new architecture whose final cause would emerge from the creative mind of the modern architect.

Anagogical Themes in Schwitters' *Kathedrale*

Figure 11.1 Kurt Schwitters, *Kathedrale des erotischen Elends* (1933).
Source: © Kurt Schwitters/VG Bild-Kunst. Copyright Agency, 2019.

Merz and the Merz cathedrals

Schwitters began to develop his Merz art and architecture shortly after the end of the First World War as a method for assembling found materials into art that he called 'MERZ' – a term coined after a word fragment in his first collage, *Das Merzbild* (The Merz Picture) from 1919 (Figure 11.2).[3] With the exception of a few collages from the same period, Schwitters' Merz works were made from discarded objects, including torn and cut pieces of printed matter, and pasted onto canvases in various angles or directions not so that they would 'be used logically in their objective relationships, but only within the logic of the work of art'.[4] It was a method Schwitters would continue to apply like a brand name to all of his activities, including architecture.

In his article 'Die Bedeutung des Merzgedankens in der Welt' (The Meaning of Merz-Thought in the World) from 1923, Schwitters compared the transformation of found objects in a Merz work to the assemblage and reassemblage of words in a piece of prose or poetry, since 'In poetry, words are torn from their former context, they are *entformelt* and brought into a new artistic context, they become formal parts of the poem'.[5] The term '*entformelt*' is a neologism that Schwitters invented, roughly translating as 'disassociation of form(s)'.[6] Schwitters' use of the term to describe the making of a poem is an elaboration of a conception he held about the assemblage of materials in a Merz work – that in the 'artistic evaluation' of found objects, 'essential is only the *Formen* (forming)'.[7] The application of these two concepts is demonstrated most clearly in *Pornographisches*

Figure 11.2 Kurt Schwitters, *Das Merzbild* (1919).
Source: © Kurt Schwitters/VG Bild-Kunst. Copyright Agency, 2019.

Figure 11.3 Kurt Schwitters, *Haus Merz* (1920).
Source: © Kurt Schwitters/VG Bild-Kunst. Copyright Agency, 2019.

i-Gedicht (Pornographic i Poem) from 1923, where Schwitters cut the printed pages of a children's story in half, and in doing so relocated the words into new contexts giving them new associations that are potentially pornographic.

The founding principle behind Schwitters' *Formung* and *Entformung* of found objects in a Merz work was based upon a conception of all materials as having a transitory invisible 'individual character' he called their '*Eigengift*'.[8] For Schwitters, in order for a found object to become useful as material for a Merz work, this *Eigengift* had to be *entmaterialisiert* in the *Entformung* of the object.[9] That is to say that in order for a found object to be used as material for making art, its *Eigengift* had to be forgotten through a mental process by which its identity or purpose changed even as the physical appearance of the thing remained unaltered. Yet, Schwitters' Merz art was not a random assemblage of objects denuded of their original purposes but rather compositions that were the result of a correspondence between the lines, colours and forms in a work of art he described as its '*Ausdruck*'.[10] For Schwitters, this expression was not brought to the work *a priori* but 'comes into being through the artistic evaluation of its elements. I know only how I do it, I know only my materials, from which I take, I know not to what *Zwecke* (ends/purposes)'.[11] Because 'every combination of lines, colours, and forms had a definite expression that cannot be put into words', it follows that the *Zweck* for Schwitters' Merz works consisted of the sensuous manifestation of an invisible content that both determined, and was determined by, the unique arrangement of found objects as art.

Shortly after the first exhibition of his Merz art in July 1919 at Der Sturm gallery in Berlin, Schwitters began experimenting with his Merz use of found materials to create Merz sculpture and architecture.[12] As he explained in his article 'Merz', this expansion into three dimensions meant to *modellieren* (to sculpt or model).[13] In the text that followed, Schwitters introduced *Haus Merz* (House Merz) as his 'first piece of Merz architecture' and included a quote from his friend, the art critic Christof Spengemann, who identified the small assemblage in his article 'Merz: Die offizielle Kunst' (Merz: The Official Art) as *die Kathedrale* (the Cathedral) (Figure 11.3).[14] Simultaneous to these events, Schwitters also began to explore the cathedral theme in a small book of eight lithographs from 1920 entitled *Die Kathedrale* (The Cathedral). It is interesting that despite its title, Schwitters did not include a religious edifice on its cover, but rather a hastily drawn flat-roofed industrial mill. The conflation of cathedral and the mill is most succinctly noted by the presence of gears in both *Haus Merz* and the lithograph drawings and watercolours he created to describe the Merz transformation of found materials into art or architecture as a kind of milling.[15]

It was during this early phase of Schwitters' Merz architecture that he began to construct another structure called a *Säule* (column) that became the model and starting point for a full-size architectural environment he referred to as a 'cathedral'. Based on an account from Richard Huelsenbeck, Schwitters started constructing the first of three columns as early as December of 1918 when he claimed it was 'all crap' – a depository for unused objects in his *Merzbilder* (Merz pictures).[16] Later, in the spring of 1920, Max Ernst also visited Schwitters and reported that he referred to it as a '*colonne de merz*' (Merz-column).[17] By 1923, Schwitters had altered the first *Merz-column* and included his collage *Der erste Tag* (The First Day) from 1918–19 on its base. The title can be considered a designation that, along with a statement from his son Ernst, implies it may have been the initial point of Schwitters' inspiration for the construction of the what he initially described as a *Merzbau*:

> His pictures would decorate the walls, his sculptures standing along the walls. As anybody who has ever hung a picture knows, an interrelation between the pictures results. Kurt Schwitters, with his particular interest in the interaction of the components of his works, quite naturally reacted to this. He started by tying strings to emphasize this interaction. Eventually they became wires, then were replaced with wooden structures, which, in turn were joined with plaster of Paris. This structure grew and grew and eventually filled several rooms on various floors of our home, resembling a huge, abstract grotto.[18]

In 1931, Schwitters claims the existence of ten columns including a third 'great column' in his article 'Myself and My Aims', which he now referred to as the *Kathedrale des Erotischen Elends*, or KdeE for short. Although no photographic record remains of this 'great column', the 1923 photo referred to as *Der erste Tag Merz-säule* (The First Day Merz-column) is the date that Schwitters claims his *Merzbau* began (Figure 11.4).[19] It can be inferred from Schwitters' statement that the *Merz-säule* was one of the ten columns that his son Ernst believes were sublimated into the *Merzbau* as a kind of a model.

As Schwitters' KdeE evolved, it took on a unique role in his own œuvre as a type of sacred structure. Although now destroyed, we know from accounts given by fellow artists and his own son Ernst Schwitters that the KdeE included numerous '*Grotten* (grottoes)', '*Höhlen* (holes, caves)' and '*Zimmer* (rooms) – designated as such by Schwitters himself – as well as containers in which materials for future *Merzbiler* and Merz constructions were kept'. Recalling his Hannover Merzbau in a letter he wrote in 1946, Schwitters states that his 'Merz tower was not confined to a single room, but spread over the whole house

 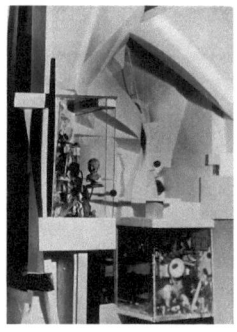

Figure 11.4 Kurt Schwitters, *Der erste Tag Merz-säule* (1923).
Source: © Kurt Schwitters/VG Bild-Kunst. Copyright Agency, 2019.

Figure 11.5 Kurt Schwitters, Gold Grotto (1925).
Source: © Kurt Schwitters/VG Bild-Kunst. Copyright Agency, 2019.

… parts of it were in the adjoining rooms, on the balcony, in two rooms of the cellar, on the second floor, in the attic' (Figure 11.5).[20] Similar to his collages, the different areas of Schwitters' *KdeE* were named after specific objects which contained or made reference to specific events in his cultural world. In published accounts of the *Merzbau*, there are at least forty different grottoes, rooms and caves.[21] The *Zimmer* referred to geographical regions, styles and mythological or historical figures in German history and culture. Conversely, the *Höhlen* are containers for objects and artefacts that were elicited – or in some cases pilfered – from the representative individuals themselves such as Sophie Täuber-Arps' cave which contained her bra, while Mies van der Rohe's cave contained a pencil Schwitters may (or may not) have been poached from Mies' drafting table. Like a Gothic cathedral reliquary, the objects in these *Höhlen* were physical evidence of the artist and their important contributions to Schwitters' cultural world.

Zukunftskathedrale

That Schwitters drew and assembled works he associated with cathedrals in Germany during the early 1920s is not to be understood as the promotion of a religious belief but rather the reinforcement of a cultural idea to inspire the development of a new German architecture. As early as 1914, Bruno Taut had proposed the Gothic cathedral as a potent paradigm for a modern unification of the arts.[22] Following Germany's defeat in the First World War, many architects sought to join with the socialists in Berlin as the Arbeitsrat für Kunst (Working Council for Art) to help forge a new German Republic.[23] Taut revived this idea of synthesizing the arts as a major component of the Arbeitsrat für Kunst's founding manifesto '*Ein Architektur-Programm*' (An Architecture Program) from March 1919, which promoted a faith in the power of architecture to create a better future, a clear commitment to breaking down the artificial divisions between the arts that had occurred following the Gothic period, and argued that the architect should have the overarching responsibility for the final design.[24] When Walter Gropius later took over as director of the Arbeitsrat für Kunst, he again used the image of a cathedral in the pamphlet for the April 1919 *Ausstellung für unbekannte Architekten* (Exhibition of Unknown Architects)[25] in Berlin and echoed Taut's original call for 'architects, sculptors and painters' to break down the barriers between the arts and be unified by the 'architect' whose work, he explained, would create a *Gesamtkunstwerk* as the *Zukunftskathedrale* (Cathedral of the future) – a crystalline expression of a spiritual idea that would metaphorically radiate its light into the design of objects for everyday life. It was this conception of the *Zukunftskathedrale* that Lyonel Feininger synthesized into his famous woodcut for the cover of the 1919 *Bauhaus Manifesto*.

Shortly after the *Arbeitsrat für Kunst*'s acceptance of the *Gesamtkunstwerk* as the model for a new German architecture, Schwitters identified a comparable aim underlying his own work claiming, 'My aim is the *Merzgesamtkunstwerk* that embraces all branches of art in an artistic unity.'[26] Notwithstanding their similarities, Schwitters was not a member of the Arbeitsrat für Kunst nor can it be certain that he had any familiarity with its members or Gropius' *Zukunftskathedrale* when he invented Merz in December 1918. Nevertheless, it is difficult to imagine that Schwitters' sudden identification of the cathedral and *Gesamtkunstwerk* as important themes in his Merz œuvre in 1920 was merely a coincidence. During the opening of his first Merz exhibition at Der Sturm gallery, Schwitters would have become familiar with members of the Arbeitsrat für Kunst and Gropius' newly founded Bauhaus school. Der Sturm was a gallery where Taut and Behne had been leading members since 1914 and Gropius had recruited many of its artists to join his new Bauhaus faculty in Weimar. Two months before writing an article on *Haus Merz*, Spengemann published a review of Taut's book, *Die Stadtkrone* (The City Crown) from 1919. The review is probably where Schwitters became familiar with Taut and his work in the Arbeitsrat für Kunst. Later, Taut himself must have recognized the resonance between Schwitters' Merz architecture to his own aims since he invited Schwitters to contribute a short article about his architectural modelling method 'Schloss und Kathedrale mit Hofbrunnen' (Castle and Cathedral with Courtyard Well) to the spring 1922 issue of his architectural journal *Frühlicht*.[27] That Schwitters created *Haus Merz* and began to construct his KdeE during this period of time is understandable when one considers his familiarity with the members of the Der Sturm gallery who embraced the Gothic cathedral of Taut and Gropius as a prototype for the construction of a new post-war German *Gesamtkunstwerk*. As the *Grotten*, *Höhlen* and *Zimmer* of Schwitters' KdeE indicate, he employed the motif of a religious structure to demonstrate his conception of architecture in a more emphatic way than Taut or Gropius. In doing so, Schwitters connected his Merz method of making art and architecture with the anagogical purpose of the Gothic cathedral.

Anagogical themes in the Gothic cathedral and in Merz

It can be asserted that no concept is more important to the design of religious experience in both the Gothic cathedral and Schwitters' KdeE than *anagoge*. Typically associated with the reading of a religious text, the term 'anagoge' refers to the interpretation of a word or passage of text as having a spiritual or mystical sense over and above its literal meaning. During the twelfth century, the French abbot Suger gave one of the most celebrated explanations of the anagogic function of the precious metals and gems in religious objects. He stated that they were to cause one to 'reflect, transferring that which is material to that which is immaterial' and to be 'transported from this inferior to that higher world in an anagogical manner'.[28] This perception of art and architecture essentially derived from a dictum attributed to the early Christian theologian Origen of Alexandria, who said that 'the visible world contains images of heavenly things in order that by means of these lower objects we may rise to that which is beyond'.[29] Much in the same way as his peers who were practising Expressionist and Dada art, Schwitters interpreted the materials that he used as having an ineffable content contributing to the making of his Merz art and architecture.

The mystical interpretation of material components in art was a popular concept of the German avant-garde during the early twentieth century. One of the primary proponents of a spiritual concept of art was Wassily Kandinsky, who outlined a theory of artistic composition based upon his concept of an 'inner necessity' in his 1912 essay 'Über das Geistige in der Kunst' (Concerning the Spiritual in Art). Herein Kandinsky argued that the juxtaposition of 'colouristic and linear forms that have an independent existence', along with musical 'dissonance', 'ugly sounds' and 'unbeautiful dance movements' could be considered beautiful, provided they were borne from an invisible determining content he referred to as an 'internal necessity'.[30] A handful of the Zürich Dadaists during this time also viewed their work as an interpenetration of material with spiritual content in order to provide an explanation for the possibility of making sense of the apparent nonsense of the fluctuating material world.[31] For one of the founders of Dada, Hugo Ball, the process by which Dada art and poetry incited the imagination to make connections between absurd and misshapen assemblies of literary and visual fragments had a precedent in the anagogic interpretation of Christian art.[32] Even when Ball first encountered the name 'Dada', he recognized a connection between it and mysticism. He wrote about this connection in his diary on 18 June 1921, explaining that 'when I met the word "Dada", I was twice called from Dionysius. D.A.-D.A. (H-------k [Huelsenbeck] wrote about this mystical birth; I did too in earlier notes. At that time, I was interested in the alchemy of letters and words)'.[33] The dating of this remark is important, because Ball made it at a time when he was working on a biography of Dionysius the Pseudo-Areopagite for his book, *Byzantinisches Christentum* (Byzantine Christianity).[34]

The Christian apologetic philosopher, Dionysius the Pseudo-Areopagite was an important early-fifth-century theologian responsible for developing the anagogical framework that influenced the design of the Gothic cathedral. In his *Celestial Hierarchy*, the Pseudo-Areopagite built upon Plotinus's theory of the One to propose an invisible source for physical things as the 'Father of lights' or God.[35] The Pseudo-Areopagite sought to use the Christian conception of creation as a metaphor to describe how one could interpret an invisible order for all things beyond the veil of visible reality.

While today the term 'anagoge' is overshadowed by its use to name a form of religious experience, contemporary dictionaries define anagoge as 'the elevation of the mind [or the adept] to divinity' in early Greek philosophy and the 'interpretation [or explanation] of texts as having [or by inserting] a higher sense, e.g. the interpretation that seeks to give a symbolic relationship to biblical words'.[36] Both the German word 'anagoge' and the English word 'anagogy' derive from the Late Greek word αναγωγη (anagoge) as an elevation (mystical or ecstatic) and ultimately from the early Greek word αναγειν (*anagein*) meaning 'to lead', and 'to elevate'.[37] The ancient Greek use of the word *anagein* to describe the elevation of something 'physically' was expanded to include the elevation of something 'intellectually' and later by extension, 'mystically' with Plato, who used a word with the same stem 'ana' as *anagein* to describe the epistemological ascent (*anabasis*) from a contemplation of physical particulars to their higher invisible archetypes or *eidos*.[38] As an example, following Aristotle's distinction, to interpret the how and why of a house was to *agagein* or to elevate an understanding of it intellectually.

The close connection between the term *anagogy* in early Greek philosophy and its later development in Christian exegesis is best revealed by Saint Thomas Aquinas, who used Aristotle's concept of causality in his *Summae Theologica* to describe Dionysius the Pseudo-Areopagite's 'God' or 'Father of Light' as the 'final cause'.[39] Here, Aquinas used Aristotle's notion of a final cause to posit God as the 'ultimate cause'.[40] Aquinas' contemporary, Saint Bonaventure, also saw an application of the four causes in Christian theology by applying them to the four forms of biblical exegesis. For Bonaventure, the four levels of the 'book of Scripture' – the literal, tropological, allegorical and anagogical – could likewise be applied to interpreting nature as a 'book of creation' having material, formal, efficient and final causes.[41]

Perhaps nowhere does an anagogical perspective of materials reappear during the twentieth century more vigorously than in the making and reception of Schwitters' Merz art and architecture. In the modern era, the term 'anagogy' has maintained a use consistent with Schwitters' Merz interpretation of found objects: to describe the elevation of the mind from a perception of visible particulars to an interpretation of the invisible content that they hold in common. In 1923, Schwitters certainly saw a connection between his work, Dada and spiritual experience when he claimed that 'Dada is the Christian spirit in the realm of art'.[42] And later, in 1944, he connected this 'Christian spirit' with his own work when he wrote to Herbert Read thanking him for describing his Merz work as having 'a mystical justification for taking up the stones which the builders rejected and making something of them'.[43] Schwitters' references to the spiritual in these instances suggest that his interest was in the anagogical role of Merz. All this aside, Schwitters never used the German term for 'anagoge' (anagogy) to describe his Merz use of found objects.

For Schwitters however, KdeE was not envisioned as a form of religious experience but a demonstration of his conception of architecture. Constructed as a representation of the Heavenly Jerusalem on earth, the primary function of geometry, the emphasis on light and use of precious materials in making a Gothic cathedral was intended to lead the mind of its user to anagogically contemplate ineffable truths about the creation of all things by a Christian god. However, Schwitters' Merz was not a religion. In his description of *Haus Merz,* Spengemann suggested that *Haus Merz* is 'not the church building' in the literal sense, but rather the 'expression of a truly spiritual intuition, of the kind that raises us to the infinite: absolute art'.[44] Like the Gothic cathedral, this anagogic reading of *Haus Merz* compares it to a church reliquary as a model for how Merz architecture should be imagined, while the *Merzbau* is likened to a prototype for how it could be constructed. Similar to the shrines and reliquaries of a Gothic cathedral the intention of Schwitters' *Merzbau* was to venerate particular individuals and events that were significant to the Merz approach towards the use of found materials to make art and architecture.

Conclusion

If there are structures that demonstrate the profound change of the sacred during the early twentieth century, Schwitters' KdeE must certainly be included among them. When Schwitters began to develop the KdeE, German Expressionist artists and architects were still exploring new approaches to the construction of art and architecture that would embrace what they perceived as the ephemeral, transitory nature of meanings in contemporary life. In this context, the Gothic cathedral's construction as a *Gesamtkunstwerk* became an ideal model for the avant-garde. It served to loosen the boundaries between the arts in order that designers might conceive and experiment with new approaches to architecture. Schwitters' sublimation of the terminology and aims of the Arbeitsrat für Kunst demonstrate that he saw Merz as an ideal method for achieving these aims and his KdeE was an attempt to make manifest and validate his ideas in physical form. Yet, only shortly after Schwitters claimed to have begun his KdeE, the Bauhaus pedagogue Mies van der Rohe, claimed in his 1924 article 'Baukunst und Zeitwille' that it was no longer time to 'build cathedrals' and called upon artists and architects to embrace 'reason and realism' as expression of the time to create structures as a 'perfect functional expression'.[45] Schwitters however, kept working on his KdeE until 1937 when he was forced to flee Nazi Germany. Although it was demolished by an Allied bombing raid in 1943, the photographs of Schwitters' KdeE persist in the cultural memory of German modernity. Never complete and continually changing, it was the celebration of modern art and architecture – the non-objective sublimation of the physical and metaphysical articles of the everyday into a representation of a modern sacred structure.

Notes

1. Bruno Taut, 'Eine Notwendigkeit', *Der Sturm* 4, nos. 196–7 (February 1914): 174–5.
2. Charles Baudelaire, *The Painter of Modern Life*, trans. and ed. Jonathan Mayne (London: Phaidon Press, 1964), 12–15.
3. Kurt Schwitters' explanation that the word 'Merz' came from an advertisement for '*KOMMERZ UND PRIVATBANK*' is found in an autobiographical text in an issue of *Merz*

titled 'Katalog'. Kurt Schwitters, 'Katalog', *Merz*, no. 20 (1927): 99–100. Reproduced in Kurt Schwitters, *Das literarische Werk*, ed. Friedrich Lach, vol. 5 (Cologne: DuMont Buchverlag, 1981), 250–4. Hereafter references made to Lach's compendium of Schwitters' writings are abbreviated as follows: *LW*, followed by a volume number and pagination.

4. Schwitters, 'Merz', *Der Ararat* 2, no. 1 (January 1921): 3–9. Reproduced in *LW*, vol. 5, 74–82. This English translation is by Ralph Manheim in *LW*, vol. 5, 404.
5. Schwitters, 'Die Bedeutung des Merzgedankens in der Welt', *Merz: Holland Dada*, no. 1 (January 1923): 8–11. Reproduced in *LW*, vol. 5, 133–54. See specifically, 134. This English translation by John Elderfield, *Kurt Schwitters* (London: Thames and Hudson, 1985), 43.
6. Ibid. This English translation by Elizabeth Burns Gamard in Gamard, *Kurt Schwitters' Merzbau* (New York: Princeton Architectural Press, 2000), 26.
7. Elderfield gives both senses to the translation of '*Entformung*'. Elderfield, *Kurt Schwitters*, 237. For Schwitters' use of the term *Formen*, see: Schwitters, 'Merz', in *LW*, vol. 5, 76.
8. *Entformelt* is the term Schwitters uses to describe the disassociation of words and objects from their original contexts and purposes. Elderfield explains the relationship between *Formung* and *Entformung* in Schwitters' work at length in: Elderfield, *Kurt Schwitters*, 237–8.
9. Schwitters, 'Die Bedeutung des Merzgedankens in der Welt', 134. With my inclusion of *Eigengift* and *Entmaterialisiert* from the original German text, this English translation by Werner Schmalenbach, *Kurt Schwitters* (Cologne: Verlag M. DuMont Schauberg, 1967), 94.
10. Ibid., 76. With my inclusion of the original German word *Ausdruck*, this English translation by Ralph Manheim in *LW*, vol. 5, 406.
11. '*Das Kunstwerk entsteht durch künstlerisches Abwerten seiner Elemente. Ich weiss nur, wie ich es mache, ich kenne nur mein Material, von dem ich nehme, ich weiss nicht, zu welchem Zwecke*'. Ibid.
12. Kurt Schwitters, 'Die Merzmalerei', *Der Sturm* X, no. 4 (July 1919): 61. Reproduced in Kurt Schwitters, *LW*, vol. 5, 37.
13. Schwitters, 'Merz', 6.
14. Christof Spengemann, 'Merz – die offizielle Kunst', *Der Zweemann* 1, nos. 8–10 (June–August 1920): 40–1.
15. Matthew Mindrup, 'The Merz Mill and The Cathedral of the Future', *Intersticies* 14 (November 2013): 49–58.
16. Richard Huelsenbeck, *Memoirs of a Dada Drummer*, ed. Hans J. Kleimschmidt, trans. Joachim Neugroschel (New York: Viking Press, 1974), 66.
17. In the spring of 1920, Max Ernst visited Schwitters at his studio and claimed that Schwitters referred to it as a 'Merz-column'. Patrick Waldberg, *Max Ernst* (Paris: Pauvert, cop., 1958), 162–3 after Elderfield, *Kurt Schwitters*, 146, n. 10.
18. *Kurt Schwitters* (Tokyo: Seibu Museum of Art and Museum of Modern Art, 1983), 142. An exhibition catalogue.
19. Schwitters, 'Ich und meine Ziele', *Merz 21: erstes Veilchenheft*, no. 21 (Hannover, 1931): 113–17. Reproduced with partial English translation by Eugène Jolas in: Kurt Schwitters, *LW*, vol. 5, 340–8 and 423–4 specifically, 345 and 424. See also: Gamard, *Kurt Schwitters' Merzbau*, 87–94.
20. After Gamard, *Kurt Schwitters' Merzbau*, 95, n. 24.
21. After Ibid., 98, n. 30.
22. Taut, 'Eine Notwendigkeit', 174–5.

23. J. Weinstein, *The End of Expressionism; Art and the November Revolution in Germany, 1918-19* (Chicago: University of Chicago Press, 1990), 1–25; I. K. Rigby, 'Critics, Artists and the Revolution', in *German Expressionism, Documents from the End of the Wilhelmine Empire to the Rise of National Socialism*, ed. R. Washton Long (New York: G.K. Hall; Toronto [etc.]: Maxwell Macmillan, cop., 1993), 173–4; Ian Boyd Whyte, *Bruno Taut and the Architecture of Activism* (Cambridge: Cambridge University Press, 1982), 95–102.

24. Bruno Taut, 'Ein Architektur-Programm', *Mitteilungen des deutschen Werkbundes* 4 (1918): 16–19.

25. Marcel Franciscono, *Walter Gropius and the Creation of the Bauhaus in Weimar* (Urbana, Chicago, London: The University of Illinois Press, 1971), 146–7.

26. Schwitters, 'Merz', 7. This English translation by R. Manheim in *LW*, vol. 5, 407.

27. Schwitters, 'Schloss und Kathedrale mit Hofbrunnen', *Frühlicht* 1, no. 3 (1922): 87.

28. Abbot Suger, *Abbot Suger on the Abbey Church of St.-Denis and Its Art Treasures,* ed. Erwin Panofsky (Princeton: Princeton University Press, 1979, (2 edn)), 46–9 and 64–5.

29. Origen, *On First Principles*, trans. G.W. Butterworth (Gloucester: Peter Smith, 1973), 278–9.

30. Wassily Kandinsky, 'On the Spiritual in Art and Painting in Particular', in Wassily Kandinsky, *Kandinsky: Complete Writings on Art*, ed. Kenneth C. Lindsay and Peter Vergo, trans. Peter Vergo (Da Capo Press, 1994), 193, 202–4.

31. Richard Shepard suggests that a number of Dadaists came to Zürich with the same question for which they had two different perspectives: 'Was a dynamic principle of order discernible within its contradictions and fluctuation or was it, in the end, just chaos?' For those who took the position of the former Shepard included Tristen Tzara, Raoul Hausmann, Hans Arp, Richard Huelsenbeck, Johannes Baader, Emmy Hennings and Hugo Ball. See: Richard Shepard, 'Dada and Mysticism: Influences and Affinities', in *Dada Spectrum: The Dialectics of Revolt*, ed. Stephen C. Foster and Rudolph E. Kuenzli (Maddison: Coda Press, 1979), 98–104 and 111–13.

32. Hans Richter, *Dada Art and Anti-Art,* trans. David Britt (London: Thames and Hudson, 1997), 51.

33. Hugo Ball, *Flight Out of Time*, ed. John Elderfield, trans. Ann Raimes (Berkeley and Los Angeles: University of California Press, 1996), 210. For a discussion of Ball's interpretation, see: Ibid., 248–51.

34. Ball, *Byzantinisches Christentum: Drei Heiligenleben* (Munich and Leipzig: Duncker & Humblot, 1923).

35. Dionysius Areopagita, *Des heiligen Dionysius Areopagita angebliche Schriften über die beiden Hierarchien*, trans. Josef Stiglmayr (Kempten and Munich: Kösel, 1911), 3; This English translation in *Dionysius the Pseudo-Areopagite*, 145–6.

36. With my inclusion of 'or the adept', 'or explanation' and 'or by inserting' into the second and third definitions of 'anagoge' in the *Brockhaus-Wahrig* dictionary to make it correspond with the *Duden* definition. *Duden: Das grosse Wörterbuch der deutschen Sprache* (Manheim, Leipzig, Wein and Zürich: Dudenverlag, 1999), 193, s.v. 'Anagogy'; Compared to the German dictionaries, the *Oxford English Dictionary (OED)* limits its definition and examples for the word 'anagogy' to a description of the interpretation of Scriptures as a 'spiritual elevation or enlightenment, especially to understand mysteries' and a 'mystical interpretation, hidden "spiritual" sense of words'. See: *The Oxford English Dictionary*, 2nd edn, vol. 2 (Oxford: Oxford University Press, 2004). s.v. 'Anagogy'.

37. *Oxford Dictionary of English Etymology*, ed. C. T. Onions (Oxford: Oxford University Press, 1966), s.v. 'Anagogy'.

38. For Plato, the mind that moves from a contemplation of visible things to knowledge of their intelligible Ideas is an 'ascent' (*anabasis*). Plato, *The Republic*, trans. Paul Shorey (Cambridge, MA: Harvard University Press; London: William Heinemann Ltd, 1969), 109–29.

39. For this passage in the *Summa Theologica*, see: Saint Thomas Aquinas, 'Question V: Of the Good in General', in *The Summa Theologica of Saint Thomas Aquinas*, trans. Fathers of the English Dominican Province, rev. Daniel J. Sullivan, vol. 1 (Chicago: William Benton, 1952), Part I, Question V, Article II, Objection I, 24. Aquinas' Commentaries on Aristotle's Physics and Metaphysics have been translated into English. See Saint Thomas Aquinas, *Commentary on Aristotle's Physics*, trans. R. J. Blackwell, R. J. Spath and W. E. Thirkel (London: Routledge and Kegan Paul, 1963); Thomas Aquinas, *Commentary on Aristotle's Metaphysics*, trans. and intro. P. Rowan (Indiana: Dumb Ox Books, 1961).

40. Aquinas argued that God is the 'ultimate cause' in Part I, Question I, Article III of the *Summa Theologica*. See: Saint Thomas Aquinas, 'Question II: Whether God Exists', in Saint Thomas Aquinas, *The Summa Theologica of Saint Thomas Aquinas,* Part I, Question II, Article III, 13.

41. Saint Bonaventure, 'Prologue', in *Breviloquium*, IV, 1 et 5; ed. min. 20–23; *In Hexaemeron*, II, 15–18, and XIII, 11-33, t. v, 338–9 and 389–92; *De reductione atrium*, 5, t. v, 321, et ed min., 372 after Etienne Gilson, *The Philosophy of Saint Bonaventure*, trans. Frank J. Sheed and Dom Illtyd Trethowan (Patterson: St. Anthony Guild Press, 1965), 208, n. 38–9.

42. '*Dada ist der christliche Geist auf dem Gebiete der Kunst*'. Kurt Schwitters, 'Tran 35, Dada ist eine Hypothese', *Der Sturm* 15, no. 1 (March 1924): 29–32. Reproduced in *LW*, vol. 5, 172–5. See specifically 174.

43. Schwitters to Herbert Read, 1 November 1944. Reproduced in Kurt Schwitters, *Wir Spielen, bis uns Tod abholt: Briefe aus fünf Jahrzehnten*, ed. Ernst Nündel (Frankfurt am Main: Ullstein, 1974), 177 and Herbert Read, London 1944, n.p. after Elderfield, *Kurt Schwitters,* 93, n. 73–4.

44. Spengeman, 'Merz – die offizielle Kunst', 40–1.

45. Ludwig Mies van der Rohe, 'Baukunst und Zeitwille', *Der Querschnitt* 4 (1924): 31–2.

CHAPTER 12
MODERN MEDIEVALISMS
CURATING THE SACRED AT THE SCHNÜTGEN MUSEUM IN COLOGNE (1932–9)
Maximilian Sternberg

In his autobiography, Frank Lloyd Wright wrote that he considered Victor Hugo's *Notre Dame de Paris* to be 'one of the truly great things ever written on architecture'.[1] And this is not an isolated testimony: time and again, modern architects of the heroic era of high modernism referred to, and at times appropriated, the medieval past in order to express their aspirations for both their own time and the future. The Middle Ages can in fact be seen to embody the archetypal historical 'Other' of Modernism; no other historical era has been derided or idealized in such recurrent and passionate forms. The advent of architectural modernism attested to a distinct and varied renewal of the modern fascination with medieval imagery that was first cultivated by those artists and writers associated with German Romanticism. It can thus be seen that modern architectural imaginings are a classic locus of medievalism more widely, defined by Lousie d'Arcens as the 'reception, interpretation or recreation of the European Middle Ages in post-medieval cultures'.[2] The idea of sacrality in modern architectural discourse in particular has frequently been framed with recourse to the medieval past, the Romantic legacy of Caspar David Friedrich's paintings being one of its many precursors and sources of inspiration.

Medievalism was especially influential in relation to modern architects' conceptions of the task of twentieth-century church design. For the leading church-architects and theorists of sacred space, including the Protestant Otto Bartning and the Catholic Rudolf Schwarz, medieval art and architecture was held up as an incontrovertible standard for assessing the cultural and spiritual conditions for the modern expressive possibilities of the sacred. Furthermore, medievalist art critics such as Wilhelm Worringer exerted considerable influence over the avant-garde, highlighting the trans-historical allure of medieval art, particularly the Gothic. Assessing modern sacred architecture by medieval standards became seminal. Particularly in German architectural discourse and in most publications on modern sacred architecture since the 1960s, the paradigm of the Gothic, the Romanesque or the medieval cathedral serve more generally to make sense of the architectural currents of the present.

This present chapter examines how the curation of Germany's most significant museum of medieval art, the Schnütgen Museum in Cologne,[3] coincided precisely with the design of the first ground-breaking modern churches to be built in the Rhineland. Given German architects' intense interest in the Middle Ages, it seems apt to study the way that museum curators actually chose to display medieval art to the public in this period. By what architectural means did the Schnütgen's first director Fritz Witte (1876–1937) hope to convey the relevance of medieval culture to contemporary society? Did the meanings he ascribed to his collection share affinities with architects' conceptions of the Middle Ages and how has this informed their understanding of the sacred in modern times? The question of how to present traditional religious art to a modern audience became a major challenge for modern architecture, and the Schnütgen Museum can significantly inform our understanding of the sacred in Modernism, insofar as it presents a very early example of a modernist approach to museum design that was to become the norm, first in Germany, then across the world, embodied most famously in institutions such as MoMA in New York.[4]

Opened as an autonomous museum in 1932, the Schnütgen was in fact the first art museum in the world to present a collection of exclusively *medieval* artefacts in a setting that comprised barren and well-lit rooms with whitewashed walls and pedestals, making no recourse to historicizing, figurative scenic props (Figure 12.1). For many contemporary observers in the West, this sort of 'white cube' architecture is one of the most familiar manifestations of quasi-sacred space.[5] By studying how a modernist architectural language came to be adopted as the most suitable conduit for the public reception of religious art, we can gain insights into how modern architecture itself was perceived to have the capacity to embody sacred meanings. Furthermore, in the Schnütgen, we can

Figure 12.1 Schnütgen Museum, St Heribert Abbey, Room 10 'Gothic wood sculpture' (1932).
Source: Rheinisches Bildachiv.

see how the rise of the whitewashed interiors of both modernist museums and churches not only developed contemporaneously but were also interconnected by processes that fed one off another. Scholars have increasingly recognized that museum design and curation were major arenas for Modernism in which art patrons, art critics and museum directors played a significant role alongside architects.[6] Museum design itself was not only influenced by but also actively contributed to the rise and popularization of modernist aesthetics. In what follows it will be argued that it was not coincidental that Witte, the Schnütgen's first director, was simultaneously an early advocate of modern museum curation *and* of modern ecclesiastical art and architecture. The fact that he occupied this pivotal position as both a medieval art historian and a passionate public mediator of medieval heritage should not be surprising, given the leading, if today largely neglected, role medievalism played in Modernism.

* * *

In 1910, the clergyman and antiquarian Alexander Schnütgen (1843–1918) bequeathed his private, and by then already internationally renowned, collection of medieval art to Cologne. The city built a new wing at the local Applied Arts Museum to house it, and in 1910 Fritz Witte was appointed as the first curator of the collection. He was then instated as director in 1918, and held that position until his death in 1937. Trained both as a Catholic priest and as an art historian in Rome and Münster, Witte also gained experience in the curation of museum collections, under the mentorship of Alfred Lichtwark in Hamburg. Lichtwark was a reforming pioneer of museum pedagogy, a connoisseur of medieval art as much as he was a leading advocate for modern art. Far from being an antiquarian, Witte engaged enthusiastically with modern art, maintaining close relations with members of the Deutsche Werkbund throughout his career. He served on the committee dedicated to the display of modern religious art in the seminal Werkbund Exhibition of 1914, and eight years later he was one of the most vocal apologists of Peter Behrens' much-debated Dombauhütte at the Deutsche Gewerbeschau in Munich. Witte was equally instrumental in the appointments of Richard Riemerschmid and Dominikus Böhm at the Cologne Applied Arts school in the 1920s.

As editor of the leading journal *Die christilche Kunst*, Witte was also a supporter of the architectural ideals of the Catholic liturgical reform movement led by Johannes van Acken and the Catholic priest Romano Guardini. Mies van der Rohe much admired Guardini, and it is well attested that he read his works carefully. While Witte was critical of modernist polemics calling for a revolutionary break with the past, warning of the proliferation of 'subjectivism and diffuse world views', he was no less firm in his condemnation of the church's 'ridiculous and untimely' patronage of doctrinaire historicism.[7] In his activities as a publicist, he regularly insisted on the affinities between medieval and modern art, postulating that 'historic religious art cannot deny its inner relationship to modern art'.[8] Clearly influenced by Worringer but also by the architectural critic Adolf Behne, Witte exclaims for instance that Matthias Grünewald, whom he takes as a medieval rather than a Renaissance painter, captures a 'soulful emotion and experience' that stands at the gates of Expressionism'.[9] Witte shared the popular Expressionist enthusiasm for the ostensibly trans-temporal qualities of medieval art.

In 1932, the Schnütgen collection was deemed to be both substantial and important enough to warrant its own museum, and it was moved to the premises of the secularized Abbey of St Heribert in Cologne-Deutz. Witte personally conceived the new display, and he was determined not only to present the artefacts as being of *art historical* significance (rather than a cultural-historical or applied arts collection) but to do so with the most explicitly modern curatorial means available. After Schnütgen's death in 1918, Witte had already begun modernizing the display in the Applied Arts Museum. Presenting the task of the design of a museum as one more *progressive* than conservative, he asserted just prior to the refurbishment that 'art history is cultural history, it is the history of the soul, the mirror of culture, and must tell the truth clearly without flattery . . . Gothic space must be shown as a whole, not broken down into its elements. Taken out of context the object loses its significance'.[10] He prioritized works of high quality and exhibited them sparsely, relegating lesser works to storerooms that now housed a study collection (Figure 12.2). The new arrangement in the Applied Arts Museum attempted to communicate historical developments to the public in a more accessible way, by following a logic that included all media, while also consistently displaying large sculptures in a way that foregrounded their monumental character. In his commitment to mediating his collection to a wider public, Witte also produced the first visitor guide and systematic scholarly catalogue

Figure 12.2 Applied Arts Museum, Cologne. Room 8 'Chapel' of the Schnütgen Wing (after 1925).
Source: Rheinisches Bildachiv.

of the museum. When he was finally delivered the opportunity to start a display from scratch in the new setting of St Heribert, Witte clearly felt the time was ripe for drawing the consequence of his own modern medievalism, enacting a far more comprehensive reconfiguration of the collection than he had been able to carry out up until that time.

The St Heribert Abbey in Deutz stands in close proximity to the banks of the Rhine, with views from its east range towards Cologne's cathedral on the other side. The original complex consisted of a double-storied, eighteenth-century baroque cloister complex adjoined by a Late Gothic abbey church. The former conventual buildings surrounding the cloister made up the core of the museum's exhibition spaces. Witte arranged the premises into fourteen rooms for the collection. By using the cloister galleries both as auxiliary exhibition spaces and as a means to organize the visitors' circulation, he respected the traditional centrality of the cloister in a monastery. According to the recommended itinerary laid out in the guide, the visitor to the exhibition started on the north side and followed a clockwise path around the cloister. The exhibits on the path were chronologically organized, opening with Romanesque sculpture and bronzes, followed by Gothic painted woodworks and miniatures, then Gothic and Romanesque treasuries, and stained glass.[11] The church that was accessed from the south-west corner of the cloister was incorporated into the itinerary. From the north-west corner, back by the main entrance, the visitor ascended stairs into the heart of the collection – 'Gothic wood sculptures' – located in the most prominent room on the first floor, which is the level on which the route concluded, with rooms for tapestries, ecclesiastical vestments and braids, finally terminating beyond the medieval epoch, in the 'Baroque art' room.

In his article for the special edition of a local newspaper dedicated to the opening, Witte underlines the modernity of his approach, defining his ambition for the project, which was 'not to show a lot but to show it well'. Making explicit reference to the concept of *Sachlichkeit*,[12] he contended that the modern visitor wants to appreciate 'one work after another', rather than 'being confronted with an amassed side-by-side'.[13] He also dismissed the attempts by others to create 'atmospheres', seeing no place for 'sensations and the artificial' in mediating the experience of art in a museum'.[14] The most striking visual feature of Witte's rooms were thus the blank, whitewashed walls.[15] The new setting was radically pared back, both in colour and in décor. The whole wherewithal of the period room, with its stone vaults, arched windows, ornate columns and timber trusses, varieties of materials, wall colours and ornamentation, was abandoned altogether. Witte held himself exclusively to white walls, simple cuboid pedestals and flat ceilings without mouldings. Display cases had fine metal frames hosting only a limited number of objects. The sobriety of the environment was further accentuated by the large amount of space left between exhibits, and the banishment of all furniture from the rooms.

In further contrast to the picturesque, historicizing rooms of the collection in the Applied Arts Museum, natural light was employed as the primary means of illuminating exhibits, in ways appropriate to their individual functional needs. For instance, Witte noted that the collection of stained glass is illuminated by daylight for the purposes of authentic experience, but also that it is kept separate so as to not interfere with the appreciation of other artworks.[16] The space left open by the placement of artefacts along the perimeter of the rooms allowed for the distribution of a bright and even daylight in them. Electric lighting was dispensed through modern light fittings. Artefacts were arranged on a single horizon line, further underlining the contrast between the spacious blankness of the walls and the objects displayed. Only works of the 'most significant artistic quality' were included,[17] and most rooms further singled out particularly outstanding objects by isolating them even further from the rest of the objects on display. Witte boldly asserted that each artwork is to be considered a world unto itself, proclaiming, 'The first and last principle in the display of the museum was to achieve the greatest possible isolation of the individual art works, as though the museum had been custom-built for each high-quality object itself.'[18]

Witte underlined the importance of making rooms capable of adaptation to future circumstances. Indeed, at one level the 'white cube' backdrop presented a pragmatic, flexible frame for the shifting needs of his collection. The white rooms made objects out of the artefacts by presenting an ambience of objectivity. However, this was achieved largely by an act of exclusion, seemingly creating a blank page. Yet the white cube is of course anything but a neutral setting. Having first appeared during the Secession in Vienna, the sobriety of the pared-back white interior was specifically intended to instil an emotive sense of the sacred in visitors' encounters with art.[19] In his classic study of the modern art museum, Bryan O'Doherty has noted the affinity of the white cube with a medieval church.[20] And it is also worth remembering that Le Corbusier attributed a spiritual value to whitewashing walls even in domestic interiors: 'there are no more dirty, dark corners. Everything is shown as it is. Then comes an inner cleanness ... Once you have put Ripolin on your walls you will be master of yourself.'[21] The spiritualizing connotations of white walls was not entirely lost on Witte as his emphasis on *Sachlichkeit* and functionality was counterbalanced by his continuing concern for the religious significance of the works.

In the written public account of his Schnütgen display, Witte in fact made reference to the late medieval mystic and native of the Rhineland, Thomas à Kempis. Witte asserted that the works of the collection originated in medieval practices of private devotion for which the monastic cell was the original paradigmatic setting. By justifying the isolation of a work of art with respect to its original religious purpose, Witte developed a more spiritualizing account of his display. Just as he had drawn a trans-temporal analogy between Grünewald and Expressionism at the beginning of his curatorial career, he implies that the Rhenish mystic tradition embodied by Thomas à Kempis anticipated the modern aesthetic turn towards a conception of art through the prism of personal experience. By acknowledging the works' religious functions, Witte also intended to enable the viewer to gain insight into 'the religious attitudes of the Rhineland's spiritual and intellectual history', and to foster a 'veneration for the ancient'[22] among the broader public. In an article published in 1920, Witte had stated that religious objects that no longer served their original purpose should be given to museums as the only place where they can 'honour the church and serve science'.[23] The strategy of isolation therefore fulfilled a range of intentions, from the functional to the aesthetic and religious.

The ambivalence of isolation as an approach to display is mirrored in the architectural character of the curation, which wavers between rationalizing sobriety and spiritualizing evocation. Particularly in the 'Gothic wood sculptures' room it becomes apparent that Witte did not renounce the communicative possibilities offered by a subtle architectural mise en scène. Along the sides of the room, Witte installed what could be termed roofless peristyles, each resting on four-square columns terminating in a flat wall, creating a semi-enclosed space behind. On one level, the installation can be read as a simple, functional frame that is consistent with Witte's strident commitment to *Sachlichkeit* and answering to the need for segregated encounters with individual artworks by creating intimate niches at regular intervals. However, on another level the resulting configuration could also be read either as cloister galleries or as a simplified and stage-set-like basilica, complete with nave, aisles and chancel.

Apprehended through the viewfinder of a camera, the association with a church interior is amplified. Generally photographed as one would a church, the view is down the 'nave' towards the implied liturgical focus in the 'chancel'. The tall windows of the large room, whose rhythm the columns take up, reinforces the sense of a skeletal, intimate interior of a medieval parish church or modest monastic oratory. There are only two objects that break up the single plane on which all other works are displayed, and both stand on axis with the stairs and 'nave'. One is a towering crucifix installed at the back of the room in the equivalent of a flat 'apse', and the other is a Mary with Christ-Child suspended from the ceiling at the top of the stairway above the 'choir screen'. Three sculptures at the base of the crucifix introduce Trinitarian symbolism of the kind commonly found in medieval apses. Without claiming to didactically 'reconstruct' the historical settings that the objects originally inhabited, Witte's display suggested a coherent liturgical backdrop. Though abstracted, the church analogy would have been apparent to the museum's educated and mostly bourgeois Christian audience, many of whom would still have regularly attended services in one of Cologne's plentiful medieval churches. While Witte may have rejected the model of the museum period room, contrary to his own claims he did in fact create a very deliberate and artificial atmosphere, aiming to engender very particular sensations.

The arrangement of the remaining sculptures evokes not only the cells of a monastery but also those private chapels that proliferated in the bays of aisles and transepts in many Gothic churches from the thirteenth century onwards. To some extent, the peristyles also broke up the uniform illumination of the white interior, bestowing upon the room a more differentiated character familiar from traditional church architecture. As visitors walked up the wide staircase to Room 10, at first they would only have seen a single artefact – the crucifix – marking a threshold and thereby conveying a sense of entry and preparing them for a special encounter. Beckoning the visitor, the placement of the crucifix creates a conscious dramatic effect, drawing on the analogy between physical and spiritual ascent made in ecclesiastical architecture. For all his stated commitment to *Sachlichkeit*, Witte here staged an experience that could be taken as a form of secular-sacred pilgrimage or devotion. Witte could in fact draw on modern calls for the renewal of the spirit of traditional architecture, such as the one that Alva Aalto made in 1925 to declutter church interiors for devotional as much as aesthetic purposes: 'A simple unpretentious room with one single detail (a crucifix on a grey lime wall) that heightens the atmosphere of devotion, is a hundred times more beautiful than columns and ornamental flourishes framing an enormous altarpiece.'[24] Witte could not have expressed his own credo as curator more succinctly.

A resulting paradox of this sanctification of museum space was a peculiar concomitant secularization of the actual existing church. The venerable Gothic chapel is simply given the label 'room 8' in the guide. The former place of worship becomes both exhibit and exhibition space, a historical testament that is aestheticized for the edification of art connoisseurs. It is incorporated in the same serene calm of the exhibition atmosphere taken to be imbued with spiritual and sacrosanct heritage values. In his foreword to the 1936 guide, Witte makes mention of both the 'modern presentation' of the collection and the layers of hagiographic, monastic and imperial history embedded in St Heribert and that are still in evidence in the fabric and furnishings of its chapel.[25] With characteristic pathos, Witte exclaims that the collection could not possibly have found a more propitious home, one in which 'Rupert of Deutz created finest Rhenish intellectual history', and where Benedictines were 'for centuries bearers of German spirit, erudition and art'.[26]

In the same special newspaper issue of 1932, the leading conservationist and fellow medievalist art historian Paul Clemen too speaks of the abbey as a 'site consecrated by history and ritual', creating a very 'special individual' of a museum.[27] Franz von Wolff-Metternich in turn praises the preservation and incorporation of the historic fabric specifically as a 'master class of *modern* architecture', 'breathing back life' into it and recusing it from its previously disfigured state.[28] Franz Rademacher speaks of a 'monastic atmosphere that still reverberates in the charming quadrangle' benefiting the ecclesiastical art on display.[29] The sense of a communicative exchange between material remains and modern staging in St Heribert is essentially the thread that runs through the variety of viewpoints presented in the special issue. Rather than merely isolating medieval artefacts so as to transform them into autonomous works of art, the modernity of the curation thus also served to mediate between the historical fabric on the one hand, and the collection of the museum of the other, since together artworks and religious artefacts manifested a living tradition. As Witte writes in the afterword of his guide: '[In the Schnütgen Museum] bridges are built from the present to the past, and on them people walk across the riverbank of history to the present.'[30] The poster for the opening of the Schnütgen at St Heribert is perhaps the most telling visual expression of this conception (Figure 12.3). The Expressionist composition sets the scene by Cologne's iconic pairing of bridge and cathedral, and presents the migration of the museum as though it was a medieval translation of relics, a sacred play publicly enacted in the city. Modern and medieval art are here characterized in their spiritual affinity, reminiscent of Lyonel Feininger's seminal woodcut for the cover of the 1919 Bauhaus manifesto.

This simultaneous heritagization and renewal of medieval art was contemporaneous with dramatic new avenues of church design in Germany, and nowhere more so than in the Rhineland. One of the most radical examples was Rudolf Schwarz's much discussed St Fronleichnam in nearby Aachen (Figure 12.4). Consecrated in 1930, the church was enthusiastically praised by Schwarz's close friend Mies van der Rohe – its blank rectilinear white interior, offset only by the dark monolithic floor, pews and altar, was revolutionary.

Modern Architecture and the Sacred

Figure 12.3 Poster for the opening of the Schnütgen Museum, St Heribert (1932).
Source: Rheinisches Bildachiv.

Figure 12.4 Rudolf Schwarz, St Fronleichnam, Aachen (1930).
Photograph courtesy of Livia Hurley.

Yet Schwarz was critical of both liturgical functionalism and techno-centric architectural rationalism. On the contrary, he shared with Guardini an interest in the mystical and contemplative aspects of liturgy and the creation of appropriate spaces of worship.[31] Furthermore, Schwarz spoke of the religious origins of the modern technical spirit and the 'unbroken lineage between gothic and technical' in his account of his Corpus Christi project.[32] Although Schwarz relinquished figurative medieval references of the kind found in the work of his erstwhile collaborator Dominkus Böhm, medieval architecture continued to be a key reference for him. For Schwarz, *Sachlichkeit* has its origins in medieval architecture, and rationalism and contemplative mysticism are in fact two sides of the same coin. While the stern whiteness of the Schnütgen Museum and St Fronleichnam serve different purposes, the justification their two authors give for them, and the spiritual connotations they embody, nevertheless bear an undeniable resemblance. In their common rejection of scenic historicism, the curator Witte and the architect Schwarz create an alternative form of austere theatricality, of a rhythmic play of dark and light informed by a modernist conception of space such as that which appears in the influential designs by the Swiss scenographer Adolphe Appia discussed by Ross Anderson in this volume.

Such affinities between church and museum, are further evidenced in Schwarz's earlier restoration works. In his very first major architectural commission, Schwarz carried out the renovation of the interiors of Burg Rothenfels (1926–8), a major centre for the Catholic reform movement aimed specifically at youth (Figure 12.5).

Figure 12.5 Rudolf Schwarz, Rothenfels Castle, refurbished communal room (1926). Photograph courtesy of Burg Rothenfels.

Schwarz was himself a member of the organization and effectively acted as the resident architect. Like Witte, Schwarz had to deal with an existing monastic complex and adapt it for modern purposes. As Witte would follow suit in 1932, Schwarz opted for the aesthetics of pared-back white interiors evocatively inserted into a medieval fabric, creating provocative juxtapositions between modern and medieval. The primary communal room was kept largely empty, with basic, moveable furniture designed to enable adaptive uses, not unlike the flexibility Witte sought to create at the Schnütgen. Schwarz suggested that the architectural poverty in fact harboured a spiritual richness. Contemporaries perceived a mystical atmosphere in these rooms which readily Schwarz readily accepted. Schwarz liked to cite Thomas á Kempis and other medieval mystics.[33] Schwarz's approach was radical and it proved seminal for subsequent modern conservation practices.[34] The work at Rothenfels that was in fact a collaboration between Guardini and Schwarz was intended to convey liturgical reform to an audience wider than its monastic origins. This again brought the character of the design and purpose of the institution of Rothenfels close to that of the Schnütgen collection in St Heribert.

* * *

The evolution of the Schnütgen collection from a private applied arts collection to a public art history museum reflects some of the leading tendencies both in the advent of modern museum staging and in the cultural production of medievalism in the interwar period in Germany. Witte's display at St Heribert followed a wider trend found in both, namely the progressive aestheticization of history. Yet Witte's curation not only aestheticized the sacred but also sacralized the aesthetic. At St Heribert this sacralization was achieved both by incorporating built heritage and by creating a modernist frame that evoked some mode of sacrality with ambiguous temporal connotations. For all of Witte's deep understanding of, and allusions to, the medieval world to which his collection belonged, he did not conjure identifiable liturgical settings with their diverse religious practices. Rather, the observers find themselves immersed in an abstracted generic setting, the conceptual domain of styles, aesthetic criteria, affinities and differences – a milieu operating between personal taste and knowledge, itself bracketed between connoisseurship and art historical knowledge. This domain, curiously, authorizes a more 'authentic' worship than traditional religion, one that is based on artistic quality.

Witte implies that the gap between everyday liturgical practice and that of taste and knowledge enjoys similarities with mystical experiences that involve a *contemptus mundi* for the sake of communion with a higher reality. This is also echoed in the ascetic church spaces advocated by Guardini and Schwarz. Witte's and Schwarz's mise en scène possess an element of modernist violence in that they erase the mediating role of historicizing architectural simulation and décor in favour of the void of the white walls, engaging in a form of creative destruction for the purposes of renewal. Abstract space comes to mediate the dispersed artefacts or worshippers, in which whiteness creates a special domain for contemplation and renewal that requires a silencing of aesthetic interference.

In many ways, Witte's museum architecture was an exemplary architectural re-enactment of the Romantic motifs out of which the modern museum originated, and which effectively transformed the museum into a privileged site of what Hölderlin has termed an 'aesthetic church',[35] while the inherited medieval church becomes a museum that retains its dignity as art and heritage even after the death of God announced by Friedrich Nietzsche. In its modernist theatricality, the Schnütgen curation of 1932 is also related to the *Gesamtkunstwerk* tradition and its attempt to reconcile art with life, as discussed in Gabriele Bryant's chapter in this volume.

Engagements with the medieval inheritance, be it in the form of a collection of art, or in terms of the claims of age-old traditions of ecclesiastical architecture, make legible the ambivalent modern conception of the sacred. The Schnütgen Museum of the 1930s, lost for all time to the aerial bombardments in the Second World War, reveals that modern Sachlichkeit was a multivalent and ambivalent concept. The fact that Witte believed the Schnütgen might play a role in a wider process of societal renewal, again reveals his affinity with modern architects' imaginary, which Iain Boyd White aptly defined as a 'coalescence of religious and mystic belief with dreams of the harmonious social collective'.[36] In pursuit of these spiritual expectations, both museum curators and church designers appropriated the white space of Modernism, teasing out different meanings for different purposes. In some instances, museum and church design juxtaposed medieval and modern, and whiteness became an alluring way of suggesting a reconciliation of tradition and modernity, of spirit and technology. Witte and Schwarz reinvent the space of the museum and church through an uncanny 'change over' in which what is in fact highly artificial – the white wall – has taken on the semblance of what is 'natural' and 'authentic', a paradoxical situation which is at the very heart of modernity. What characterized the examples discussed here is the unusually explicit and reflective manner in which this was enacted. Medievalism is arguably a privileged, though largely ignored, window into these tensions at the very heart of Modernism.

Notes

1. Frank Lloyd Wright, *An Autobiography* (Warwick: Pomegranate, 2005), 78.
2. Lousie d'Arcens, ed., *The Cambridge Companion to Medievalism* (Cambridge: Cambridge University Press, 2016), 5.
3. For a history of the collection see: Nancy Netzer and Virginia Reinburg, eds, *Devotion. Fragmented Devotion: Medieval Objects from the Schnütgen Museum* (Chicago: Chicago University Press, 2000).
4. Alexis Joachimides, *Die Museumsreformbewegung in Deutschland und die Entstehung des modernen Museums, 1880-1940* (Dresden: Verlag der Kunst, 2001), chapter 5.
5. Gretchen Townsend Buggeln, Crispin Paine and S. Brent Plate, eds, *Religion in Museums: Global and Multidisciplinary Perspectives* (London: Bloomsbury Academic, 2017), 14.

6. Katherine Kuenzli, 'The Birth of the Modernist Art Museum: The Folkwang as Gesamtkunstwerk', *Journal of the Society of Architectural Historians* 72 (2014): 503–29. Anthony Vidler, 'The Space of History: Modern Museums from Patrick Geddes to Le Corbusier', in *The Scenes of the Street and Other Essays* (New York: Monacelli Press, 2011), 294–316.
7. Fritz Witte, 'Neue Zeiten, neue Ziele', *Zeitschrift für christliche Kunst* 32 (1919): 3–4.
8. Ibid., 7.
9. Ibid.
10. Ibid., 5.
11. Fritz Witte and Hermann Schnitzler, *Führer durch das Schnütgen-Museum der Hansestadt Köln* (Cologne: Schnütgen-Museum, 1936).
12. Witte, 'Was wir wollen, und was wir sollen', *Kölnische Volkszeitung*, 19 March 1932.
13. Ibid.
14. Ibid.
15. The argument for adopting white walls for art museums across the board had been formulated in the early 1920s by the art critic Karl Scheffler. He justified his call for the white wall in the art historical museum by invoking the ostensibly whitewashed interior of the artist's atelier. Alexis Joachimides has aptly termed this new approach the 'atelier-space simulation'; see: Joachimides, *Museumsreformbewegung*, 252–3.
16. Witte, 'Was wir wollen'.
17. Ibid.
18. Ibid.
19. Joachimides, *Museumsreformbewegung*, 135.
20. Bryan O'Doherty, *Inside the White Cube* (Berkley: University of California Press, 1986), 14–15.
21. Le Corbusier, *The Decorative Art of Today* [1925] (London: Architectural Press, 1987), 188.
22. Witte, 'Was wir wollen'.
23. Fritz Witte, 'Ein ernstes Wort über Restaurierung', *Zeitschrift für christliche Kunst* 33, no. 4 (1920): 58.
24. Alvar Aalto, 'Finish Church Art', in *Alvar Aalto in His Own Words*, ed. Göran Schildt (Helsinki: Otava, 1997), 38.
25. Witte and Schnitzler, *Führer*, 7.
26. Ibid., 6–7.
27. 'Randglossen und Zeitstimmen zum Problem Museum von Heute', *Kölnische Volkszeitung*, 19 March 1932.
28. 'Schnütgen-Museum und Denkmalpflege', *Kölnische Volkszeitung*.
29. 'Vom Römerkastel zum Museum', *Kölnische Volkszeitung*.
30. Witte and Schnitzler, *Führer*, 87.
31. Richard Kieckhefer, *Theology in Stone, Church Architecture from Byzantium to Berkley* (Oxford and New York: Oxford University Press, 2008), 234–9.
32. Rudolf Schwarz, 'Erneuerung des Kirchenbaus?' *Die Form* 21/22 (1930): 546.
33. Wolfgang Pehnt, *Rudolf Schwarz 1897-1961: Architekt einer anderen Moderne* (Ostfildern: G. Hatje, 1997), 16, 36–43.

34. Wolfgang Pehnt, 'Die ganze Raumform: Dominkus Böhm und Rudolf Schwarz, ein Doppelportrait', in *Dominikus Böhm: 1880-1955*, ed. Wolfgang Voigt and Ingebord Flagge (Tübingen: Ernst Wasmuth, 2005), 30.
35. Anette Gilbert, 'Die "ästhetische Kirche." Zur Entstehung des Museums am Schnittpunkt von Kunstautonomie und Kunstreligion', *Anthaneum* 19 (2009): 45–85.
36. Iain Boyd Whyte, ed., *Modernism and the Spirit of the City* (London and New York: Routledge, 2003), 5.

CHAPTER 13
ARCHITECTURE, POLITICS AND THE SACRED IN MILITARY MONUMENTS OF FASCIST ITALY
Hannah Malone

Introduction

Benito Mussolini's Fascist regime in Italy served its political ends through architecture that was at once sacred and modern. This chapter explores that conjunction of religion and modernity through a group of ossuaries (bone depositories), which were built to house the remains of Italian soldiers who fell in the First World War. Whereas, initially, Italians who died fighting in the war were buried in makeshift cemeteries close to the battlefields, in the 1920s and 1930s their remains were disinterred and reburied by the Fascist regime within large ossuaries. Located along the former front in north-eastern Italy, the Fascist ossuaries are unique among European memorials for their vast scale and monumentality. Innovative in form, they drew on architectural elements of European modernism and Italian rationalism, as evidenced by a tendency towards abstraction, simplification and reduction of ornament. At the same time, Catholic symbolism was deployed in order to imbue the monuments with sacred power and to serve a political agenda. As secular sites of pilgrimage, the ossuaries fostered veneration of fallen soldiers through imagery that was explicitly religious. They depicted the dead as martyrs and their death as a sacrifice for the redemption of the fatherland. By imposing a narrative that spoke of salvation, they also helped to silence discordant memories of the Great War as pointless slaughter. As well as bolstering support for the Fascist dictatorship, the monuments were meant to prepare the Italian population to fight in future wars. Their combination of religious and political iconography was in the line with the way Fascism acted as a 'political religion' or an ideology that adopted religious strategies of propaganda. As the Fascist authorities operated in a deeply Catholic culture, they borrowed tools of persuasion that belonged to the church. At the same time, they endorsed modern architectural styles as emblematic of the modernity of Fascism. This suggests how, far from disappearing from modern architecture, the sacred was reinvented in new and meaningful ways to serve political functions.

The architecture of Fascist Italy contradicts a stereotypical view of modern architecture as a secular movement that is focused on function, technology and rationalism.[1] Rather, Mussolini's regime engendered buildings that were both sacred and modern, or which drew simultaneously on religion and Modernism to serve political goals. Italian rationalism was exceptional among interwar movements in modern architecture in that

Architecture, Politics and the Sacred

it was simultaneously 'cosmopolitan and nationalistic, politically progressive and yet fully committed to the political program of Fascism'.[2] As such, it was ideally suited to Fascist ambitions both to modernize Italy and to revive its national traditions – a paradox that also reflected the coexistence of revolutionary and reactionary factions within the regime. After the conquest of Ethiopia and the foundation of the Fascist empire (1936), there was a turn towards traditionalism in ideology, as in architecture. However, the ossuaries emerged from an earlier period in which the Fascist authorities endorsed a range of styles and a unique blend of Modernism and tradition.

This chapter will show how religious symbolism and modern aesthetics might work together to carry messages of political propaganda. As such, the ossuaries are particularly interesting as they exemplify how religion can be not only integral to modern aesthetics but also expressive of modernity. The monuments are ideal spaces for the modern reinvention of the sacred, in part, because of their nature as burial sites. While cemeteries are closely bound to ideas of the sacred, they are also sites for architectural experimentation because of the limited functional requirements of a dead body. To show how modernity and holiness coexisted within the ossuaries, this chapter has three sections: the first section looks to the context in which they were built; the second shows why they were built or the aims that they were meant to serve; and the third focuses on how modern architecture used the sacred to fulfil those aims.

Context

Between 1915 and 1918, more than 650,000 Italian soldiers died fighting against Austro-Hungarian and German forces in a relatively small area, which stretches across the north-eastern corner of Italy into what is now Slovenia. Initially, those who fell in battle were buried wherever possible in makeshift cemeteries or mass graves close to the battlefields. Immediately after the war, those burial places were rearranged into small cemeteries scattered along the former front lines, and which looked like minor civilian cemeteries.[3] In 1927, two years after the establishment of the Fascist dictatorship, the authorities declared those modest cemeteries to be unsatisfactory and launched a vast campaign to award honourable burial to the war dead. The regime exhumed the remains of over 300,000 soldiers who had died in battle and reburied them in new ossuaries, which were built close to the earlier burial grounds and to the former battlefields. The older cemeteries were then demolished.

The authorities summarized the campaign to rebury the fallen with one word: 'centralization'.[4] Whereas before the dead were scattered among a large number of small burial grounds, the Fascists' programme for reburial meant that remains were concentrated within fewer, large ossuaries. For instance, the ossuary of Montello is quite small by comparison with some of the others, but still it contains over 9,000 bodies gathered from 130 cemeteries in the surrounding area (Figure 13.2). The geographical concentration of the fallen was accompanied by a process of political centralization in that the campaign was run entirely by a military commission under the Ministry of War.

Previously, the commemoration of the fallen had been left to mourners, local councils and Veterans' groups. However, from 1927, measures were introduced that supressed local initiatives and curtailed the rights of private citizens to erect monuments and to hold ceremonies in honour of the dead. Effectively, the Fascist regime monopolized the right to pay homage to the fallen and brought remembrance under the control of the state. By demolishing the older front line cemeteries, the authorities were going against the wishes of many of the bereaved, and they met with resistance, particularly from the clergy as a group that had a stake in commemoration. Clearly, the aim was not to provide solace or consolation, but to gain political advantages from commemoration. Hence, the sacred was used in a way that placed the Fascist cause above the spiritual needs of mourners.

As to the architects, the military commission that was charged with the construction of the ossuaries had the power to appoint favoured architects without holding competitions. These architects were part of a select group and were chosen either because they were veterans of the Great War, or because they were active within the Fascist party. After General Ugo Cei took over as head of the commission in 1935, he awarded all projects to his favourites – the architect Giovanni Greppi and the sculptor Giannino Castiglioni. Working in partnership under Cei's direction, Greppi and Castiglioni developed original forms that advanced the ossuary as a building type. Although they were at one time prominent, or at least part of the establishment, the designers of the ossuaries have since fallen into oblivion, perhaps because of a tendency to banish to the sidelines of history those who were tainted by association with the Fascist dictatorship. Despite their current obscurity, these architects created innovative designs that drew on the sacred in new ways.

Aims

It is important to grasp the purpose of the ossuaries in order to understand how spirituality and modernity served together to further that purpose. The obvious answer to the question of why the ossuaries were built, or why the Fascist state went to great effort and expense to exhume the fallen, is that it helped advance specific political aims. Having seized control in 1922 by undemocratic means, the Fascist authorities needed to legitimize and strengthen their power, and one of the ways in which they did so was through the commemoration of the dead. In particular, they used the ossuaries to serve two political objectives. The first was to 're-write' the memory of the First World War, as a highly contentious and divisive event in Italian history. Few Italians had wanted the war, and many thought that, although Italy was on the winning side, the nation had lost much and gained little.[5] The peace negotiations brought disappointment, and deepened the divisions between those for whom the conflict was a triumphant victory and others for whom it represented a pointless slaughter. The Fascist leadership drew strength from that societal facture and, once in power, imposed its own memory of the past. Thus, the conflict became a keystone of Fascist ideology. As monuments to the 'sacrifices and glory of the fatherland', the ossuaries were part of Fascist propaganda that was meant to restore the nation's dignity, after the conflict exposed Italy's weaknesses in its military skills, foreign relations and international standing.[6] They expressed a positive vision of the war, which served to prepare the nation for future military engagements – a function that became more important with Italy's invasion of Ethiopia in 1935. Of course, as much as the ossuaries helped to remember history, they were also about forgetting, in that they repressed negative memories of the war and silenced dissenting voices, particularly among pacifists and neutralists.

The second political objective was to foster a cult of fallen soldiers as martyrs for the fatherland. That cult was a useful political instrument because it helped to bind the living together through a common memory of the dead, and to build unity among a population that had been divided by the First World War. The celebration of the death of honourable men helped to enhance Italy's self-image and to reinforce the honour of a nation shaken by conflict. Clearly, any prestige awarded to the nation could be harvested in turn by the Fascist authorities. Moreover, the celebration of the fallen served as a call to arms, as the living were led to believe that they owed it to the dead to fight for their fatherland. At the inauguration of one of the ossuaries in 1938, the chief of staff, General Pietro Badoglio, stated that 'to be worthy of the fallen . . . all Italians must be ready to follow their example [and to die for Italy]'.[7] This kind of rhetoric was used to prepare the Italians for new wars and to promote an agenda based on militarism and imperialism.

Tellingly, the Fascist cult of the dead was expressed through the language of Catholicism. The fallen were described as martyrs; their martyrdom was a sacrifice for the redemption of the fatherland; the ossuaries were called *sacrari* or shrines because they enclosed 'relics'. Thus, Fascist propaganda 'spoke' in a Catholic vocabulary that was familiar and accessible to the majority of the Italian population. Christian images of sacrifice pervade the ossuaries, such as the palms of martyrdom at the ossuary of Fagarè, or the statue of Risen Christ at Passo del Tonale (1936). At Pian di Salesei, the low-rise blocks of the ossuary were arranged to form a cross-shaped plan in the forecourt of a pre-existing church. In that each of the blocks represents a battle in the surrounding area, the deaths are cast as necessary sacrifices for the resurrection of the nation. For the Fascists, it was a way to recast the war's losses as having been necessary for Italy's rebirth. The aim was to promote future wars of conquest by promising the fallen eternal life in the national memory.

The Christian paradigm of martyrdom and redemption has long offered a model for noble and meaningful death. The patriotic variant of that paradigm was not a Fascist invention, but rather had emerged during Italy's fight for independence in the nineteenth century as a foundation of national identity.[8] Fascist propaganda also cast as martyrs those who had died fighting for the regime, thus connecting Fascist heroes with Italy's founding fathers.[9] This propaganda operated through myths of which Catholicism was a major source. However, the religious element went beyond rhetoric since Fascism was conceptualized as the 'religion of the fatherland', in which the nation replaced God as the object of faith. This convergence of politics and religion has been described as the sacralization of politics – a process whereby, with the rise of modern nationalism, politicians borrowed ideological instruments that belonged to religion and the clergy.[10]

It shows how, with the rise of modern secularization, the sacred migrated from the religious sphere to that of politics.

On the one hand, the Fascists relied on the persuasive powers of religion and the political support of the Catholic Church. On the other, tensions emerged between church and state, as Fascism encroached upon the domain of religion and threatened the autonomy of the clergy. Through the Lateran Pacts of 1929, the Fascist state entered an official alliance with the Vatican, which was meant to resolve conflicts dating back to the Risorgimento, or the struggle for Italian unification.[11] In reality, the pacts were a marriage of convenience, dictated by mutual self-interest, rather than ideological alignment. Whereas the Vatican planned to use the regime to 're-Christianize' Italian society, the Fascists expected the clergy's support for plans of imperial conquest.[12] Both sides hoped to dominate the balance of power, but were ultimately disappointed. While the Vatican looked to the Fascist authorities to protect its power, the regime depended on the clergy to shape public opinion, particularly among rural communities that lived outside of the sphere of national politics and were more open to religious indoctrination than to nationalist messages. Very shortly after the signing of the pacts, the church encouraged Catholics to vote 'yes' in a plebiscite in support of the Fascist regime.[13] In the end, the pacts failed to reconcile church and state because of the fundamental incompatibility of Catholicism and Fascism, as totalizing ideologies that demanded complete control over the hearts and minds of Italians.[14]

As a tradition dear to many Italians, the commemoration of the dead presented an opportunity to exercise public influence, which made it a source of conflict and rivalry between the Fascist and clerical authorities. The regime's efforts to control the commemoration of fallen soldiers jeopardized the role played by clergy in that commemoration since the war years.[15] However, in exchange for backing the regime, the clergy was granted a position in Fascist rituals of remembrance. Around the time of the Lateran Pacts, a compromise emerged that apportioned the dead between the church and the state according to the location of death.[16] In broad terms, those who fell on the front lines were buried by the regime in ossuaries close to the former battlefields, whereas those who died behind the front were accommodated in urban churches, which were partly or completely funded by the state, but administered by the clergy. Thus, the Fascist authorities appeased the Vatican, while retaining control over the remains of those who died in action – a category awarded the highest position in the hierarchy of fascist propaganda.[17] Geographically, it meant that the church tended to urban burial sites, while the regime had the opportunity to build new ossuaries on empty sites along the former front lines – on which this chapter focuses.[18]

Means

Around twenty new ossuaries were built in the short period of time between 1929 and 1938. Some were constructed at the sites of existing churches, as at Caporetto, Pian di Salesei, Bezzecca, Timau and Schio, but most were created entirely from scratch. In terms of their architectural form, they are remarkably varied and draw on various historical traditions. For instance, the adoption of classical models, albeit in a simplified form, can be seen in the portico at Fagarè (1935) and the triumphal arch of Asiago (1936). Roman classicism had a particular significance for Fascism as the language of empire and of Italian greatness and, in that sense, the monuments were part of efforts to establish a national style and to export classicism from the capital to Italy's remote northern territories. During the Fascist period, Italians architects turned more often to antiquity, than to the Middle Ages, in search of a national idiom.[19] However, the Middle Ages were also a source of inspiration and a number of the ossuaries are reminiscent of medieval castles or fortresses – in line with their martial character and their position as guardians of Italy's borders. For instance, the ossuary at Caporetto recalls a medieval fortress, and the monument at Oslavia takes the form of cylindrical towers interconnected by battlements (Figure 13.1). This reflected a pan-European trend of medievalist war memorials since the nineteenth century, which ennobled warfare through suggestions of medieval chivalry. In late-nineteenth-century Italy, ossuaries were built for the fallen of the wars of independence in the form of medieval turrets. After the First World War, the need to counter a sense of rupture reasserted this tradition.[20] In fact, the Fascist ossuary at Oslavia was modelled on the sixth-century mausoleum of King Theodoric near Ravenna. Across Europe, medieval references were powerful not only because they could idealize modern warfare but also because they could imbue commemoration with a sense of the sacred because of associations with Christianity.

Crucially, tradition is always reinvented in a modern form in the ossuaries. At Montello (Figure 13.2), classical elements, such as the columns and temple front, are updated or modernized. Equally, the ossuary at Pocol is a modern variation on the theme of the medieval tower in that the historical precedent is stripped to its essentials. As seen in these examples, ornament is limited and the sculpture is subordinated to the architecture. This tendency towards simplification, abstraction and plain geometrical forms reflected the influence of the Modern Movement. Specifically, it showed how Italian rationalism adapted elements of the International Style to suit a Fascist context, for instance by adopting simple geometries that were rooted in Italian heritage.[21] As well as supporting Mussolini's image as the leader of a modern revolution, the limitation of decoration served to reduce costs – a major concern of the fascist administration. In line with modern aesthetics, the ossuaries were shaped by a process that minimized detailing to expose the essential form of architectural types. For example, the ossuaries at Pocol and Pasubio are abstract renditions of a tower; Asiago and Stelvio draw on the arch; Fagarè takes the form of a portico; Rovereto recalls a circular temple; and Monte Grappa and Redipuglia are arranged as stairs. The monuments capture the essence of familiar types in order to harness their symbolic capital – particularly with reference to the sacred. The references have an abstract or generic quality, in that they do not refer to a specific source, but help to evoke timelessness and sacrality. Overall, the ossuaries were shaped by a typically Fascist interplay between tradition and modernity, which stemmed from a desire to create architecture that was at the same time Italian and modern, or which was both rooted in Italy's history and suited to its new status as a Fascist dictatorship.[22] This

Figure 13.1 Oslavia (1938).
Photograph by Hannah Malone, 2014.

conjunction of tradition and innovation was manifested through architecture that was modern and religious, or which drew on both Modernism and Catholicism.

The ossuaries evoke the sacred mainly in two ways. On the one hand, the presence of chapels, altars, crucifixes and Stations of the Cross makes them explicitly Catholic, reflecting the alliance between church and regime, and the role of the clergy as officiators

Figure 13.2 Montello (1935).
Photograph by Hannah Malone, 2014.

in Fascist rituals. On the other hand, there is a subtler sense of transcendence within the ossuaries, which is not overtly religious, although it draws on the well-worn strategies of Catholicism. This implicit sacrality expresses the nature of Fascism as a religious ideology and as a rival to Catholicism. Although the distinction is between a Catholic and Fascist spirituality, the line between the two is blurred and it is difficult to say where one ends and the other begins. It is also important not to think of 'political' and 'religious' as distinct categories because even the most manipulative propaganda may have appealed to the spiritual feelings of Italians. Moreover, the ossuaries embodied a range of motivations associated with the many agents involved in their design and construction – including military and state leaders, architects, builders and local authorities. In any case, the sacred, as evoked by the ossuaries, was truly modern in that it drew force from mass politics, rather than from institutional religion.

The ossuaries deployed the sacred to serve political ends primarily through their function, form and location. They harnessed the power of religion through their intended function as sacred sites and as destinations to which the masses would flock in secular pilgrimage to pay their respects or to participate in large ceremonies. This intention was supported by the process of concentrating millions of bones within few locations, but also through the construction of new railways and roads to render the monuments more accessible. Battlefield tourism was a booming industry in the 1920s and 1930s, and was greatly encouraged by the Fascist regime as a 'pious and sacred . . . duty for every Italian'.[23] The ossuaries became stations on battlefield tours that were arranged by schools, universities and Fascist clubs for adult recreation. Their sacred aura was enhanced by means of guidebooks, pamphlets, films, photographs, newspaper articles and other forms of publicity, which were targeted particularly at veterans and young people.²⁴ Until the Second World War impeded travel, large numbers of people visited the ossuaries under Fascism. Although it is difficult to know whether visitors really thought of the ossuaries as sacred sites, the high numbers of visitors suggest some success in turning them into pilgrimage destinations. That said, a public official complained in 1938 that the war zones, although 'spiritually sacred to Italians', were being ruined by scavengers searching for scrap metal.²⁵

In terms of their form, the ossuaries drew on religious symbolism, often in combination with military imagery. For example, the monument at Redipuglia is composed of a giant staircase with three crosses at the top that were intended to represent the 'Calvary' of the fallen (Figure 13.3). Akin to Christ, the dead were seen to have sacrificed their lives to redeem the nation and their sacrifice is re-enacted through religious iconography. The sacred imagery interweaves with military symbolism as the dead are represented in military formation. The monument at Redipuglia is the largest of its kind, containing body parts from over 100,000 corpses, of which approximately 60,000 were unknown or unidentifiable. While the unidentified remains were massed within a crypt, the small boxes containing the known dead were slotted into small niches or alcoves within a grid. Among this great mass, six tombs stand apart: the largest, which is at the front, is that of the commander, the Duke of Aosta, Emanuele Filiberto di Savoia, a cousin of the king, who would later become a fervent Fascist. Behind him are his five generals. Behind them, the rest of the fallen are arranged in serried ranks, as in an army risen from the dead that is ready to march into battle under the leadership of its commanders (who in real life were seldom at the front). As described in 1941, 'Redipuglia is not a Cemetery, but a rally of devout sons and warriors . . . of the Fatherland'.²⁶ The soldiers' readiness to fight is suggested by the obsessive repetition of the word PRESENTE that runs horizontally along the risers of the ascending steps (Figure 13.4).²⁷ This refers to the Fascist ritual of the *appello* or roll call, when a leader calls out the name of the dead and his comrades answer 'presente' to suggest that the dead are forever present in the memory of the living and always ready to serve their country. Yet, at Redipuglia, the actual identities of the fallen

Figure 13.3 Redipuglia (1938).
Photograph by Hannah Malone, 2014.

Figure 13.4 Redipuglia, detail.
Photograph by Hannah Malone, 2014.

are practically annihilated, as the dead are not remembered as husbands, fathers and sons, but only as soldiers. There is no sense of the fact that, unlike the 100,000 soldiers, the commanders did not die in battle, but passed away peacefully in post-war Italy. Thus, Redipuglia illustrates how Fascism borrowed opportunistically from Catholicism to bolster a militarist ideology.

The designers of the ossuaries turned to ecclesiastical architecture for practical, aesthetic and communicative solutions. In many ways, churches offered an ideal model for the ossuaries, not only for their capacity to evoke the sacred but also because of their nature as political places where power is asserted and negotiated.[28] While many forms of public and private space express social power, ecclesiastical architecture is special because that power is underpinned by a sense of the supernatural. By dividing between holy and profane space, church architecture demarcates community. Equally, Fascism sought to redefine the boundaries of the national community – an ambition reflected in the ossuaries and the depiction of the fallen as a cohesive group united by common beliefs. Church design also establishes a hierarchical order based on proximity to the divine or power source. A key principle of Fascist ideology, hierarchy was embodied in ossuaries, for instance at Redipuglia in the arrangement of the fallen by rank. In general, ecclesiastical architecture offered a blueprint for how the ossuaries might convey sacred meanings, establish rituals, coordinate large groups of people and establish community and hierarchy.

As sacred buildings, the ossuaries stand out and create space, rather than fitting in with their surroundings.[29] This is achieved by delimiting the ossuary by fences or walls, which serve a symbolic as well as practical function in that they denote the *zona sacra* (sacred area) around the monument. The enclosure is a traditional element of both ecclesiastical and funerary architecture in that it marks the boundary between the sacred and the profane – between the world of the living and the dead. Given the need to accommodate mass gatherings, they designed the monuments with an eye to voids as well as solids, much like Italian baroque churches. This space-focused approach created theatrical stages for Fascist events, such as funerals and inaugurations, which affirmed the sacredness of Fascism and re-enacted the victory of the Great War. For instance, the balconies at Montello were designed for 'religious rituals' (Figure 13.2).[30] As in ecclesiastical architecture, the ossuaries also incorporated routes for rituals and ceremonies, which might be exterior, as the staircases ascending the terraces in the ossuary of San Candido, or interior, as at the concentric balconies that ascend the interiors at Oslavia, Pocol and Montello. Processional routes served to retain the memory of sacred rituals, even when they were not taking place.

A spectacular route leads to the ossuary of Caporetto (Kobarid), now in Slovenia. As the site of a humiliating defeat in 1917, Caporetto took on particular significance in Fascist propaganda as Italy's Passion, or as death that brought ultimate triumph. The symbolism of the Passion pervades the ossuary at Caporetto, which is located on a hill above town and connected to it by a *Via Sacra* (Sacred Way). Two pillars stand at the beginning of the *Via Sacra* in the main square of Caporetto, bearing the star of Italy and the Cross, which represent Catholicism and patriotism as the two symbolic pillars of Fascism. The route is flanked by the fourteen Stations of the Cross, which are marked with carved slabs by the sculptor Giannino Castiglioni and small piazzas where visitors can stop and pray on their ascent to the ossuary.[31] Castiglioni deployed the motif of the *Via Crucis* at the ossuaries of Caporetto, Rovereto and Redipuglia, as a link between Catholic tradition and the cult of the fallen as Christ-like saviours of the nation.[32] Designed by the architect Gianni Greppi, the ossuary at Caporetto developed around a seventeenth-century church at the apex of the hill as a structure of ascending octagonal terraces that recall military bastions. As noted by the historian Vanda Wilcox, 'The new Fascist memorial was constructed around the old chapel just as the Fascist symbolism and iconography were built onto and around the Catholic faith.'[33] Whereas the terraces accommodate niches for the remains of over 7,000 dead, a massive staircase continues the route to the entrance of the church. By integrating Catholic and Fascist iconography, the designers managed to imbue the ossuary with a powerful message of redemption. Thus, each battle, and the resulting losses, represent a step on the path leading to the salvation of the nation. Similarly, at Asiago, the ossuary was built as a gigantic triumphal arch on a small hill, which was linked to the town via an axial route culminating in a monumental staircase.

As seen at Caporetto, Asiago and elsewhere, staircases are prominent in the design of the ossuaries. Their function is to create long, taxing routes, which visitors were meant to ascend to give thanks for the sacrifices of the dead, and to express their faith in that for which lives have been lost. The ossuary at Redipuglia is a 'staircase to heaven', too big to be climbed, but visitors ascend by smaller, criss-crossing stairs at the sides of the monument (Figure 13.4).[34] The fact that paths are unnecessarily long, wide and steep shows that ritual, rather than practicality, was the main concern. Often, the stairs lead to balconies where visitors could pause to admire the view, as is the case at Oslavia, Rovereto and Montello (Figure 13.2). Demanding routes require commitment of the visitor, as a symbolic sacrifice to the dead and a re-enactment of the Calvary. The obvious precedent is the *Scala Sancta* (Holy Stairs), a recreation of the staircase that Christ ascended before his interrogation by Pontius Pilate, which Catholic pilgrims climb on their knees as an act of penance – the most famous example of which is in the Lateran Palace in Rome. The *Scala Sancta* inspired the design of Giuseppe Terragni's memorial to First World War (1928–32) at Erba Incino near Como, which the architect described as 'the first modern monument to the fallen built in Italy'.[35] Formed of a vast staircase ascending to a hilltop shrine, the memorial is steeped in references to ascension. In that visitors climb to a terrace where they can pause and admire the view, there is an evident link with the ossuaries. The motif of the staircase may also be connected to Jacob's ladder – a biblical reference to heaven-bound ascent that Le Corbusier used in a design for a villa.[36] In fact, the ossuaries may be read in Le Corbusian terms as '*promenades architecturales*' (architectural promenades) where circulation structures the viewer's impressions in a way that conveys meaning.[37] In general, Terragni's architecture is emblematic of how the designers of the ossuaries, and other architects of the period, harnessed the sacred to express Fascist power.[38] In line with a conception of Fascism as a new religion, Terragni sought to create 'mystical space' through geometrical forms and abstract references to ecclesiastical architecture.

Ideally, the route is always upward so as to evoke ideas of spiritual ascension. Clearly, architects were making the most of sloping terrains, as the sites where Italian soldiers fought, and where later the ossuaries were built, are largely mountainous. However, they were also drawing on a long-standing tradition of verticality in religious architecture, as represented by the vertiginous heights of Gothic cathedrals. Through verticality, designers pursued a 'spiritual beauty', according to the head of the commission that built the ossuaries.[39] There are connections with the *sacro monte* (literally, sacred mountain), an Italian Renaissance tradition whereby chapels were set within a landscape, typically along an ascending pathway, and accommodated life-size statuary that depicted religious scenes.[40] Located largely in the regions of Lombardy and Piedmont, the *sacri monti* are a relatively unique phenomenon in religious architecture, which sprung from a desire to offer an alternative destination for pilgrims in the late fifteenth century, when travel to the Holy Land was becoming increasingly hazardous. The Fascist ossuaries are akin to the *sacri monti* in that the visitor is engaged by means of an uphill route that is articulated through architecture and sculpture. Similarly, in 1920–2, the architect Eugenio Baroni designed a modern *sacro monte* to serve as a monument to the *Fante*, or infantryman, which was to be built on the former battlefield of Mount San Michele.[41] The design represents the soldier's path to war and death through a succession of grouped statues that are arranged along a staircase. By depicting the sacrifice of the fallen as a Via Crucis, Baroni sought to create 'a route of prayer, purification, with slow pauses for meditation'.[42] In that the project focused on the suffering of soldiers, rather than the triumph of the nation, it was eventually blocked by Mussolini as incompatible with Fascist propaganda. However, its combination of the *sacro monte* and the *Scala Sancta* acted as a model for the ossuaries – with the difference that they shifted focus from death to 'resurrection'.

In their upward thrust, the ossuaries differ from an opposite tradition in funerary architecture that burrows into the earth. That tradition is represented by the cemetery designs of eighteenth-century French revolutionary architects, such as Claude-Nicolas Ledoux, Étienne-Louis Boullée and Jean-François Blondel.[43] In the Fascist party headquarters in Como, Terragni placed the floor of the shrine of Fascist martyrs on a slightly lower level than the atrium from which it is accessed in order to heighten a 'sense of funerary religiosity'.[44] This 'buried architecture' (to use Boullée's expression) suggests descent into the underworld, rather than ascent towards the heavens.[45] By contrast, the ossuaries are more triumphant than mournful.

As evidenced by these examples, sacred symbolism was not just appended to the ossuaries through ornament but expressed through the buildings' volumetric forms. This meant that religion was a constituent element of the modern aesthetics of the ossuaries – part of what made them look modern. As religious traditions converged with modernist aesthetics, designers engaged with models of church architecture, which traced a line between the simple, white spaces of medieval Cistercian monasteries and the architecture of the Modern Movement. Since the late eighteenth century, the sacred expanded from ecclesiastical architecture to other building types, such as museums, libraries or government buildings, which could be endowed with a holy aura because of their cultural value.[46] As monuments to the dead, performing a largely symbolic function, the ossuaries were ideally suited to take on sacred connotations. They show how, with the decline of organized religion, the sacred could shift from the sphere of religion to that of politics.

Another way in which the monuments evoked the sacred was through their location in the landscape – grouped along the former front lines, the ossuaries contributed to an official Fascist policy to turn the battlefields into sacred sites. The battle grounds were accorded special status in a decree of 1922, which describes their role as a 'temple' for the teaching of the 'new religion of the fatherland' (i.e. Fascism).[47] Following the conventions of Fascist propaganda, the battlefields were consecrated by the blood spilt for the redemption of the fatherland. As well as acting as geographical markers of the landscape of war, many of the monuments were placed in areas that previously belonged to the Austro-Hungarian empire, and which Italy gained as a consequence of the First World War. Thus, they staked a claim on land acquired through the loss of military lives and justified the price paid for the new territory. They were also part of efforts to 'italianize' the Slavic and German populations of those areas, which involved the brutal repression of local languages and cultures.[48] Whereas the ossuaries were described as 'sentinels of the fatherland' protecting Italy's new borders, their role was really as admonishments to the local population and as 'outposts' for a future conquest of the Balkans.[49]

A number of the monuments are located high on mountains that were of strategic importance during the fighting, since both sides sought to gain the high ground. For instance, the ossuary on the apex of Monte Grappa, at an altitude of almost 2000 metres, is a powerful symbol of the Italian victory, in that here the Italians fought uphill against the Austro-Hungarian forces (Figure 13.5). The location had religious, as well as military, significance. Before the First World War, in 1901, the Catholic Church declared Monte Grappa a 'sacred mountain' and placed at its peak a statue of the Madonna. During the war, when Monte Grappa was the site of some of the bloodiest battles, Italian soldiers adopted the Madonna as an object of veneration. After the establishment of the dictatorship in 1925, the Fascist authorities wanted to create their own monument to victory. Thus, Monte Grappa became a contested site for two competing forms of holy propaganda, as church and state both sought to place their mark on the mountain.

An early project for the ossuary of Monte Grappa shows how, initially, the Fascist leadership agreed to preserve the statue of the Madonna at the centre of the composition. However, a later project presents a compromise, as the statue of the Madonna is kept intact, but it is shifted to a new location on top of a new chapel. In effect, this second design reframes, or recontextualizes, the religious monument. Significantly, there is also a new arrival in this second project in the form of a colossal statue of Italy, personified as an Amazonian woman and escorted by a smaller foot soldier. With the appearance of Italy, the Madonna has a rival. In this second design, the cult of the Madonna and the cult of Italy (or of the motherland) are placed in opposition. Eventually, the ossuary was built following a third and final project, and the original chapel of the Madonna was demolished. While the statue itself was kept, it was hidden within a new chapel of Fascist design. The clergy protested and threatened that there would be a popular

Figure 13.5 Monte Grappa (1935).
Photograph by Hannah Malone, 2014.

insurrection, but the Fascist state had won the argument. By enclosing the Madonna in a new structure, the regime effectively managed to convert a space of the church into a monument of the state. The ossuary of Monte Grappa is evidence of the power that the Fascist state had acquired by the early 1930s.

The case of Monte Grappa is emblematic of the struggle between secular and clerical powers for monopoly over the spiritual. It illustrates how the Fascist regime appropriated religious symbols to serve political ends and how those symbols were couched in modern architecture. The ossuary is imbued with spiritual connotations, in that it is shaped like a 'tower of Babel' with ascending and concentric rings (Figure 13.5). Once more, a staircase ascending to a hilltop chapel evokes the idea of heavenly ascent. A triumphal route runs long the crest, on each side of which a flanking monument commemorates an individual battle (Figure 13.6). As at Pian di Salesei, this *Via Sacra* is intended to represent Italy's route to victory in the First World War. As the hilltop location evokes the idea of ascension, the vistas are integral to the experience of visiting the monument. Moreover, in that signs of the war remain in the craters below, the landscape suggests a sacred cycle of death and rebirth, or of sacrifice and regeneration. At the inauguration of the ossuary of Asiago, the head of the commission that built the monuments described 'a sacred land, sown with the dead, for the blossoming of the Victory'.[50] Whereas at Monte Grappa the stripped-back aesthetic suited the image of a modern dictatorship, the spiritual suggestions drew on religious traditions; thus, the modern and the sacred worked together to convey Fascist power.

Figure 13.6 Monte Grappa.
Photograph by Hannah Malone, 2014.

With the fall of Mussolini's regime in 1945, the ossuaries were 'de-Fascistized', or stripped of some of the Fascist symbols, but by no means all of them. Today, they occupy an ambiguous position in Italian heritage. Although they have lost their original function as instruments of Fascist propaganda, they retain their sacred power. Some of the ossuaries have been reinvented as national monuments and are used to accommodate state and military ceremonies. Others are appreciated for their architectural qualities and their value as memorials to the fallen. It is interesting that, although the monuments have been reinterpreted in the light of current politics and culture, their religious content has not been entirely effaced. The ossuary of Redipuglia is significant in this respect in that, despite its militaristic symbolism, it has been adopted as a monument to peace by the Catholic Church and other religious groups, which points to the persistence of religion as a lens through which to view modern architecture.

Conclusion

Italy's ossuaries demonstrate how, under Mussolini's regime, modern architecture evoked the sacred as an instrument of propaganda. Principally, the monuments had two aims: one, to rewrite the history of the First World War and second, to foster a cult of the fallen to serve political ends. To fulfil those aims, they harnessed both modern aesthetics and spiritual imagery. In particular, they deployed the power of religion through their function, form and location. The ossuaries illustrate the nature of Fascism as a quasi-religious ideology that drew opportunistically on Catholicism. More importantly, however, they highlight the role played by spirituality in modern architecture. They testify to the fact that modernity and religion were not mutually exclusive languages, but rather worked together to serve the political ends of the Fascist regime. Today, the ossuaries are still an important part of Italy's architectural heritage and illustrate the enduring presence of the sacred in contemporary culture and in the interpretation of modern buildings. Now, as under Fascism, the ossuaries demonstrate how spirituality is fundamental to the aesthetics and meaning of modern architecture.

Notes

1. Richard A. Etlin, *Modernism in Italian Architecture, 1890–1940* (Cambridge, MA: MIT Press, 1991), xiii; Julio Bermudez, 'Introduction', in *Transcending Architecture*, ed. Julio Bermudez (Washington, DC: CUA Press, 2015), 6.
2. David Rifkind, *The Battle for Modernism: Quadrante and the Politicization of Architectural Discourse in Italy* (Venice: Marsilio, 2012), 10, see also 11–13.
3. Lisa Bregantin, *Per non morire mai: la percezione della morte in guerra e il culto dei caduti nel primo conflitto mondiale* (Padua: Il Poligrafo, 2010), 193–233.
4. Archivio del Commissariato Generale per le Onoranze ai Caduti, 'Memoria sulla sistemazione definitiva delle salme dei militari italiani caduti in guerra', 11 March 1930.

5. Giovanni Sabbatucci, 'La Grande Guerra come fattore di divisione', in *Due nazioni: Legittimazione e delegittimazione nella storia dell'Italia contemporanea*, ed. Loreto di Nucci and Ernesto Galli della Loggia (Bologna: Il Mulino, 2003).
6. '*dei sacrifici e della gloria della Patria*', plaque at the foot of the monument.
7. '*degni*', '*si sentano sempre pronti a seguirne il mirabile esempio*', *Il Comune di Asiago per la inaugurazione del Monumento ai caduti: Altipiano dei Sette Comuni* (Padua: Tip. del Messaggero di S. Antonio, 1938), 10.
8. Lucy Riall, 'Martyr Cults in Nineteenth-Century Italy', *The Journal of Modern History* 82, no. 2 (June 2010): 255–87, https://doi.org/10.1086/651534; Hannah Malone, *Architecture, Death and Nationhood: Monumental Cemeteries of Nineteenth-Century Italy* (London: Routledge, 2017), 104–18.
9. Roberta Suzzi Valli, 'Il culto dei martiri fascisti', in *La morte per la patria: la celebrazione dei caduti dal Risorgimento alla Repubblica*, ed. Oliver Janz and Lutz Klinkhammer (Rome: Donzelli, 2008), 101–7.
10. Emilio Gentile, *The Sacralization of Politics in Fascist Italy* (London: Harvard University Press, 1996); Emilio Gentile and Robert Mallett, 'The Sacralisation of Politics: Definitions, Interpretations and Reflections on the Question of Secular Religion and Totalitarianism', *Totalitarian Movements and Political Religions* 1, no. 1 (1 June 2000): 18–55, https://doi.org/10.1080/14690760008406923.
11. John F. Pollard, *The Vatican and Italian Fascism, 1929-1932: A Study in Conflict* (Cambridge: Cambridge University Press, 1985), 1–6.
12. Ibid., 104, 167–8, 191.
13. Ibid., 57–8.
14. Ibid., 191.
15. Patrizia Dogliani, 'Constructing Memory and Anti-memory, the Monumental Representation of Fascism and Its Denial in Republican Italy', in *Italian Fascism: History, Memory, Representation*, ed. R. J. B. Bosworth and Patrizia Dogliani (New York: St. Martin's Press, 2001), 15; Oliver Janz, 'Mourning and Cult of the Fallen (Italy)', *1914–1918 Online: International Encyclopaedia of the First World War*, 4, https://encyclopedia.1914-1918online.net/article/mourning_and_cult_of_the_fallen_italy.
16. Bregantin, *Per non morire mai*, 262–3.
17. A text of 1925 (quoted in Bregantin, *Per non morire mai*, 92) differentiates between the 'fallen' who were killed in action and the 'dead' who died away from the battlefields.
18. After the signing of the Lateran Pacts in February 1929, the clerical and Fascist authorities agreed to build the ossuaries of Treviso and Mantua, respectively, in April and June of that year (Bregantin, *Per non morire mai*, 256–8).
19. There are exceptions under the form of references to the medieval city-state: Richard A. Etlin, 'Nationalism in Modern Italian Architecture, 1900-40', in *Nationalism in the Visual Arts*, ed. Richard A. Etlin (Hanover and London: National Gallery of Art, Washington, 1991), 88–109.
20. George L. Mosse, *Fallen Soldiers: Reshaping the Memory of the World Wars* (Oxford: Oxford University Press, 1990), 100–3; ibid., 286.
21. Rifkind, *The Battle for Modernism*, 16.
22. Etlin, *Modernism*, xvii, xxiii, 377–90; Ruth Ben-Ghiat, *Fascist Modernities: Italy, 1922-1945* (Berkeley: University of California, 2001), 136–7.

23. Consociazione Turistica Italiana, *Sui Campi di Battaglia: Il Cadore, la Carnia e l'alto Isonzo* (Milan: CTI, 1937), 8, cited in Vanda Wilcox, 'From Heroic Defeat to Mutilated Victory: the Myth of Caporetto in Fascist Italy', in *Defeat and Memory: Cultural Histories of Military Defeat in the Modern Era*, ed. Jenny Macleod (London: Palgrave, 2008), 55. See also: Dogliani, 'Constructing Memory and Anti-memory', 18.

24. See, for instance, footage of the burial of General Gaetano Giardino in the ossuary of Monte Grappa in 1936, https://youtube/4D2qtocBS94.

25. Archivio Storico dell'Ufficio dello Stato Maggiore dell'Esercito, Fondo L3, VIII, 6, cartella 259, letter from the Gen. Renato Michelesi to Direzione Generale TCI, 10 March 1938.

26. 'Redipuglia non è, dunque, un Cimitero, ma una adunata di figli devoti, di guerrieri . . . della Patria', Attilo Fuiabo, *Credo nella resurrezione degli Eroi* (Milan: Corticelli, 1941), 227. See also: Ministero della Difesa, *Sacrari Militari della Prima Guerra Mondiale: Redipuglia* (Rome: Ministero della Difesa, 1988), 7.

27. The PRESENTE motif originated with the martyrs' shrine that was designed by Adalberto Libera and Antonio Valente for the exhibition of the Fascist revolution in Rome in 1932 (Etlin, *Modernism*, 414–15).

28. Jeanne Halgren Kilde, *When Church Became Theatre: The Transformation of Evangelical Architecture and Worship in Nineteenth-Century America* (Oxford University Press, 2005), 9–21; *Sacred Power, Sacred Space: An Introduction to Christian Architecture and Worship* (Oxford: Oxford University Press, 2008), 3–11.

29. See Karla Cavarra Britton's chapter in this volume.

30. '*funzioni religiose*', Archivio Commissione Generale Onoranze ai Caduti, Sezione Tecnica, Montello, 'Progetto disegni, dettagli per la costruzione, Felice Nori', 18 July 1931.

31. '*atmosfera mistica*', Archivio Commissione Generale Onoranze ai Caduti, Sezione Tecnica, Caporetto, Atti amministrativi 1935–9, 'Capitolato ditta Vittorio Marchioro', 22 August 1936.

32. Anna Maria Fiore, 'La monumentalizzazione dei luoghi teatro della Grande Guerra: I sacrari di Giovanni Greppi e Giannino Castiglioni (1933-1941)' (PhD diss., IUAV, 2001), 77.

33. Wilcox, 'From Heroic Defeat to Mutilated Victory', 56.

34. Richard A. Etlin, 'In Face of Death: Calming the Mind, Mining the Soul', in *Der bürgerliche Tod: Städtische Bestattungskultur von der Aufklärung bis zum frühen 20. Jahrhundert/Urban Burial Culture from the Enlightenment to the Early 20th Century*, ed. Claudia Denk and John Ziesemer (Regensburg: Verlag Schnell and Steiner/ICOMOS Nationalkomitee der Bundesrepublik Deutschland, 2007), 41.

35. Letter written by Giuseppe Terragni to Pietro Maria Bardi in 1932, quoted in Bruno Zevi, *Giuseppe Terragni* (London: Triangle Architectural Publishing 1989), trans. Luigi Beltrandi, 42; see also Etlin, *Modernism*, 522; Daniele Vitale, '1926-1932, Monumento ai caduti di Erba Incino', in *Giuseppe Terragni: opera completa*, ed. Giorgio Ciucci (Milan: Electa, 1996), 307–12. Terragni also incorporated a staircase into the tomb (1934–5) commissioned by Margherita Sarfatti, Mussolini's lover and influential figure in the art world, for her son Roberto, who had fallen in the First World War: Alessandra Muntoni, '1934-1935, Monumento a Roberto Sarfatti, col d'Echele', in Ciucci (ed.), *Giuseppe Terragni*, 445–51.

36. Flora Samuel, 'Architectural Promenades through the Villa Savoye', in *Architecture and Movement: The Dynamic Experience of Buildings and Landscapes*, ed. Peter Blundell Jones and Mark Meagher (London: Routledge, 2014), 44–9, here 46; Ross Anderson, 'All of Paris, Darkly: Le Corbusier's Beistegui Apartment, 1929-1931', in *Le Corbusier, 50 years later: International Congress* (Valencia: Universitat Politecnica de Valencia, 2015), 4. DOI: http://dx.doi.org/10.4995/LC2015.2015.928

37. Samuel, 'Architectural Promenades', 44–5. Thomas L. Schumacher noted how Terragni applied the promenade structure of Le Corbusier's villas to the design of tombs: *Il Danteum di Terragni: 1938* (Rome: Officina, 1980), 80–2; 'Tra, intorno e dentro i monumenti e le tombe di Terragni', in *Giuseppe Terragni: opera completa* (Milan: Electa, 1996), 229–39, here 229.

38. Etlin, *Modernism*, 445, 447, 522–4. The project for a Danteum (1938), or monument to Dante, by Terragni and Libera is another example of an ascending, spiritual journey, articulated by architecture.

39. '*bellezza spirituale*', Archivio Commissione Generale Onoranze ai Caduti, Sezione Tecnica, Monte Grappa, Letter of Gen. Giovanni Faracovi to Valentino Pellizzari, 10 May 1929.

40. Rudolf Wittkower, '"Sacri Monti" in the Italian Alps', in *Idea and Image: Studies in the Italian Renaissance* (London: Thames & Hudson, 1978); Mauro Quercioli, *I Sacri Monti* (Rome: Istituto poligrafico e Zecca dello Stato, Libreria dello Stato, 2005).

41. Massimiliano Savorra, 'La rappresentazione del dolore e l'immagine dell'eroe: il monumento al Fante', in *L'architettura della Memoria in Italia: Cimiteri, Monumenti e Città, 1750-1939*, ed. Maria Giuffré et al. (Milan: Skira, 2007); republished as 'Il monumento al Fante sul monte San Michele al Carso, 1920-1922', in *Le pietre della memoria. Monumenti sul confine orientale*, ed. Paolo Nicoloso (Udine: Gaspari, 2015), 71–91; Quinto Antonelli, *Cento anni di Grande guerra. Cerimonie, monumenti, memorie e contromemorie* (Rome: Donzelli, 2018), 58–61.

42. '*una via di preghiera, di purificazione, a soste lente di meditazione*', Eugenio Baroni, 'Il bozzetto 'Fante'. Nel concorso nazionale per il monumento-ossario al Fante sul monte San Michele', 1920-1, quoted in Franco Sborghi, ed., *Eugenio Baroni (1880–1935)* (Genoa: De Ferrari, 1990), 90.

43. Richard A. Etlin, *Symbolic Space: French Enlightenment Architecture and Its Legacy* (Chicago: University of Chicago Press, 1994), 172–80 and 'In Face of Death', 35–45.

44. Giuseppe Terragni, 'Il Sacrario dei Martiri comaschi nella Casa del Fascio di Como', *Quadrante* 35/36 (October 1936): 52, quoted in Etlin, *Modernism*, 447.

45. Étienne-Louis Boullée, 'Architecture, Essay on Art', trans. Sheila de Vallée, in *Boullée & Visionary Architecture*, ed. Helen Rosenau (New York: Academy Editions, 1976), 90; see also Etlin, 'In Face of Death', 37.

46. Bermudez, *Transcending Architecture*, xiii; see also Karla Cavarra Britton's chapter in this volume.

47. '*tempio*', '*nuova religione di Patria*', Archivio Storico dell'Ufficio dello Stato Maggiore dell'Esercito, Fondo L3, VIII, 6, cartella 259, 'Decreto-legge che dichiara "monumentali" alcune zone . . . del teatro di Guerra italo austriaco 1915-1918', 20 October 1922. Soon after taking power in 1922, Mussolini signed a decree that originated under the previous government, and which declared the battlefields to be 'monumental sites'. The original proposal was for the battlefields to be 'sacred', but this proved to be too difficult so the wording was changed: Archivio Storico dell'Ufficio dello Stato Maggiore dell'Esercito, Fondo L3, VIII, 6, cartella 259, 'Proposta per la consacrazione dell'Altopiano Carsico a monumento della Guerra nazionale', 12 November 1920; Bregantin, *Per non morire mai*, 223–9.

48. Anna Vinci, *Sentinelle Della Patria: Il Fascismo Al Confine Orientale: 1918-1941* (Rome: Laterza, 2011), 161–8.

49. Dogliani, 'Constructing Memory and Anti-memory', 15.

50. '*santa terra seminata di morti per il germogliare fecondo della Vittoria*', quotation by Ugo Cei in *Il Comune di Asiago*, 12.

CHAPTER 14
ATMOSPHERE OF THE SACRED
THE AWRY IN MUSIC, CINEMA, ARCHITECTURE
Michael Tawa

Discomfiture

There is a troubling condition at the core of Christian theology: Christ leaves and leaves us be – forsaken, abandoned to oblivion and exposed to the withdrawal of God. And yet, hope against hope, in the words of the Apostles' Creed, we 'look to the resurrection of the flesh (*carnis resurrectionem*) and the life everlasting (vitam *aeternam*)'.[1] Hope is all we are left with, and that hope is invested as a sustained theological tradition of light and transcendence, translated architecturally, at least since the Gothic, through luminosity, levity and dematerialization of the built fabric of the church. A theology of obscurity is admitted, and finds its architectural expression in the gloom, or better, in the gloaming spaces of shadow, dim reflection and obscurity. There is a *via negativa*, an apophatic theology – a theology of deferral, circumspection and silence – that counters the *via positiva* of kataphatic or affirmative theology of speech, and that is commonly associated with mysticism. But Christianity predominantly develops the sacred through a theology of light and affirmation that marginalizes obscurity, uncertainty and doubt.

What is 'the sacred', though? Generally, it only exists in oppositional terms, over against a counterpart – the profane or the secular – to which it remains distantiated and irreconciled. In some respects, this oppositional construal serves to maintain the privilege, authority and power of the first over the second; or else the sacred is unacknowledged, as it is in modern architecture where a resolute secularization (or aestheticization) of conditions historically associated with the sacred are displaced into the phenomenological, haptic or experiential. In all this, normative oppositional thinking has left unexplored the constitutive identity between sacred and secular.

Fundamentally, both are a matter of sequestration. A clue is in the etymological root *SEG, to cut (one region/territory from another). Hence, sacred and secular have to do with the borderline, the limit, and, at the same time, with measure, with segmentation. Likewise, the temple (Latin *templum*, Greek *temenos*) – that is, sacred space as such – is a place reserved and withdrawn by being cut off from the everyday, from existential temporality and spatiality. 'Temple' is from the etymon *TEM and Greek *temnein*, to cut, in the sense of being cordoned-off and 'held' (Latin *tenere*) by a stretched string (*ten-*) that demarcates a boundary. This demarcation produces sacred and secular in the one gesture of sequestration.

Following Giorgio Agamben and Jacques Derrida, between sacralization and profanation there is only the most infinitesimal shade of sense – a shift of register

Figure 14.1 Gloaming space of shadow, dim reflection and obscurity. (War Memorial, Canberra). Photograph by Michael Tawa, 2015.

Figure 14.2 Uncanny circumambience. (Anish Kapoor, *Cloud Gate*, Chicago, 2006). Photograph by Michael Tawa, 2014.

maybe, or of scale, power, tint or nuance.[2] So it is that humanity creates the two terms, and the opposition between them, in order to then either join or separate, reconcile or estrange them at will. The two regions or conditions are initiated by the same gesture of sequestration that separates and removes, safeguards and abandons, secures and consigns to oblivion.[3] Unsurprising, then, that the rational, secular project at the heart of modernity remains interminably haunted by the spectre of the sacred and incessantly looks for means of sanctification – for example in proportioning systems that intimate transcendent order; in pervasive narratives of peregrination and journeying towards light; and in alchemical references to base and transcendent, ignoble and noble materialities.

The troubling condition I began with – the simultaneous presence and absence of Emmanuel (God with us) – is not therefore antinomical, dichotomous or complementary. It is not black and white, nor either-or. Rather, it is both-in-both, in the sense that the gloaming of twilight is characterized by a mutual presence and transactional exchange of darkness and light, gloom and gleam. Likewise, the moment between in and out breathing, the slack sea between high and low tide or the point of contra flexure in a structural system – when one condition gives way to its counterpart, or lets its other, its ulterior or alterity, be.

This genuinely spiritual Christian experience – that the faithful is irreconcilably both forsaken and redeemed, in a state of both doubt and certainty – might well owe something to the traces of Greek philosophy and tragedy in Christian theology; but effectively, it means that the Christian confronts an irremediable condition characterized by longing – that is, by love and desire for union. The love might be unrequited (the relationship between humanity and divinity is evidently not symmetrical or reciprocal), but faith sustains it. Neither light nor dark, absent nor present, forgotten nor remembered, the faithful inhabits an interstitial, ambiguous region suspended between obscurity and clarity, knowing and unknowing, doubt and certainty, fullness and emptiness, poverty and abundance, fructification and barrenness, and so on. Neither one nor the other, and at the same time both: heard and ignored, admitted and excluded, saved and condemned. This is the particular spiritual tenor, mood or ambience that Christianity brings to the sacred experience.

Atmosphere of the Sacred

My aim here is to venture an architectural equivalent of this tenor – that is, to ask what might be the spatial and material conditions that produce such an ambience and that in turn make it possible for the human being to become aware of and to have a lived and embodied, haptic experience of this theological (or intellectual) and religious (or emotional) moment. The distinguishing quality of this moment – the primary characteristic of the uncanny region that environs the Christian experience – has a spatial correlate, a marked circumambience in which two or more radically different, irreconcilable conditions produce between them a palpable sense of indeterminacy. The ambience is uncanny since familiar and alien, comforting and discomfiting at the same time. And it is awry in that the normative conditions of experience are in it distorted and rendered unfamiliar.

Awry

In John Tavener's *Nativity of the Mother of God*, from the 1988 composition for cello and orchestra *The Protecting Veil*, there is a pivotal moment when the music goes awry.[4] The sustained melody of the first movement is interrupted, in the second, by glissando figures that slide from consonant to discordant tuning, introducing a strange and uncanny element. This thaumaturgical intervention – this wonder-work that alienates and discomfits the familiar – accompanies a significant threshold in the narrative: the birth of Mary. A structural alteration from consonance to dissonance, from consistency to distention within the musical fabric, signals a structural change in the fabric of the world: a patent intervention of heaven into the affairs of the earth, of the sacred in the normative conditions of human being. A kind of extensive porosity between worlds opens and unsettles things.

Yet the shift from one to the other is not bordered by any schism. Nor do the two conditions inhabit distinct temporalities or timeframes – one is not before or after the other. That is to say, the awry is present from the very beginning, as an unexercised potential that is systematically augmented and eventually overtakes the opening figures.

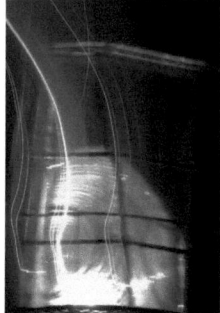

Figure 14.3 Things go awry. (Lighthouse, Trial Bay).
Photograph by Michael Tawa, 2015.

Figure 14.4 Extensive porosity. (Mirror, Venice).
Photograph by Michael Tawa, 2016.

In other words, the awry is not a condition that *befalls*, arrives from outside or develops in time. Rather, the awry is always already there.

Being sensitive to the awry – to the uncanny undertow that distorts and disorients – is also being open to the possibility of awe. Now awe is not an isolated experience but always shadowed by its foundational counterpart – terror or dread. For Martin Heidegger, 'close by essential (ontological) anxiety, in the terror of the abyss, there dwells awe. Awe clears and embraces that place of being essentially human within which one abides at home in the abiding.'[5] Awe (*Scheu*) is a fundamentally uncanny (*unheimlich*) ambience, since in it is produced the precarious, indeterminate and irresolvable double mood (*Stimmung*) of simultaneous angst and curiosity – in the words of Rudolf Otto, a *mysterium tremendum et fascinans*, that remain in permanent suspension.[6] This undecidability between terror and awe gives wonder its uncanny register.

In Taverner's *Nativity*, the intrusion of another register into the circumstantial world is marked by intervening musical figures – glissando and zigzag themes that tend towards but do not touch the keynotes; sharps and flats over against the anticipated harmony given at the outset; all typical of Romani music, the music of Gypsies, Hindus, Arabs and Jews for example, or the Rembetika music of depression-era Greece. These discords produce distance, suspension and irreconcilability within the musical fabric. They also produce a sense of longing and lamentation, accompanying a sustained melancholia – usually for a lost time or place, either *Heimat* or *Himmel*, Homeland or Heaven.

Here, then, sacred and profane do not constitute an opposition, a dichotomy or complementarity, but a constitutive alteration of one in the other that marks their intimate selfsameness: a change of register or state; a dilation or intensification; an augmentation or dissimulation. In our encounter with the discrepant, awry and uncanny, something happens, something takes place – logically, structurally and materially – to render the one alien to itself.

Such alienation derives from an inherent discrepancy that creates distance and dilation between different parts, dimensions, phases or powers within an entity – a piece

Figure 14.5 Indeterminate borderlines. (James Turrell, *Within without*, National Gallery of Australia, Canberra, 2010). Photograph by Michael Tawa, 2015.

Figure 14.6 Alien or deviant presence. (Bút Tháp Temple, Vietnam, thirteenth century). Photograph by Michael Tawa, 2015.

of music, a film, a narrative, a building. The discrepancy disestablishes the being, taking its various registers into a state of suspension and undecidability. Because these become ambiguous, they begin first to waver, and then begin to interact and conjugate so as to produce new assemblages that gather temporarily before dispersing and reassembling differently and interminably. Each assemblage has its own palpable ambience and mood, but also integrity and logic – that is, its own consilience. In the circumambience proper to atmosphere, affects or systems coexist simultaneously, but without coincidence or alignment. The discrepancy between them produces porosity, slippage or dissonance within a texture that remains strangely consilient and consistent.

Undecidable

The final sequence in Paolo and Vittorio Taviani's film *Kaos* (1984) recounts the narrator's conversation with (the ghost of) his mother, in which she recounts an event in her youth. Fleeing Sicily by boat the family stops at the island of Lipari to rest. On the beach the children head for the high pumice cliffs that back the sea. She is older and has to remain with her ailing mother. Seeing her sadness, the mother eventually signals for her to join her siblings. They climb to the top of the blinding white cliffs and, filmed by a rear shot taken diagonally down to the azure sea that excludes the horizon line, they slowly sidestep and dance down the pumice slopes, eventually merging with the ocean. The soundtrack to this extraordinary scene is Barbarina's aria *L'Ho perduto, me meschina* from Mozart's *The Marriage of Figaro*.

What is the aura, the ambience of this scene? How is it produced? The atmosphere of the sequence results from several discrete but coincident conditions inherent within the cinematic set-up. First, the narrator, the author Luigi Pirandello whose short stories the film is based on, visits his empty family home after his mother has passed away. He remembers a story that his mother used to tell him when he was young. He is in a reverie of recollection, tracing evanescent memories, making sense of who he is.

The film then shifts to that earlier time and the narrative voice becomes the mother's. There are several overlapping stories and voices – the narrator's journey into the past, Pirandello's stories, the narrator's mother in her penultimate years, the same woman as a young girl at the pumice beach.

And then there is the Mozart aria. *L'Ho perduto, me meschina* means 'Woe is me, I have lost it'.[7] The libretto refers to a brooch that the peasant girl Barbarina was to give to the countess' maid but which she has lost. A trifling moment in the scheme of things, sung by a minor character, but which Mozart scores to produce extraordinary emotional intensity. How is this achieved?[8]

The affective quality of the music could be ascribed to its being set in the minor mode (F minor). The key of F minor has four flats, and flat keys were often associated with grief and dejection in the vocabulary of the time. The presence of diminished seventh chords and three-note figures produces sharp dissonances, also associated with grief and sadness, while the use of chromatic chords (which include notes extraneous to the mode

 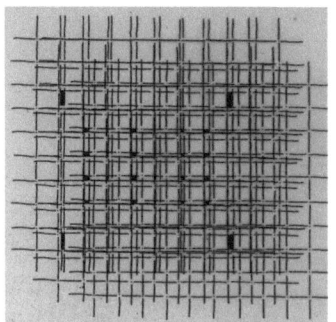

Figure 14.7 Shudder. (Lighthouse keepers' cottages, Trial Bay). Photograph by Michael Tawa, 2015.

Figure 14.8 Consilient discrepancy. Photograph by Michael Tawa, 1995.

or key of the piece, hence producing an 'alien' or 'deviant' presence) adds harmonic complexity or 'colour'.

The vocal line is fragmented, with short sighing gestures set against the persistent quaver figures of the accompaniment that together convey a sense of bewilderment and powerlessness. Contributing to the quality of unfulfilled and perhaps unfulfillable desire is the dissonance at the first '*me-SCHI-na*': the resolution at '*na*' being only partial and the resulting chord being unstable according to the norms of tonality. In fact, the piece never comes properly to an end because of Figaro's interruption.

At one level, there is a disparity between Barbarina's trifling distress and the deep scale of sadness in the music. At another, the dissonant (or internally disparate) modality of the music accentuates the emotional tension in the filmic narrative, contributing a great deal to its *Stimmung*. This modal disparity is at odds with the sublimely enveloping imaging of the landscape and the eventual absorption of the children's joyful abandon into the azure field.

In the film's exquisite conjunction of narrative, image and sound, these disparities parallel the narrator's desire to recollect his past, his desire for the mother and her youth, the mother's desire to relive and retell the story, the child's desire to join her siblings, the desire of the children's falling and mergence with the sea, and an overarching and tragic desire for surrender and release. These multiple simultaneous layers produce a disseveral texture that reverberates but never totalizes into a single reading. Rather, they produce a narrative ambience of insinuation and allusion indefinitely open to interpretation and consequently always novel and surprising.

Shudder

Before turning to architecture, and to the spatial, material and haptic correlates of atmosphere in theology, music and cinema, there are four motifs that I would like to retain from the foregoing. First, atmosphere is produced by a state of consilient discrepancy. Second, consilient discrepancy results from the simultaneous coexistence of several parallel, independent parts – spatialities, temporalities, degrees or conditions – which maintain their separateness in a state of suspension, while also potentially gathering into emergent wholes. Third, the experience of consilient discrepancy is itself ambiguous and wavering. It is characterized by a sense of the uncanny, the disturbing and the discomfiting and, at the same time, of the familiar, the reassuring and the comforting. Fourth, this experience parallels a theological figure that is foundational for Christianity and for a particular experience of the sacred: an absent presence that disturbs the normative coordinates of the everyday world and intimates something of the otherworldly inherent to it.

In fact, atmosphere is properly a species of mood or temporality, rather than a physical environment or spatiality – although it does pivot on a kind of temporalization or mobilization of the spatial. We are all familiar with atmosphere as the anticipation of a moment to come, the circumambience that frames an event yet to unfold, or a virtuality yet to be actualized – a game of sport, a concert, a marriage. Atmosphere is this open (and, critically, this *shared*) attentiveness to what might come to pass, what might at any moment take place. It is a collective witnessing of being-in-the-moment and anticipation that is not passive but has effective agency in the sense that a collective can mobilize the latent – that is, it can activate the multiple suspended registers, promote their assemblage and unclench their eventuation.

The undecidability in the texture of consilient discrepancy is manifest and experienced as a kind of shuddering or shaking, since the indeterminate cannot rest on one or another of its factors and must interminably shuttle between them. We see this in the films of David Lynch for example, where parallel registers coincident in the one world open to each other, and in Alfred Hitchcock's films, too, where the two worlds of reality and dream – the oneiric that is more real than the real – become indeterminate. We also saw this in the musical texture of Tavener's *Protecting Veil* and in the overlaid visual and acoustic registers in the film. But what might be the architectural counterpart of these discrepant textures, of this shuddering?

The characteristic of atmosphere, founded on unaligned yet coherent multivalency, can be instantiated in architecture, which like music and cinema, has the capacity to set up productive conditions based on incommensurable, discrepant assemblages. This is possible across several registers. One is the underlying spatial or geometric system that directs relative arrangement, scale, proportion, symmetry, rhythm, patterns and shape. Another is the material and tectonic system of connections and joints that regulate the formal, volumetric and technical assemblage of parts. A further register relates to the spatial sequences, narratives and experiences enabled through the spatial and tectonic set-up. There is also a semantic register through which architecture engages allegorical, metaphorical or symbolic referents, thus relating built form, spatiality and temporality to broader conditions and currents of human knowledge and experience – metaphysical, philosophical, religious, ethical, political, social, scientific and aesthetic among others.

The degree to which these different registers are aligned, coordinated and resolved within a single work contributes substantially to its character and complexion. Where different registers and references are mobilized to circulate and wander (to wend or wind their way through the fabric of a building), they will gather, disperse and condense into semantic ambiances that give the architectural setting a distinctive atmosphere. This then triggers an ongoing process of curiosity, inquiry and discovery that seeks to understand and relate them to each other, to see how they connect and fit together across the gaps and discontinuities established between them. Consequently, a work will always produce unexpected resonances, open up new readings and generate new patterns of meaning.

In what follows I would like to explore instances of consilient discrepancy that build into an atmosphere of the sacred by analysing Sigurd Lewerentz's Church of St Peter at Klippan, Sweden (consecrated 1966), in terms of the four registers mentioned earlier – geometry, materiality, narrative and allegory – respectively through the overlay of several discrepant alignments, axialities, orientations and disposition of component elements; through the masonry fabric of the building that shuttles between gravity and levitation; through a spatial narrative that is inherently destabilized; and through the concatenation of different allegorical and symbolic references to Christian theology.[9]

At St Peter, consilient discrepancy is evident within each of these four registers as well as between them. For example, there are several unaligned geometric systems within the spatial set-up, as there are discrepancies between the geometric system, the material conditions, the spatial narrative and the allegorical references. These incommensurabilities within the total architectonic montage construct a complex and dense assemblage that is open to multiple readings and interpretations. These are set within the circumambience of a very particular Protestant tenor of collective worship and individual religious experience, influenced by the aesthetics of the Romantic and the sublime – but also, following Raymond Williams' reading, according to a distinctive 'Modern' sensibility, emergent in the late nineteenth century and equally engaging Romantic motifs: 'the general apprehension of mystery and of extreme and precarious forms of consciousness; the intensity of a paradoxical self-realisation in isolation';[10] as well as a concern for the problematics of language, authorship and representation; discontinuous narrative; strangeness, estrangement and mystery; disconnection and unsettlement, alienation and loss.

In his reading of Lewerentz's late work, particularly in the geometrical disposition of St Peter, Peter Blundell Jones discerns a deliberative departure from strict classicism:

> From the beginning of his career, he was interested in irregularity and conflicting orders rather that in the calm finality sought by Mies . . . and if, like Mies, Lewerentz still held to a concern for geometry and proportion visible in the completely orthogonal plan with its square within a square and carefully modulated dimensions, the three-dimensional composition of St Peter's is untidy, asymmetrical, contextual, contingent; its irregularities are not repressed but relished. Despite the Classical rigor of an early masterpiece like his Chapel of the Resurrection of 1926, Lewerentz seems in his late work to have returned increasingly to the National Romanticism of his youth, reworking it in an entirely new form. [11]

Colin St John Wilson likewise notes Lewerentz's ambiguous tectonics, utilizing discrepancy and obliquity, as an 'abandonment' of classical architectural syntax – though he sees it as having both programmatic and symbolic functions, the latter producing an enigmatic, insistent strangeness that engages metaphysical and religious dimensions of the sacred:

> In the Church of St Peter . . . an unprecedented austerity of means prevails. But this austerity is not an end in itself – it is the means by which the tragic aura of the Mass envelops us with a breathtaking primitiveness. Once again there is the element of strangeness . . . The building's mystery lies in the discrepancy between its apparent straightforwardness and its actual obliqueness. The harder you look, the more enigmatic it becomes.[12]

The plan of the main chapel at St Peter is square and thus centralized, not linear. In a square space, no single direction predominates. But here Lewerentz introduces several axial systems across the space. The altar is asymmetrically positioned against one of the walls rather than in the middle of the space, and the centre is inaccessible since taken up by a large steel column assembly. Located opposite the main west entry door, the altar also sets up a shallow axiality responding to the processional tradition of church architecture. Consequently, the room is simultaneously centralized and axial, focused and lengthened, stable and unstable, symmetrical and asymmetrical.

At least four systems are overlaid in the main chapel space, each with its own discrete implied centre and axes – in Figure 14.10, the square plan described by the four walls with its geometrical centre (Cr); the four doors that lead into the space (D1–D4); the central column (Cl) and the altar (A). None of these systems coincide. The four entrances are differently sized and do not line up across the space. They do not accord with the room's geometrical cross axes (A1) or relate to anything in the four quadrants of the space. Each door is associated with a different function. The entry axis through the western door (A4) – the chapel's civic address and the largest of the four – follows the layout of traditional churches. The northwest entry from the wedding chapel (D2) adjoins the baptismal font (B). The northeast entry (D3) between organ (O) and choir (Ch) is for the clergy and is positioned not quite opposite its counterpart, the southeast entry (D4), which is smaller, close to the altar and reserved for the church community. The axis (X1) linking the centre of the western entry door (D1) and the altar (A) aligns neither with the entry axis central on the door and normal to the square space (A4), the geometric cross axis of the space (A1), the cross axis passing through the central column (A2), the cross axes through the organ (X2) and baptismal font (X3) nor with the centre of the room (Cr). These multiple geometric alignments, some shifted imperceptibly in relation to others, produce a complex zoning of the space and an elusive, subtle discrepancy within what otherwise appears to be a self-consistent formal programme.

Lewerentz builds further ambiguity between the apparently commensurable, stable square plan of the chapel and a number of infinitesimal variations and misalignments that contest and destabilize it. The central column – marginally central in a space that

Modern Architecture and the Sacred

Figure 14.9 Sigurd Lewerentz, St Peter, Klippan (1962–6), interior view from the western entry door towards the altar.
Photograph by John Gamble, 2008.

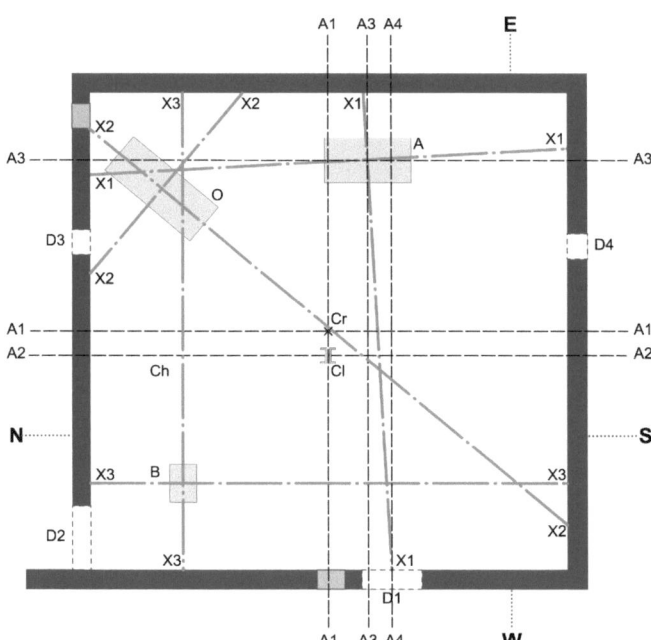

Figure 14.10 Axial discrepancies in the plan of Sigurd Lewerentz's St Peter, Klippan.
Drawing by Michael Tawa, 2018.

is not quite square – supports a pair of steel beams positioned asymmetrically above it, delivering greater openness and thus greater communitarian emphasis to the western half of the room. This tactic creates a virtual separation and distention between the congregation and the altar, while at the same time unifying priest and worshipper, divinity and humanity in the centralized space. The apparatus that achieves these complex and ambiguous relationships – the monumental column and beams that metaphorically read as the cross of Christ: the implement of suffering and redemption, sin and salvation – functions as a mechanism that simultaneously connects and separates, enables and disables. The offsetting of geometric systems and patterns between walls and column, column and beams, beams and vaulted ceiling, entry doors, windows, congregation and priest, choir, altar and organ effectively build up a web of tensions that equally burden and relieve the space.

The spatial narrative prompted at St Peter flows from its particular geometric and material tectonics. Imperceptibly unaligned spatial systems convey a sense that everything is not as it seems, that the stable is haunted by a palpable disestablishment. The familiarity of the set-up – centralized space, altar, processional sequence, accessibility, organ, baptismal font, pews – is paralleled by a discomfiting unfamiliarity. The known takes on an uncanny attunement. In this way, architecture engages with the strange and enigmatic qualities we identified in *Kaos* and *The Protecting Veil*. These have aesthetic dimensions, but here they work to imbue the space with otherworldliness: a sense that the divine is incident yet unseen; that a transformative, spiritualizing presence is immanent, eminent and imminent.

Such a narrative resonates with allegorical aspects of liturgy and worship. The tectonic and kinaesthetic experience of the chapel's architecture infers and indicates symbolic referends. The allegorical – literally what is 'spoken otherwise', saying one thing in place of another – is not duplicitous or disingenuous, however. Rather, it is in respect of the nature of things, so as not to violate them, cognisant that some can only be said otherwise, differently, indirectly, by deferral and detour.

Figure 14.11 Lewerentz, St Peter, Klippan, interior view from the baptistery towards the southeast entry door.
Photograph by John Gamble, 2008.

Figure 14.12 Lewerentz, St Peter, Klippan, brick-vaulted ceiling.
Photograph by John Gamble, 2008.

Several experiential qualities – characterized by non-oppositional and non-contradictory conditions – prompt such a reading. The space is centralized *and* axial. Consequently, the liturgical emphasis is indeterminately both communitarian and hierarchical – the celebrant is at once among the community of worshippers who surround the performance of the sacrament, in their midst, *and* before them, in Christ's stead; God is immanent *and* transcendent; salvation is a gift (vertically, down from 'above'), the outcome of faith ('up' from 'below') *and* of good works (towards others, horizontally).

The geometry of the space is orthogonal, apparently equal-sided and symmetrical. Yet it is also riddled with inequalities, made up of distinct systems that don't quite align and whose infinitesimal discrepancies and deferred reconciliations quietly animate the space by rendering its apparent quadrate fixity indeterminate and disestablishing its material density: the burden of existence is leavened by grace.[13]

In material and tectonic terms, the gravity of the heavy masonry building lends the interior spaces a particular enigmatic luminosity or gloaming that shifts emphasis from the bright light of day to the twilights, when night and day become indeterminate, where the delineating boundaries of things become ambiguous, and in whose dusk actuality is reabsorbed into potentiality: 'God is light'[14] *and* 'dwells in thick darkness'.[15]

Now the liturgical elements that properly furnish an atmosphere of the sacred – the temporality of ceremonial substances (pervasive incense, density of fragrance, condensation, recitation, music, reverberation, descant); the iridescence of sacramental objects (gold, silver, metal thread jacquards); the scintillation of surfaces (gold-leaf, stained glass, icons, glazed tiles) – are enabled, in combination, to produce two radically different but simultaneous and heady affects: materialization of the immaterial circumambience of space and dematerialization or vaporization of architecture.

There is the chapel's resolute interiority and radical sequestration from the outside. The space reads as a lithic clearing, a hollow or cavern carved out of masonry. Since the floor, walls and ceiling are made of the one material, the common distinction between ground, midspace and sky, or between earth, world and heaven is dissolved. At the same time, window openings are detailed in such a way that the boundaries of the

Figure 14.13 Lewerentz, St Peter, Klippan, brick floor and baptistery.
Photograph by John Gamble, 2008.

Figure 14.14 Lewerentz, St Peter, Klippan, baptistery.
Photograph by John Gamble, 2008.

room are turned inside-out and the interior is exteriorized so that it reads as a delimited portion of the outside. The light they admit is not the calculated light of analysis and discrimination that determines the lineaments and edges of form. Rather, light gleams and glows, scintillates and, as it increases or decreases due to ambient conditions outside, brings a tidal fluctuation to the perceived scale of the space that consequently appears to expand or contract, to have its dimensions relativized, rendered indefinite and thoroughly obfuscated. A world apart, the room now hovers in an intermediate region, uncoupled from the coordinates, dimensions, conditions and laws of normative existence. Consequently, the force of gravity is eased and the weight of the architecture leavened. Again, there is a simultaneous coexistence of apparent contraries: heft *and* levity, mass *and* porosity, immobility *and* vitality.

Then there is the extraordinary undulating ground plane that wells up as an emergent telluric undertow, reminiscent of Michelangelo's Capitoline Hill in Rome, which references the *Umbilicus Caput Mundi* or *Omphalos* of Delphi – the navel of the world: a weal or welt signifying the source or origin of creation *and* a gateway enabling Heaven, Earth and Underworld to communicate.[16] This nexus brings together two symbolic figures: solidity and liquidity – concavity, hollowness and porosity making possible the flow of water as a spring or font. Mass is disestablished, dematerialized and liquefied; the immobile is mobilized; substance is transmuted and essentialized.

It is important to recognize that these qualities are achieved in Lewerentz's design entirely through the tectonic fabric of the architecture – that is, by the (conventional) working of geometry, space, contour, form, materials, connections and light – rather than by overt representational, iconographic or other explicit religious signs and references; or indeed by any (radical) volumetric innovation. The semantic dimension of the architecture is delivered by its physical constitution and presence, rendered open and available to experience and interpretation. The coincidence of tectonics and meaning is construed here through consilient discrepancy between multiple unaligned systems, whose conjugational potential is calibrated to the metaphysical, philosophical, ethical, religious and aesthetic dimensions of Christian worship. These systems are overlaid in oppositional patterns – fundamentally undecidable and incommensurable – to produce a barely perceptive yet affective shuddering or shimmering of the architectural fabric. This in turn affords an experience of the awry, an enigmatic and simultaneous presence *and* absence of divinity; the insistent gravity, weight *and* simultaneous reconstitution of the material world; and the discomfiture, grief *and* simultaneous joy in noticing that the destiny of human being is an irremediable state of suspension between abandonment and recuperation, oblivion and solicitude.

Notes

1. Christian Classics Ethereal Library. '*Creeds of Christendom, with a History and Critical Notes, Volume II. The History of Creeds*', http://www.ccel.org/ccel/schaff/creeds2.iv.i.i.i.html (retrieved 26 February 2018).

2. See Giorgio Agamben, *Profanations*, trans. Jeff Fort (New York: Zone Books, 2007); and Jacques Derrida, *The Beast and the Sovereign, Volume I*, trans. Geoffrey Bennington (Chicago: Chicago University Press, 2009).

3. The etymon is *SEQ, which produces a complex double network of sense – on the one hand, divisional: section, segment, segregate, secateurs, secrete, and on the other connective: segue, sequel, sequence, secure, secret. *SEQ can be read as the reflexive pronoun *se-*, apart, aside + the etymon *KREI – sieve, separate, discriminate, cure, create. Every creation is founded on sequestration, and more so architecture, whose foundational gesture is the segregation or secreting of an inside over and above an abyssal, abandoned outside.

4. The word 'awry' is from the etymon *WER, turn, bend. The awry is the wry, crooked, skewed, distorted, twisted or deviant; a doubling of the surface, a turning inside-out that shows what is normally concealed, excluded or forgotten. The word 'wonder' is cognate – from *WEND, (to move by) winding, turning, weaving (wander, wend, go, move) + *TER, term, boundary, borderline: what makes the borderline turn (to reveal its outer face/side to the inner; and vice versa; to become other, alter ego . . .). The awry and the abject are in that sense correlates – hence the uncanny affect that blends fascination and fright, admiration and dread, terror and veneration, awe and wonder.

5. Martin Heidegger, *Pathmarks*, trans. William McNeill (Cambridge: Cambridge University Press, 1998), 307.

6. Rudolf Otto, *The Idea of the Holy: An Inquiry into the Non-Rational Factor in the Idea of the Divine and Its Relation to the Rational*, trans. John W. Harvey (London: Oxford University Press, 1923), 13–24.

7. The lyrics are as follows: L'ho perduta, me meschina! Ah chi sa dove sarà? Non la trovo. L'ho perduta. Meschinella! E mia cugina? E il padron, cosa dirà? (I have lost it, woe is me! Ah, who knows where it is? I can't find it. I have lost it. Miserable little me. And my cousin? And the boss, what will he say?).

8. I am indebted to my counterparts at the Sydney Conservatorium of Music, David Larkin and Lewis Cornwell, who generously provided the musicological detail in what follows.

9. The following extends my previous analyses of this building and other precedents. See my *Agencies of the Frame: Tectonic Strategies in Cinema and Architecture* (Newcastle upon Tyne: Cambridge Scholars Publishing, 2010), 252–7, 305–9.

10. Raymond Williams, *The Politics of Modernism: Against the New Conformists* (London: Verso, 1993), 40.

11. Peter Blundell Jones, 'Sigurd Lewerentz: Church of St Peter, Klippan, 1963-66', *arq: Architectural Research Quarterly* 6, no. 2 (2002): 159–73.

12. Colin St John Wilson, 'Sigurd Lewerentz: The Sacred Buildings and the Sacred Sites', in *Sigurd Lewerentz 1885-1975*, ed. Nicola Flora, Paola Giardiello and Gennaro Postiglione (Milan: Electa, 2001), 16, 21.

13. 'For it is by grace you have been saved, through faith – and this is not from yourselves, it is the gift of God – not by works, so that no one can boast'. Eph. 2. 8-9. Biblical citations are from the King James Version available at http://www.gasl.org/refbib/Bible_King_James_Version.pdf (retrieved 23 February 2018).

14. 1 Jn 1. 15.

15. 1 Kgs 8. 12.

16. See Rene Guenon, 'The Omphalos and Sacred Stones', in *The King of the World*, trans. Henry D. Fohr (Hillsdale: Sophia Perennis, 2004), 54–61.

BIBLIOGRAPHY

Aalto, Alvar. 'Finish Church Art'. In *Alvar Aalto in His Own Words*, edited by Göran Schildt, 37–8. Helsinki: Otava, 1997.
Aalto, Alvar. 'Viaggio in Italia'. *Casabella Continuità* 200 (1954): 4–7.
Acken, Johannes van. *Christozentrische Kirchenkunst: Ein Entwurf zum Liturgischen-Gesamtkunstwerk*. Gladbeck i. W.: A. Theben, 1923.
Acking, Carl-Axel. 'Artist and Professional: Glimpses of Asplund's Last Years'. In *Erik Gunnar Asplud: Architect*, edited by Claes Caldenby and Olof Hultin, 17–21. Stockholm: Arkitektur Förlag, 1985.
Adams, Nicholas. *Gunnar Asplund's Gothenburg: The Transformation of Public Architecture in Interwar Europe*. State College, PA: Penn State University Press, 2014.
Adler, Gerald. *Robert Maguire & Keith Murray*. London: RIBA Publishing, 2012.
Agamben, Giorgio. *Profanations*. Translated by Jeff Fort. New York: Zone Books, 2007.
Airio, Tuula. *Lappeen hautausmaa Lepola. Ilmari Wirkkalan 1930-luvun hautausmaaideaali*. Tallinn: Lappeen kotiseutuyhdistys, 2010.
Amery, Colin. 'Nikolaus Pevsner's "Pioneers of the Modern Movement", 1936'. *The Burlington Magazine* 151, no. 1278 (2009): 617–19.
Anderson, Ross. 'All of Paris, Darkly: Le Corbusier's Beistegui Apartment, 1929–1931'. In *Le Corbusier, 50 Years Later: International Congress*. Valencia: Universitat Politecnica de Valencia, 2015. http://dx.doi.org/10.4995/LC2015.2015.928.
Anderson, Ross. 'Minimal Ritual: Mies van der Rohe's Chapel of St. Savior, 1952'. In *Modernism and American Mid-20th Century Sacred Architecture*, edited by Anat Geva, 15–30. London: Routledge, 2018.
Anderson, Ross. 'The Appian Way'. *AA Files* 75 (December 2017): 163–82.
Anderson, Stanford and Gail Fenske, eds. *Aalto and America*. New Haven, CT: Yale University Press, 2012.
Ansermet, Ernst. 'La Gymnastique Rythmique a Hellerau'. *SIM* 97 (July–August 1913): 57–9.
Antonelli, Quinto. *Cento anni di Grande guerra. Cerimonie, monumenti, memorie e contromemorie*. Rome: Donzelli, 2018.
Antonini, Debora. *Le symbolique, le sacré, la spiritualité dans l'oeuvre de Le Corbusier*. Paris: Fondation Le Corbusier and Editions de la Villette, 2004.
Appia, Appia. 'Darsteller, Raum, Licht, Malerei (1919)'. In *Texte zur Theorie des Raums*, edited by Stephan Günzel, 117–21. Stuttgart: Reclam, 2013.
Appia, Adolphe. *L'œuvre d'art Vivant*. Paris: Edition Atar, 1921.
Appia, Adolphe. *Œuvres Complètes, Volume I: 1880–1894*. Edited by Marie L. Bablet-Hahn. Lausanne: L'Age d'homme, 1983.
Appia, Adolphe. *Œuvres Complètes, Volume II: 1895–1905*. Edited by Marie L. Bablet-Hahn. Lausanne: L'Age d'homme, 1986.
Appia, Adolphe. *Œuvres Complètes, Volume III: 1906–1921*. Edited by Marie L. Bablet-Hahn. Lausanne: L'Age d'homme, 1988.
Appia, Adolphe. *Œuvres Complètes, Volume IV: 1921–1928*. Edited by Marie L. Bablet-Hahn. Lausanne: L'Age d'homme, 1992.
Aquinas, Thomas. *Commentary on Aristotle's Metaphysics*, trans. and intro. P. Rowan. Indiana: Dumb Ox Books, 1961.

Bibliography

Aquinas, Saint Thomas. 'Question V: Of the Good in General'. In *The Summa Theologica of Saint Thomas Aquinas*, trans. Fathers of the English Dominican Province, rev. Daniel J. Sullivan, vol. 1. Chicago: William Benton, 1952.

Atkinson, Harriet. '"The First Modern townscape?" The Festival of Britain, Townscape and the Picturesque'. In *Alternative Visions of Post-War Reconstruction: Creating the Modern Townscape*, edited by John Pendlebury, Erdem Erten and Peter J Larkham, 72–89. Abingdon: Routledge, 2016.

Baatz, Ursula. *Hugo M. Enomiya-Lassalle. Jesuit und Zen-Lehrer: Brückenbauer zwischen Ost und West*. Freiburg im Breisgau: Herder, 2004.

Bachin, Robin F. *Building the South Side: Urban Space and Civic Culture in Chicago, 1890–1919*. Chicago: University of Chicago Press, 2004.

Ball, Hugo. *Byzantinisches Christentum: Drei Heiligenleben*. Munich and Leipzig: Duncker and Humblot, 1923.

Ball, Hugo, *Flight Out of Time*. Edited by John Elderfield, translated by Ann Raimes. Berkeley and Los Angeles: University of California Press, 1996.

Bardi, P. M. et al. *Quadrante 35–36 Documentario sulla Casa del Fascio di Como*. [1936] Como: Tipographia Editrice Cesare Nani, 1989.

Barry, Fabio. *Painting in Stone: Architecture and the Poetics of Marble from Antiquity to the Enlightenment*. New Haven, CT: Yale University Press, 2020.

Bartning, Otto. *Vom neuen Kirchenbau*. Berlin: Verlag Bruno Cassirer, 1919.

Baudelaire, Charles. *The Painter of Modern Life*. Translated and edited by Jonathan Mayne. London: Phaidon Press, 1964.

Beacham, Richard. *Adolphe Appia: Artist and Visionary of the Modern Theatre*. Reading: Harwood Academic Publishers, 1994.

Beacham, Richard. *Adolphe Appia: Texts on Theatre*. London: Routledge, 1993.

Behne, Adolf. *Eine Stunde Architektur*. Berlin: Archibook, 1984.

Behne, Adolf. *The Modern Functional Building by Adolf Behne*. Santa Monica, CA: The Getty Research Institute, 1996.

Beil, Ralf and Regina Stephan, eds. *Joseph Maria Olbrich 1867–1908. Architekt und Gestalter der frühen Moderne*. Ostfildern: Hatje Cantz, 2010.

Bell, Catherine, *Ritual Theory, Ritual Practice*. New York and Oxford: Oxford University Press, 1992.

Belting, Hans. *Likeness and Presence: A History of the Image before the Era of Art*. Translated by Edmund Jephcott. Chicago: University of Chicago Press, 1994.

Bender, Thomas. *Toward an Urban Vision: Ideas and Institutions in Nineteenth-Century America*. Louisville: University of Kentucky Press, 1975.

Benjamin, Walter. *Das Kunstwerk im Zeitalter seiner technischen Reproduzierbarkeit*. Frankfurt/Main: Suhrkamp, 2003.

Bermudez, Julio, ed. *Transcending Architecture: Contemporary Views on Sacred Space*. Washington: CUA Press, 2015.

Betsky, Aaron. *James Gamble Rogers and the Architecture of Pragmatism*. Cambridge, MA: MIT Press, 1994.

Bialostocki, Jan. 'The Renaissance Concept of Nature and Antiquity'. In *The Renaissance and Mannerism, vol. 2, Studies in Western Art: Acts of the Twentieth International congress of the History of Art*, edited by Millard Meiss, 19–30. Princeton, NJ: Princeton University Press, 1963.

Birksted, Jan K. *Le Corbusier and the Occult*. Cambridge, MA: MIT Press, 2009.

Blaeser, Werner. *Mies van der Rohe: The Art of Structure*. Translated by D. Q. Stephenson Basel: Birkhäuser, 1993.

Block, Jean F. *The Uses of Gothic: Planning and Building the Campus of the University of Chicago, 1892–1932*. Chicago: University of Chicago Library, 1983.

Bibliography

Bluestone, Daniel. *Constructing Chicago*. New Haven, CT: Yale University Press, 1991.

Blumberg, Hans. *The Legitimacy of the Modern Age*. Translated by Robert M. Wallace. Cambridge, MA: MIT Press, 1983.

Blundell Jones, Peter. *Architecture and Ritual: How Buildings Shape Society*. London and New York: Bloomsbury, 2016.

Blundell Jones, Peter. 'Sigurd Lewerentz: Church of St Peter, Klippan, 1963–66'. *arq: Architectural Research Quarterly* 6, no. 2 (2002): 159–73.

Bock, Manfred, Vladimir Stissi, and Sigrid Johanisse, eds. *Michel de Klerk: Architect and Artist of the Amsterdam School, 1884–1923*. Rotterdam: NAi Publishers, 1997.

Boesiger, Willy, ed. *Le Corbusier: Œuvre Complète 1946–1952*. Basel: Birkhäuser, 1953.

Bognar, Botond. *Togo Murano: Master Architect of Japan*. New York: Rizzoli, 1996.

Böhme, Gottfried. *Atmosphäre: Essays zur neuen Ästhetik*. Frankfurt/Main: Suhrkamp, 2013.

Borts, Barbara. 'Mouths Filled with Song: British Reform Judaism through the Lens of Its Music'. PhD diss., Durham University, 2014.

Boullée, Étienne-Louis. 'Architecture, Essay on Art'. Translated by Sheila de Vallée. In *Boullée & Visionary Architecture*, edited by Helen Rosenau, 82–116. New York: Academy Editions, 1976.

Boyer, John W. *The University of Chicago: A History*. Chicago: University of Chicago Press, 2015.

Bradley, Simon and Nikolaus Pevsner. *London 1: The City of London*. New Haven, CT and London: Yale University Press, 2002.

Brämer, Andreas, Mirko Przystawik, and Harmen H. Thies, eds. *Reform Judaism and Architecture*. Petersberg: Imhof, 2016.

Brandlhuber, Margot and Michael Buhrs, eds. *Im Tempel des Ich: Das Künstlerhaus als Gesamtkunstwerk*. Ostfildern: Hatje Cantz, 2013.

Bregantin, Lisa. *Per non morire mai: la percezione della morte in guerra e il culto dei caduti nel primo conflitto mondiale*. Padua: Il Poligrafo, 2010.

Britton, Karla. *Auguste Perret*. London: Phaidon, 2001.

Britton, Karla. 'Auguste Perret's Notre Dame du Raincy'. In *The Cambridge History of Religious Architecture of the World*, edited by Richard Etlin. Cambridge: Cambridge University Press, forthcoming.

Britton, Karla, ed. *Constructing the Ineffable: Contemporary Sacred Architecture*. New Haven: Yale University Press, 2010.

Britton, Karla and Daniel Ledford. 'Paul Rudolph and the Psychology of Space: The Tuskegee and Emory University Chapels'. *Journal of the Society of Architectural Historians* 78, no. 3 (September 2019): 327–46.

Britton, Karla and Kyle Dugdale. 'Theoretical A/gnosticisms: Paul Tillich, Colin Rowe, and the Theology of Architecture'. In *Routes of Knowledge: Journeys and Vehicles of Architectural Theory*, edited by Elke Couchez, Rajesh Heynickx, and Ricardo Agarez. London: Bloomsbury Academic, 2021.

Brown, Callum. *The Death of Christian Britain: Understanding Secularisation, 1800–2000*. London: Routledge, 2001.

Brown, Neave, Alan Colquhoun, James Gowan, Peter Smithson et al. *Lyons Israel Ellis Gray: Buildings and Projects 1932–1983*. London: Architectural Association, 1988.

Brülls, Holger. *Neue Dome: Wiederaufnahme romanischer Bauformen und antimoderne Kulturkritik im Kirchenbau der Weimarer Republik und der NS-Zeit*. Berlin and Munich: Verlag für Bauwesen, 1994.

Bryant, Gabriele. 'Gothic of the Murdered God: From the Crystal Creed to the Spirit of Abstraction in Modern German Architecture'. In *Phenomenologies of the City: Studies in History and Philosophy of Architecture*, edited by Maximilian Sternberg and Henriette Steiner, 181–93. London: Ashgate, 2015.

Bucciarelli, Piergiacomo. *Fritz Höger. Hanseatischer Baumeister 1877–1949*. Berlin: Vice Versa, 1992.

Bibliography

Bücher, Karl. *Arbeit und Rhythmus*. Leipzig: Hirzel, 1896.
Burke, Peter. *Cultural Hybridity*. Cambridge: Polity Press, 2009.
Burkert, Walter. *Greek Religion*. Translated by J. Raffan. Oxford: Basil Blackwell, 1985.
Burkert, Walter. *Savage Energies: Lessons of Myth and Ritual in Ancient Greece*. Translated by Peter Bing. Chicago: University of Chicago Press, 2001.
Bushart, Magdalena. *Der Geist der Gotik und die expressionistische Kunst*. Munich: Schreiber, 1990.
Came, Daniel, ed. *Nietzsche on Art and Life*. Oxford: Oxford University Press, 2014.
Campo-Ruiz, Ingrid. 'Equality in Death: Sigurd Lewerentz and the Planning of Malmö Eastern Cemetery 1916–1973'. *Planning Perspectives* 30, no. 4 (2015): 639–57.
Canepa, Matthew. 'Distant Displays of Power: Understanding Cross-Cultural Interaction among the Elites of Rome, Sasanian Iran, and Sui-Tang China'. *Ars Orientalis* 38 (2010): 121–54.
Carl, Peter. '"The Godless Temple": Organon of the Infinite'. *Journal of Architecture* 10, no. 1 (2005): 63–90.
Carl, Peter. 'On Depth: Particular and Universal, Fragment and Field'. In *Fragments, Architecture and the Unfinished, Essays Presented to Robin Middleton*, edited by Barry Bergdoll and Werner Oechslin, 23–42. London: Thames and Hudson, 2006.
Carus, Carl Gustav. *Nine Letters on Landscape Painting*. Translated by David Britt. Los Angeles: Getty Publications, 2002.
Casey, Edward S. *The Fate of Place*. Berkley, CA: University of California Press, 1997.
Cassirer, Ernst. *Die Philosophie der symbolischen Formen*, 3 vols. Berlin: B. Cassirer, 1923–29.
Cassirer, Ernst. *The Philosophy of Symbolic Forms*. 3 vols. Translated by Ralph Manheim. New Haven, CT: Yale University Press, 1955.
Castroriadis, Cornelius. 'The Retreat from Autonomy: Post-modernism as Generalised Conformism'. *Democracy & Nature* 7, no. 1 (2001): 17–26.
Cêtre, Jean-Pierre and Franz Graf. 'Les hangars: un type pleinement ouvert à l'expérimentation technique'. In *Encyclopédie Perret*, edited by Jean-Louis Cohen, Joseph Abram and Guy Lambert, 93–100. Paris: Editions du Moniteur, 2002.
Cherry, Bridget and Nikolaus Pevsner. *London 3: North West*. New Haven, CT and London: Yale University Press, 2002.
Christ-Janer, Albert. *Eliel Saarinen: Finnish-American architect and Educator*. Chicago: University of Chicago Press, 1979.
Christ-Janer, Albert and Mary Mix Foley. *Modern Church Architecture: A Guide to the Form and Spirit of 20th Century Religious Buildings*. New York: McGraw Hill, 1962.
Ciucci, Giorgio, ed. *Giuseppe Terragni: Opera completa*. Milan: Electa, 1996.
Clark, Michael D. 'Ralph Adams Cram and the Americanization of the Middle Ages'. *Journal of American Studies* 23, no. 2 (1989): 195–213.
Cohen-Mushlin, Aliza and Harmen H. Thies, eds. *Jewish Architecture in Europe*. Petersberg: Imhof, 2010.
Cohen-Mushlin, Aliza and Harmen H. Thies, eds. *Synagogenarchitektur in Deutschland: Dokumentation zur Ausstellung*. Petersberg: Imhof, 2008.
Cohen, Jean-Louis. *The Future of Architecture Since 1889: A Worldwide History*. London: Phaidon, 2012.
Coleridge, Samuel Taylor. 'On Poesy or Art'. In *Modern Criticism Theory and Practice*, edited by Walter Sutton and Richard Foster, 36–41. New York: Irvington Publishers, 1988.
Colquhoun, Alan. 'The Modern Movement in Architecture'. *British Journal of Aesthetics* 2, no. 1 (1962): 59–65.
Condit, Carl. *Chicago 1910–1929: Building, Planning and Urban Technology*. Chicago: University of Chicago Press, 1973.
Conron, John. *American Picturesque*. University Park, PA: Pennsylvania State University Press, 2000.

Curl, James Stevens. *A Celebration of Death: An Introduction to Some of the Buildings, Monuments, and Settings of Funerary Architecture in the Western European Tradition*. London: Constable, 1980.
Curl, James Stevens. *Victorian Churches*. London: Batsford, 1995.
Curtis, William J. R. *Le Corbusier: Ideas and Forms*. London: Phaidon, 1986.
Curtis, William J. R. *Modern Architecture since 1900*. Oxford: Phaidon, 1982.
d'Arcens, Lousie, ed. *The Cambridge Companion to Medievalism*. Cambridge: Cambridge University Press, 2016.
Dalley, Stephanie. *The Mystery of the Hanging Garden of Babylon*. Oxford: Oxford University Press, 2013.
Davila, Carl. 'Fixing a Misbegotten Biography: Ziryab in the Mediterranean World'. *Al-Masaq, Journal of the Medieval Mediterranean* 21, no. 2 (2009): 121–36.
Demus, Otto. *Byzantine Mosaic Decoration*. New Rochelle, NY: Caratzas Brothers, 1976.
Derrida, Jacques. *The Beast and the Sovereign*, 2 vols. Translated by Geoffrey Bennington. Chicago: Chicago University Press, 2009–2011.
Descola, Philippe. *Beyond Nature and Culture*. Translated by Janet Lloyd. Chicago: University of Chicago Press, 2013.
Dickie, James. 'The Palaces of the Alhambra'. In *Al-Andalus: The Art of Islamic Spain*, edited by Jerrilynn D. Dodds, 135–51. New York: Metropolitan Museum of Art, 1992.
Dino, Alfieri and Luigi Freddi, eds. *Mostra della Rivoluzione Fascista*. Milan: IGIS spa., 1983.
Dionysius, Areopagita. *Des heiligen Dionysius Areopagita angebliche Schriften über die beiden Hierarchien*. Translated by Josef Stiglmayr. Kempten and Munich: Kösel, 1911.
Dogliani, Patrizia. 'Constructing Memory and Anti-memory, the Monumental Representation of Fascism and Its Denial in Republican Italy'. In *Italian Fascism: History, Memory, Representation*, edited by R. J. B. Bosworth and Patrizia Dogliani, 11–30. New York: St. Martin's Press, 2001.
Dormoy, Marie. *Souvenirs et portraits d'amis*. Paris: Mercure de France, 1963.
Dupré, Louis. *Passage to Modernity, an Essay in the Hermeneutics of Nature and Culture*. New Haven, CT: Yale University Press, 1993.
Durisch, Thomas, ed. *Peter Zumthor 1985-2013: Buildings and Projects*. Zurich: Scheidegger & Spiess, 2014.
Durth, Werner, Wolfgang Pehnt, and Sandra Wagner-Conzelmann. *Otto Bartning: Architekt einer sozialen Moderne*. Berlin: Akademie der Künste and Wüstenrot Stiftung, 2017.
Eckardt, Wolf von. *Eric Mendelsohn*. New York: George Braziller, 1960.
El Lissitzky. *Russia: an Architecture for World Revolution*. Translated by Eric Dluhosch. Cambridge, MA: MIT Press, 1970.
Elderfield, John. *Kurt Schwitters*. London: Thames and Hudson, 1985.
Eliade, Mircea. *The Sacred and the Profane: The Nature of Religion*. Translated by Willard R. Trask. New York: Harper Torchbooks, 1957.
Enomiya-Lassalle, Hugo M. *Zen Meditation for Christians*. Translated by John Maraldo. La Salle, IL: Open Court, 1974.
Etlin, Richard, ed. *The Cambridge Guide to the Architecture of Christianity*. Cambridge: Cambridge University Press, forthcoming.
Etlin, Richard A. 'In Face of Death: Calming the Mind, Mining the Soul'. In *Der bürgerliche Tod: Städtische Bestattungskultur von der Aufklärung bis zum frühen 20. Jahrhundert/Urban Burial Culture from the Enlightenment to the Early 20th Century*, edited by Claudia Denk and John Ziesemer, 35–45. Regensburg: Verlag Schnell and Steiner/ICOMOS Nationalkomitee der Bundesrepublik Deutschland, 2007.
Etlin, Richard A. *Modernism in Italian Architecture, 1890–1940*. Cambridge, MA: MIT Press, 1991.

Bibliography

Etlin, Richard A., ed. *Nationalism in the Visual Arts*. Washington and Hanover, NH: National Gallery of Art and University Press of New England, 1991.

Etlin, Richard A. *Symbolic Space: French Enlightenment Architecture and Its Legacy*. Chicago: University of Chicago Press, 1994.

Euripides. *Iphegenia among the Taurians*. Translated by Anne Carson. Chicago: University of Chicago Press, 2013.

Falassi, Alessandro, ed. *Time Out of Time, Essays on the Festival*. Albuquerque, NM: University of New Mexico Press, 1987.

Favro, Diane. *The Urban Image of Augustan Rome*. Cambridge: Cambridge University Press, 1996.

Fernandez Ordoñez, José. *Eugène Freyssinet*. Paris: Éditions du Linteau, 2013.

Fiore, Anna Maria. 'La monumentalizzazione dei luoghi teatro della Grande Guerra: I sacrari di Giovanni Greppi e Giannino Castiglioni (1933–1941)'. PhD diss., IUAV, 2001.

Fischer, Theodor. 'Was ich bauen möchte'. *Hohe Warte*, no. 3 (1906–7): 326–8.

Flora, Nicola, Paola Giardiello, and Gennaro Postiglione, eds. *Sigurd Lewerentz 1885–1975*. Milan: Electa, 2001.

Foster Stephen C. and Rudolph E. Kuenzli, eds. *Dada Spectrum: The Dialectics of Revolt*. Maddison, WI: Coda Press, 1979.

Frampton, Kenneth. *Modern Architecture: A Critical History*. London: Thames and Hudson, 1980.

Frampton, Kenneth. *Studies in Tectonic Culture: The Poetics of Construction in Nineteenth and Twentieth Century Architecture*. Cambridge, MA: MIT Press, 2001.

Franciscono, Marcel. *Walter Gropius and the Creation of the Bauhaus*. Urbana, IL and London: University of Illinois Press, 1971.

Frank, Hartmut and Karin Lelolek, eds. *Behrens, Peter. Zeitloses und Zeitbewegtes. Aufsätze, Vorträge, Gespräche 1900–1938*. Munich and Hamburg: Dölling & Galitz, 2015.

Frankfort, Henri. *Kingship and the Gods*. Chicago: Chicago University Press, 1978.

Fredrikson, Erkki. *Lyseotalon vuosisata – Jyväskylän Lyseon päärakennuksen ja opinkäynnin vaiheita 1900-luvulla*. Jyväskylä: JYLY ry, 2002.

Freundenberg, Caterina, Christa Thorau, and Immo Wittig. *Die Gustav-Adolf-Kirche in Berlin-Charlottenburg und ihr Architekt Otto Bartning*. Gifhorn, Balthauser Verlag, 2009.

Fuiabo, Attilo. *Credo nella resurrezione degli Eroi*. Milan: Corticelli, 1941.

Funkenstein, Amos. *Theology and the Scientific Imagination from the Middle Ages to the Seventeenth Century*. Princeton, NJ: Princeton University Press, 1986.

Gadamer, Hans-Georg. 'Education Is Self-Education'. *Journal of the Philosophy of Education* 35, no. 4 (2001): 529–38.

Gadamer, Hans-Georg. *Reason in the Age of Science*. Translated by Frederick G. Lawrence. Cambridge, MA: MIT Press, 1981.

Gadamer, Hans-Georg. *The Relevance of the Beautiful and Other Essays*. Edited by Robert Bernasconi and Translated by Nicholas Walker. Cambridge: Cambridge University Press, 1986.

Gadamer, Hans-Georg. *Truth and Method*. Translated by Garrett Barding and John Cumming. London: Sheed and Ward, 1975.

Gamard, Elizabeth Burns. *Kurt Schwitters' Merzbau*. New York: Princeton Architectural Press, 2000.

Gamble, John. 'Alvar Aalto: Formal Structure and a Methodical Development of an Inclusive Architecture'. PhD diss., University of New South Wales, 2014.

Gargiani, Roberto and Anna Rossellini. *Le Corbusier: Béton Brut and Ineffable Space, 1940–1965: Surface Materials and Psychophysiology of Vision*. London: Routledge, 2011.

Geertz, Clifford. *The Interpretation of Cultures*. London: Fontana, 1993.

Gentile, Emilio. *The Sacralization of Politics in Fascist Italy*. Cambridge, MA and London: Harvard University Press, 1996.
Gentile, Emilio and Robert Mallett. 'The Sacralisation of Politics: Definitions, Interpretations and Reflections on the Question of Secular Religion and Totalitarianism'. *Totalitarian Movements and Political Religions* 1, no. 1 (2000): 18–55.
Geva, Anat, ed. *Modernism and American Mid-20th Century Sacred Architecture*. London: Routledge, 2018.
Giedion, Sigfried, *Space, Time and Architecture*. Cambridge, MA: Harvard University Press, 1941.
Gieselmann, Reinhard and Werner Aebli, *Kirchenbau*. Zürich: Verlag Girsberger, 1960.
Gilbert, Anette. 'Die "ästhetische Kirche": Zur Entstehung des Museums am Schnittpunkt von Kunstautonomie und Kunstreligion'. *Anthaneum* 19 (2009): 45–85.
Gilbert, James. *Perfect Cities: Chicago's Utopias of 1893*. Chicago: University of Chicago Press, 1991.
Gilson, Etienne. *The Philosophy of Saint Bonaventure*, Translated by Frank J. Sheed and Dom Illtyd Trethowan. Patterson, NJ: St. Anthony Guild Press, 1965.
Gintoff, Vladimir. 'These Churches Are the Unrecognized Architecture of Poland's Anti-Communist "Solidarity" Movement'. *ArchDaily*, 7 March 2016, https://www.archdaily.com/782902/these-churches-are-the-unrecognized-architecture-of-polands-anti-communist-solidarity-movement.
Gisbertz, Olaf. 'Experiment, Utopie und Wirklichkeit: Die Mathildenhöhe und das Neue Bauen in der Weimarer Republik'. In *'Eine Stadt müssen wir erbauen, eine ganze Stadt!': Die Künstlerkolonie Darmstadt auf der Matildenhöhe*, edited by Markus Harzenetter and Jörg Haspel, 251–60. Stuttgart: Theiss, 2017.
Gisbertz, Olaf. 'Experiment, Utopie und Wirklichkeit: Die Mathildenhöhe und das Neue Bauen in der Weimarer Republik'. *Icomos: Hefte des deutschen Nationalkomitees* 64 (2018): 251–60.
Golia, Vittorio. 'La città dei morti, un cimitero di Alvar Aalto'. *ArtWort*, 12 April 2014, https://www.artwort.com/2014/04/12/architettura/citta-dei-morti-cimitero-alvar-aalto/.
Goodspeed, Thomas Wakefield. *A History of the University of Chicago*. Chicago: University of Chicago Press, 1916.
Grant, Iain Hamilton. *Philosophies of Nature after Schelling*. London: Continuum, 2008.
Griffin, Roger. *Modernism and Fascism*. Houndmills and New York: Palgrave Macmillan, 2007.
Gropius, Walter. *Manifest und Programm des Staatlichen Bauhauses*. Weimar: Bauhaus, 1919.
Groys, Boris. *Gesamtkunstwerk Stalin: Die gespaltene Kultur in der Sowejtunion*. Munich and Vienna: Hanser, 1988.
Guénon, René. *The King of the World*. Translated by Henry D Fohr. Hillsdale, NY: Sophia Perennis, 2004.
Gusdorf, George. *Du Néant à Dieu dans le Savoir Romantique*. Paris: Payot, 1983.
Haar, Sharon. *The City as Campus: Urbanism and Higher Education in Chicago*. Minneapolis, MN: University of Minnesota Press, 2011.
Halgren Kilde, Jeanne. *Sacred Power, Sacred Space: An Introduction to Christian Architecture and Worship*. Oxford: Oxford University Press, 2008.
Halgren Kilde, Jeanne. *When Church Became Theatre: The Transformation of Evangelical Architecture and Worship in Nineteenth-Century America*. Oxford: Oxford University Press, 2005.
Hammer-Schenk, Harold. 'Edwin Opplers Theorie des Synagogenbaus: Emanzipationversuche durch Architektur'. *Hannoversche Geschichtsblätter* 32, nos. 1–3 (1979): 101–17.
Hammond, Peter, ed. *Towards a Church Architecture*. London: The Architectural Press, 1962.
Hammond, Peter. *Liturgy and Architecture*. New York: Columbia University Press, 1960.
Hardie, Phillip. *Virgil's Aeneid, Cosmos and Imperium*. Oxford: Clarendon Press, 1986.
Harper, Prudence O., Evelyn Klengel-Brandt, Joan Aruz, and Kim Benzel. *Discoveries at Ashur on the Tigris, Assyrian Origins*. New York: Metropolitan Museum of Art, 1995.

Bibliography

Hawthorne, Christopher. 'Swiss architect Peter Zumthor, 65, is 2009 Pritzker laureate'. *Los Angeles Times*, 12 April 2009, https://latimesblogs.latimes.com/culturemonster/2009/04/swiss-architect-peter-zumthor-65-is-2009-pritzker-laureate.html.
Heathcote, Edwin. *Monument Builders: Modern Architecture and Death*. Chichester: Academy, 1999.
Heathcote, Edwin and Iona Spens. *Church Builders*. Chichester: Academy, 1997.
Heidegger, Martin. *Being and Time*. Translated by John Macquarrie and Edward Robinson. Oxford: Basil Blackwell, 1980.
Heidegger, Martin. *Hölderlin's Hymn 'The Ister'*. Translated by William McNeill and Julia Davis. Bloomington, IN: Indiana University Press, 1996.
Heidegger, Martin. 'Language'. In *Poetry, Language, Thought*, edited and translated by Albert Hofstadter, 185–208. New York: Harper & Row, 1975.
Heidegger, Martin. *Pathmarks*. Translated by William McNeil. Cambridge: Cambridge University Press, 1998.
Heidegger, Martin. 'The Age of the World-Picture'. In *The Question Concerning Technology and Other Essays*, translated by W. Lovitt, 115–54. New York: Harper & Row, 1977.
Heidegger, Martin. 'The Origin of the Work of Art'. In *Basic Writings: Martin Heidegger*, edited and translated by David F. Krell, 139–212. London: Routledge, 1993.
Heinold, Erhardt and Günther Großer, eds. *Hellerau leuchtete: Zeitzeugenberichte und Erinnerungen*. Dresden: Verlag der Kunst, 2007.
Hejdjuk, Renata and Jim Williamson, eds. *The Religious Imagination in Modern and Contemporary Architecture: A Reader*. New York: Routledge, 2011.
Helms, Mary W. 'Sacred Landscape and the Early Medieval European Cloister'. *Anthropos* 97, no. 2 (2002): 435–53.
Hendrich, Jörn-Hanno. 'Alfred Fischer-Essen. 1881–1950. Ein Architekt für die Industrie'. PhD diss., RWTH Aachen, 2010.
Heschel, Abraham Joshua. *Man Is Not Alone: A Philosophy of Religion*. New York: Farrar, Straus & Giroux, 1951.
Higgott, Andrew. *Mediating Modernism*. New York: Routledge, 2007.
Hillman, Judy. 'Assimilation by Design: London Synagogues in the Nineteenth Century'. In *The Jewish Heritage in British History: Englishness and Jewishness*, edited by Tony Kushner, 171–209. London: Cass, 1992.
Hiß, Guido. *Synthetische Visionen: Theater als Gesamtkunstwerk von 1800 bis 2000*. Munich: Epodium, 2005.
Hoff, August, Herbert Muck, and Raimund Thoma. *Dominikus Böhm*. Munich: Verlag Schnell & Steiner, 1962.
Hollinshead, Mary B. 'The North Court of the Erechtheion and the Ritual of the Plynteria'. *American Journal of Archaeology* 19, no. 2 (2015): 177–90.
Horkheimer, Max. *Gesammelte Schriften*. Frankfurt/Main: Fischer, 1988.
Howard, Rob and Ernst Petersen. 'Visualisation of Unbuilt Buildings in Their Landscape'. *Proceedings of the IEEE International Conference on Information Visualization* (1999): 110–15.
Huelsenbeck, Richard. *Memoirs of a Dada Drummer*. Edited by Hans J. Kleimschmidt. Translated by Joachim Neugroschel. New York: Viking Press, 1974.
Huovinen, Eero. *Kuolemattomuudesta osallinen: Martti Lutherin kuoleman teologian ekumeeninen perusongelma*. Helsinki: Suomalainen Teologinen Kirjallisuusseura, 1981.
Hurwitt, Jeffrey M. *The Athenian Acropolis: History, Mythology and Archaeology from the Neolithic Era to the Present*. Cambridge: Cambridge University Press, 1999.
Huse, Norbert. *'Neues Bauen' 1918 bis 1933. Moderne Architektur in der Weimarer Republik*. Munich: Heinz Moos Verlag, 1975.
Hytier, Jean. *The Poetics of Paul Valéry*. Translated by Richard Howard. New York: Doubleday, 1952.

Lorenz, Mario and Monika Finger, eds. *In einem Neuen Geiste/ In a New Spirit: Synagogen von/ The Synagogues of Alfred Jacoby*. Frankfurt am Main: Deutsches Architektur Museum, 2002.
Jaenicke, Dieter and Ralph Lindner, eds. *Rekonstruktion der Zukunft*. Leipzig: Spector Books, 2017.
James-Chakraborty, Kathleen. *Erich Mendelsohn and the Architecture of German Modernism*. Cambridge: Cambridge University Press, 1997.
James-Chakraborty, Kathleen. *German Architecture for a Mass Audience*. London: Routledge, 2000.
James-Chakraborty, Kathleen. 'Modern German Church Architecture'. In *The Cambridge History of Religious Architecture of the World*, edited by Richard Etlin. Cambridge: Cambridge University Press, forthcoming.
Janssen, Joks. 'Religiously Inspired Urbanism: Catholicism and the Planning of the Southern Dutch Provincial Cities Eindhoven and Roermond, c. 1900 to 1960'. *Urban History* 43, no. 1 (2016): 135–57.
Janz, Oliver. 'Mourning and Cult of the Fallen (Italy)'. *1914-1918 Online: International Encyclopaedia of the First World War*, https://encyclopedia.1914-1918-online.net/article/ mourning_and_cult_of_the_fallen_italy.
Jarrassé, Dominique. *Guide du patrimoine juif parisien*. Paris: Parigramme, 2003.
Joachimides, Alexis. *Die Museumsreformbewegung in Deutschland und die Entstehung des modernen Museums 1880-1940*. Dresden: Verlag der Kunst, 2001.
Joas, Hans. *Die Macht des Heiligen: Eine Alternative zur Geschichte von der Entzauberung*. Berlin: Suhrkamp, 2017.
Johnson, Paul. *The History of the Jews*. London: Phoenix, 2001.
Jones, Lindsay. *The Hermeneutics of Sacred Architecture: Experience, Interpretation, Comparison*, 2 vols. Harvard, MA: Harvard University Press, 2000.
Jordan, Kate and Ayla Lepine, eds. *Modern Architecture and Religious Communities, 1850-1970: Building the Kingdom*. London: Routledge, 2018.
Jung, Carl G. *Gesammelte Werke*. Olten: Walter, 1976.
Kadish, Sharman. 'Constructing Identity: Anglo-Jewry and Synagogue Architecture'. *Architectural History* 45 (2002): 386–408.
Kadish, Sharman, *Jewish Heritage in Britain and Ireland: An Architectural Guide*. Swindon: Historic England, 2015.
Kadish, Sharman, *The Synagogues of Britain and Ireland*. New Haven, CT and London: Yale University Press, 2011.
Kandinsky, Wassily. *Kandinsky: Complete Writings on Art*. Edited by Kennith C. Lindsay and Peter Vergo. New York: Da Capo Press, 1994.
Kantorowicz, Ernst. *The King's Two Bodies*. Princeton, NJ: Princeton University Press, 1957.
Keel, Othmar. *The Symbolism of the Biblical World: Ancient Near Eastern Iconography and the Book of Psalms*. Translated by Timothy J. Hallett. Winona Lake: Eisenbrauns, 1997.
Kelly, Jessica. 'Vulgar Modernism: J.M. Richards, Modernism and the Vernacular in British Architecture'. *Architectural History* 58 (2015): 229–59.
Kerdeman, Deborah. 'Hermeneutics and Education: Understanding, Control and Agency'. *Educational Theory* 48, no. 2 (1998): 241–66.
Kessler, Katrin. *Ritus und Raum der Synagoge: liturgische und religionsgesetzliche Voraussetzungen für den Synagogenbau in Mitteleuropa*. Petersberg: Imhof, 2007.
Kessler, Katrin and Alexander von Kienlin, eds. *Jewish Architecture – New Sources and Approaches*. Petersberg: Imhof, 2015.
Kidder Smith, George E. *The New Churches of Europe: An Illustrated Guidebook and Appraisal*. Cleveland, OH: World Publishing Company, 1961.
Kieckhefer, Richard. *Theology in Stone, Church Architecture from Byzantium to Berkley*. Oxford and New York: Oxford University Press, 2008.

Bibliography

Kimmelman, Michael. 'The Ascension of Peter Zumthor'. *New York Times*, 11 March 2011, https://www.nytimes.com/2011/03/13/magazine/mag-13zumthor-t.html.
Kinold, Klaus and Wolfgang Jean Stock. *Rudolf Schwarz: Church Architecture*. Munich: Hirmer Verlag, 2018.
Kivinen, Paula. *Tampereen Tuomiokirkko*. Porvoo: WSOY, 1986.
Klinger, Cornelia. *Flucht–Trost–Revolte: Die Moderne und ihre ästhetischen Gegenwelten*. Munich: Hanser, 1995.
Koerner, Joseph L. *Caspar David Friedrich and the Subject of Landscape*. London: Reaktion Books, 2009.
Koskenniemi, V. A. *Elegioja ynnä muita runoja*. Porvoo: WSOY, 1917.
Krinsky, Carol Herselle. *Synagogues of Europe: Architecture, History, Meaning*. Mineola, New York: Dover, 1996.
Kröger, Maite. *Theodor Fischers architektonisches Prinzip am Beispiel der Ulmer evangelischen Garnisonkirche*. Munich: Grin Publishing, 2012.
Kuenzli, Katherine. 'The Birth of the Modernist Art Museum: The Folkwang as Gesamtkunstwerk'. *Journal of the Society of Architectural Historians* 72, no. 4 (2014): 503–29.
Kunin, Seth Daniel. *God's Place in the World: Sacred Space and Sacred Place in Judaism*. London and New York: Cassell, 1998.
Kushner, Tony, ed. *The Jewish Heritage in British History: Englishness and Jewishness*. London: Frank Cass, 1992.
Küster, Heinrich. 'Die städtischen Markthallen in Breslau'. *Zentralblatt der Bauverwaltung* 29 (1909): 74–8.
Lahtinen, Tuomo. *Polttohautaus Suomessa. Aatehistoria ja kehitys*. Åbo: Åbo Akademi, 1989.
Laine, Marja. 'Siunauskappeli arkkitehtuurina ja tilakokemuksena'. MA thesis, University of Jyväskylä, 2011.
Lampugnani, Vittorio and Romana Schneider. *Moderne Architektur in Deutschland 1900–1950: Expressionismus und Neue Sachlichkeit*. Stuttgart: Hatje, 1994.
Langer, Susanne. *Feeling and Form*. London: Routledge & Kegan Paul, 1953.
Le Corbusier. *Correspondance: Lettres à la famille, 1900–1925*, vol. 1. Paris: Infolio, 2011.
Le Corbusier, *Étude sur le movement d'art décoratif en Allemagne*. La Chaux-de-Fonds: Exole de L'Art, 1912.
Le Corbusier, *Le poème de l'angle droit*. Paris: Teriade, 1953.
Le Corbusier, *Modulor 2: Let the User Speak Next*. Translated by Peter de Francia and Anna Bostock. London: Faber and Faber, 1958.
Le Corbusier, *The Nursery Schools*. Translated by Eleanor Levieux. New York: Orion Press, 1968.
Le Corbusier, *The Decorative Art of Today*. Translated by James I. Dunnett. London: Architectural Press, 1987.
Le Corbusier, *Vers une architecture*. Paris: Georges Crès, 1923.
Lears, T. J. Jackson. *No Place of Grace: Antimodernism and the Transformation of American Culture, 1880–1920*. New York: Pantheon Books, 1981.
Lehmann, Niels and Christoph Rauhut. *Fragments of Metropolis Rhein & Ruhr: Das Expressionistische Erbe an Rhein und Ruhr*. Munich: Hirmer, 2016.
Lehtimäki, Terhi and Hanna Lyytinen. *Siunauskappeli rakennustyyppinä: Evankelis-luterilaisten seurakuntien siunauskappelit 1917–2000*. Tampere: Arkkitehtitoimisto Hanna Lyytinen Oy, 2015.
Lerch, Helmut and Jürgen Bredow. *Otto Bartning: Materialen zum Werk des Architekten*. Darmstadt: Das Beispiel, 1983.
Lesk, Alexandra, 'A Diachronic Examination of the Erechtheion and Its Reception'. PhD diss., University of Cincinnati, 2004.
Lewis, Michael J. *The Gothic Revival*. London: Thames & Hudson, 2002.

Bibliography

Lloyd Wright, Frank. *An Autobiography*. Warwick: Pomegranate, 2005.
Löwith, Karl. *Meaning in History: The Theological Implications of a Philosophy of History*. London: University of Chicago Press and Cambridge University Press, 1949.
Maak, Niklas. *Le Corbusier: The Architect on the Beach*. Munich: Hirmer, 2011.
Macarthur, John. '"The revenge of the picturesque", Redux'. *The Journal of Architecture* 17, no. 5 (2012): 643–53.
Machor, James L. *Pastoral Cities: Urban Ideals and the Symbolic Landscape of America*. Madison, WI: University of Wisconsin Press, 1987.
Maguire, Robert. 'Church Design since 1950'. *Ecclesiology Today* 27 (2002): 2–14.
Mallarmé, Stéphane. *A Throw of the Dice will Not AbolishCchance*. [1914] Translated by Robert Bononno and Jeff Clark. Seattle: Wave Books, 2015.
Malone, Hannah. *Architecture, Death and Nationhood: Monumental Cemeteries of Nineteenth-Century Italy*. London: Routledge, 2017.
Mann, Barbara E. *Space and Place in Jewish Studies*. New Brunswick, NJ and London: Rutgers University Press, 2012.
Marx, Leo. *The Machine in the Garden: Technology and the Pastoral Ideal in America*. Oxford: Oxford University Press, 1964.
Maulsby, Lucy. *Fascism, Architecture and the Claiming of Modern Milan, 1922–1943*. Toronto: Toronto University Press, 2014.
Maynard, W. Barksdale. *Princeton: America's Campus*. University Park, PA: Pennsylvania State University Press, 2012.
McKenzie, Judith. *The Architecture of Alexandria and Egypt 300BC – AD 700*. New Haven, CT and London: Yale University Press, 2007.
McLaughlin, Niall. 'Incarnation: Bishop Edward King Chapel Cuddesdon'. In *Modern Religious Architecture in Germany, Ireland and Beyond: Influence, Process and Afterlife since 1945*, edited by Lisa Godson and Kathleen James-Chakraborty, 117–37. New York: Bloomsbury Academic, 2018.
Meier, Albert, Alessandro Costazza, and Gerard Laudin, eds. *Kunstreligion: Ein ästhetisches Konzept der Moderne in seiner historischen Entfaltung*, 3 vols. Berlin: De Gruyter, 2010–2014.
Menin, Sarah and Flora Samuel. *Nature and Space: Aalto and Le Corbusier*. London and New York: Routledge, 2003.
Mercer Ursula and Charlotte Benton, *A Different World: Émigré Architects in Britain 1928–1958*. London: RIBA Heinz Gallery, 1995.
Merleau-Ponty, Maurice. *Phenomenology of Perception*. Translated by Colin Smith. London: Routledge & Kegan Paul, 1962.
Mertins, Detlef. *Mies*. London: Phaidon, 2014.
Mies van der Rohe, Ludwig. 'A Chapel'. *Arts and Architecture* 70, no. 1 (January 1953): 18–19.
Mies van der Rohe, Ludwig. 'Baukunst und Zeitwille'. *Der Querschnitt* 4 (1924): 31–2.
Miller Lane, Barbara. *Architecture and Politics in Germany, 1918–1945*. Cambridge: Harvard University Press, 1968.
Miller Lane, Barbara. *National Romanticism and Modern Architecture in German and the Scandinavian Countries*. Cambridge: Cambridge University Press, 2000.
Miller, Naomi. *Heavenly Caves: Reflections on the Garden Grotto*. New York: Braziller, 1982.
Mindrup, Matthew. 'The Merz Mill and The Cathedral of the Future'. *Intersticies* 14 (2013): 49–58.
Mintz, Alan. 'Prayer and the Prayerbook'. In *Back to the Sources: Reading the Classic Jewish Texts*, edited by Barry W. Holtz, 403–29. New York: Summit, 1984.
Morris, William. *Hopes and Fears for Art*. Cambridge: University Press, 1905.
Morton, Timothy. *Dark Ecology*. New York: Columbia University Press, 2016.
Mosse, George L. *Fallen Soldiers: Reshaping the Memory of the World Wars*. Oxford: Oxford University Press, 1990.

Bibliography

Mumford, Eric. *The CIAM Discourse on Urbanism, 1928–1960*. Cambridge, MA: MIT Press, 2000.
Nairn, Ian and Nikolaus Pevsner. *Sussex*. Harmondsworth: Penguin, 1965.
Nerdinger, Winfried. *Theodor Fischer: Architekt und Städtebauer 1862–1938*. Berlin: Ernst, 1988.
Netzer, Nancy and Virginia Reinburg, eds. *Devotion. Fragmented Devotion: Medieval Objects from the Schnütgen Museum*. Chicago: Chicago University Press, 2000.
Neumeyer, Fritz. *The Artless Word: Mies van der Rohe on the Building Art*. Cambridge, MA: MIT Press, 1994.
Nicolisen, Dörte. *Das andere Bauhaus: Otto Bartning und die Staatliche Bauhochschule Weimars*. Berlin: Kupfergraben, 1996.
Nieminen, Pertti. *Uurnat. Runoja*. Helsinki: Otava, 1958.
Nietzsche, Friedrich. *Kritische Studienausgabe*. Edited by Giorgio Colli and Mazzino Montinari, Munich: dtv, 1988.
Northedge, Alistair. 'An Interpretation of the Palace of the Caliph at Samarra (Dar al-Khilafa or Jawsaq al-Khaqni)'. *Ars Orientalis* 23 (1983): 143–70.
Novalis, 'Isn't the Cosmos then in Ourselves?' In *Pollen and Fragments*, edited and translated by Arthur Versluis. Grand Rapids, MI: Phanes Press, 1989.
O'Doherty, Bryan. *Inside the White Cube*. Berkley, CA: University of California Press, 1986.
Oliver, Richard. *Bertram Grosvenor Goodhue*. Cambridge, MA: MIT Press, 1983.
Origen. *On First Principles*. Translated by G. W. Butterworth. Gloucester, MA: Peter Smith, 1973.
Orhanen, Outi. 'Siunauksen tilat: Pohjalaiset siunauskappelit ja hautaushuoneet'. MA thesis, University of Jyväskylä, 2015.
Otto, Frei. 'Eero Saarinens jüngste Arbeiten'. *Bauwelt* 46, no. 6 (1955): 104–7.
Otto, Rudolf. *Das Heilige: Über das Irrationale in der Idee des Göttlichen und sein Verhältnis zum Rationalen*. Munich: C. H. Beck, 2014.
Otto, Rudolf. *The Idea of the Holy: An Inquiry into the Non-Rational Factor in the Idea of the Divine and Its Relation to the Rational*. Translated by John W. Harvey. London: Oxford University Press, 1923.
Ozuf, Mona. *Festivals and the French Revolution*. Translated by Alan Sheridan. Cambridge, MA: Harvard University Press, 1988.
Paavilainen, Simo, ed. *Nordic Classicism, 1910–1930*. Helsinki: Finnish Museum of Architecture, 1982.
Pakoma, Katariina. 'Cemetery and Chapel of Rest, Lyngby-Taarbaek'. In *Drawn in Sand – Unrealised Visions by Alvar Aalto*, edited by Aila Kolehmainen and Esa Laaksonen, 48–9. Helsinki: Alvar Aalto Museum and Alvar Aalto Academy, 2002.
Palagia, Olga and Bonna D. Wescoat, eds. *Samothracian Connections: Essays in honour of James R. McCredie*. Oxford: Oxbow Books, 2010.
Pallasmaa, Juhani. 'Hapticity and Time: Notes on Fragile Architecture'. *Architectural Review* 207 (2000): 78–84.
Pallasmaa, Juhani. 'Kuoleman kuvat arkkitehtuurissa'. In *Mikään ei häviä. Kirjoituksia kuolemankulttuurista*, edited by Tiina Huttunen, Cia Kiiskinen, Riitta Tuominen, and Julia Weckman, 115–33. Helsinki: WSOY, 2006.
Pallister, James. *Sacred Spaces: Contemporary Religious Architecture*. London: Phaidon, 2015.
Panofsy, Erwin, ed. *Abbot Suger on the Abbey Church of St.-Denis and Its Art Treasures*. Princeton: Princeton University Press, 1979.
Papadaki, Stamo. *Oscar Niemeyer*. New York: George Braziller, 1960.
Parnell, Steve. 'AR's and AD's Post-war Editorial Policies: The Making of Modern Architecture in Britain'. *The Journal of Architecture* 17, no. 5 (2012): 763–75.
Pehnt, Wolfgang. *Deutsche Architektur seit 1900*. Ludwigsburg: Wüstenrot Stiftung, 2005.

Pehnt, Wolfgang. 'Die ganze Raumform: Dominkus Böhm und Rudolf Schwarz, ein Doppelportrait'. In *Dominikus Böhm 1880–1955*, edited by Wolfgang Voigt and Ingebord Flagge, 29–43. Tübingen: Ernst Wasmuth, 2005.

Pehnt, Wolfgang. *Rudolf Schwarz 1897–1961: Architekt einer anderen Moderne*. Ostfildern: G. Hatje, 1997.

Pehnt, Wolfgang and Hilde Strohl. *Rudolf Schwarz, 1897-1961: Architekt einer anderen Moderne*. Stuttgart: Gerd Hatje, 1997.

Pelkonen, Eeva-Liisa. *Alvar Aalto: Architecture, Modernity, and Geopolitics*. New Haven, CT and London: Yale University Press, 2009.

Pendleton-Jullian, Ann M., *The Road That Is Not a Road and The Open City*. Chicago and Cambridge, MA, London: Graham Foundation for Advanced Study in the Fine Arts and MIT Press, 1996.

Pentikäinen, Juha. *Suomalaisen lähtö. Kirjoituksia pohjoisesta kuolemankulttuurista*. Pieksämäki: Suomalaisen Kirjallisuuden Seuran toimituksia, 1990.

Pérez Oyarzun, Fernando and Rodrigo Pérez de Arce. *Valparaíso School Open City Group*. Basel: Birkhäuser, 2003.

Pérez Oyarzun, Fernando, Pedro Bannen Lanata, Hernan Riesco Grez, Maria del Pilar Urrejola Dittborn. *Iglesias de la modernidad en Chile, precedentes europeos y Americanos*. Santiago: Ediciones ARQ, 1997.

Pérez Oyarzun, Fernando, Rodrigo Pérez de Arce, Horacio Torrent and Malcom Quantrill, eds. *Chilean Modern Architecture since 1950*. College Station, TX: Texas A&M University Press, 2010.

Perret, Auguste, *Contribution à une théorie de l'architecture*. Paris: Cercle d'études architecturales, 1952.

Petit, Jean, ed. *Le Corbusier lui-même*. Geneva: Editions Rousseau, 1970.

Pevsner, Nikolaus. *Pioneers of Modern Design: From William Morris to Walter Gropius*. New York: Museum of Modern Art, 1949.

Pfammatter, Ferdinand. *Betonkirchen*. Zurich: Benziger Verlag, 1948.

Picard, Joseph. *Modern Church Architecture*. London: Orion Press, 1960.

Plato. *The Republic*. Translated by Paul Shorey. Cambridge, MA and London: Harvard University Press and William Heinemann, 1969.

Pollard, John F. *The Vatican and Italian Fascism, 1929–1932: A Study in Conflict*. Cambridge: Cambridge University Press, 1985.

Pollitt, J. J. *Art in the Hellenistic Age*. Cambridge: Cambridge University Press, 1986.

Portoghesi, Paolo, Flavio Mangione, and Andrea Soffitta, eds. *L'Architettura delle Case del Fascio*. Florence: Alinea Editrice, 2006.

Pöykkö, Kalevi. 'Kuolema ja arkkitehtuuri'. In *Synty ja kuolema*, edited by Simo Lahtinen, Tapani Pennanen, Rostislav Holthoer, and Roger Luke, 84–93. Tampere: SKSK, 1989.

Price, Jay M. *Temples for a Modern God: Religious Architecture in Postwar America*. Oxford: Oxford University Press, 2012.

Proctor, Robert, *Building the Modern Church: Roman Catholic Church Architecture in Britain, 1955 to 1975*. Farnham: Ashgate, 2014.

Quercioli, Mauro. *I Sacri Monti*. Rome: Istituto poligrafico e Zecca dello Stato, Libreria dello Stato, 2005.

Radford, Antony and Tarkko Oksala. 'Alvar Aalto and the Expression of Discontinuity'. *The Journal of Architecture* 12, no. 3 (2007): 257–80.

Ragon, Michel. *The Space of Death: A Study of Funerary Architecture, Decoration, and Urbanism*. Translated by Alan Sheridan. Charlottesville: University Press of Virginia, 1983.

Raith, Frank-Bertholt. *Der Heroische Stil: Studien zu Architektur am Ende der Weimarer Republik*. Berlin: Verlag für Bauwesen, 1997.

Bibliography

Ranney, Victoria Post. *Olmsted in Chicago*. Chicago: RR Donnelley & Sons, 1972.

Rehm, Rush. *Understanding Greek Tragic Theatre*. London and New York: Routledge, 2017.

Riall, Lucy. 'Martyr Cults in Nineteenth-Century Italy'. *The Journal of Modern History* 82, no. 2 (June 2010): 255–87.

Richards, J. M. *An Introduction to Modern Architecture*. Harmondsworth: Penguin, 1940.

Richards, Robert J. *The Romantic Conception of Life: Science and Philosophy in the Age of Goethe*. Chicago: Chicago University Press, 2004.

Richter, Hans. *Dada Art and Anti-art*. Translated by David Britt. New York: Thames and Hudson, 1997.

Rifkind, David. *The Battle for Modernism: Quadrante and the Politicization of Architectural Discourse in Fascist Italy*. Venice: Marsilio, 2012.

Robinson, Joel. 'Death and the Cultural Landscape (On the Cemetery as a Monument to Nature)'. *Proceedings of the Forum UNESCO University and Heritage 10th International Seminar 'Cultural Landscapes in the 21st Century'* (2005): 1–8.

Romain, Jonathan A. *Faith and Practice: A Guide to Reform Judaism Today*. London: RSGB, 1991.

Rossi, Paulo. *The Dark Abyss of Time*. Translated by Lydia G. Cochrane. Chicago: Chicago University Press, 1984.

Rosso, Michela. 'Between History, Criticism and Wit: Texts and Images of English Modern Architecture (1933–36)'. *Journal of Art Historiography* 14, no. 1 (2016): 1–22.

Rousseau, Jean-Jacques. *Reveries of the Solitary Walker*. Trans. Russell Goulbourne. Oxford: Oxford University Press, 2011.

Rüedi, Peter. 'Peter Zumthor: Architekt'. *Neue Zürcher Zeitung*, February, 2001.

Ruhl, Carsten, Chris Dähne and Rixt Hoekstra, eds. *The Death and Life of the Total Work of Art: Henry van de Velde and the Legacy of a Modern Concept*. Berlin: Jovis, 2015.

Ruth, Ben-Ghiat. *Fascist Modernities: Italy, 1922–1945*. Berkeley, CA: University of California Press, 2001.

Rykwert, Joseph. 'The Churches We Deserve?' *New Blackfriars* 37 (1956): 71–175.

Rykwert, Joseph. *Remembering Places: A Memoir*. Abingdon and New York: Routledge, 2017.

Sabbatucci, Giovanni. 'La Grande Guerra come fattore di divisione'. In *Due nazioni: Legittimazione e delegittimazione nella storia dell'Italia contemporanea*, edited by Loreto di Nucci and Ernesto Galli della Loggia, 107–25. Bologna: Il Mulino, 2003.

Sachs, Curt. *World History of the Dance*. Translated by Bessie Schonberg. London: Allen & Unwin, 1937.

Sacrari Militari della Prima Guerra Mondiale: Redipuglia. Rome: Ministero della Difesa, 1988.

Sadler, Michael Ernest, ed. *The Eurhythmics of Jaques-Dalcroze*. Boston: Small Maynard and Company, 1913.

Samuel, Flora. 'Architectural Promenades through the Villa Savoye'. In *Architecture and Movement: The Dynamic Experience of Buildings and Landscapes*, edited by Peter Blundell Jones and Mark Meagher, 44–9. London: Routledge, 2014.

Samuel, Flora and Inge Lindner-Gaillard, *Sacred Concrete: The Churches of Le Corbusier*. Basel: Bikhaüser, 2013.

Savorra, Massimiliano. 'Il monumento al Fante sul monte San Michele al Carso, 1920–1922'. In *Le pietre della memoria. Monumenti sul confine orientale*, edited by Paolo Nicoloso, 297–310. Udine: Gaspari, 2015.

Sborghi, Franco, ed. *Eugenio Baroni (1880–1935)*. Genoa: De Ferrari, 1990.

Scapolo, Barbara. '"Eupalinos o l'architetto" o del fare consistente'. In *Paul Valéry Eupalinos o l'architetto*, edited by Barbara Scapolo, 89–117. Milano-Udine: Mimesis Edizioni, 2011.

Scheffler, Karl. 'Das Haus'. In *Der Rhythmus Ein Jahrbuch* 2, no. 1 (Jena: Eugen Diederichs Verlag, 1913): 2–13.

Schelling, Friedrich W. J. *Sämmtliche Werke*, edited by Karl F. A. Schelling. Stuttgart and Augsburg: Cotta, 1856–61.

Bibliography

Schelling, Karl Friedrich Wilhelm. *Ideas for a Philosophy of Nature*. Translated by Errol E. Harris and Peter Heath. Cambridge: Cambridge University Press, 1988.
Schelling, Karl Friedrich Wilhelm, *Philosophy of Art*. Translated by Douglas W. Stott. Minneapolis, MI: University of Minnesota Press, 1989.
Schildt, Göran. *Alvar Aalto: The Complete Catalogue of Architecture, Design and Art*. New York: Rizzoli, 1994.
Schiller, Friedrich. *Letters on the Aesthetic Education of Man*. Translated Elizabeth M. Wilkinson and L. A. Willoughby. Oxford: Clarendon, 1982.
Schiller, Friedrich. *Werke in vier Bänden*. Vienna: Caesar, 1980.
Schlegel, Friedrich. *'Athenäums'-Fragmente und andere Schriften*. Stuttgart: Reclam, 2005.
Schlegel, Friedrich. *Philosophical Fragments*. [1798] Translated by Peter Firchow. Minneapolis: Minnesota University Press, 1991.
Schmalenbach, Werner. *Kurt Schwitters*. London: Thames and Hudson, 1967.
Schnell, Hugo. *Twentieth Century Church Architecture in Germany*. Regensburg: Schnell & Steiner, 1974.
Schulze, Franz. *Mies van der Rohe: A Critical Biography*. Chicago: The University of Chicago Press, 1985.
Schumacher, Thomas L. *Il Danteum di Terragni: 1938*. Rome: Officina, 1980.
Schuyler, David. *The New Urban Landscape: The Redefinition of City Form in Nineteenth- Century America*. Baltimore: John Hopkins University Press, 1986.
Schwarz, Rudolf, *The Church Incarnate: The Sacred Function of Christian Architecture*. Translated by Cynthia Harris. Chicago: Henry Regnery Company, 1958.
Schwarz, Rudolf. 'Erneuerung des Kirchenbaus?' *Die Form* 21/22 (1930): 545–57.
Schwitters, Kurt. 'Die Bedeutung des Merzgedankens in der Welt'. *Merz: Holland Dada* 1 (1923): 8–11.
Schwitters, Kurt. 'Die Merzmalerei'. *Der Sturm* 10, no.4 (1919): 61.
Schwitters, Kurt. 'Ich und meine Ziele'. *Merz: erstes Vielchenheft* 21 (1931): 113–17.
Schwitters, Kurt. 'Katalog'. *Merz* 20 (1927): 99–100.
Schwitters, Kurt. *Kurt Schwitters: Das Literarische Werk*. Edited by Friedrich Lach, vol. 5, *Manifest und kritische Prosa*. Cologne: DuMont Buchverlag, 1981.
Schwitters, Kurt. 'Merz'. *Der Ararat* 2, no. 1 (1921): 3–9.
Schwitters, Kurt. 'Schloss und Kathedrale mit Hofbrunnen'. *Frühlicht* 1, no. 3: 87.
Schwitters, Kurt. 'Tran 35, Dada ist eine Hypothese'. *Der Sturm* 15, no. 1 (1924): 29–32.
Schwitters, Kurt. *Wir spielen, bis uns der Tod abholt: Briefe aus fünf Jahrzehnten*. Frankfurt/Main: Ullstein, 1974.
Scully, Vincent. 'The Earth, the Temple, and Today'. In *Constructing the Ineffable: Contemporary Sacred Architecture*, edited by Karla Britton, 26–48. New Haven, CT: Yale School of Architecture, 2010.
Seddon, Jill. 'The Architect and the "Arch-Pedant": Sadie Speight, Nicolaus Pevsner and 'Design Review'. *Journal of Design History* 20, no. 1 (2007): 29–41.
Shapiro, Edward S. *A Time for Healing: American Jewry since World War II*. Baltimore, MD: The Johns Hopkins University Press, 1992.
Shearman, John. *Mannerism*. Harmondsworth: Penguin, 1967.
Singler, Sofia. 'Constructing Country, Community and City: Alvar Aalto's Cross of the Plains'. In *Territories of Faith: Religion, Urban Planning and Demographic Change in Post-War Europe, 1945–75*, edited by Sven Sterken and Eva Weyns. Leuven: Leuven University Press (forthcoming).
Singler, Sofia and Maximilian Sternberg. 'The Civic and the Sacred: Alvar Aalto's Churches and Parish Centres in Wolfsburg (1960–68)'. *Architectural History* 62 (2019): 205–36.
Siry, Joseph. *Beth Sholom Synagogue: Frank Lloyd Wright and Modern Religious Architecture*. Chicago: Chicago University Press, 2012.

Bibliography

Siry, Joseph. *Unity Temple: Frank Lloyd Wright and Architecture for Liberal Religion*. Cambridge: Cambridge University Press, 1998.
Smith, Henry Justin. 'The University Chapel – Its relations to Chicago'. *University of Chicago Magazine* 20, no. 9 (1928): 476–80.
Solà-Morales, Ignasi de. *Differences: Topographies of Contemporary Architecture*. Cambridge, MA: MIT Press, 1997.
Solomonson, Katherine. *The Chicago Tribune Tower Competition: Skyscraper Design and Cultural Change in the 1920s*. Cambridge: Cambridge University Press, 2001.
Spence, Basil. *Phoenix at Coventry*. London: Butler & Tanner Ltd Frome, 1962.
Spengemann, Christof. 'Merz – die offizielle Kunst'. *Der Zweemann*, no. 8, 9, 10 (1920): 40–1.
Spinoza, Baruch. *Ethics*. Translated by Edwin Curley. London: Penguin, 1996.
Spotts, Frederic. *The Churches and Politics in Germany*. Middletown, CT: Wesleyan University Press, 1973.
Stadler, Edmund. 'Jaques-Dalcroze et Adolphe Appia'. In *Émile Jaques-Dalcroze*, edited by Frank Martin, 412–59. Neuchatel: Eds de la Baconnière, 1965.
Stavagna, Michele. 'Begräbniskapelle auf jüdischem Friedhof: Den Erstling wiederentdeckt'. *Bauwelt* 23 (2014): 24–7.
Steane, Mary Ann. *The Architecture of Light: Recent Approaches to Designing with Natural Light*. Abingdon and New York: Routledge, 2012.
Steane, Mary Ann, David Jolly and David Luza. 'Found in Translation? Reconfiguring the River Edge of Cochrane, Patagonia, a Travesía Project of the Valparaíso School Led by David Jolly and David Luza, November 2013'. *Brookes e-journal of Learning and Teaching* 8, no. 1–2 (2016): accessed June 2019. http://hejlt.org/article/found-in-translation-reconfiguring-the-river-edge-of-cochrane-patagonia-a-travesia-project-of-the-valparaiso-school/.
Steane, Mary Ann, David Jolly Monge and Marcelo Araya Aravena. 'The Origins of City: Paseo'. *arq: Architectural Research Quarterly* 16, no. 4 (2012): 325–37.
Stephan, Regina, ed. *Erich Mendelsohn: Architect, 1887–1953*. New York: Monacelli, 1999.
Sterken, Sven. 'A House for God or a Home for His People? The Church-Building Activity of Domus Dei in the Belgian Archbishopric (1952–82)'. *Architectural History* 56 (2013): 387–425.
Sternberg, Maximilian and Henriette Steiner, eds. *Phenomenologies of the City: Studies in History and Philosophy of Architecture*. London: Ashgate, 2015.
Stewart, David B. *The Making of a Modern Japanese Architecture: 1868 to the Present*. Tokyo: Kodansha International, 1987.
Stock, Jean Wolfgang. *European Church Architecture: 1950–2000*. Munich: Prestel 2002.
Stock, Wolfgang Jean, ed. *European Church Architecture 1900–1950: Towards Modernity*. Munich: Prestel, 2003.
Suzzi Valli, Roberta. 'Il culto dei martiri fascisti'. In *La morte per la patria: la celebrazione dei caduti dal Risorgimento alla Repubblica*, edited by Oliver Janz and Lutz Klinkhammer, 101–17. Rome: Donzelli, 2008.
Taut, Bruno. 'Ein Architektur-Programm'. *Mitteilungen des deutschen Werkbundes* 4 (1918): 16–19.
Taut, Bruno. 'Eine Notwendigkeit'. *Der Sturm* 4, no. 196–7 (1914): 174–5.
Tawa, Michael. *Agencies of the Frame. Tectonic Strategies in Cinema and Architecture*. Newcastle upon Tyne: Cambridge Scholars Publishing, 2010.
Taylor, Charles. *A Secular Age*. Cambridge, MA: Belknap Press of Harvard University Press, 2007.
Tishler, William H, ed. *Midwestern Landscape Architecture*. Champaign: University of Illinois Press, 2000.
Torgerson, Mark A., ed. *An Architecture of Immanence: Architecture for Worship and Ministry Today*. Grand Rapids, MI: WM. B. Eerdmans, 2007.

Tournikiotis, Panayotis. *The Historiography of Modern Architecture*. Cambridge, MA: MIT Press, 1999.
Townsend Buggeln, Gretchen and Barbara Franco, eds. *Interpreting Religion at Museums and Historic Sites*. Lanham: Rowman & Littlefield Publishers, 2018.
Townsend Buggeln, Gretchen, Crispin Paine, and S. Brent Plate, eds. *Religion in Museums: Global and Multidisciplinary Perspectives*. London: Bloomsbury Academic, 2017.
Tresch, John. *The Romantic Machine: Utopian Science and Technology after Napoleon*. Chicago, University of Chicago Press, 2012.
Turner, Harold W. *From Temple to Meeting House: The Phenomenology and Theology of Places of Worship*. The Hague: Mouton Publishers, 1979.
Turner, Paul Venable. *Campus: An American Planning Tradition*. New York: Architectural History Foundation, 1984.
Turner, Victor. *The Ritual Process: Structure and Anti-structure*. Chicago: Aldine, 1969.
Underwood, David. *Oscar Niemeyer and Brazilians Free-form Modernism*. New York: George Braziller, 1994.
Valéry, Paul. *Amphion: Mélodrame*. Paris: Lerolle, 1931.
Valéry, Paul. 'Eupalinos, or the Architect'. In *Dialogues*, vol. 4, *Collected Works*, edited by Jackson Matthews. Princeton: Princeton University Press, 1962.
Valéry, Paul. 'Introduction to the Method of Leonardo da Vinci'. In *Leonardo, Poe, Mallarmé*, vol. 8, *Collected Works of Paul Valéry*, edited and translated by Malcom Cowley and James R. Lawler, 3–63. Princeton, NJ: Princeton University Press, 2015.
Valéry, Paul. *The Art of Poetry*. Translated by Denise Folliot. Princeton, NJ: Princeton University Press, 1958.
Vesely, Dalibor. 'Mathesis Universalis in the Jesuit Tradition'. In *Bohemia Jesuitica 1556–2006*, vol. 2, edited by Petronilla Cemus, 701–15. Prague: Univerzita Karlova v Praze, 2010.
Vial Armstrong, Jose, Jorge Sanchez, and Alberto Cruz. 'Reconstrucción Parroquia de Corral'. *CA, Ciudad y Arquitectura* 32 (1982): 28–33.
Vidler, Anthony. 'The Space of History: Modern Museums from Patrick Geddes to Le Corbusier'. In *The Scenes of the Street and Other Essays*, 294–316. New York: Monacelli Press, 2011.
Vinci, Anna. *Sentinelle della Patria: Il Fascismo al Confine Orientale: 1918–1941*. Rome: Laterza, 2011.
Vitale, Daniele. '1926-1932, Monumento ai caduti di Erba Incino'. In *Giuseppe Terragni: opera completa*, edited by Giorgio Ciucci, 307–12. Milan: Electa, 1996.
Vogt, Von Ogden. 'The University Chapel: Fabric and Idea'. *University of Chicago Magazine* 21, no. 2 (December 1928): 67–72.
Voigt, Wolfgang, ed. *Gottfried Böhm*. Berlin: Jovis, 2006.
Voigt, Wolfgang and Ingeborg Flagge, eds. *Dominikus Böhm, 1880–1955*. Tübingen: Wasmuth, 2005.
Volbach, Walter and Richard Beacham, eds. *Adolphe Appia: Essays and Scenarios and Designs*. London: UMI Research Press, 1989.
Voßkamp, Wilhelm, ed. *Utopieforschung: Interdisziplinäre Studien zur neuzeitlichen Utopie*. Frankfurt am Main: Suhrkamp, 1985.
Wagner, Monika, Dietmar Rübel and Sebastian Hackenschmidt, eds. *Lexikon des künstlerischen Materials: Werkstoffe der modernen Kunst von Abfall bis Zinn*. Munich: C. H. Beck, 2010.
Wagner, Richard. *Dichtungen und Schriften: Kommentierte Jubiläumsausgabe in zehn Bänden*. Edited by Dieter Borchmeyer. Frankfurt/Main: Insel, 1983.
Waldberg, Patrick. *Max Ernst*. Paris: Pauvert, 1958.
Wang, Tamar, ed. *The Synagogue at Sixty*. London: Belsize Square Synagogue, 1999.
Wang, Wilfried and Daniel E. Sylvester, eds. *Hans Scharoun: Philharmonie Berlin, 1956–1962*. Berlin: Wasmuth, 2013.

Bibliography

Washton Long, Rose-Carol, ed. *German Expressionism: Documents from the End of the Wilhelmine Empire to the Rise of National Socialism*. New York and Toronto: G. K. Hall and Maxwell Macmillan, 1993.

Weber, Max. *Wissenschaft als Beruf*. Munich: von Duncker & Humblot, 1919.

Weinstein, Joan. *The End of Expressionism: Art and the November Revolution in Germany, 1918–19*. Chicago: University of Chicago Press, 1990.

Whyte, Iain Boyd. *Bruno Taut and the Architecture of Activism*. Cambridge: Cambridge University Press, 1982.

Whyte, Iain Boyd, ed. *Modernism and the Spirit of the City*. London and New York: Routledge, 2003.

Whyte, William. 'The Englishness of English Architecture: Modernism and the Making of a National International Style: 1927–1957'. *Journal of British Studies* 48, no. 2 (2009): 441–65.

Wiebenson, Dora. *The Picturesque Garden in France*. Princeton, NJ: Princeton University Press, 1978.

Wiedmann, August K. *The German Quest for Primal Origins in Art, Culture and Politics, 1900–1933*. Lampeter: The Edwin Mellen Press, 1995.

Wilcox, Vanda. 'From Heroic Defeat to Mutilated Victory: The Myth of Caporetto in Fascist Italy'. In *Defeat and Memory: Cultural Histories of Military Defeat in the Modern Era*, edited by Jenny Macleod, 46–61. London: Palgrave, 2008.

Williams, Raymond. *The Politics of Modernism: Against the New Conformists*. London: Verso, 1993.

Wischnitzer-Bernstein, Rachel. *The Architecture of the European Synagogue*. Philadelphia: Jewish Publication Society of America, 1964.

Witte, Fritz. 'Neue Zeiten, neue Ziele'. *Zeitschrift für christliche Kunst* 32 (1919): 3–4.

Wittkower, Rudolf. '"Sacri Monti" in the Italian Alps'. In *Idea and Image: Studies in the Italian Renaissance*. London: Thames & Hudson, 1978.

Wolner, Edward W. *Henry Ives Cobb's Chicago: Architecture, Institutions, and the Making of a Modern Metropolis*. Chicago: University of Chicago Press, 2011.

Young, Victoria M. *Saint John's Abbey Church: Marcel Breuer and the Creation of a Modern Sacred Space*. Minneapolis, MI: University of Minnesota Press, 2014.

Zevi, Bruno. *Erich Mendelsohn: The Complete Works*. Basel: Birkhäuser, 1999.

Zevi, Bruno. *Giuseppe Terragni*. Translated by Luigi Beltrandi. London: Triangle Architectural Publishing, 1989.

Zumthor, Peter. *Architektur Denken*. Basel: Birkhäuser, 2010.

Zumthor, Peter. *Atmosphären*. Basel: Birkhäuser, 2006.

Zumthor, Peter. 'Key Projects by Peter Zumthor'. *De Zeen Magazine*, 18 April 2009, https://www.dezeen.com/2009/04/18/key-projects-by-peter-zumthor/.

Zumthor, Peter. *Peter Zumthor 1985-2013: Buildings and Projects*. Edited by T. Durisch, 5 vols. Zurich: Scheidegger & Spiess, 2014.

Zumthor, Peter. '"Sie stehen auf der Erde, aber Sie spüren die Öffnung zum Himmel": Peter Zumthor über seine Arbeit an der Bruder-Klaus-Kapelle in Mechernich'. Interview with Dina Netz. *kulturwest*, July 2007, http://www.kulturwest.de/architektur/detailseite/artikel/sie-stehen-auf-der-erde-aber-sie-spueren-die-oeffnung-zum-himmel/.

Zumthor, Peter. 'Wir Schweitzer sind nicht so änfällig für Moden'. *Spiegel Online*, 29 May 2009, http://www.spiegel.de/kultur/gesellschaft/stararchitekt-zumthor-wir-schweizer-sind-nicht-so-anfaellig-fuer-moden-a-627167.html.

INDEX

Page numbers in italic indicate a figure on the corresponding page.

Aalto, Aino   73
Aalto, Alvar   2, 3, 5, 64, 66, 73–85, 86 nn.3, 11, 87 n.16, 120, 214
Abbey of St Heribert, Cologne-Deutz   7, 211, 212, 215, *216*, 218
Abd ar-Rahman II   20
Absolute/absolute   24, 39
abstract form   56
abstract geometry   22
abstraction   57
Acropolis, Athens   *15*, 15–17, 75, 155
Actor Network Theory   36 n.79
Aeneid (Virgil)   14
Aesthetic Education of Man, The (Schiller)   25
aestheticization   7, 41, 241
    of politics   38
    progressive   218
aesthetics   181
    abstraction   152
    elements   147
    emotion   152
    form   120
    modern   43, 210, 223, 227, 234, 237
affirmative theology   241
afterlife   4, 78, 84
Agamben, Giorgio   241
Aglauros cave   15
agoras   101
Alabaster altar of Tukulti-Ninurta I   13–14, *14*
'Albigensian dualism'   154
alchemy   50–1
Alexander the Great   19
alienation   42, 92, 243, 244, *244*
allegories   22, 248
Altes Museum, Berlin (1823–30)   4, 37–8, *38*, 40–1, *41*
American Jews   56
Amidah ('standing prayer')   116, 121 n.12
Amphion: Mélodrame (Valéry)   151
amphitheatre-form burial zones   74, 75, 77
anagein   203
'anagoge' (anagogy)   201–3
Anastasis Rotunda   19
ancient Near Eastern temples   14, 15
Anderson, Ross   217

Angell, James Roland   132, 133, 138
Anglican Cathedral, Coventry   163, *164*, 165–7
anthropology   108
Antonin, Raymond   143–4
Antonius Church, Ickern   59
aphorisms   150
Aphrodite and Eros cave   15
apophatic theology   241
Apostles' Creed   241
Appia, Adolphe   6, 181–2, 184–6, 188–90, 192, 193 nn.2, 4, 217
Applied Arts Museum, Cologne   210, *211*, 211–15
apse mosaic of Santa Pudenziana   *19*, 19–20
Arbeitsrat für Kunst (Working Council for Art)   196, 200, 201, 204
arche and *eschaton*   24
Architects' Journal, The   159, 161–3, 165–7, 170, 171, 173, 173 n.2, 176 n.36
Architectural Review, The   159–63, 165–8, 170, 171, 173, 173–4 n.2
architecture   38, 42, 91, 189, 247
    American   64, 127
    'banality'   151
    British   171
    buried   73, 234
    church   214
    culture   120, 161, 171, 173, 176 n.43
    discourse   3, 6, 159, 163, 164, 170, 171, 173, 208
    ecclesiastical   73, 84, 108, 145, 147, 151, 210, 214, 219, 231–4
    education   92–3, 103, 105
    European   19
    Fascist   29, 222
    French   145, 148, 149
    funerary   73, 74, 77–9, 81, 232, 234
    German   200, 201, 208
    Gothic   5, 51–2, 60, 194 n.35
    hermeneutics   109
    lightweight   101, 103, 104
    medieval   22, 166, 217
    modern   1–4, 6–8, 43, 56, 57, 69, 73, 143–4, 148, 149, 151, 163, 164, 166, 171, 181, 190, 196, 204, 208, 209, 222, 236, 237, 241
    monumental   144, 145, 223

Index

practice   56, 151
  as 'precursor of redemption'   40, 42
  relationship with poetry   91, 93, 94, 149–51
  religious   66, 69, 85, 143, 147, 153, 159–1, 163, 166, 170, 173, 233
  Roman   18
  Romanesque   60, 68
  sacred   1–3, 7, 8, 22, 56, 57, 66, 68, 73, 103–5, 109, 150, 196, 208
  and spirit   154–6
  style   31, 51, 52, 56, 69, 114, 125, 222
  symbolic   20
  synagogue   111
  Western   1, 51
  'white cube'   96, 209, 213
Ariés, Philippe   87 n.34
Aristotle   20, 32 n.22, 196, 203
Ark (*Aron HaKodesh*)   5, 111–20, 124 n.39
art   52, 196. *See also* sacralization
  Baroque   212
  Christian   202
  creation   37
  ecclesiastical   210
  forms   42, 49
  fusion/replaces with religion   37, 39, 40
  German   160
  history   38
  medieval   7, 208–10, 215
  modern   38, 41, 42, 148, 152, 204, 210, 215
  museum   40
  Nordic Christian   78
  religious   152, 161, 177 n.54, 209, 210
  sacred   154
  spiritual concept of   202
  Western   51
  works   42, 43, 212–15
artefacts   7, 17, 18, 209, 211–13, 215
asceticism   49, 96
Ascher, Felix   60
Ashkenazi Jews   114
Ashkenazi tradition   112
Asiago triumphal arch (1936)   227, 232, 236
Asplund, Erik Gunnar   66, 80, 83, 120
Ateliers d'art sacré (1919)   154
Athena Polias   15–17
atmosphere   7, 42–3, 51, 247, 248, 252
Augustan Campus Martius   30
Augustus   18
aura   43, 110, 111, 113, 155, 229, 234, 245, 249
Ausdruck (expression)   196, 198
austerity   7, 64, 68, 92, 93, 96, 104, 249
avant-garde/avant-gardism   160, 164, 208
  German   196, 202
  Modernism   125
  movements   40, 204
  programme   42

Avis, Joseph   113
awry   243–5, 253, 254 n.4

Bachelard, Gaston   13
Badoglio, Pietro   225
Baeza, Arturo   96
Baixas, Juan   106 n.24
Baker House (1946–8)   66
Bakhoum, Michel   148
Ball, Hugo   4, 37, 202
Ballu, Albert   145
Band, Karl   147
Banham, Reyner   161, 165–7, 171, 176 n.43
Baroni, Eugenio   233
Bartning, Otto   2, 57, 58, 61, 62, 64–6, 208
Baruël, Jean-Jacques   74, 78, 81
Basilica of Saint-Jeanne-d'Arc de Paris   147
battlefield tourism   229
Baudelaire, Charles   196
Bauhaus   4, 56, 61, 188, 204
Bauhaus Manifesto (1919)   201, 215
Behne, Adolf   42, 160, 201, 210
Behrens, Peter   3, 40, 210
Being   22, 23, 25
Bellalta, Jaime   96
Belsize Square synagogue (1958)   117–20, *118*, 123 n.35
Benjamin, Walter   38
Betonkirche (Pfammatter)   147
Bet Tfila ('House of Prayer')   108
Beuys, Joseph   49
Bevis Marks, London (1761)   113, 122 n.21
Bildung/formación   5, 25, 26, 91, 92, 103–5
Bildungsanstalt für rhythmischen Erziehung (Institute for Rhythmic Education)   183, 184, *184*, 186
bimah   5, 108, 111–20, 124 n.39
Bletter, Rosemarie Haag   160, 161
Blomstedt, Pauli   73
Blondel, Jean-François   234
Böhm, Dominikus   2, 4, 57–9, 61, 62, 64–8, 210, 217
Böhm, Gottfried   43, 68, 69
Boissonnas, Frédéric   184, 186
Bosslet, Albert   68
Boullée, Étienne-Louis   234
Bourdelle, Antoine   150
Braque, Georges   152
Bridgewater Conference (1947)   163
Britain   170
  discourse   160
  post-war modernism in   161–3
British House of Commons   113
British Reform movement   114
Brod, Michael   118
Bronze Age   15

Index

Bruder Klaus Field Chapel (2005–7)   4, 39, 42
   construction process   47–9, *48*, 50
   design   49, 51
   entrance   44, *45*, *46*
   and German expressionist architecture   52
   and its landscape   43–4, *44*
   number symbolism of   49–50
   Peter Zumthor's early drawings   47
   primitive cave in   52–3
   teardrop-shaped oculus   44, 45, *46*, 50
   themes in   49, 50
Brülls, Holger   68
Brunelleschi, Filippo   34 n.43
'brutalism'   69, 109, 117
Bryggman, Erik   83
Bücher, Karl   183
Buenos Aires cathedral (1936)   147
building
   Christian   5
   civic   125
   modern   237
   religious   3, 6, 144, 145, 154, 159, 163, 171
   sacred   4, 52, 69, 143, 155, 231
   synagogue   5
Building Design Partnership (BDP)   117
Building Illustrated   165
Buildings of England, The (Pevsner)   109
'Building the Modern Church' (Proctor)   168
Burg Rothenfels (1926–8)   217, *217*, 218
burial ground   73–9, 223, 226
Burkert, Walter   18, 27
Burnham, Daniel   137
Burns, Cecil   147
Burton, Ernest DeWitt   133, 134
Byzantine architecture   19
Byzantine Mosaic Decoration (Demus)   33 n.42
Byzantinisches Christentum (Ball, Byzantine Christianity)   202

Camus, Albert   31
Capitoline Hill, Rome   253
Capitol Park, Chandigarh   30
Caporetto ossuary, Kobarid   227, 232
Cáraves, Patricio   106 n.24
'carousel of hegemonies'   148
Carré, Maison Louis   76
Carus, Carl Gustav   24–7
Caryatid portico   17
caryatids   75
Casa del Fascio, Como   27–30, *28*
Cassirer, Ernst   112
Castiglioni, Giannino   224, 232
Castroriadis, Cornelius   159
Cathedral for World Peace, Hiroshima (1954)   4, 66–7, *67*
Cathedral of Oran (1908)   145, 148
Cathedral of Our Lady of the Immaculate Conception, Maputo (1936)   148
Cathedral of Peace (1954)   68
'Cathedral of the Midway' project   136
Catholic reform movement   217
Catholic University   92
cave   51–3
Cei, Ugo   224
Celestial Hierarchy (Dionysius the Pseudo-Areopagite)   202
cemetery   74, 77, 78, 85, 222, 223
ceremony   14, 15, 20, 22, 185
   convocation   130, 131
   death   224
   substances   252
Chagall, Marc   152
Chapel for the Women's Christian College, Tokyo (1932)   148
Chapelle du Rosaire, Vence   148
Chapel of the Holy Cross (1940)   80
Chapel of the Resurrection (1926)   248
Château de Glérolles, Lake Geneva   181, *183*, 186
Chicago   132–4, 137
Chicago Plan Commission   137
Chicago Tribune   136
Chicago Tribune Tower   125, *126*
Chile   91, 93, 96
Christ   19, 50, 83, 233, 241
Christ and Magdalene (painting, 1890)   78
Christ-centred church art   58, 59
Christianity   25, 91, 113, 120, 125, 148, 227
   liturgical concepts   110
   post-medieval   23
   theology   19, 203, 241, 242, 247, 248
Christians
   European   56
   German   56
Christian Science Church, Tunbridge Wells (1933)   147
Christian Trinity   50
Christ Lutheran Church, Minneapolis (1949)   4, 64, 64–6, *65*, 67
Christ the King Cathedral, Liverpool   167
Christ the King Church, Hauenstein (1932)   68
church   108, 217
   aesthetic   219
   American   66, 170
   architecture   60, 96, 110, 149, 154, 159, 167, 171, 231, 234
   avant-garde   68
   British   171
   building   5, 6, 58, 69, 91, 104, 109, 110, 145, 148, 150, 159, 163, 165, 171, 173, 175 n.21
   construction   57

Index

contemporary   66, 114, 171
design   92, 104, 147, 148, 173, 177 n.54, 215, 219, 231
European   170
function   168, 170
German   68
Gothic   214
interwar   58, 61, 62
medieval   214
modern   56, 62, 69, 148, 165, 167, 208
parish   109, 165, 168, 171
progressive design   170
rehabilitating   163
structure   69
traditional   167
twentieth-century   159, 171, 208
Church at Stevenage   162, *162*
Church of Christ the King, Bischofsheim (1926)   4, 58–9, 62, 68
Church of England, England   114, 117
Church of Larerello, Pisa (1956–7)   147
Church of Light, Osaka   156
Church of Sainte-Elisabeth, Cologne-Muhlheim (1951–2)   147
Church of Santa Maria, Porto (1996)   155–6
Church on the Water, Hokkaido   156
'Church Triumph' (Powers)   171
Cirlot, Juan Eduardo   13
Cistercian monasteries   234
'*città dei morti*'   78, 85
city planning   147
civic life   104, 132, 133
Claudel, Paul   154
Clemen, Paul   215
Cobb, Henry Ives   125, 128, 130
Cohen, Jean-Louis   148
Coleridge, Samuel Taylor   24, 26, 27
collective life   30, 85, 93
collective memory   49, 51, 53
Collegiate Gothic   125
Combaz, Jean   147
commemoration   18, 224, 226, 227, 236
Committee on Building and Grounds   133
competition   73–4, 163, 165, 167, 168
conceptual thinking   27
congregation   57, 61, 66, 96, 109, 112, 115–17, 148, 251
Congrès Internationaux d'Architecture Moderne (CIAM)   56, 160, 163
Conkling, Wallace E.   190
Conservative movement   119
Constantinople   20
Constitution of the Sacred Liturgy (1963)   177 n.54
construction   136, 149, 150, 196
  issues   163

process   47, 48, 50
techniques   75, 160
Contribution à une théorie de l'architecture (Perret)   150
Coolidge, Charles   126, 128, 133
Corporación Amereida   101
Corpus Christi, Aachen (1930)   65, 217
Couturier, Marie-Alain   148, 152
Cram, Ralph Adams   125, 126
creative process   149, 151, 155
crematoria and cremation   74, 77, 81–3
Critique of Judgement (Kant)   24
Cruz, Alberto   91–7, 106 n.24
culture
  Catholic   7, 222
  civic   139
  history   49, 53
  Italian   29
  secular   23
Cyriacus of Ancona   18

Dada   202, 203, 206 n.31
d'Arcens, Lousie   208
'dark ecology'   25
Das Merzbild (The Merz Picture, 1919)   197, *198*
Davis, Henry David   114, 116
death
  Nordic iconography of   78
  rituals   73, 81–5
deities and human   14, 15, 18
de Klerk, Michel   58
Delgado Chapel project, Caracas (1951)   153
Demus, Otto   33 n.42
Denis, Maurice   147, 150, 154
Der erste Tag Merz-säule (The First Day Merz-column, 1923)   199, *200*
Der Rhythmus (1911)   186, *187*, 188
Derrida, Jacques   241
Der Sturm gallery   198, 201
Descartes, René   34 n.43
design teaching   91, 93, 105
de Solà-Morales, Ignasi   191
Deutsche Gewerbeschau   210
Deutscher Werkbund   184, 210
Devotio Moderna   23
diaspora   144
Dickerson, J. Spencer   136
Dictionary of Symbols, A (Cirlot)   13
didactic monuments   18, 24
Die christliche Kunst   210
Die Kathedrale (The Cathedral, Schwitters)   199
Die rhythmische Gymnastik und das Theater (Appia)   186
Die Stadtkrone (The City Crown, Taut)   201
Diocese of Paris   147

Index

Dionysius the Pseudo-Areopagite   20, 202, 203
'disciplined civilisation'   18, 27
Disraeli, Benjamin   114
divine   17–19, 69
   and human   18, 19
   transcendence   22
Dohrn, Wolf   183, 186, 188
Dombauhütte   210
domed tetrapylon   20
domus dei   110
domus ecclesiae   110, 113
Dormoy, Marie   150
dualism   24, 26, 50
Dudok, Willem Marinus   120
Dumas, Fernand   147
Durand, Claude Nicholas   26
Duval, Charles   147

Early Christian Church   96
Eastern Orthodoxy   113
Ecclesia Militans   29
economic theory   23
ecumenicalism   65
Edelfelt, Albert   78
edifices   18
église-tour (tower church)   147, 148
Eigengift   198
'Ein Architektur-Programm' (An Architecture Program, 1919)   200
Einheitskunstwerk   188
Einstein, Albert   152
Elegy to Loneliness (Koskenniemi)   81
Eliade, Mircea   13, 15, 31 n.8
Eliot, T. S.   149
Ellis, Tom   120
Emanuel, Barrow   114, 116
Emanuele Filiberto di Savoia   230
embodiment   13, 18, 27, 30, 31, 83, 155
Enlightenment   3, 5, 13, 18, 23, 108
'*entformelt*'   197, 205 n.8
ephemerality   13, 15, 50, 103, 196
Erechtheion   15, 17, 18, 75
Erechtheus   15, 17
Erichthonios   15, 17
Ernst, Max   199
Espaces rythmiques   6, 181, 182, *182*, 184, *184*, 192
Eupalinos, or the Architect (Valéry)   144, 149, 150, 154, 155
eurhythmics   182, 183, 185, 186, 192, 193 n.4
Euripides   189
Europe   13, 67, 85, 96
   architects   18
   northern   66
   Renaissance   18, 73
'exclusive humanism'   23, 31

Exhibition of the Fascist Revolution (1933)   27
Existenzminimum   93
extensive porosity   243, *243*

façade   58, 62, 67, 75, 84, 162
Fagarè ossuary (1935)   225, 227
Fascism   7, 27, 29, 68, 222–7, 229–33, 237
Fascist ossuaries   222–37
Fascist propaganda   224–6, 234, 237
Feininger, Lyonel   188, 201, 215
Festival of Britain (1951)   165
festival time   92, 101, 103, 104
Festsaal   185, 185–6, *187*
Fêtes   24
Final Judgement   24
Finnish Cremation Association (*Polttohautausyhdistys*)   83
Firminy church (2006)   151
First World War   7, 222, 224, 225, 227, 233–7
Fischer, Alfred   59
Fischer, Theodor   58, 184
Fletcher, Banister   109
flexible standardisation   80
Fondation Le Corbusier   191, 192
Frampton, Kenneth   69, 156
France   26, 77, 148, 153, 170
Friedmann, Robert   60
Friedrich, Caspar David   25, 52, 208
Frings, Josef Cardinal   58, 59
Frühlicht   201
Functionalism   160, 161
funerary chapels   73–81, 84, 85
furniture   80

Gadamer, Hans-Georg   8, 17, 92, 103, 104, 185, 192
garden city, Hellerau   183–4
Gallis, Yvonne   154
Garrison Church, Ulm (1910)   58
Geertz, Clifford   108
Geneva Music Conservatory   182
genius loci   165
geometric systems   247, 248, 251
German Expressionism   3, 38, 50–2, 69, 204, 211, 213
German Idealism   37, 41
German Reform community   117
Germany   57, 114, 170, 208, 209, 215, 218. *See also* Weimar Republic
   cathedrals   200
   church architecture in   60
Gesamtkunstwerk (total work of art)   7, 38, 39, 42, 43, 49, 52, 53, 97, 196, 201, 204, 219
Gibberd, Frederick   163, 165, 167
Gide, André   150

277

Index

Giedion, Sigfried   2, 31, 66, 152, 160
Gilkey, Charles W.   134
Girola, Claudio   101
Gluck, Christoph Willibald   186
God   23, 241, 252
   Christian   24
   death   37
   identification with Nature   24
   philosophical   27
Goethe, Johann Wolfgang von   40
Golia, Vittorio   86 n.11
Gonse, Emmanuel   147
Goodhue, Bertram Grosvenor   5, 126, 127, 129–34, 138, 139, 140 n.22
Gothic Saint Michael's, Coventry   163
Gothic style   208, 212
   buildings   128, 137
   cathedrals   7, 52, 69, 125, 132–4, 136, 138, 188, 196, 200–4, 233
   forms   127
   models   125
   Modern   126, 127, 133, 134, 136, 138
   precedent   132–4
   space   211
   structures   126
   tradition   134, 139
   typologies   132
   wood sculptures   *209*, 212, 214
Gowan, James   119
Gray, David   119
Great Chain of Being   23, 25
Great Mosque, Cordoba   33 n.34
Great Transition   23
Greece   76–7, 81
Greek Orthodox Churches   33 n.42
Greek philosophy   203, 242
Greek temples   14, 155
Greek tragedy   17, 32 n.22, 242
Greenough, Horatio   161
Grenfell-Baines, George   117
Greppi, Giovanni   224, 232
Gropius, Walter   58, 61, 188, 201
Grotten (grottoes)   199–201
Grünewald, Matthias   210, 213
Guardini, Romano   3, 210, 217, 218
Gustav Adolf Church, Berlin (1934)   61–3, *62*, *63*

Hammond, Peter   120, 147, 154, 168, 170
Handwerk (crafts)   43
Hannover Merzbau   199
harmony   43, 183
Harper, William Rainey   126, 128
Haskalah ('Jewish Enlightenment')   114
Haus Merz (House Merz)   198, *198*, 199, 201, 204
Heidegger, Martin   14, 24, 25, 27, 244

Hellenism   18, 20, 144
Helsinki University of Technology   86 n.3, 87 n.16
Hephaistos   15
Hermeneutics of Sacred Architecture, The (Jones)   109
Heschel, Abraham   153
hierarchy   20, 40, 109, 226, 231
hierophany/theophany   31 n.8
Higgott, Andrew   160, 161
History of Architecture, A (Fletcher)   109
Hitchcock, Alfred   247
Hitchcock, Henry-Russell   160
Hoddesdon Conference (1951)   163
Höger, Fritz   58
Höhlen (holes, caves)   199, 201
Hölderlin, Friedrich   219
Holl, Steven   155
Holy Family   22
Homer   15
Honegger, Denis   147
Hood, Raymond   125
Horkheimer, Max   37
hospederías (guesthouses)   101
Hôtel de Ville   147
House of Commons   119
House of the Arrhephoroi   15, 17
Huelsenbeck, Richard   199
Hugo, Victor   208
human
   being   20
   and divine   18, 19
   finitude   20, 22, 25, 29
humanism   5, 22, 84
humanity   171, 251
Hunstanton school   162
Huré, Marguerite   147
Husserl, Edmund   152
Hyde Park   127
Hytier, Jean   150

industrial
   age   160, 161
   city   134, 137, 139
   production   160
'ineffable space' (*espace indicible*)   6, 144, 151–6
Institute for the History of German Jews   108
'insular utopias'   53
Interior of the Temple (1926)   190, *190*
International Style   57, 66, 84, 160, 227
International Style: Architecture since 1922, The (Hitchcock)   160
intramundane eschatology   27
Iommi, Godofredo   91, 93
Italy   76–8, 235
   culture/tradition   27, 29

Fascist regime in 7, 222, 223, 236
  heritage 237
  invasion of Ethiopia (1935) 223, 225
Iversen, Henrik 74

Japan 67
Jaques-Dalcroze, Émile 182–4, 186, 188
Jay, A. B. 136
Jeanneret, Albert 188
Jeanneret-Perret, Marie Charlotte Amélie 154
Jerusalem 22
Jerusalem Temple 110, 111
Jewish Cemetery Chapel, Königsburg (1927) 4, 60–1, *61*
Jewish Chronicle 116
Jews 116
  communities 120
  diaspora 110, 111
  emancipation 110
  identity 5, 108
  life 110, 112
  'public' service 111
  sacred spaces 108
John Cassian 22
John of Damascus 22
Johnson, Philip 160, 162
Jolly, David 93, 107 n.25
Jones, Lindsay 109
Jones, Peter Blundell 248
Jordan, R. Furneax 166
Joseph, Delissa 117
Jubilee Church, Rome (2003) 155
Judaism 120
  British 114
  modern 111–13
Judson, Harry Pratt 129, 132, 140 n.22
Jugendstil 38, 51
Jung, Carl Gustav 51
Juvonen, Helvi 83
Jyväskylä Funerary Chapel (1925) 73, 76, 78, 84
Jyväskylä Lyceum 87 n.31

Kadish, Sharman 114, 120
Kaleva Church (1966) 84
Kandinsky, Wassily 196, 202
Kant, Immanuel 24, 25
Kaos (1984) 245, 251
Kathedrale des erotischen Elends (KdeE, The Cathedral of Erotic Misery) 196, *197*, 199–201, 203, 204
Kekrops 15–17
Kelly, Jessica 174 n.2
Kenzo Tange 67, 68
Kiefer, Anselm 50
kinaesthetic experience 251

King's College Chapel, Cambridge 134
Koskenniemi, V. A. 81
Krinsky, Carol Herselle 111
Kristallnacht 60
Kunin, Seth 113
Kunstreligion (Art-religion) 4, 37–41, 49
Kuoleman puutarha ('The Garden of Death,' painting, 1906) 81

La Ciudad Abierta, Open City (1971) 100–1
Landschaftsseele 181
Langer, Susanne 112
Lansbury Estate 165
la phalène 100
L'Architecture d'aujourd'hui 152
L'Art Sacré 148, 152, 154
La Sainte-Baume basilica, Provence (1946–60) 153, 154
La salle, cathédrale de l'avenir? (Jeanneret) 188
Las Condes Monastery 93
Lassalle, Hugo 68
Lateran Pacts (1929) 226
Lateran Palace 233
Latour, Bruno 36 n.79
La Tourette monastery (1953–61) 151
Le Corbusier 3, 6, 18, 25, 26, 30, 57, 68, 84, 111, 132, 143–5, 148, 151–6, 188, 189, 192, 213, 233
Ledoux, Claude-Nicolas 234
Léger, Fernand 152
Le poème de l'angle droit (Le Corbusier) 25, 153, 155
Le Raincy Church 145, 147, 148
Lerup, Lars 111
Lesk, Alexandra 17
'L'Espace indicible' (Le Corbusier) 152
Le Tremblay Church (1929) 153
Lewerentz, Sigurd 77, 248, 249, 253
L'Ho perduto, me meschina (Barbarina) 245
Lichtwark, Alfred 210
light/lighting 60, 65, 66, 80, 84, 102–5, 151, 153, 189, 253
  cube of 95
  experimentation with 97
  issues 103
  natural 91, 94, 95, 101, 212
  restructuring space and 98–100
  role in design 92, 94–5, 97, 98, 100
  structuring power of 95, 96
  theology of 241
Liljequist, Bertel 83
Lindqvist, Selim A. 74
Liturgical Reform Movement 58, 96, 117, 120, 170, 171, 210, 218
liturgy 2, 95, 96, 108, 110–14, 116, 152, 153, 165, 166, 170, 177 n.54, 214, 217, 218, 251, 252

279

Index

Liturgy and Architecture (Hammond)   170
'lived understanding'   92, 103, 105
Liverpool Anglican Cathedral   167, 168, *169*
Liverpool Cathedral   133, 134
L'oeuvre d'art Vivant (The Work of Living Art, Appia)   188, 189
London County Council   164
Los Angeles Central Library   126
Los Pajaritos Chapel, Santiago (1953)   93–8, *94, 95*
Ludwig Mies van der Rohe Archive   191, 192
Lutheranism   23, 64, 77, 82
Luza, David   107 n.25
Lynch, David   247
Lyngby-Taarbaek Funerary Chapels and Cemetery   74–5, *75*, 77–84, *82*
Lyons, Edward   119, 120
Lyons Israel Ellis   117, 119

Maak, Niklas   154, 155
Mabille, Pierre   13
Madonna statue   235, 236
Maguire, Robert   170, 171
Maimonides   153
Malmi Cemetery, Helsinki (1934)   73
Malmö Eastern Cemetery   77
Mamuk architecture   148
Manifest und Programm (Gropius)   188
Mann, Barbara   120
Manplan 5: Religion   171, *172*
Mariendom Church, Neviges (1968)   69
Market Square and town centre   165
Markus, Thomas   176 n.49
The Marriage of Figaro (Mozart)   245
martyrdom   27, 29, 30, 225
Mary the Mother of God, Ronchamp   154
masonry   15, 22, 136, 252
Massachusetts Institute of Technology   66
materiality   27, 49, 149, 242, 248
materialization   252
materials   49, 56–8, 66, 69, 80, 84, 144, 150, 196, 197, 202–4, 252
mathematical physics   25
Matisse, Henri   148
Maximus Confessor   22
May, Ernst   58
medieval cathedrals   136, 139, 166, 208
medievalism   208–10, 212, 218, 219
Meier, Richard   155
Mendelsohn, Erich   4, 59–62, 64–6
Merleau-Ponty, Maurice   152
Mertins, Detlef   3
Merz art/architecture   196, 201–4
  cathedrals   197–200
Merzbau project   7, 199, 200, 204

metamorphosis   22, 29
metaphysics   39, 186, 204
Michael (archangel) depiction   20–2, *21*
Michelluci, Florentine Giovanni   147
Middle Ages   208, 209, 227
Midway Plaisance   127–31, 136
Mies van der Rohe, Ludwig   3, 6, 58, 132, 190–2, 194 n.35, 200, 204, 210, 215, 248
militarist ideology   231
military commission   223, 224
Miller, Naomi   51
minimalism   49
Ministry of Education, Rio de Janeiro   68
Ministry of War   223
Mirror of the Marvelous (Mabille)   13
modal disparity   246
Modern Architecture Research Group (MARS)   163, 170
modernism   2, 5–7, 37, 39, 41, 67, 69, 84, 96, 108, 109, 125, 138, 150, 159–60, 164–5, 167, 170, 171, 173, 174 n.2, 208–10, 219, 222, 223, 228
  early   161
  'orthodox'   29, 66
  post-war   161–3
modernity   1, 4, 5, 7, 27, 38, 108, 109, 125–7, 136, 138, 144, 174 n.3, 181, 192, 196, 204, 212, 215, 219, 222–4, 227, 237, 242
Modern Movement   144, 160, 167, 227, 234
modern nationalism   225
Modulor (Le Corbusier)   152
Modulor 2 (Le Corbusier)   152
modulor theory   153, 155
monastery   148, 212, 214, 218
Monte Grappa ossuary (1935)   227, 234–6, *235*
Montello ossuary (1935)   223, 227, *229*, 232, 233
monuments and monumentality   29, 30, 76, 224, 227, 229, 234–7
Morrison, Hugh S.   125
Morton, Tim   25
mortuary   73, 74, 82
Moser, Karl   143, 147
mosques   56, 69, 108
Mount Rokko chapel, Kobe   156
Mount Zion synagogue, St Paul (1954)   60
Murano, Tōgo   4, 66–8, 144, 148
Murray, Keith   170
museum   214, 217
  architecture   219
  curation   7, 210, 213, 215
  design   209–11
  modern   41, 218, 219
  space   215
Museum of Modern Art (MOMA)   191, 209
museum-temple   40
music   243–5

280

Index

Mussolini, Benito   7, 27, 30, 222, 227, 237
Mystagogia (Maximus Confessor)   22
mysticism   29, 202, 217, 241
myths and mythology   15–17, 49, 53

Nabu   14
National Party of Fascism (PNF)   27, 29, 30
National Romanticism/Romanticists   66, 248
Nativity of the Mother of God (Tavener)   243, 244
natura naturans   24, 26
nature   25, 74, 77–9, 83, 84
 and Mind   24, 26–7
Naturphilosophie (Schelling)   24, 25, 31
Nebraska State Capitol   126
Nègre, Abbé Félix   145
Nehru, Jawaharlal   30
Neoplatonic conception   19
Neues Bauen (New Building)   61
Neumann, Balthasar   34 n.43
New Brutalism   119
New Church Research Group (NCRG)   170, 171
New Testament   20
'New-Town' projects   162
New Towns Act (1946)   162
New Towns Commission   164
New World of Space (Le Corbusier)   152
New York Times Magazine   145
Niemeyer, Oscar   68
Nieminen, Pertti   73
Nietzsche, Friedrich   31, 37–9, 51, 52, 219
nonconformism   111
Nordenswan, Mikael   86 n.6
Notre Dame, Raincy   6, 61, 143, 145, *146*, 147, 150, 156
Notre Dame de Paris (Hugo)   208
Notre-Dame-du-Haut Chapel, Ronchamp (1955)   3, 57, 84, 144, 151, 153–6
Nożyk synagogue, Warsaw   115
Nuestro Señora del Tránsito church, Corral (1961)   93, 97–100, *99*
'numinous'   42
Nuska   13, 14

Oberstrasse Synagogue, Hamburg (1930)   60
obscurity   241, *242*
O'Doherty, Bryan   213
Odyssey (Homer)   15
Œuvre complète (Le Corbusier)   189
oikistes   16
Olbrich, Josef Marie   58
Old Testament   20, 22
Olmsted, Frederick Law   127, 128, 137, 138
On the Aesthetic Education of Man (Schiller)   4
On the Divine Images (John of Damascus)   22

Open City   104
 co-operative life   100–1
 oratory   101–2, *102*
Origen of Alexandria   202
ornament and ornamentation   15, 18, 19, 22, 57, 58, 83, 84
Orpheus and Eurydice   186, *187*
Orphic harmony   153, 154
Orthodox United Synagogue   117
Oslavia ossuary (1938)   227, *228*, 232, 233
Otaniemi University Chapel (1956)   84
Otto, Rudolf   42, 215, 244

Paattionlehto Chapel (1960)   79
'The Painter of Modern Life' (Baudelaire)   196
paintings
 of Caspar David Friedrich   25–6
 kunstreligiös   52
Palatine Chapel of Roger II, Palermo   23
Palazzo della Ragione, Padova   22
Panathenaea   15
Pandroseon   17
pantheistic agnosticism   83, 84
Parish Church of Saint-Pierre, Firminy-Vert   153
park and boulevard system   127, 128, 136, 137
Parks Movement   137
Parnell, Steve   173 n.2
Parthenon   18, 155
Pasubio ossuary   227
patriotism   232
Patterns in Comparative Religion (Eliade)   13
Pausanias   16
Peace Center, Hiroshima   67, 68
pedagogy   91, 92
Pehnt, Wolfgang   58
Pendleton-Jullian, Ann   91
Pentateuch (Five Books of Moses)   111
Pentikäinen, Juha   87 n.34
Perez, Fernando   96
Perret, Auguste   6, 61, 143–5, 147–51, 156
Pevsner, Nikolaus   2, 109, 114, 119, 154, 160, 162, 165, 167, 173
Pfammatter, Ferdinand   147
Philharmonie, Berlin (1963)   69
Philo   153
Pian di Salesei   225, 236
picturesque   165, 167
Pietilä, Raili   84
Pietilä, Reima   84
Pioneers of the Modern Movement (Pevsner)   2, 160, 173
Pirandello, Luigi   245
Plague, The (Camus)   31
Plan of Chicago (Burnham)   137
Plato   14, 51

281

Index

Plum, Harald   74
Pocol ossuary   227, 232
Poelzig, Hans   51
poesía del ha lugar (poetry of place)   100
Poetics (Aristotle)   32 n.22
Poland   69
political
   centralization   223
   ideologies   40
   propaganda   223
Pontius Pilate   233
Portinari, Candido   68
Poseidon   15, 17
Power and Production Pavilion   117
Powers, Alan   171
'presence'   43
Prière sur l'Acropole (Renan)   18
'primitivism'   152
primordial claim   15
'the priority of the question'   17
Proctor, Robert   168, 176 n.32
progressive Catholicism   59
The Protecting Veil (Tavener)   243, 247, 251
Protestant Church   57, 61, 66
Protestants/Protestantism   83, 110
pulpit   63, 66, 115, 117, 131
Purcell, Juan   101, 106 n.24
Purism   153

Rademacher, Franz   215
Ragot, Gilles   153
Rationalism   217, 222, 227
Raumstil (spatial style)   183, 192
Raymond, Antonin   148, 154
Read, Herbert   206
Reason in the Age of Science (Gadamer)   103
reburial programme   223
'reconstructive surgery'   98
redemption   225, 232, 234, 242, 251
Redipuglia ossuary   227, *230*, 230–3, *231*, 237
Reform Judaism   117
Reifenberg, Heinz Walter   117
'*Reigen*'   112
reinforced concrete construction   144, 145, 149
religion   222
   devotion   56
   fusion/replaces with art   37, 39, 40
   iconography   76, 127
   indoctrination   226
   observance   56
   political   40
   power   229
   practices   3, 13, 218
   symbol   236
   traditional   181

truth   42–3
typologies   131
Renan, Ernest   18
Research Institute for Jewish Architecture   108
resurrection   77, 82, 84
Resurrection Chapel, Turku (1939)   83
Resurrection Church, Essen (1930)   62
Rhenish mystic tradition   213
Richards, J. M.   160, 161, 165–7, 173
Riemerschmid, Richard   210
Risen Christ statue, Passo del Tonale (1936)   225
rituals   15, 185
   death   73, 81–5
   Fascist   229, 230
   religious   232
   sacred   232
Robinson, Joel   77
Rockefeller, John D   126–9, 134
Roehampton Estate   162
Roman Catholic Cathedral, Liverpool   163
Roman Catholic churches   57, 59, 65, 168, 170, 177 n.54, 226, 235, 237
Roman Catholicism   3, 92, 105, 113, 225, 226, 228, 229, 231, 232, 237
Roman classicism   227
Romanesque   208, 212
Romanticism   3, 4, 24, 25, 27, 31, 37, 41, 50, 83, 208
Rome   18
Rousseau, Jean-Jacques   26
Rovereto ossuary   227, 232, 233
Rowe, Colin   143
Royal Institute of British Architects (RIBA)   162
Rudolph, Paul   156
Rüedi, Peter   49
Rutan, Charles   128
Rykwert, Joseph   115, 175 n.21

Saarinen, Eero   64, 66
Saarinen, Eliel   4, 57, 64–7
Sachlichkeit   1, 3, 212–14, 217, 219
sacrality   3, 13, 27, 37, 208, 218, 229
sacralization   7, 38–41, 218
   of politics   225, 226
Sacrario of the Martyrs of Como   27, *28*, 29, 30
sacred   4, 13, 15, 17–20, 23, 24, 29, 42, 109, 111, 149, 152, 209, 227, 231, 241
   atmosphere   241–53
   experience   242
   form   143, 144, 151, 156
   language   143–4, 156
   living   27
   and modern art   41
   practices   31
   role in modern times   38

Index

sites   229, 230, 234
space   66, 113, 125–7, 144, 152, 168, 208, 241
structure   199, 204
themes   37
tradition   131
sacro monte   233, 234
St Antonius Church, Basel (1927)   147
St. Augustine   19
Saint Bonaventure   203
Sainte-Marie de la Tourette Monastery   153
St Engelbert, Cologne (1932)   65, 66
Saint Francis of Assisi, Belo Horizonte (1943)   68
St François des Capuchins church, Beirut (1955)   148
St Fronleichnam, Aachen   215, *216*, 217
St. Ignatius Chapel, Seattle (1997)   155
St John the Baptist Church, Neu-Ulm   68
St Joseph Church, Le Havre (1954)   145, 147–8
St Mark's Coptic Cathedral, Cairo   148
St Mary and Joseph Roman Catholic Church   165
St Michael Church, Hildesheim   68
Stoic conception   19
St Pantaleon Church, Cologne   68
St Paul's Bow Common Church, London   170
St Peter Church, Klippan (1966)   248, 249, *250*, 251, *251*, 252, *252*
St Pierre à Roye Church, Somme (1931)   147
St Salvator Church, Münsterschwarzach (1938)   68
St. Savior Chapel, Chicago   190–1, *191*
St Suzanne Church, Brussels (1928)   147
Saint Thomas Aquinas   203
San Candido ossuary   232
Sanchez, Jorge   101, 106 n.24
Santa Clara Chapel, Greater Santiago   93
Sassanid architecture   19
Scala Sancta (Holy Stairs)   233, 234
scenography   182
Scharoun, Hans   69
Scheffler, Karl   52, 184, 220 n.15
Schelling, K. F. W.   24, 25, 31, 39
Schiller, Friedrich   4, 25, 26, 29, 37, 52, 181
Schinkel, Karl Friedrich   4, 37, 38, 40, 41, 52
Schlegel, Friedrich   37, 39
Schlegel, August Wilhelm   37, 39
Schleiermacher, Friedrich   39
Schmidt, Karl   183, 188
Schnütgen, Alexander   210, 211, 219
Schnütgen Museum, Cologne   7, 208–9, *209*, 211, 213, 217–19
Schwarz, Rudolf   2, 57, 58, 64–6, 120, 208, 215, 217–19
Schwippert, Hans   65
Schwitters, Ernst   199
Schwitters, Kurt   7, 196–204

Scott, Adrian Gilbert   165
Scott, Giles Gilbert   133, 167, 176 n.32
Scully, Vincent   143, 155
Second Vatican Council   69, 96, 117, 153–4, 170, 177 n.54
Second World War   230
Secular Age, A (Taylor)   3
secularization   3, 4, 38, 241
self-education   103
Sephardi Jews   114
   practice   115
   synagogues   112
Shearman, John   51
Shemoneh Esreh. See Amidah ('standing prayer')
Shepard, Richard   206 n.31
Shepley, George   128
Siemensstadt   61
Simberg, Hugo   81
Simões de Freitas e Costa, Marcial   148
Sipari, Osmo   78–9
Sirén, Heikki   84
Sirén, Kaija   84
'Site of special scientific interest' (SSSI)   100
Siza, Alvaro   155
skene   17, 18
Smith, Adam   23
Smith, Henry Justin   138
Smithson, Alison   162, 167
Smithson, Peter   154, 162, 167
Sogn Benedetg Chapel, Switzerland (1985–8)   47
South Hackney synagogue, London (1897)   114–17
South Hampstead United synagogue (1959–62)   117–20, *119*, 124 n.39
'sovereign shelter' (*l'abri souverain*)   6, 143–5, 147–9, 156
space   7, 24, 27, 29, 37, 43, 69, 151–3, 189, 252
   conception   31, 47
   exhibition   37, 41
   geometry of   252
   infinity   25
   modernist concept   22
   organization   58
   quality of   97
   religious   109, 145
   spiritual   108
   utopian aspects of   25
Space, Time and Architecture (Giedion)   2, 66
spatiality   29, 247
Special Park Commission (1905)   137
Spence, Basil   163, 166, 167, 176 n.36
Spengemann, Christof   198, 201, 204
Spinoza, Baruch   24
spirit of the machine   160
spiritual
   ambitions   181

Index

ascension   233
culture   184
intensity   22
transformation   50
spirituality   1, 37, 49, 58, 69, 96, 125, 135, 144, 152, 154, 186, 188, 213, 217, 224, 229, 237, 242
sponsorship   164, 165
staging   182, 186, 188
Stelvio ossuary   227
Stimmung (mood)   40, 43, 244, 246
Stirling, James   119, 154
Strabo   18
Sublime   24
Suger (abbot)   202
Sullivan, Louis   138
Summae Theologica (Saint Thomas Aquinas)   203
Summerson, John   175 n.21
Sunset (painting, Caspar David Friedrich)   23
Swift, Harold   134
symbols and symbolism   13, 16–18, 22, 49–50
  Catholic   222
  civic   139
  Fascist   232, 237
  militaristic   230, 237
  of Passion   232
  religious   6, 7, 148, 222, 230
  sacred   234
  Trinitarian   214
Synagogue Council   116
synagogues   56, 59
  British   116
  characteristics   109–11
  contemporary American   118
  design   4, 5, 108, 120
  modern Judaism and their   111–13
  orthodox   117, 119, 122 n.18

Tabet, Antoine   148
Tadao Ando   156
Tampere Cathedral   81
Täuber-Arp, Sophie   200
Taut, Bruno   3, 58, 196, 200, 201
Tavener, John   243, 247
Taviani, Paolo   245
Taviani, Vittorio   245
Taylor, Charles   3, 23, 31
Taylor, Nicholas   167
Technische Hochschule   184
technology   160, 219
  innovation   30, 31
  modern   57
tectonic system   8, 247, 251–3
temporality   15, 16, 22, 24, 29, 185, 247, 252
Terragni, Giuseppe   27, 29, 233, 234

Tessenow, Heinrich   6, 184, 192
Thies, Harman   111, 114
Third Reich   61, 68
Thomas à Kempis   213, 218
The Three Crosses Church, Vuoksenniska (1958)   83
Torah   111–13, 115
Towards a Church Architecture (Hammond)   170
tradition   5, 108, 109, 127, 136, 138, 219, 223, 227, 228
  English   167
  Italian Renaissance   233
  Judeo-Christian   153
  premodern English   164
  religious   132, 135, 234, 236
  synthesis of   126
  and technological innovation   30
transcendence   22, 29, 49, 192, 229, 241
travesía   92, 102–4, 107 n.25
Trinitas, Malmi Funerary Chapels, Finland (1950)
  ancient typologies and topographies   73–7, *76*
  ritual and representation   81–4
  walled enclosures   77–81, *79*
Trinity Congregational Church, Lansbury (1951)   165, *166*
Trouin, Edouard   154
Turner, Harold   108–10
Turner, Victor   108
Tuskegee university chapel, Alabama (1960–9)   156

Umayyad architecture   19
UNESCO World Heritage   191
United Church of Christ, Osaka (1928)   148
Unité d'habitation, Marseille   189, 190
United States   66, 67, 125
United Synagogue   117
Unity Temple   66
University Chapel (1928)   5, 126–30, *127*, *130*, 132–9, *135*, *137*
University Chapel, Fribourg (1941)   147
University of Chicago   125–7, 138. *See also* University Chapel (1928)
  Academic Avenue   128, *128*, 130
  Campus   129, *129*
  Garden   131, *131*
  library   128
University of Chicago Magazine   125
Universum Cinema, Berlin (1928)   60
Upper Berkeley Street synagogue, West London   114–17, *115–16*
urban culture   125, 148
urbanity   84–5
urban metropolis   163
urban primitivism   5, 85
urn burials   73, 76, 78, 82, 83

Index

Valéry, Paul   143, 144, 149–51, 154–6
Valparaíso School of Architecture   5, 91–3, 96, 97, 102–5, 107 n.25
van Acken, Johannes   58, 59, 69, 210
Vatican II. *See* Second Vatican Council
Vers une Architecture (Le Corbusier)   111, 154, 189
Via Crucis   232, 233
Vial, José   96
Via Sacra (Sacred Way)   232, 236
Ville Radieuse   26
Virgil   14, 18
visual arts   23
Voegelin, Eric   4
Voelcker, John   161
Vogt, Von Ogden   134
von Klenze, Leo   18
von Salzmann, Alexander   185
von Wolff-Metternich, Franz   215

Wackenroder, Wilhelm Heinrich   39, 40
Wagner, Richard   37, 38, 42, 69
watering and catafalques   81–3
Weber, Max   39
Wedding Tower, Darmstadt   58
Weimar Republic   57, 59, 68
Werkbund Exhibition (1914)   210
White, Iain Boyd   3, 219
white walls   93, 95, 212, 213, 218, 219, 220 n.15
Wilcox, Vanda   232
Williams, Raymond   248
Wilson, Colin St John   249
Witte, Fritz   209–15, 217–19
Woodland Cemetery chapels   83
Worringer, Wilhelm   52, 208, 210
Worth Abbey Church (1964–75)   *172*
Wright, Frank Lloyd   66, 132, 138, 208
Wright, Lance   171

Zeitgeist   159
Zeus Polieus   16
Zimmer (rooms)   199, 201
Ziryab   20
Zukunftskathedrale (Cathedral of the future)   200–1
Zumthor, Peter   4, 39, 42, 43, 47, 49–53